Ray E. Nadeau
Purdue University

A modern rhetoric of speech-communication

Second edition

Addison-Wesley Publishing Company
Reading, Massachusetts · Menlo Park, California · London · Don Mills, Ontario

This book is in the
ADDISON-WESLEY SERIES IN SPEECH

FREDERICK W. HABERMAN
Consulting Editor

The first edition of this book was published under the title *A Basic Rhetoric of Speech-Communication*. Copyright © 1969; Philippines copyright 1969.

Copyright © 1972 by Addison-Wesley Publishing Company, Inc. Philippines copyright 1972 by Addison-Wesley Publishing Company, Inc.

All rights reserved. No part of this publication may be reproduced, stored in a retrieval system, or transmitted, in any form or by any means, electronic, mechanical, photocopying, recording, or otherwise, without the prior written permission of the publisher. Printed in the United States of America. Published simultaneously in Canada. Library of Congress Catalog Card No. 74-167994.

HA 2/73 04999

To Frances

Preface

A Modern Rhetoric of Speech-Communication is *rhetoric* in the original tradition of purposeful human communication concerned with man, his codes, and his commitment to democratic government. It is a rhetoric of *speech*-communication as distinguished from *written* communication and other modes, including the newspaper and mass media in general. It is *modern* in the sense that it provides an up-to-date base for the beginning course.

The writer recognizes the fact that, similarities notwithstanding, basic courses vary in purpose, content, and kinds of experiences offered. They are designed to meet local needs within the framework of other complementary courses. *A Modern Rhetoric* is traditional in that it can readily be used for courses placing a continuing emphasis on speaker-listener interaction in the public address situation. At the same time, the basic course is often the one and only exposure of a student to the problems of speech-communication. A basic text written in that context should include materials that provide a base for experience in the wider range of speech-communication situations in which the "one-course student" finds himself (and will continue to find himself) in his daily life. It is in that spirit that *A Modern Rhetoric* also takes due notice of conversations, interviews, small-group process, and large-group decision-making.

Organizational plan

Part 1 consists of four chapters with a focus on the *theory common to all forms* of speech-communication. Chapter 1 is based on man's age-old concepts of speech-communication as defined, tested, and supplemented by empirical studies in this century. The remaining three chapters deal with language symbolism, processes of reasoning, and psychological factors relevant to this area of communication.

Part 2 exposes the student to *initial experiences in communication* and offers additional information and suggestions on coping with some of the general problems encountered in human interaction.

Part 3 further extends the discussion of theory and practice through *communicative situations commonly recognized as characteristic* in modern life. Separate chapters cover the problems to be solved in forms of direct human communication, ranging from friendly conversation through parliamentary procedure with all its complexities.

The emphasis throughout the book is on the responsibilities of speaker *and* listener and on the theories and practices facilitating communication between them. While this book obviously fits no particular course plan, it is organized so that it can readily be adapted to a number of different plans. (No instructor's manual accompanies this text because the materials ordinarily included in one are considered to be valuable to students as well. All such materials are consequently to be found in the text proper.)

New features in this edition
1. Material on *the self-concept* has been expanded and given additional emphasis in Chapter 4 of Part 1.
2. To help the student attain a better grasp of communication theory, *comprehension questions* and *demonstration options* have been inserted at proper intervals in the four chapters of Part 1.
3. The original chapter on *listening critically* has been broadened to include *listening actively* and *listening self-defensively*. As Chapter 8, "Listening: modes and methods," the expanded chapter has been moved to Part 2.
4. A chapter entitled "Acquiring initial experience" has been added to Part 2.
5. Material on *one-to-one communication* has been given separate treatment as Chapter 9, "Interacting Person-to-Person," in Part 3.
6. The original chapter on influencing beliefs and attitudes has been reorganized and expanded. The title of the revised chapter in Part 3 is now "Changing listener attitudes."
7. To provide an appropriate balance in suggested student activities, a series of *listening options* has been added to the speaking options in Part 3.
8. Typical examples of *student communication* (information, discussion, persuasion) have been substituted for speeches, debates, and activities featuring diplomats, executives, presidents, and other notables.

Finally, like the earlier edition, *A Modern Rhetoric* has been written in the continuing hope that students will find the book useful in achieving better understanding of themselves and of the central part communication plays in the relations of man with man.

Lafayette, Indiana R. E. N.
October, 1971

Acknowledgments

The writer is indebted to Professors Frederick Haberman, University of Wisconsin, and Gustav Friedrich, Purdue University, for their interest and counsel; to Professor Bruce Kendall (1922–1969), Purdue, for his comments on the section dealing with parliamentary procedure; to Professor Charles Stewart, Purdue, for his suggestions on the preparation and handling of resolutions in student assemblies; to Professor John Pacilio, Jr., University of Arizona, for his cooperation in providing outlines of student speeches and the edited text of the student discussion in Chapter 11; to the many others whose contributions to the various chapters are noted in the text proper or in footnotes to it; to Mrs. Charles (Jennie) Bishop for expert typing of the manuscript; and to the colleagues and students with whom it has been my good fortune to be associated over the years.

Contents

	Introduction Communication: Our Hope for the Future	1
PART 1	SPEECH-COMMUNICATION IN THEORY	
Chapter 1	The Process of Speech-Communication	9
Chapter 2	Language: Power and Peril	24
	Words and the meanings of words	25
	The right words in the right places	29
	Problems in abstraction, classification, and definition	34
	Fact, inference, and judgment	38
Chapter 3	Common Sense in Reasoning	42
	Fundamental concepts in reasoning	42
	The materials of reasoning	48
	Practical patterns in reasoning	50
	Checking reasoning	55
Chapter 4	Perception, Motivation, Cues, and Rapport	60
	Perception and communication	60
	Perception and the self-concept	62
	Person perception	65
	Motivation and goals	68
	Cue selection and attention	72
	Rapport	75

PART 2 SPEECH-COMMUNICATION IN PRIMARY PHASES

Chapter 5 Acquiring Initial Experience — 81

The short introduction — 81
Interaction for mutual enjoyment — 85
The impromptu talk — 86
Presenting one's point of view — 88

Chapter 6 Planning with the Listener in Mind — 91

What am I going to say? — 91
How am I going to say it? — 94
Transitions — 100
Introductions and conclusions — 101

Chapter 7 Earning Listener Confidence — 104

The dry-run stage — 104
The on-your-feet stage — 106
The day-arrives stage — 111

Chapter 8 Listening: Modes and Methods — 114

Listening actively — 114
Listening self-defensively — 117
Listening analytically — 121

PART 3 SPEECH-COMMUNICATION IN ACTION

Chapter 9 Interacting Person-to-Person — 131

Interaction in conversations — 135
Interaction in interviews — 136

Chapter 10 Presenting Information — 140

The informational talk — 142
Visual aids — 145
Example of skeleton outline on explanation of a concept — 159
Representative informational speech — 160

Chapter 11 Planning and Participating in Discussion — 165

Preliminary distinctions — 165
The task environment — 169
The interpersonal environment — 172
Model of factors affecting group behavior — 173
Finesse in discussion — 175
Planning the discussion series — 178
Evaluating discussion — 180

	Typical open-ended discussion questions	184
	Example of learning discussion guide	185
	Example of problem-solving discussion guide	186
	Model student discussion	188
	Examples of resolutions	206

Chapter 12	**Changing Listener Attitudes**	**209**
	Attitudes, beliefs, and opinions	209
	Attitude-changing and the communication process	213
	Factors affecting attitudes toward the message	215
	Factors affecting attitudes toward the speaker	220
	Factors affecting attitudes toward the situational surroundings	223
	Listener response and observable effects	226
	Analyzing listeners and their attitudes	227
	Example of outline of problem-and-solution persuasive speech	232
	Representative student speeches aimed at changing attitudes	234

Chapter 13	**Debating Issues in a Free Society**	**243**
	What is freedom of speech?	244
	Two key decisions on freedom of speech	245
	Decisions in a free society	246
	The student and freedom of speech	247
	Friendly persuasion in public debate	248
	Approaches to case organization and defense	250

Chapter 14	**Decision-Making in Parliamentary Procedure**	**254**
	Basic motions and examples	255
	Special-problem motions	259
	Administration and order of business	260
	Duties of "assembly" members	264

Appendix A	**Use of the Library**	**269**
Appendix B	**Library Aids**	**272**
Appendix C	**Focus on Common Materials**	**274**
Appendix D	**Topical Bibliographies**	**277**
Appendix E	**Bibliography of Speech Collections**	**280**
	General Bibliography	**282**
	Index	**289**

*Baby, this is an age of ferment
in which the whole question of dialogue
is critical.*

Louis Lomax

Introduction
Communication: our hope for the future

Our decade seems to offer promise that the nuclear powers do now see some disadvantages in mutual annihilation and may even come to agree on arms limitation, but the development, testing, and manufacture of bombs and missile systems continue. The poor, the underprivileged, the disenfranchised, and the discriminated-against are making some progress in achieving equality in education, job opportunities, and political rights; open-housing ordinances are being belatedly passed by city councils and township boards, while some state legislatures avoid the issue in the hope that the problem, if long enough ignored, will eventually go away. Football stadiums are jammed on pleasant, sunny weekends, while thousands of young men—and some not so young—are with the armed forces. There are strikes by teachers, strikes by steelworkers, strikes by automotive workers. Arguments about pollution increase in intensity; city air is often filled with "dirt"; the land is so heavily treated with chemicals, pesticides, and insecticides that animal, bird, and insect life barely survives; Lake Michigan is so wholly polluted at its southern end that there is danger of "losing the lake." This is the age of the street march, the demonstration, and the parading with signs. Is smoking marijuana a criminal act or is it a personal matter equivalent to drinking bourbon or some other alcoholic beverage? What makes some individuals abandon generally accepted standards to embrace new and seemingly eccentric groups and movements? How do you account for accelerating crime rates? Why do we have almost as many of our people in mental hospitals as in the colleges and universities?

The foregoing enumeration of problems and questions is intended to highlight one point: We cannot solve problems or answer questions without communication, and some of the problems and questions are so serious that the world holocaust which we so much fear may still erupt. We make gigantic strides in the world of science; we have already put spacemen on the moon, and it is only a matter of time before we put them on one or more of the other planets, but in the crucial business of handling interpersonal relations, we are less efficient and less successful.

What is communication? For the moment, let us agree that . . .

Communication is social

As Colin Cherry says, "Communication is essentially a social affair."[1] Its function is to enable men to associate with one another and to work together cooperatively for the common good. It is a direct avenue to the reduction of those tensions over which man has control. (We cannot do much about heavy rains and the threat of a landslide, but we can do something about corruption in politics.) It is appropriate to note that man's early efforts at making recognizable sounds were direct responses to stimuli at the same level represented by the utterances of birds and animals watching the approach of threat in the form of man or other birds and animals. In the same way, primitive man certainly used verbalizations of one kind or another as an aid to establishing rapport with his fellows or, conversely, to give warnings or make it clear that intruders were unwelcome. Modern man continues to use language at this elementary, presymbolic level. For instance, we have all had the experience of going through a reception line in which "receivers" and "received" smile pleasantly and utter vapid nothings which say, in effect, "I'm friendly," but no one remembers what is said long enough to make forgetting a problem. Neighbors run into one another regularly at bus stops or in supermarket parking lots. Unless they are close friends, convention dictates that they smile pleasantly and exchange short greetings. If one violates the code by stopping and attempting, without some very obvious reason, to engage the other in a lengthier exchange, the latter often spends an inordinate amount of time trying to guess at the motive for the change in behavior. As you are cutting the lawn, a new neighbor of your own age may stop by and observe, "It's a hot day to be cutting a lawn." Both he and you know that his observation is accurate, and both you and he know that it is not intended to convey any information; it is just a way of saying, "Perhaps we can be friends." The conversation may, after a few other trial balloons, move to questions about the location of the nearest beach, availability of dates, and so on. In other words, language is often irrelevant or totally inconsequential; it serves in such instances to preserve an existing relationship or to establish rapport for a new one. Hayakawa makes the point that sometimes large groups (e.g., cocktail parties, singing groups, conventions, pep rallies, rituals of any kind) "make noises together"[2] of a similarly irrelevant nature.

If the kind of language we have been talking about is primarily presymbolic (i.e., having as its purpose the establishment or maintenance of lines of communication through sympathetic noise rather than through dependence on the "meanings of words"), what is symbolic language? It is the language which "separates the men from the animals." *It is man's unique ability to make things stand for other things.* For example, the word "donkey" calls to mind whatever your image of a donkey may be, but the word is not the donkey, the word is not the thing represented. The word is a symbol having no necessary or inherent connection with the animal. If we could agree that, henceforth, the word "donkey" would be used for that object to which we now give the name "chair," and that "chair" would be used to indicate the animal, the only changes would be in the

---

1. Cherry, p. 3. (All abbreviated footnotes are references to books listed alphabetically by author in the Bibliography at the end of this volume.)
2. Hayakawa, p. 71.

symbols and not in the objects. Why is this important? We live in a symbol-saturated society in which we are constantly exposed to suggestions, pressures, and blandishments aimed at convincing us that we can be "happy" only if we have the "right address," "a new car (preferably two) every year," membership in the "right organizations," etc.

We must come to understand that the symbolic process of making things (words included) stand for other things has built into it a very natural "confusion of symbols with the things symbolized."[3] We cannot think clearly or handle our language efficiently if we believe, for example, that the possession of a car in the Cadillac class necessarily indicates affluence, or that the smoking of a Marlboro automatically confers rugged strength and virility upon the smoker (it may confer something entirely different), or that one becomes a man of impeccable and discriminating taste by letting it be known that he drinks "only Scotch."

We are safe in this wonderful world of symbols so long as we remember that it *is* a world of symbols. Symbols are, of course, extraordinarily useful. We cannot learn everything by firsthand experience, and we therefore depend on words (symbols) as the carriers of information amassed through the centuries; we use this information daily and depend on it for our planning of the future. In fact, it is man's ability to symbolize that makes it possible for him to record the past, discuss the present, and predict the future. Without symbolism as a time-binding and socializing cement, there could be no civilization as we know it. Without symbolism and the efficiency in communication which it makes possible, the relations of man to man would indeed be seriously handicapped.

Communication is political

Embedded in our federal Constitution and in the Bill of Rights with the Amendments are our freedoms of worship, of assembly, of the press, and of speech, as well as a catalog of rights more numerous and detailed than those enjoyed by the citizens of any other country. How many of us know what those documents have to say about our freedoms? How many of us have read the Human Rights Declaration of the United Nations, that great tribute to the human spirit passed by the General Assembly in December of 1948? It has been estimated that a "... quarter of the human race lives today under the aegis of Communism, which literally defies the Charter of the United Nations. It is probable that another fifty percent of the world's population has no intelligent comprehension of the Charter and their rights under it."[4] What are we doing to insist on the protection of human rights in our own country, let alone elsewhere in the world? How many of us see the free elections of our system as a privilege? Do we know what a system of "checks and balances" means? Do we have any idea how our own government at the local level operates? Do we do anything more than vote on candidates and issues? Or do we prefer to "leave it to Charlie," and run the risk of waking up some day to discover that Charlie has "taken over" and decided to suspend some of our rights?

---

3. *Ibid.*, p. 28.
4. George P. Rice, Jr., *Law for the Public Speaker* (Boston: Christopher, 1958), p. 131. Reprinted by permission.

Communication is also vitally political in that it is the alternative to violence as an avenue to change. No one seriously questions the right to dissent. The problem seems to be to dissuade dissenters from resorting to violence if their arguments or demands are not instantaneously met. If the wishes of minorities must always immediately prevail, democracy as we know it will collapse. On the other hand, when the basic right of freedom of speech is only tolerated by the established orders to provide an "outlet for pent-up emotions," when over an extended period it fails to lead to alleviation of demonstrable social inequities and injustices, no one should be amazed that appeals to law and order are regarded with jaundiced eye. We are fortunate; democratic principles and tradition in America remain strong in the face of many problems. We must convince *all* our citizens that open discussion of issues continues to be the best way to arrive at consensus and that such discussion is the only way to reach social and political goals within the concept that "majority decisions are in the best interests of all citizens of a democracy."

A citizenry trained and skilled in communication is better able to withstand the rhetoric of violence, better able to criticize the rhetoric of reaction, better able to keep open the channels to orderly change, and better able to keep our political system in tune with the times.

Communication is practical

The difference between the successful man and the unsuccessful man is frequently the superior ability of the first to communicate, to talk well and to listen well. In the free world there are now almost 4,000 Toastmaster Clubs (and hundreds of Dale Carnegie groups) through which thousands of men and women, recognizing at last the critical importance of oral communication, belatedly attempt to fill in this gap in their education. However skilled they may be in their chosen fields, they have come to understand that knowledge is not enough to get ahead in this world; one must also be able to think clearly, to speak effectively, to listen sensitively. These people have also come to realize that skill in communication is not something that "just comes naturally" or by osmosis; it comes more readily and consistently from intensive study of the principles of communication followed by experience in them.

In 1926, a study by Paul T. Rankin, at that time supervising director of research and adjustment for the Detroit public schools, indicated that 68 adults spent 70 percent of their waking day in some form of communication and that 75 percent of this communication time was devoted to talking and listening, 25 percent to reading and writing. (The Rankin study has been criticized on the ground that it depended on estimates by the subjects themselves of the time spent in communication and in its different modes.) More recently, in the issue for June 1967, *Nations's Business* (p. 16) reported a survey of 700 executives who were asked to make estimates of the ways in which they spent their communication time. Although this survey is open to the same criticism as the Rankin study, there is nonetheless significance in the fact that these executives said 80 percent of the day was spent in oral communication (talking and listening), and the remaining 20 percent was spent in planning, reading, and writing. In the March 27, 1967, issue (pp. 132 ff.) of *Chemical Engineering*, Robert Haakenson, a community relations expert, estimated that we spend "substantially more than a quarter of our lives" in the process of talking and listening. Each of us can conduct his own personal survey and discover that, on the average, an American speaks a hundred words for every one he may write. With the admitted exception of Calvin Coolidge, there have been few successful men, especially in public life and the professions, who have not had in their backgrounds some formal training in speech-communication.

Throughout our lives, but especially in times of crisis, we try to "make a good impression." We all know that the educated man has a better chance of accomplishing that objective than the uneducated man. Common sense also tells us that the test of whether or not a man is really educated lies in his ability to unify what he had learned and to communicate what he knows effectively to other people. Knowledge that cannot be communicated is of doubtful value. There is little point in investing in a college or university education if the student and his advisors do not include in the "plan of study" at least one course aimed at enabling the individual to put what he knows to use in his dealings with other people. A fine car is useless without the key to the ignition.

We also know that it is impossible to go through a day without extensive use of language for control purposes. At breakfast, in addition to the usual presymbolic "Good morning" addressed to anyone present, we ask someone to pass the salt, inquire about the latest weathercast, etc. We spend the rest of the day urging, suggesting, demanding, proposing, protesting, cajoling, commending, flattering, coaxing, claiming, instructing, approving, praising, and so on. All of us use language as an instrument of social manipulation; our purpose is to reduce the incidence of unpleasant events to an absolute minimum while increasing the number of pleasurable "transactions." We all aim at success in our various endeavors, and the primary tool in our kits is the ability to interact in a sympathetic way with those we meet and to modify their behavior through the use of appropriate language and signs.

Opportunities for getting to know ourselves, our strengths and our weaknesses, are all too few; not many classes in a college or university offer a better chance for self-revelation, self-development, and discovery of one's potential than a class in speech-communication. Those coming into such a class enter it with their share of "fears of the unknown," but with the study of speech-communication comes an understanding of human behavior and a confidence that one has come closer to his potential in successful human relationships.

"Man creates himself" and in large part what we create is our own choice.

Harry Weinberg

Communication is hope

Finally, communication is a willingness to listen, an honest attempt to put oneself in another's place in the effort to understand him, a determination to delay labeling or evaluating until "all the returns are in," a habit of looking to the advantages, benefits, and possible effects of proposals before arriving at judgments on their merits, a deep interest in talking *with* people rather than *at* or *to* them, a feeling for and an understanding of the dignity of each person as an individual, a concern for his welfare. A prime prerequisite to communication between man and man is an emphasis on humaneness. That emphasis is still very much alive among college and university students (witness the commitment of so many thousands to humanitarian programs); without that emphasis, there would be little hope for the future of the human race, little hope that man could learn, before it is too late, to work with man to solve his problems.

I am a man, and nothing which relates to man can be a matter of unconcern to me.

Terence in The Self-Tormentor

Part 1 / Speech-communication in theory

1 / The process of speech-communication

You have undoubtedly had the experience of trying to talk with someone who had "something else on his mind." If a professor is working against time to prepare a lecture for the following day, you may find him a little reluctant to discuss your progress in the class. If your father, deep in an easy chair in front of the television set, is watching World Series baseball or his favorite professional team in any sport, you are going to have some trouble "communicating" with him. You already know the importance of "the first impression"; you make some immediate judgments the first time you meet students, professors, and others, and you are very much aware that they are going through the same initial evaluative process. With some new acquaintances, you quickly find yourself compatible; with others, you don't. When you suggest to your roommate that clothes on hangers last longer, stay cleaner, and generally contribute to a sense of well-being and orderliness in a room, he may say, "Mind your own business," or "You take care of your clothes and I'll take care of mine," or "Your point is well taken and I'll do better from now on." The reaction you get will depend on what you say, how you say it, the general state of mind and mood of the roommate, his general background, his attitude toward you, the availability of other accommodations and roommates, and an interpretation of your attitude ("He wants to get rid of me," or "He is genuinely concerned about our getting along together in rather cramped quarters"). You will also recall that, in the Introduction, we made some general observations about the crucial importance of communication in the modern world and about its significance to the individual and to society. We turn now to the business of more exact and detailed definition.

First of all, let us admit that we "... are still immensely ignorant about the communication process."[1] From Greek and Roman times down through the Middle Ages and the Renaissance, speeches were ordinarily classified as those common to legislative assemblies (deliberative speeches on questions of policy), those common

---

1. Brown and Van Riper, p. 76.

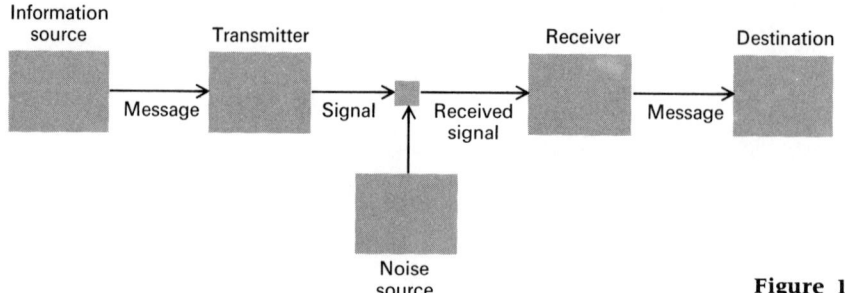

Figure 1.1

to the courts (forensic speeches of accusation or defense), and those designed for other occasions (funeral orations, addresses of welcome and farewell, speeches praising rulers, empires, and cities, declamatory exhibitions of virtuosity in speech-making on topics of every description, etc.). The three types, aimed primarily at persuasion and obviously based on the kinds of audiences before which they were to be delivered, served to help a speaker focus his approach on the problems and requirements of a specific speaking situation. Centuries later, George Campbell (*Philosophy of Rhetoric*, 1776) represented a departure from the classical tradition in that he abandoned separate "types of speeches" and listed four aims from the standpoint of *audience responses* desired: to inform, to please the imagination, to arouse the emotions, and to persuade. Campbell took the position that any one aim could be the principal objective in a speech, but that no speech need be restricted to one aim throughout. In this respect, he was in agreement with the ancients that a speech could, for example, be primarily a legislative proposal of policy ("Let's rebuild the docks at Piraeus") and still include accusations of the kind normally heard in a court, as well as praise of individuals or communities, as in speeches for special occasions. Then, in 1915, James Winans published a text on *Public Speaking* which placed a heavy emphasis on audience attention and on the general psychology of communicating ideas and emotions. Influenced by William James, Winans may be said to be a forerunner of modern approaches to communication theory. In other words, Campbell and Winans are two of the many theorists who, from the time of the early Greeks down to our own day, have indeed contributed a body of principles, arrived at subjectively and intuitively and tested by centuries of experience. However, it is only in this century that we have really begun the task of testing our assumptions empirically and of exploring descriptively and experimentally new hypotheses aimed at improving communication among men.[2]

---

2. Schramm gives four scholars primary credit for the trend toward research in the social science aspects of communication: (1) Paul Lazarsfeld, the Vienna-trained sociologist; (2) Kurt Lewin, the Vienna-trained Gestalt psychologist; (3) Harold Lasswell, the University of Chicago-trained political scientist; and (4) Carl Hovland, the Yale psychologist. Names in the next rank would be those of Leon Festinger, Irving Janis, Colin Cherry, Nathan Maccoby, and others. See Schramm, *The Science of Human Communication*, pp. 2–5. Some of the findings of these and other researchers are, of course, woven into the texture of this book.

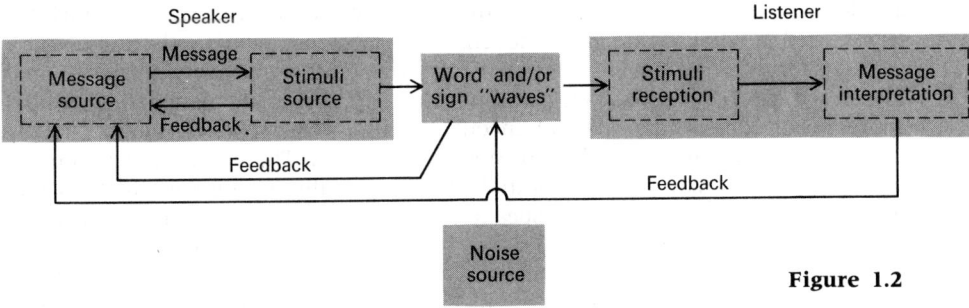

Figure 1.2

Fundamentally, communication may be interpreted to mean simply "that information is passed from one place to another. Whenever communication occurs, ... the component parts involved in the transfer of information comprise a communication system."[3] A diagram of the components of such a system is that designed by Shannon and Weaver (Fig. 1.1).[4] Originally intended as a model to be used in connection with engineering problems, the general communication system diagrammed is less than satisfactory when applied to the complexities of human communication. Nevertheless, with obvious limitations, it may be adapted to at least a part of the speech-communication process, as shown in Fig. 1.2.[5]

The fault in any diagram like that in Fig. 1.2 is the danger that it may be interpreted as some kind of action-reaction pattern. On the contrary, "When we talk about communication we are not talking about a situation in which John acts and Mary reacts to John's action and in turn John reacts to Mary's action in some simple, ongoing, one-after-another sequence.... John does not communicate to Mary, and Mary does not communicate to John; Mary and John engage in communication."[6] The point to be stressed is that streams of message stimuli, verbal and/or nonverbal, are *simultaneously* and *continuously* passing between speaker and listener. The messages continue even if the participants in the encounter never begin to talk or, after doing so, lapse into total silence. As Goffman says, one "cannot say nothing."[7] An individual who seems to be saying nothing is consciously, subconsciously, or unconsciously sending and receiving nonverbal "messages" whenever he is in the presence of another individual.

On condition that we have a clear understanding that speech-communication is a *continuous, two-way, ongoing process*, it is possible to say, in partial and admittedly one-sided explanation of the diagram, that a speaker may be regarded as conceiving

---

3. From *Language and Communication* by George A. Miller, p. 6. Copyright 1951. Used with permission of McGraw-Hill Book Company.
4. Claude E. Shannon and Warren Weaver, *The Mathematical Theory of Communication* (Urbana: University of Illinois Press, 1949), p. 5. Diagram reproduced by permission.
5. For another adaptation of the "engineers' model of communication," see Eisenson, Auer, and Irwin, p. 168.
6. Ray L. Birdwhistell, *Kinesics and Context: Essays on Body Motion Communication* (Philadelphia: University of Pennsylvania Press, 1970), p. 12. Reprinted by permission.
7. Goffman, *Behavior in Public Places*, p. 35.

an idea which he formulates into words and/or signs (nonverbal signals) which are transmitted in whole or in part to the senses of the listener, who translates or decodes the message to come up with an idea which may or may not match exactly the original idea of the speaker. The message is complicated by the fact that, along with its verbal components, the speaker is simultaneously sending—as well as receiving—many nonverbal signals (tone, facial expression, gesture, etc.). The message, then, consists of a stream of verbal and *other* stimuli. Fundamentally, no message really passes between speaker and listener; the speaker tries, through the manipulation of symbols of various sorts, to induce in the listener meanings as close as possible to his own. Sometimes he succeeds and sometimes he does not. The extent to which he succeeds largely depends on the experience which speaker and listener have in common. The set of symbols (words and other signs) which the speaker uses to express an idea is determined by the particular point of view from which *he* sees a particular "object, event, or situation" and by his "background experiences and attitudes."[8] Similarly, the listener's determination of the meaning of the message is affected by *his* point of view and by *his* background and attitudes. The more speaker and listener have "in common" (language, culture, tastes, beliefs, attitudes, etc.), the better chance there is that "communication" will be accurately interpreted.

Human communication is, of course, not simply a matter of a speaker's formulating a "message" and hoping that it will mean essentially the same thing to the listener. *Feedback* is an integral part of the process; it may be described as consisting of "return signals" or responses which have a continuing regulatory effect on the speaker in the course of his message-production. In Fig. 1.2, the speaker is shown to be receiving feedback from (1) some of "his own" stimuli (vocal apparatus and other muscle systems), (2) the sound of his voice, and (3) the listener.

For example, the speaker monitors the movement of the musculatures required to produce word sounds, and his being aware of what his muscles are doing tells him not only what subsequent sound is feasible, but also what he has to do to produce it. You know from your own experience that, as you speak, you discard some word combinations in favor of others which are easier to produce and which "go well together." By contrast, the familiar "tongue-twister sentences" are amusing because they contain difficult combinations of sounds which one would normally avoid. Furthermore, we do "see ourselves in action" and control and adjust general bodily movement as well as specific gestures in what we hope are ways appropriate to a particular communicative effort.

An external source of feedback is the sound of the speaker's voice. He listens to himself and uses what he hears to rephrase sentences, repeat significant words, increase volume, change rate and pitch. He also hears the message itself and may, in turn, be influenced by it.

A third source of feedback, also external, is the listener. Before a speaker actually keeps an appointment to meet a listener or before he stands before a scheduled assembly of any size, he is already (or should be) enjoying the advantages of feedback in that he is being influenced in his preparation for the event by his perceptions of the "audience makeup"—who will be in it, what

---

8. Both quotations from Alexander, pp. 13, 16.

their views and values are, etc. The speaker adjusts his preparation behavior to fit his image of the audience-to-be. Later, the speaker also modifies his on-the-scene behavior in the light of his interpretation of signs from an individual, a group, or an entire audience. At the same time that he is sending messages, he is constantly receiving verbal and/or nonverbal signals from the listener (frowns, smiles, negative shaking of the head, nods of approval, inattention, applause, argument, heckling, enthusiasm, resignation, doubt, encouragement, etc.). As the speaker transmits his messages, then, he simultaneously receives and interprets signals coming back to him, and he tries—or should try—to use those interpretations to improve the efficiency of his communication. In your speech-communication class, for example, your knowledge of the students in it can help you reach decisions on what materials to use in your attempts to communicate with the class. During the communication event itself, you will be in a position (1) to watch the members of the group for whatever "responses" you can detect and (2) to try to react to them. In other words, feedback from the class will be available to you both *before* and *during* your communicating with its members. (We are assuming, of course, that you classmates have been encouraged to be normal listeners rather than critics or analysts.)

At the same time that all the interactions above are taking place, other interactions are occurring within the listener. In spite of what the speaker intends, his language patterns and word combinations stimulate images and concepts peculiar to the listener alone. As these images and concepts are aroused in the listener, his beliefs may be interacting with his evaluative attitudes, with resulting modifications in his beliefs and/or attitudes. The "proofs" he hears may be solely logical, but they may be contributing substantially to raise his estimate of the credibility of the speaker. The listener's interpretations of the meaning of the speaker will further depend on whether or not he considers the speaker to be physically energetic, competent in his field, aggressive, weak, and so on. Thus we have a host of stimuli operating within the listener and affecting message reception, interpretation, and reaction.

Finally, a variety of "noises" often stand between speaker and listener to affect or garble the message in some way. No matter how much speaker and listener have in common, the latter's interpretation of the message will be less than accurate if he is irritated by the speaker's voice, or by the excessive heat of the summer day, or by his personal relationship to the speaker, or by any other factor outside the message and outside the control of the communicators. The room may be too hot, and the chairs may be too stiff. A majority of the listeners may be hungry or physically exhausted. A jackhammer may be chattering away on a nearby construction project, or music may be filtering through the walls or heating vents. Any number of such factors, having nothing to do with the messages or with the attitudes and prejudices of the participants, may interfere with the successful sending and receiving of those messages.

Conversely, outside factors may reinforce the message; for instance, the playing of patriotic music and the displaying of the flag can do much to establish a favorable environment for a speech honoring a national hero or dignitary. Sun streaming through stained-glass windows at a wedding is a happier augury than torrential rain. Thus place, time, and general atmosphere often have a direct bearing on the success or failure of a speaking-listening event.

Presence in the context of the diagram shown as Fig. 1.3 includes "present" controlled and uncontrolled personal factors and attributes as apprehended by the listener

14   The process of speech-communication

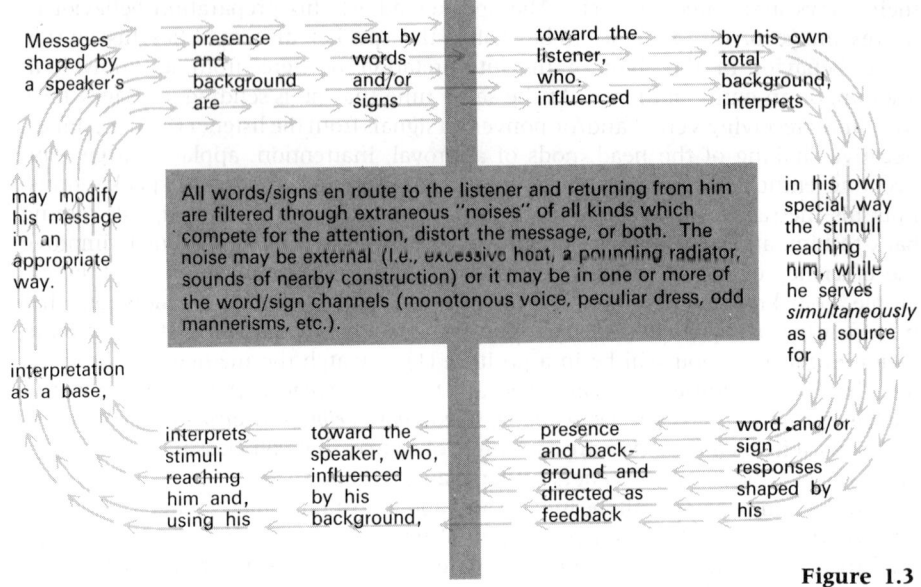

Figure 1.3

(e.g., height, weight, voice, expression, general appearance, age, dress, position); *background* encompasses one's total past: earlier environment, education, and experience, together with the beliefs and attitudes stemming from them. Although no diagram can do justice to the constant multichannel two-way flow of the process, the one in Fig. 1.3 serves again to remind us of the extreme complexity of speech-communication and the "noises" of affecting it.

At this point, although the two speech-communication diagrams (Figs. 1.2 and 1.3) and the accompanying discussion have been centered on "the speaker" and "the listener," the reader has certainly surmised that any number of people may be involved in the kinds of speech-communication with which we are concerned. The individual conducting debate within himself on the *pros* and *cons* of a certain course of action is engaged in *intrapersonal* communication. Two persons engaged in a conversation are taking part, obviously, in *interpersonal* communication, a phrase also used to describe the interaction taking place between and among individuals in any relatively small group. Although speaker-with-audience interaction may also be described as interpersonal, a greater separation and somewhat less intimacy are ordinarily involved, and as a consequence, many theorists prefer to use *person-to-group* or *public* communication in describing that situation. On the other hand, *mass* communication (radio, television, film, and journalism), the effort to reach "the masses" through one or more of a major media, has little to do with the kind of direct face-to-face communication with which we are concerned in this book; it is mentioned, however, in a section of Chapter 8 devoted to the need for using every test one can think of to protect oneself when reading or listening to the mass media.

For our purposes (and at considerable risk of oversimplification), we may define speech-communication as follows:

Speech-communication is a transactional process in which the communicator-speaker interacts with communicator-listener(s) in the attempt through words and signs to influence behavior.

Let us now use that definition as a base for further discussion of the complexities of speech-communication.

"Speech-communication is a transactional process..."

In this context, *transactional* is intended to suggest the ideally supportive and satisfying communication relationship in which it is obvious to the listener that the speaker is really trying to communicate with him, and it is equally obvious to the speaker that the listener is cooperating with him, at least to the extent of giving his undivided attention. One of the dictionary meanings of *transaction* is "mutually profitable exchange." That is the basic idea behind the process of communication; there is no mutually profitable exchange if the speaker directs a memorized talk *at* you and is not prepared to engage in any kind of communicative transaction *with* you. To paraphrase and quote from Holtzman,[9] the student who comes *prepared to speak* is in a far better position "to deal with new audience influences" than the student whose purpose is *to give a speech*. The first is ready to engage in "a transaction with his listeners." He is trying "to induce a particular response," and he is also keyed "to listen" to his listeners. The second student is more likely to be a "mere message deliverer" with little or no chance of real communicative exchange with his listeners.

To most of us, the word *process* suggests a continuing, ongoing, and developing activity directed toward some end. In holding that speech-communication is a process, we can begin with the recognition that life is a never-ending series of man's responses to stimuli in a continuous effort to cope with his environment. Asleep or awake, he continues to respond, and in or out of the actual presence of other human beings, most of his "coping" depends on his relative success in interacting with his fellowman. However, the beginnings and endings of his interactions are difficult, if not impossible, to detect. A teetotaler's reaction to an offer of a drink springs as much from earlier experiences as it does from the immediate stimulus of the offer. When he says, "No, thank you," is the communication finished? Psychologists agree that it goes on as both individuals adjust to each other's behavior. When did the communication begin and when did it end? Nobody knows. Similarly in lengthier and more formal exchanges, speech-communication is truly a process in that it is an ongoing succession of stimulus-response interactions having no discernible beginning and no apparent ending. When does a speech begin? With an initial call to engage the speaker? With eager or not-so-eager anticipation of his coming by prospective members of his audience? With prespeech discussion of and argument on his proposed topic? With his introduction to the group? With his opening remarks? And when does the speech end? As soon as the audience decides it was a waste of time to come out to hear him in the first place? When he sits down? Does the speech extend through the

---

9. For a thorough discussion of the idea of transaction in the communicative process, see Holtzman, pp. 27–37.

speaker's continuing influence and the changes he has induced? Does the speech continue through the impetus generated for additional talks and discussions by other speakers and groups? Questions like the foregoing serve to reinforce earlier statements in this chapter on the complexities of speech-communication, as well as to emphasize the fruitlessness of any quest to determine just exactly when it begins or ends.

That speech-communication is *process* can also be demonstrated from your own experience. You have undoubtedly noticed that your positions and reactions have fluctuated *during* conversations, conferences, or speeches. An interesting demonstration of this particular aspect of speech-communication is reported by Brooks and Scheidel in a study of the *ethos* of a speaker.[10] Instead of using the familiar prespeech registration of audience attitude followed by postspeech measurement of attitude change, they devised an experiment which permitted the registration of fluctuations of attitude at intervals *during* the presentation of the message, in this case a recorded speech of Malcolm X. It was found that the ethical appeal of the speaker increased dramatically at the beginning of his comments and then, through a series of shifts, that it steadily *diminished* until he concluded his remarks. Standard before-and-after measurements, on the contrary, indicated that the *ethos* of the speaker had *increased* between the time his remarks began and the time they ended. In other words, the from-one-point-in-time-to-another-point-in-time measurement of the speaker's *ethos* failed to give a true picture of what was actually happening during the ongoing process. The experimenters concluded that analysis *through* time did— in this instance, at least—provide a "truer description of audience response" than could have been obtained through traditional procedures. Therefore, in addition to the fact that speech-communication is an extremely complex "happening" *as it occurs*, we see that the process is also a timeless and continuing phenomenon which encompasses pre-event, concurrent-with-event, and post-event changes with no discernible beginnings or endings.

". . . the communicator-speaker interacts with communicator-listener(s) . . ."

The terms *communicator-speaker* and *communicator-listener* appear in the definition to highlight the fact that both speaker and listener are active participants in the process of communication. In reinforcement of the earlier stress on transaction, *interacts* is a verb signifying the interrelated quality of the continuous and reciprocal responses —listener-to-speaker and speaker-to-listener—which are inextricably a part of human communication and are characteristic of efficient communication. In other words, the listener is not a passive object toward which the speaker directs whatever message he has in mind. The listener is communicating constantly and supplying *feedback* useful to the speaker. The sensitive speaker, attuned as he is to the verbal and/or nonverbal "responses" of one listener or many, adjusts his messages to fit those "responses." His adjustments (e.g., change of tactics, more proof, a joke or two, additional illustrations) account, in turn, for a series of favorable or unfavorable reactions among his listeners. In other words, there is a constant two-way barrage of stimuli affecting both speaker and listener and causing them to vary their messages and responses accordingly.

---

10. Robert D. Brooks and Thomas M. Scheidel, "Speech as Process: A Case Study," *Speech Monographs*, **35** (March 1968), pp. 1–7.

"... in the attempt through words and signs..."

We have the impression that *words* are really the stuff that communication is made of, and it is true that speech-communication depends in part on language consisting of single words or numbers of words strung together in intelligible fashion. However, we seldom think about—or have a tendency to discount—the modifying force of nonverbal *signs*, such as tone, facial expression, feeling, timing, accent, and vocal sounds of kinds other than recognizable words.

Insofar as nonverbal communication[11] directly associated with "spoken language" is concerned, you know from your own experience that it is possible to say "No" and clearly mean "Yes." One can say, "I'm certainly eager to get to my biology class today," and mean exactly the opposite. When the flying instructor remarks, "Don't fly off on your first solo with my new jacket in the plane," his words carry an overtone not indicated in the *word* message. The tone of an assent can carry along with it a very obvious reluctance; the tone of a command can indicate uncertainty and entreaty; the tone of a refusal can show regret. "When you say that, pardner, smile!" is not just a part of our Western lore; it is also very much a part of our daily life. Friends can insult each other in a bantering way which totally negates the meaning of the words. We also know that the "meaning" of a sentence depends in part on the emphasis given to a word or words in it. For instance, "I am going to St. Louis" can be said in such a way as to indicate that (1) *you* are going there, (2) you are *determined* to go, (3) you are going to St. Louis in preference to any other place, (4) you are going *to* and not *from* that city, (5) you're going there but you don't relish the idea, (6) you are going and others should follow your lead, (7) anyone who thinks you're going there is out of his mind, and so on.

Other examples of meaning-interpretation modified by nonword aspects of speech: When you ask a favor of someone, he may smile as he replies, "I'll think it over." If you interpret the smile to be very friendly and permissive, you feel that the cause is essentially won; if he answers with a frown or trace of anger, you know that he is putting you off, perhaps permanently. "Shut the door!" can be said in such a way that it carries one or more of several emotional implications—love, hate, sarcasm, fear, and so on.[12] If you have somehow failed to carry out some directions for the completion of a certain task, you will be able to tell from the tone (irritated?) and timing (very precisely spaced words?) of a supervisor's corrections how he feels about your errors. If you have a telephone conversation with a stranger who has an accent, you will probably arrive at some inferences about his background, and they will affect your response to his verbal message. A secretary from the South may have some difficulty getting a good post in the North because her speech pattern is considered slow and imprecise; a secretary from the North may have similar problems in the South because her speech is regarded as too clipped and rapid. An audible class-wide moan may follow the announcement of a particular assignment;

---

11. The discussion of nonverbal communication in this text is based primarily on distinctions found in Argyle, pp. 91–126.

12. According to Flora Davis in *The Rhetoric of Nonverbal Communication*, edited by Haig A. Bosmajian (Glenview, Ill.: Scott, Foresman, 1971), p. 4, "Psychologist Albert Mehrabian has devised a formula to explain the emotional impact of any message: total impact = 7 percent verbal + .38 percent vocal + .55 percent facial."

the instructor doesn't need to hear any words to interpret the meaning of that kind of "speech." In other words, "how one sounds" is clearly an integral part of the word message and clearly affects the interpretation which the listener places upon it.

It is also possible to "speak" without words or vocalizations of any kind. In the hypothetical example of the supervisor's offering some corrective advice, you would not have to say anything to give him a fairly accurate impression of your reaction to his criticism. Or moving to the world of job applications, businessmen generally like to have applicants appropriately dressed and prepared to make the best impression possible. If the job applicant appears on the scene in sport clothes and doesn't seem to have the manners associated with business transactions, he is treated to some routine questions and pleasantries and then escorted to the door with the familiar "Don't call me, I'll call you." What is said in such an exchange has *nothing* to do with the result. Or let us say that every time you encounter a particular student, he looks and acts in an unpleasant manner. No matter what he says on any of these occasions, you "get the message," and it is unlikely that you will vote for him when he runs for a class office. If you are late in arriving at a meeting, you will feel more welcome if someone smiles and shows you to a chair. Is there a message in the way in which you stand or sit when talking with someone? What is your reaction when another student takes what you consider to be *your* seat in a class? Or when someone grabs *your* seat on a bus after a rest stop? At times, "actions do speak louder than words."

We see, then, that messages are made up of words *and* signs and that it is a practical impossibility in speech-communication to have language unaccompanied by nonverbal components. It is also possible, as we have seen, to have a message conveyed through nonverbal communication alone or through nonverbal communication accompanied by language which has little or nothing to do with the basic message.

Further, the scientists and psychologists tell us that words reach us more slowly than signs because of the time involved in saying words and in interpreting verbal messages. The signs (what we *see* and *sense*) reach us first and carry their own implications, which may or may not be in support of what is being said. And so we come to realize that words are only a part of the message and that we have a veritable battery of nonverbal cannon that fire signs toward the listener faster than the words which are usually considered to be the primary carriers. Over some of these signs we have control; over others we have none. Some may reinforce what we have to say, some may detract from it, and some may contradict it.

Each of us, then, brings to the communication situation physical attributes, mode of dress, mannerisms, educational background, attitudes, prejudices, voice, regional intonations and pronunciations, habits of gesture and body movement, and a host of other qualities which make up his personality and character. The message is unbelievably complex; the words used by the speaker "mean" one thing to him and, as often as not, something ranging from slightly different to grossly different to the listener. As for the latter, the eyes tell their own story of acceptance, belligerence, guile, trust, rejection; the speaker's facial expressions are "interpreted"; his gestures support, contradict, or interfere with the message and its interpretation; vocal intonations, accents, pitch patterns, and rate of speaking help win over one listener and repel another. Whatever the central message may be in the mind of the speaker, it reaches the hearer in a state modified by (1) the many other messages, usually supportive but sometimes contradictory, simultaneously dispatched by the speaker, and (2) the hearer's own attitudes and prejudices. The hearer's response is similarly conditioned by his background, and, received as feedback by the speaker, it is further conditioned or modified by the speaker's background.

Not only are there interactions of various kinds in the speech-communication process, but different *levels* of interaction may also be noted. In his book, *The Process of Communication,* Berlo distinguishes four levels of interactive response or communicative interdependence.[13] He uses the term "definitional-physical interdependence" to describe a situation in which two people in conversation are both so intent on their own problems and messages that neither really hears or reacts to what the other is saying. They are interdependent only in the physical sense that each needs the other to provide an object at which the messages can be directed. If your own message is so important to you that you can't wait until the other fellow is finished "with whatever it is that he's saying," and if he feels the same way about you and your messages, you are both in the sad state of definitional-physical interdependence. By contrast—and one step up the ladder—in "action-reaction interdependence" each person in a communication setting uses *feedback* (described earlier in this chapter) as a guide in the preparation of succeeding messages. In explaining the rules of bridge to some friends, you will be careful to react to what they say, how they look (puzzled, happy, disappointed), and they, in turn, will be equally attentive to your comments, questions, and advice. Sometimes the *feedback* is clear but to no avail; witness the notebook comment (*Time,* October 20, 1967, p. 27) of Ernesto Guevara, the Cuban revolutionary, on Bolivian peasants: "You talk to them, and in the depths of their eyes it can be seen that they don't believe." In any event, however skilled we are at recognizing and using a listener's reactions, there is always room for improvement along lines suggested for the third level, which is "interdependence of expectations: empathy." When a college or university student wants something of material value, it is common for him to broach the subject to the parent from whom he expects a more ready acceptance of the idea. It is also possible that the one parent will volunteer to discuss the matter with the other because "I know how to handle him/her." In some situations, as Berlo says, we "... do more than act and react. We develop expectations about others which affect our actions—before we take them."[14] We feel that we understand another person or group of persons so well that we can put ourselves in their places and predict with some accuracy what they will do in a given situation. For another example, a student will act in one way in his relations with one professor and in an entirely different way with another. What accounts for the difference? His image of the one obviously calls for one kind of relationship; another kind is called for by the second. Fourth and finally, perfect communicative interdependence is attained only through complete and total "interaction," a rare phenomenon indeed. It occurs when people simultaneously succeed in seeing things from one another's viewpoint, simultaneously predict one another's responses, simultaneously experience total rapport with one another. Trying to sit in one another's chairs and trying to view the world from one another's vantage points are valuable

---

13. Berlo, pp. 106–131.
14. *Ibid.*, p. 121.

approaches to understanding. Those who succeed in the attempt—and they are few—reach true "interaction: the goal of human communication."[15]

"... to influence behavior."

Ways and means of influencing behavior will be the subjects of subsequent chapters. For the moment, our purpose is restricted to (1) a listing of the broad categories of influences which speech-communicators try to exert and (2) a brief explanation of a distinction between "belief" and "attitude," terms which appear in those categories.

Modern theorists generally agree that, in the effort to influence behavior, we undertake one or more of three communicative objectives: (1) to present information; (2) to introduce, strengthen, or change belief or attitude; and/or (3) to call for some kind of action.[16] These goals are not mutually exclusive; they may appear singly or in combination. For instance, the professor talking on the subject of preparation of a special approach to some aspect of insurance-selling is presenting information on a process; he may also be endeavoring to introduce a certain attitude toward a particular selling problem, and he may be suggesting one course of action in preference to any other. The historian lecturing on the "facts" (more on this subject in Chapters 2 and 3) may encounter some resistance to his interpretations and as a consequence may find himself moving from the presentation of "information" to an attempt to change the attitudes of his listeners.

Although the phrasing of the goals above is orthodox, some comment on a useful distinction between "belief" and "attitude" is in order. Building on earlier work by Osgood, Suci, and Tannenbaum, Martin Fishbein takes the carefully reasoned position that "... an individual's attitude toward any object is a function of his beliefs about the object ... and [of] the evaluative aspect of those beliefs...."[17] By way of extension of what he means, it is possible for two individuals, both strongly opposed to the convention system of nominating candidates for elective office, to have entirely different ideas on the nature of the convention system, on its operational detail, and on what should be done about it. These individuals are alike in their *attitude* or evaluative response of overall opposition toward the system but different in their *beliefs* about it. For example, one individual may believe that the system is a waste of time and money, the other that it thwarts the democratic process.

It is also possible, of course, for people to be similar in their beliefs and different in their resulting attitudes. For instance, Fishbein cites the hypothetical case of an Oriental who has no high opinion of "White men."[18] If he expresses the belief that "Negroes are equal to White men," the negative attitude implied in that sentence is obviously not the same as the positive attitude indicated by the same statement when made either by "White men" or by Negroes. The point of this greatly simplified version

---

15. Berlo., p. 129.
16. The same theorists recognize that it is possible to influence behavior by the simple act of attentive and sympathetic listening, a habit of behavior encouraged in this volume.
17. Martin Fishbein, "An Investigation of the Relationships Between Beliefs About an Object and the Attitude Toward That Object," *Human Relations*, **16** (August, 1963), p. 233.
18. Example cited in Martin Fishbein, "A Consideration of Beliefs, Attitudes, and Their Relationships," in Steiner and Fishbein, p. 112.

of the Fishbein hypothesis is this: If we can discover and accurately interpret the beliefs which are the bases for an attitude, successful effort to change or modify the beliefs should result in a change or modification of the attitude. Conversely, if a change in one's attitude is effected because of a desire to adopt a position taken by a respected speaker or because of social pressure or any other kinds of stimuli, a corresponding change in underlying beliefs will normally occur. (For further discussion of beliefs and attitudes, see Chapter 12.)

. . . .

Comprehension checks

Can a smile change the meaning of a message? Give an example. Do the same for frown, eyes staring into space, stance, tone. Can a smile interfere with a message? Explain. Does the way you look or dress in a given situation affect meaning? Examples? It is possible to pass along a face-to-face message without words? Without signs? Demonstrate. Are telephone conversations oridnarily as satisfactory as direct person-to-person conversations? Do any signs come through the phone? What kinds?

Are you aware of having any mannerisms which contribute to or detract from your efforts to communicate? Describe or demonstrate. Do you know of any prominent public figure who has some uniquely characteristic habits of gesture? Describe. Do you use the same language patterns in talking about a problem with a friend as you do in talking about it with a professor or counselor? Is there any inconsistency or dishonesty involved in being a slightly different person in different situations? Would any other student in the class see a particular problem in exactly the same way and use exactly the same language in talking about it? How do you account for the differences?

Do you listen very well when you are uncomfortably hot? Or after you hear an end-of-class signal? Mention some other distractions or interfering "noises" you have experienced. Does your mind wander to other subjects during a class lecture? How do you account for this? Any recent examples? In this class? Are there any situations in which the force of a message is enhanced by music, portraits, flags, other symbols, atmosphere? Cite some.

Do you listen more attentively to some people than to others? Why? Do you "turn off" some people? Why? Does your acceptance of a message ever depend on how a person looks and acts? Or on what you personally think of him? Or on whether he is superior or inferior (in your opinion) to you in any way? Examples? Does the word "home" carry exactly the same meaning for you as for the student next to you? How about words like "democracy" and "truth"? Do they mean the same things to everyone? Why not? When did you last say, "What I meant was...."? Under what circumstances?

What is feedback? What is the importance of feedback in a communicative situation? Do people who have not studied speech-communication use feedback? Do you use feedback as a partial guide to what you are saying or going to say? What do you think are the advantages of being consciously aware of feedback?

Have you ever begun asking someone for a favor and then decided "in midstream" to drop the matter as a lost cause? Was that decision a result of feedback?

Describe the incident. Describe other instances of feedback you have encountered in your conversations with individuals. How did you react to the feedback? Did you make changes to improve reception of your messages? What changes? Successfully?

Does the pitch of your voice go up slightly when you are nervous or under stress? Do you try to lower it? When you sing, are you using feedback to help you to carry the tune? When you are trying to make an impression on someone, do you consciously vary volume, pitch, or rate in conversation with that person? Have you taken part in any skits or plays? What part has the sound of your own voice played in your performance?

When you walk into a classroom, are you "saying" anything? When did your saying begin? As you came through the door? Earlier? Explain. When you hear that a well-known expert on pollution is scheduled for a lecture, has his "communication" already begun? Or does it begin when he utters the first words of the lecture? Is it possible for a man to "talk" before he actually begins saying anything? When you expect someone to walk in with either good or bad news, do you get a part of the "message" before the news is passed on in words? Is it possible for a speaker to be sending one message or set of messages with words and another *contrary* message with signs? Can someone affect your behavior in some way without saying anything to you? How? Can that person tell what your reaction is without your reacting verbally? How?

Demonstration options

1. Try to get the members of the class to reproduce on paper a relatively simple geometrical drawing. Do not show them the drawing and do not use gestures. Use words only.

   Go through the same routine but permit questions from your listeners.

   Go through the same routine but use gestures as well as words.

2. Present to the class a short impromptu monologue in which you play the role of telling a close friend about some problem, real or fictitious, that you have had in one of your courses. Imagine that the scene changes to the instructor's office; tell him about the same problem. Let the class comment on the difference, if any, in the two presentations.

3. Describe a situation in which "noise" made communication difficult if not impossible. Or describe one in which "noise" enhanced and improved communication.

4. With another student in the class, play the role of a counselor giving a very short pep talk or "bit of advice." The task of the other student is to interject *aloud* his personal reactions to what is being said to him. For example: "What does he mean?" "If he thinks I'd fall for that line!" "He's got something there!" "Why me?" Etc.

5. Describe any speaker reaction to feedback which you have witnessed or experienced.

6. When someone is talking "artificially," it is a feedback which makes possible that kind of talk; give examples or imitations of people intentionally controlling the voice in a certain way for a certain purpose.

7. Explain to the class why your having a casual conversation with friends is (or is not) an attempt to influence behavior.
8. Either describe a situation in which the words in a message conflicted with the signs, or attempt to present a message to the class while contradicting it with signs. An example: Describe how eager you are to get a particular event (class, concert, game, etc.) while at the same time indicating through tone, inflection, and the way you "look" that you are not at all eager to get there.

. . . .

In the first part of this chapter the emphasis was on the complexity of the *process* of speech-communication, on the interactions *between* communicator-speaker and communicator-listener, and on the interactions *within* both communicators. Then a short but specific definition of speech-communication was followed by a discussion of the parts of that definition.

To communicate effectively, then, one must develop sensitivity in human interaction. A part of successfully relating to others obviously depends on understanding (1) typical modes of expression through language, (2) common ways of reasoning, and (3) other factors affecting speaker-listener relationships. These topics are the subjects of the next three chapters.

2 / Language: power and peril

What's in a name? That which we call a rose
By any other name would smell as sweet.

Shakespeare

In the summer of 1967, President Johnson of the United States and Premier Kosygin of Russia made a small New Jersey town famous overnight by making it the scene of two conferences. Both men were "on their best behavior," and in view of the barriers to communication (neither spoke the language of the other), the conferences at least served to convince the people of the world that there must still be hope for peace so long as the leaders of these two powers were willing to sit down and try to communicate with one another. Their *willingness* alone was a communication of hope.

If Johnson and Kosygin could have conversed directly in English or Russian, would their problems in communication have been solved? Hardly. In addition to our recognizing the problems posed by differences in backgrounds, perceptions, goals, values, and other difficulties inherent in human relations, we must also understand that "the structure of the language one habitually uses influences the manner in which one understands his environment."[1] Different languages provide different views of the world, not only through having different words or more words or no words for the same things but through differences in the ways that the words are put together. Stuart Chase gives us the very simple but illuminating example of the experience of Edmund Glenn in his studies of translation problems at the United Nations: "An English speaker...says 'I assume'; the French interpreter renders it 'I deduce'; and the Russian interpreter 'I consider'—By that time the assumption idea is gone with

---

1. Stuart Chase in the Foreword to *Language, Thought, and Reality*, by Benjamin Lee Whorf, edited by John B. Carroll (Cambridge, Mass.: MIT Press, 1956), p. vi. Reprinted by permission.

the wind!"² Through the words and thought patterns characteristically available to him through his culture and language, the American has one view of his surroundings; a person speaking another language has a different set of words, not duplicating either the vocabulary or American ways of saying, thinking, or looking at things. We have to remind ourselves that the "categories and types that we . . . [discern are not] there because they stare every observer in the face; on the contrary, the world is presented in a kaleidoscopic flux of impressions which has to be organized by our minds—and this means largely by the linguistic system in our minds."³

Unfortunately, the struggle to communicate is not just one existing between two persons speaking different languages; it is one affecting any two or more speaking the same language. For instance, in talking about the generation gap, one often says with considerable truth that old and young "do not speak the same language." Or a highly educated person finds it difficult to find the right words for communicating with a workman with little or no education. "I can't find a word for it" is a common complaint; the statement correctly implies that the individual is held captive within the bounds of his own language, and he is further handicapped by what he does not know about his own language—because no one of us has complete command over English. Our language, then, "is not merely a reproducing instrument for voicing ideas but rather is itself the shaper of ideas. . . ."⁴ How well we shape them depends on us. We often use our language so carelessly and inaccurately that any two of us might just as well be talking two languages!

This chapter presents a discussion of accuracy and sensitivity in the choice and handling of words. (Although the focus here is on words, you already know that verbal communication is accompanied by nonverbal signs; comment on the uses of language cannot take place, therefore, without implicit or explicit acknowledgment of the pervasive existence of such signs.) You must not only become more sensitive and accurate in your own word management; it is equally imperative that you develop a second sense in the interpreting of what others "mean" in their uses of words and verbal patterns. Interacting sensibly—difficult enough under favorable circumstances—becomes appreciably easier if, as a part of your effort to understand "man," you try to understand some of his problems in expressing himself.

Words and the Meanings of Words

Of all the achievements of man, none is as significant as language, without which it is no exaggeration to say that his other accomplishments would have been impossible or, at best, long delayed. Among the creatures inhabiting the earth, man is the only being capable of using word-symbols, names standing for material things (e.g., blueberry jam), as well as for abstract concepts (honor, integrity, love, etc.). We have already seen that the words and ideas which we project are the product of our own special and individual experiences, attitudes, and beliefs. Messages we send are, in

---

2. *Ibid.*, pp. vii–viii.
3. Whorf, *Language, Thought, and Reality*, p. 213. Reprinted by permission.
4. *Ibid.*, p. 212.

turn, screened through another and different set or sets of personal "filters." The meanings we attach to words are seldom, if ever, identical to those attached to the same words by others. The meanings of words are *in us*, not in the words. The words you use "call up words (or some other symbols) which the listener formulates into a pattern that makes sense to *his* needs."[5] As we learned in the preceding chapter, the listener interprets, translates, infers, and comes up with a message which may closely resemble yours, may resemble it to some extent, or may resemble it not at all. Here, then, are five ideas for developing greater accuracy in handling words.

Become sensitive to context

For a beginning, we can become aware of the contexts or settings which affect the meanings of words. Cherry gives examples of 10 different meanings of the word "meaning."[6] Beardsley notes 55 distinct senses of "point" and 109 for "run."[7] We have to be equally careful about interpretations of quoted phrases, sentences, and paragraphs. Someone can be quoted as saying, "Women are by nature better coordinated than men," when the actual statement was "One thesis which cannot be defended is this: Women are by nature . . . ." If we are context-conscious, we become careful about both interpreting words *in* context and accepting them *out of* context.

Become sensitive to slanting

A second problem is the detection of slanting. A speaker can quite easily choose to use or report only those facts favorable to his point of view, or he can report the full story but color it in such a way that he is able to manipulate the impressions and inferences drawn from his talk. In two descriptions of a riot incident, it is not too difficult, while keeping the facts constant, to make the policeman the villain in one version and the hero in the other. Rap Brown, the agitator, had a viewpoint toward the police which was unlike that of the mayor of the town at the time of the Cambridge, Maryland, disturbances. "Clark Kerr, president of the University of California, refused to meet the student delegation," as reported in one account, may appear in another as "The president was unwilling to meet the students, because he wanted more time to assemble the facts on political activity near the Sather Gate." For your own edification, read the coverage of some controversy in any two current news magazines. Underline the adjectives and adverbs, and note the choice of words in general. You will find that descriptions of the same event are often slanted in order to favor positions held by publishers, editors, or syndicated writers of some particular political persuasion. The same slanting can and does occur in conversations, conferences, and speeches. We should be aware of our own responsibility for straightforward communication, and we should remember that a speaker has great power of selectivity in choosing to say only what he wishes to say in the way he chooses to say it.

Become sensitive to "allness"

Third, we should try to inoculate ourselves against the allness-affliction. We say things like "All Irishmen have bad tempers," or "Every time he leaves the room, he forgets

---

5. Brown and Van Riper, p. 60 (italics mine).
6. Cherry, p. 115.
7. Beardsley, p. 153.

to turn off the light," or "Governor Andrews never says an intelligent thing." Be wary of such words as *everybody, nobody, all, always, never, first, last, every,* and *constantly.* Think in terms of *normally, sometimes, a few, almost, quite, occasionally,* and so on.

Become sensitive to labeling

Fourth, most of us recognize that labeling or name-calling, even in political campaigns, is not a very highly regarded activity. We are less aware that thoughtlessly attaching a label of any kind, however innocuous it may seem, to a thing or individual is often a form of automatic name-calling. Any label automatically suggests to us and to others a particular set of perceptions and attitudes. For example—and depending on the circumstances—these are name-calling words and phrases: *Communist, Protestant, Democrat, Yankee, Catholic, well-dressed, missionary, intellectual, Mexican, agnostic, liberal, Negro, janitor, Republican, maid, Madison Avenue, activist*; the list is of course endless. Just as some of our own citizens do not want to be called "foreigners," so students object to being called "foreign." What may be a convenient tag for some people is often a derogatory term to others. Man likes to classify and to place persons and things in neatly arranged pigeonholes; he doesn't realize that he is sometimes guilty of name-calling without knowing it.

Become sensitive to self-qualification

Finally, since "truth" and "fact" are truth and fact only in your mind or to the extent that someone agrees with you, it is appropriate to recognize that you could be wrong and that, even if you are convinced that you are right, it would be inappropriate to say so in a condescending or alienating way. Therefore, the novice speaker soon learns that it is possible to be more accurate and to protect himself at the same time by using self-qualifiers, such as *it seems to me, in my opinion, from my particular point of view, although others may have reason to think differently, the facts seem to indicate, apparently, my impression is that, a tentative conclusion, I currently believe, the evidence suggests, perhaps we can infer, there is some justification, available information seems to point in this direction.* Conversely, be sure you are smiling if, like some overconfident debater, you have the temerity to say, "I'm going to prove without a shadow of a doubt that . . . ."

Learning to use language intelligently begins by learning not to be used by language.

John C. Condon, Jr.

. . . .

Comprehension checks

Is it possible to determine what a word means when it is cited by itself? Take a simple word like *chisel*. Can you decide what it means without knowing how it is used in a particular sentence or situation? Does a dictionary give you all the meanings of a word? Are the given meanings necessarily correct? Why? Why not? Is it possible to determine whether or not your listener has the same meaning for a word that you do? How? Of what value is such a determination?

When someone neglects to point out that the house he is trying to sell has a leaky basement, is he slanting? Do you often hear a candidate for public office say that his opponent from another party has done anything right during his term of office? Do people tend to present evidence unfavorable to a cause they are supporting?

Can you cite any "allness" statements or questions that you regularly hear? Will your talking about them help you eliminate them? If you eliminate them, your language will be more accurate; will there by any other short- or long-range benefits?

Is it possible to be guilty of name-calling without being aware of it? Is it possible for two persons to use exactly the same term and for only one of them to be name-calling? Cite an example. What has *feeling* to do with labeling? Are you inclined to fit people you meet into broad classifications or groups? What are the dangers in doing so?

Isn't it a weakness to admit that one could be wrong? If you don't appear to be sure about a particular conclusion, can you expect listeners to have confidence in your position? Benjamin Franklin used to say that the way to convince another is to state your case accurately and fairly and then shake your head and say that that is the way it seems to you but that, of course, you may be mistaken. What do you think of that approach? Have you noticed how hard it is to change your mind after you have openly committed yourself to one specific position? Would it be easier and less embarrassing to change your mind if you did not take so positive a stand in the first place? Since we can seldom be 100 percent right, is there some advantage in regularly using self-qualifiers as possible "escape hatches" if we should need them?

Demonstration options

1. Write five short sentences in which you use *one* of the following words (or another of your choice) in five different ways: *give, slow, mean, clean, file, get, need, base, fine, high, small.* Then read one of the five sentences in such a way that it has two or three different meanings.
2. Read the coverage of some current controversy in any two news magazines or in any two newspapers. Underline the adjectives and adverbs, and note the differences in the choices of words generally. You should find that the facts in both accounts are essentially the same; you may find that the descriptions are not only different but that they are slanted to favor positions held by the publishers, editors, or syndicated writers. Report your observations to the class.
3. Read the coverage of some current controversy in any two syndicated columns in a newspaper (or in any two editorials from different newspapers). Compare the two for agreement or nonagreement on the facts. Then compare them by underlining adjectives, adverbs, etc., as indicated above. Report your observations.
4. Find some letters to the editor in any newspaper. Underline the allness words in your selection of one or two of the letters. Report on the appropriate or inappropriate use of those all-or-none words. When you are critical of the use, suggest a word which could have been used.
5. Make a record of the allness statements or questions you hear in the course of one full day. Report your observations and your suggestions for better ways to say the same things.

6. Cite the qualities which you feel are characteristic of the people in some profession or walk of life (e.g., teachers, insurance salesmen). Then describe an individual who fits your stereotype. Or one who does not. Or one who does fit it in some ways and not in others. Close with some conclusions on the advantages and dangers of classification in the particular case cited.
7. Find a no-qualification letter to the editor in a local newspaper or popular magazine. In other words, the writer must be one who has taken the position that only his stand is right and that is "all there is to it." Be prepared to read the letter or parts of it to the class. Suggest places where the writer could have used self-qualification to advantage.

Note: Students and instructors will find fascinating options for further investigation and discussion in Salomon, pp. 146–171.

The Right Words in the Right Places

In addition to exercising word care and caution in the ways described above, there are certain positive steps which we can take to increase listener understanding through skill and variety in the phrasing of our messages.

Appealing to the senses

Since we depend so heavily on our senses—sight, sound, touch, smell, and taste—to provide us with the experiences we find so useful in life, it follows that ability to re-create sensory experiences for listeners is a very valuable asset in communicating with them.

How successfully do you think Dorla Hill, University of Iowa student, added to understanding through the re-creation of sensory impressions in this short passage?

> This uneasiness people feel [in dealing with handicapped persons] is manifested in various ways. For instance, when you talk to a handicapped person, do you talk to him, or do you talk to a set of metal braces? When you look at a handicapped person, do you look him in the eye, or do you look at the spokes of a wheelchair? And when you greet a handicapped person, do you greet him with a smile, or with a look of pity that says, "You poor thing, what happened to you?"[8]

Here are two more short excerpts, both taking advantage of our common ground of sensory experience.

> Last October I was nearly the victim in a four-car auto accident. Only the driver who caused the original head-on collision was hurt. Hurt isn't the word; his whole right side of his head was caved in and blood was gushing from one eye. In about half an hour a local funeral-home ambulance arrived. Both attendants were

---

8. The examples used to illustrate points in this section are all reprinted by permission of the Interstate Oratorical Association from collections of student speeches published annually. The excerpt above is from "Cures, Not Coddles," 1969, p. 12.

dressed neatly in suits, which was fine, except that they let bystanders put the injured person on the stretcher with no covering and made no attempt to dress his wounds. The next day the patient died. Whether this accident victim could have been saved I do not know, but I am convinced that a patient's chances in a medical emergency can be pretty slim.[9]

and . . .

In the next few weeks will you ever want to cut your classes and just feel the first warm rays of the sun on your bare arms? Or smell the fragrance of new life in the air. You probably won't do it. You won't miss that student senate meeting or that faculty coffee break, or that TV program either. But you could. Why don't you? Just sit down for about five minutes and think about the things around you. Just once last winter did you notice the sparkle of snow in the white light of a moonlit night?[10]

Evoking word-pictures

You have said (or have heard it said), "He describes things so well that you can actually 'see' what he's talking about." The power of "drawing word pictures" contributes heavily to listener interest; it is also one that each of us can acquire in some degree, especially since good models of description are relatively easy to find. The excerpt below is from "Killer Davis—Who's He?" by Ann Stueve of the University of Michigan.

Wish you could meet Killer Davis—five foot two, wiry, born, bred, and wed in East-side Detroit, talks big, talks constantly, talks to anyone. You'd like him—except for one thing—Killer's 88 years old, and an 88-year-old man is ugly—he has stooped shoulders, sunken cheeks, clammy skin; he's obsolete—he doesn't work, only increases our taxes by collecting welfare; and he's odd sometimes—he papers his room with playing cards and strings twine from corner to corner to hang pictures. In the afternoon Killer just sits in the corner cafe, staring at people. And when he doesn't show up, someone inevitably asks "Is Killer dead yet?" but that someone rarely waits for an answer, and even when he does, there's rarely anyone who knows.[11]

Relying on action words

You probably already know that it is more interesting to the listener to say "The giraffe munches leaves" than "Leaves are munched by the giraffe." In other words, it is generally better to use verb forms describing direct action rather than duller passive forms of the same words. It is also better, again from the standpoint of the listener, to use words showing shades, degrees, or different levels of an action rather than the common, easiest-to-come-by form. For example, instead of a word like "walk," it is better to substitute one of these more descriptive equivalents: *saunter, hurry, stride, amble, tramp, tread, stroll, strut, swagger, limp, hobble,* etc. The passage below, from a

---

9. From "Accidental Care" by True Trueax of Montana College of Mineral Science and Technology, 1968, p. 29.
10. From "Take Time" by Jerry Clausen of Dakota Wesleyan University, 1968, p. 90.
11. 1969, p. 21.

talk by Richard K. Whitney, a Dakota Wesleyan University student, describes a New York City riot scene in 1863.

> The police, some fifty in number, arrived in a scene smacking of macabre slapstick. The Brooks Brothers clothing store was surrounded by a screaming mob of looters. Shaggy thugs were trying on modish suits, frowsy women were scurrying into the night with armloads of fancy shirts and underwear, and haberdashery literally rained from the second-floor windows. The police clubbed their way to the front door, only to discover that many in the mob were armed and willing to fight. The officers, in desperation, drew their pistols and fired volley after deadly volley into the crowd, till it broke, and finally fled.[12]

Expressing feeling

If you look up "feeling" in a dictionary, you will find synonyms like *emotions, sentiment, sympathy, empathy, affection, love, warmth, cordiality,* and any number of words describing man's human and humane relationships with all living things. A friendly smile is an expression of feeling; so is a frown. And listeners normally react with corresponding smiles or frowns. When you feel strongly about someone or something, others who know you or who hear you are "moved" to the same sentiment. If, in addition to feeling a certain way about someone or something, you are able to put your feelings into words and signs, you will more quickly establish close rapport with your listeners, and they will be more ready to listen sympathetically.

In the passage below, would you agree that Susan Adair of Ohio University, describing a situation she encountered as a volunteer worker in a nursing home, is speaking with the kind of feeling to which listeners would respond?

> Some lady had begun screaming—which was a usual occurrence, but today it irritated me—and I decided I would do what I could to quiet her. So I went charging into her room feeling like Jonathan Edwards might have if he'd glanced up from his pulpit and caught a couple kissing in the back pew. But my indignation quickly deflated when I saw her. She looked terribly like anybody's grandmother as she sat there, strapped in her wheelchair, staring at me. In a meek voice I asked her what was wrong.
>
> Immediately her eyes grew wild and she began babbling very fast, very loudly—all the while pointing at a magazine in her lap.
>
> "What about the magazine?" I asked.
>
> She stopped and looked at me as though she couldn't believe I was still there and not off on some more important errand. Then she began a methodical struggle for communication—a struggle which I finally realized was probably the result of nominal aphasia, a possible consequence of a stroke in which the victim *thinks* one word but *says* another. Her screams had been a desperate attempt to *force* communication.
>
> At last she paused and looked up at me with sad, hopeless eyes. I smiled. "Yes, there *is* a girl on the cover of *Look*, isn't there?"

---

12. 1969, p. 99.

She grasped my hand. There were tears in her eyes. "God bless you," she said—her only completely intelligible sentence.[13]

Adopting a "direct style"

Lengthy sentences, "big" words, and the formality of the essay approach are unsuited to listeners in any speech-communication situation. When someone speaks in long and complicated sentences, the listener "gets lost." It is good practice to speak in relatively short sentences and to depend on *words common to you*, meaning those you normally use in conversation. You will find it easier to use the shorter sentences and the common words if you make a habit of using as many personal pronouns as possible. It is difficult to be "stuffy" when your messages include such words as "you," "we," "us," "I," "me," etc.; further, the use of a *personal pronoun style* automatically contributes to the interaction which we all try to achieve with listeners. Note the direct and personal approach to the listener in this short selection.

> We can stop blaming the criminal, start blaming ourselves, and figure out where we've gone wrong. We can't blame crime on that all-encompassing bad guy, the Society—because *we are* the Society, and our will is the Society's will.
>
> The crucial question remains: Can we establish empathy?
>
> Put yourself back in the place of the newly formed criminal. Crime has become reinforcing to you. Through it, you have satisfied the secondary needs—for status, style, and maybe even subsistence—generated in you since childhood.
>
> Then suddenly you are confronted by a policeman in the act of committing a crime. You have a gun. Stop!
>
> Because we have allowed crime to become your way of life, the policeman is threatening your status, your identity, and your life.
>
> Will you shoot?
>
> *Do you have an alternative?*[14]

A final word on using "the right words in the right places": your success will largely depend on how realistically you *visualize and re-create listener experiences* in the real world as well as in the world of idea. What is "right" for you may not be "right" for your audience. Your choices in language (and signs) should be those you consider best suited for helping listeners to achieve vivid recall of individual or collective "happenings" and perceptions. Your task is to stimulate their imaginations in such a way that they find it easy to make their contributions to the communicative process.

. . . .

Comprehension checks

Is a word which appeals to your senses necessarily one which will appeal to the senses of a listener? What bearing should the experiences of the listener have on your choice

---

13. 1969, p. 38.
14. From "Where Criminal is Victim" by Brenda Depew of Depauw University, in 1969, p. 10.

of "vivid language"? How can you determine what those experiences are? To how many different senses do the first three speakers quoted (under "Appealing to the Senses") appeal? Is the language in each instance the sort which would arouse the memories of college and university undergraduates?

Does the passage on Killer Davis evoke a picture for you? Do you think it evokes the same picture for everyone who reads it? If there are differences in the pictures evoked, how do you account for them? Do you know any 88-year-old people? Is it reasonable for the speaker to take it for granted that you do?

What words in the description of the 1863 riot do you consider "action words"? Are any of them especially vivid to you? Why? Are there any improvements you could make in the speaker's choice of words? Would these improvements necessarily be better choices for everyone else in the class?

There are three direct quotations in the passage on the elderly lady in the nursing home. How do you think each of these was said? Would your "oral interpretation" of each sentence be the same as that of others in your class? Why not? Are there emotional overtones and feelings in those sentences? In the passage as a whole? How would you describe or identify them? Are there times when emotion is a stronger "argument" than reason? When?

The passage about blaming ourselves instead of the criminal is a good example of the "direct style." How many personal pronouns are used? Is the passage easy to understand? What makes it so? What changes would you make? Why?

Demonstration options

1. Find a paragraph from some piece of literature, editorial, or speech in which the "composer" has made good use of sensory appeals. Discuss what he has done.
2. Find a paragraph which totally lacks such appeals to "the listener." Suggest how it could be improved.
3. Write your own short appeal to the listener's sensory experiences. (It could be a description of a favorite dish or dessert.)
4. You have been to a lookout point, vista platform, scenic viewing point, or you have been to a ghost town, a restored village, or some other place of historical or aesthetic interest. Write one or two short paragraphs describing what you saw; re-create in language adapted to and for the class a total picture or some part of it. Then read it to the members of the class for their reaction.
5. Write a short description of any place (local building, park, auditorium, museum, etc.) familiar to most of the students in the class. Let the class members comment on important items missed or improperly described from *their* point of view.
6. Write a description of some well-known picture, portrait, drawing, painting, or statuary on the campus. Compare your description with that of other students. How do you explain the differences in the descriptions?
7. Find a paragraph or two of "action" in a speech, short story, article, or novel. Jot down the best action words in a column, and in the same order on another sheet, write an overworked and common equivalent for each of the action words. Trade columns of ordinary words with another student, and then try separately

to come up with new sets of matching action words. Compare with the original lists to see if, by accident, a few of the original words have been "recovered."
8. Write an original "action passage" on some incident that happened to you, that you know about, or that you witnessed. Make it as class-oriented as you can, and be prepared to read it to the class.
9. Find a passage in any speech or literary work in which you see an emphasis on feeling. Read it aloud to the class, and explain what feeling or feelings you detect in it.
10. At some time in your life you have been emotionally affected. Perhaps one such occasion occurred when your family moved from one community to another. Try to describe such an event in terms which will help members of the class to "feel with you" about what happened.
11. Choose an essay or composition of some kine that you wrote for another class. On the assumption that the style in it is more formal than the direct style we are talking about, rewrite a paragraph or two in personal-pronoun, common-word, speech-communication style. Be prepared to read both the formal and the less formal versions in class.
12. Select a paragraph or two from one of your class textbooks, and change them into the more direct style suited to listeners rather than readers. Be prepared to read both passages in class.

. . . .

Problems in Abstraction, Classification, and Definition

A story is told of two elderly farmers listening to an itinerant preacher. One, a little deaf, asks the other, "What's he sayin'?" and the other replies, "He don't say." Students listening to lectures sometimes have the same problem; a professor may be so enamored by the principles of his particular discipline that he never "comes down to earth," and students are at a loss to know what he is talking about. The opposite extreme is the professor who very engagingly and entertainingly tells story after story —not all of them necessarily relevant—gives example after example, and finds it almost impossible to get to the point. The difficulty is that such professors are literally stuck at particular levels of abstraction without realizing that the way to be interesting and effective is to move "up and down the ladder." Principles can be made meaningful only by examples and data; examples and data make little sense unless they are used as a base for principles or conclusions at a higher level.

Abstraction. In the preceding sections of this chapter, we examined ways to use words accurately and in the right places. Names are descriptive words requiring additional attention, because, as you undoubtedly realize, names are a form of elementary abstraction; for example, "chair" is a word covering many different kinds and styles of units to which one could point to designate a chair. If we wish to go "up the ladder" of abstraction, we may successively say "chair, seat, furniture, furnishing, property, estate, and wealth." (If you look closely at a legal brief or speech outline, you will see that the process of organizing either is normally one of collecting materials and arranging them according to relative levels of abstraction.) Abstraction, then, may be regarded as a "process of leaving out details"[15] as you move to progressively higher levels. The higher you get, the farther behind you leave the objects and the sense data which gave rise to the original name-level abstraction. We have many choices of what to call something; a measure of our language sensitivity is our choice of that level of abstraction which best meets our needs in a specific set of circumstances. There are Indians and an Indian, students and a student, South Africans and a South African, cars and a car, New Yorkers and a New Yorker, airlines and an airline, and any other pairs you can think of. We have to be careful about confusing our stereotypes of the Indian with the individual Indian standing before us. What is regarded as true of a group (and gives rise to an abstraction) is not necessarily true of the unit or individual. You may buy a car because the product has a reputation for reliability; yet that car may prove to be a "lemon." We must be aware that our concept of the members of a given race as a class should have little if anything to do with our relationship with or evaluation of a particular member of that race. Like the word or name, a higher-level abstraction is *not the thing* it is supposed to represent; when we speak with an individual or group, we must use abstractions carefully and demonstrate at the same time that we are using them with a full knowledge of their advantages and limitations.

Classification. Classifications are often described as higher-order abstractions which we choose to use as convenient "catchall" labels for people or things having similar characteristics. For example, "furniture" is one of the possible levels of abstraction as we go from "chair" to "wealth." We can decide to make that level serve as a more or less stabilized classification for items like tables, desks, bookcases, sofas, and other units required to equip rooms for living. Or stated another way, classification may be regarded as the abstractive process of labeling or sorting people or things into groups and subgroups on a basis of their similarities and differences. For instance, among the Indo-European languages of the world are the families classified as Germanic, Celtic, Baltic, Slavic, Romance, and others. In the Romance classification are such languages as Portuguese, Spanish, French, Italian, and Romanian. Within each language there are a number of dialects. Although the classifications resulting from the studies of languages (or the species of bear) are of a scientific order, the relation to up-the-ladder-down-the-ladder abstractive processes is clear. The problem is that we sometimes forget that *classifications are static, man-made products of convention* which are subject to change. The word "furniture" means whatever we want it to mean. College athletes are called amateurs, although they receive compensation of various kinds. We classify them as amateurs, *because it pleases us to do so.* Russia directly and openly pays its athletes; in our view they are not truly amateur, because they do not fit our special classification of amateur. In the United States, the line between the golf amateur and the golf professional is so thin that it now takes a legal expert to determine one's status. And Hayakawa makes the point that we classify as "Negro" anyone with a small amount of Negro blood and that it would be just as reasonable to classify as white anyone with a small amount of white blood.[16] The first classification of Negro exists

---

15. Johnson, p. 151.
16. Hayakawa, p. 217.

only because it suits the purpose of the white majority. We must get used to the idea that classifications are made by individuals and groups to serve *their* needs; classifications can be and often should be changed. What something or someone is called should depend on one's particular vantage point at the time. For example, we should not label Harvey McDuff of the University of Southern California simply as a psychologist. When he is practicing in Pasadena, he is a clinical psychologist; when he is lecturing on the campus, he is a professor of psychology; when he is writing a novel, he is a novelist; when he is writing short stories, he is a short-story writer; when he is playing the violin, he is a violinist; when he is skating, he is a skater.

Man's "proclivity to classify" frequently gets him into trouble. Parents label a child "stubborn," and from that time forward the child takes pride in being stubborn. Schoolteachers and administrators label an adolescent as a potential dropout and soon have a dropout in fact. On the basis of initial and incomplete evidence at the beginning of a semester, a student is labeled "top caliber," "average," or "below average," and he proceeds to perform at the expected level. "As you are classified, so will you often perform" is a frightening truism. The moral is twofold: We must remember (1) that classifications should be approached warily and (2) that classifications, once made, are neither sacred nor inflexible. In Aristotle's time, qualities were typically regarded as properties belonging to the thing or person under scrutiny; in our day, qualities are considered to be inventions springing from the mind and eyes of individual beholders. Earlier we said that meanings of words are not in the words but *in us*; it is equally true that classifications are not in the items observed but *in us*.

Definition. Definition has points in common with both abstraction and classification. When you consult "pocket dictionaries"—or, for that matter, *Roget's Thesaurus*—for the meaning of a word, you will usually find synonyms but no other information; in other words, such works take the short and easy road of staying on the same level of abstraction as the word for which you want a definition. Even less fruitful is the attempt to define by moving up the abstraction ladder because, as we have already seen, going in that direction leads to our being progressively more and more general. The only other route to take is down the ladder, and it does lead toward some understanding of the "meaning" of a word because, in this instance, we are moving toward more specific elements and examples. If we try to define "furniture" in terms of "wealth," we are not of much help to someone who has never heard the word being defined. But if we show that person items of furniture in a Sears catalog or, better still, in a local furniture store, he will quickly understand what that word means to many of us. Consider the term "foreign aid." We can go up toward "idealistic philanthropy," or come down toward "sending agricultural experts only to non-Communist countries making formal requests for such help."

In addition to defining by citing pocket-dictionary synonyms or moving down the abstraction ladder toward examples, we can adopt a listing of attributes as a third mode of definition. For instance, a lawyer could be giving a talk on wills and find it necessary to define an "executor" by listing his duties. An architect discussing the services of his firm might want to delimit a "mechanical engineer" by briefly outlining the part he plays on a planning team. A civic worker interested in the council form of city government would have to describe the characteristics of that form in some detail before moving on to questions of advantage and disadvantage.

There are other kinds of definition (e.g., explaining the usage of a word or term by citing it in a variety of contexts), but those closely associated with abstraction and classification are, in the opinion of this writer, best suited to the needs of the speaker. As for the importance of skill in definition, one need only remind himself of how recently he has heard two or more persons argue strenuously, and perhaps heatedly, for a half hour or more, only to find that they were "talking about different things." Care in definition keeps our speaking in focus and saves time and energy for everyone concerned.

Comprehension checks

What is "the ladder of abstraction"? Does this question represent a problem in abstraction: "Why doesn't he give us an example?" Or this one: "When is he going to tell us what those examples are supposed to show?" Is the word "car" an abstraction? What would be a possible choice of name for the next rung *up* the abstraction ladder? And for the next rung *down*? Of what use are abstractions? Do they have any disadvantages?

Who makes classifications? Is the word "patriot" a classification? Assuming that it is, does it always mean the same thing to all people? Do classifications ever change? Are "catchall labels" and "stereotypes" ever useful? Sometimes bad? Always to be avoided? Or are they useful but subject to certain reservations when we use them? What reservations?

There is a definition of speech-communication in Chapter 1. Does it answer the question "What is speech-communication?" to your satisfaction? Does it leave anything out? Is it redundant? What is the value of any definition? Are some concepts impossible to define? Can you give examples? Does difficulty of exact definition increase as one goes up the ladder to higher and higher abstractions? Explain why.

Demonstration options

1. From any source, select a single statement followed by a clarifying example. The meaning of the statement must be obvious enough to require *no explanation* on your part. If it is not so clear as you would like it to be, the example should do all the clarifying necessary. (Best statement and accompanying example can be be determined by class vote.)
2. Look for bad examples used to support ideas and select the worst one you can find. State the exact source.
3. Find an example which seems to support nothing in some passage. State the source.
4. Find a statement or series of statements with no clarifying examples. State the source.
5. Demonstrate a "ladder of abstraction" without referring to or using any of the examples in this text. Start on the lowest rung with a single item and move on up to the highest rung possible. Or start at the top and work down. Or choose a category "in between" and cite abstraction levels up and down from the rung chosen.

6. Name a classification which has a different meaning for two or more groups. For example, as noted earlier, *amateur* means one thing to us and another to people in the Soviet Union. Or cite a classification name which now replaces one which was formerly in popular use for the same group. In either case, fully explain the differences and the reason(s) for them.
7. Find a definition in any source except this text. Explain the method of definition in this particular instance, and suggest any possible improvements you would make in the definition itself or in the method used.

. . . .

Fact, Inference, and Judgment

Fact. A popular comic postcard carries the photograph of a smug-looking baby saying, "My mind is made up; don't confuse me with facts." The creative genius who conceived the line and illustration did not have to be a trained psychologist. Any careful observer of the passing scene knows that the "mind made up" is often the "mind lost to reason." However, "facts" are not always as reliable as they may seem, nor are they always good reason to change one's mind. Furthermore, it takes a good man to recognize a fact when he meets one.

In the earlier decades of this century, the fact that "Christopher Columbus discovered America in 1492" was rather generally accepted. Of course, there was already a lunatic fringe impiously suggesting that the Norsemen had settled, however precariously, on the edges of Labrador, and some were even so bold as to say that the Norsemen had established settlements along the New England coast and had even penetrated the interior of the continent as far as present-day Minnesota. It is now believed that the Norsemen did indeed come to America about the year 1000 A.D., and that they remained for some considerable period afterward. Where does this "new fact" leave Columbus? It all depends on how you define "discovered." But the real point of this paragraph is that a fact is a fact so long as an individual *believes* or a group of individuals *agree* that it is a fact. Man is so constituted that he proceeds according to what *he* regards as fact, whether or not others agree with him and whether or not the item under scrutiny is indeed "a fact" in anyone's mind but his own. Furthermore, "facts" are being continually displaced, as illustrated above, by new facts.

Let us assume that you have just witnessed an accident. Will your *statement of the facts* be the same in detail as those presented by the drivers of the two cars involved? We all know that it is possible, even probable, that you and each of the drivers will have entirely different versions of the incident. When the businesslike detective on a television program interrupts with "Let's stick to the facts, ma'am," it would be bad theatre but good semantic practice to add, "as you see them." *Facts are personal* and they often vary in direct proportion to the number of "reporters." Each of us has his own set of capabilities for observation, his own past experiences, and his own system of values, and all of these elements are *continually changing*. Little wonder that we differ in our "reports." As various accounts go through the second, third, and subsequent stages of "editing," resemblances to the original version are sometimes only coincidental. A popular parlor game is built on the idea that it is fun to see how a simple message is distorted as it is passed from person to person and back to its originator. Participation in this game usually has a salutary effect on "communicators"; it makes them less sure of the infallibility of the fact.

Inference. To look at facts with a quizzical eye is a habit useful to the student both during his undergraduate days and for the rest of his life. Of course, we do necessarily use facts as a basis for arriving at inferences. You can walk into a professor's office without knowing his field of interest and yet, if he has the usual collection of books, monographs, and scholarly journals therein, make a fairly accurate guess (inference) about his specialty. The number of books is an ascertainable fact—though you may miss a few he has in the drawers of his desk and under sheaves of papers—and the titles are also readily available. Similarly, if you have confidence in your source of statistics and see that the tonnage of wheat going to Russia from all other countries has been increasing each year for the past ten years, you can infer that Russia's need for wheat is steadily increasing. (Before you do so, however, it would be wise to try to find out what she has been doing with the wheat.) In other words, much of our knowledge is the result of our ability to move from facts which we consider reliable to a reasonable inference or generalization based on those facts (and sometimes from one set of inferences to still another higher-ranking generalization). The process is quite readily seen in an examination of the "need for a change" section in a debate brief; the "facts" normally lead to subpoints at the inference level, and a collection of such inferences leads to a main-point inference at a higher level.

What has been said about wariness toward "facts" applies to inferences as well. For example, a considerable amount of historical inference simply "ain't so." Was Lincoln really interested in freeing the slaves, or was the Emancipation Proclamation simply another maneuver to bring the South to its knees? Was our invasion of Mexico in the Mexican War justified? Was our invasion of Cuba in the Spanish-American War justified? Your viewpoint on these and similar issues will depend largely on whose accounts you read and accept.

To return to the professor's office and the inferences you would draw, a friend could go into the same office and come out with a higher—or lower—count of the items and a more exact—or less exact—idea about the specialty of the professor. Your background might lead you to classify him as "an English teacher"; his, "an expert on lyric poets of the Puritan and Restoration periods."

We should think of facts, therefore, as personal or reported *observations* subject to error in both the observing and the reporting. We should regard inferences as *guesses* aimed at deriving knowledge from facts; sometimes these guesses are "educated" and sometimes they are not. Your estimates of the reliability of the facts and of the validity of the inferences, your own and those of others, will be fallible at best. Above all, be careful not to confuse facts with inferences and inferences with facts. For the sake of example, let us assume that "the old oaken bucket," the traditional trophy awarded annually to the winner of the Purdue-Indiana football game, has disappeared from a display case in the Purdue Memorial Union. And let us further assume these facts: The bucket is missing and three young men were seen departing from the Union with a "bedroll" about the time it disappeared. The inference: Indiana University students took the bucket. However logical the inference may seem, it would be folly to treat it as a fact.

Judgment. Since the oaken bucket was removed from its place of honored repository in the Union Building (fact), and we assume that the removal was accomplished by students from Indiana University (inference), it is possible to draw the conclusion (judgment) that three students from that institution have no apparent reverence for the traditional Purdue-Indiana rivalry. You understand, of course, that there could be error in the "fact" (missing items often turn out not to be missing—a point you can check at the nearest police station), or in the inference (the bucket could have been taken by young factory workers, by students from one or more of a dozen nearby colleges and universities, by students from Purdue, or by a custodian wanting to polish the brass bands on the bucket) or, obviously, in the judgment based on the fact(s) and/or inference(s).

A judgment is a personal evaluation of an event, person, or thing. Judgments may be expressed as conclusions based on facts or as conclusions based on inferences; or they may be buried in almost any kind of expression. Examples of judgments: "He *adamantly* refused to continue negotiations." "Give your *kleptomaniacal* roommate a tie of his own." "She *minced* her way through the crowd." Of the Queen Elizabeth legend Hilaire Belloc once said, "A more monstrous scaffolding of poisonous nonsense has never been foisted upon posterity." Judgments at any level should be approached with care; *a good speaker assumes responsibility for precision* in his statements of facts, inferences, and judgments in either "pure" or mixed forms. The listener must also be able to recognize these distinctions if he would listen intelligently and critically.

He that judges without informing himself to the utmost that he is capable cannot acquit himself of judging amiss.

John Locke

. . . .

Comprehension checks

Do facts ever change? Under what circumstances? In the world of sense experiences and impressions (including what you read on the printed page), is there such a thing as *an absolute fact*? Name one and defend your position on it. If you see a student wearing a blue sweater, can you be positive it's blue? Why? Why not? Early in this century, an explorer named Cook claimed to have been the first to reach the North Pole. Some people believed him. Was his claim a fact for those who did? And not one for those who didn't? If he actually did reach the Pole before Peary, what is the fact? Some Eskimos still believe Cook was first. Is our fact better than their fact? Why? Why not? Does the source of a fact have any bearing on whether or not it is one? How careful should we be in the wording of facts? Why?

What is an inference? Something more than "an educated guess"? Something less? Have you ever "arrived at an inference" which later turned out to be unjustified? What were the circumstances? If it is wise to be careful about "the facts," should you be just as careful about the inferences you draw from them? More careful? Why? If an inference makes sense to you, are you free to assume that it will also make sense to your listeners?

"A judgment is a personal evaluation of an event, person, or thing." Are value judgments which are acceptable to you necessarily those acceptable to an audience? Is there such a thing as a "universal value," one acceptable to everyone, including you? Cite one. When you hear a statement about someone (e.g., "He is from Sicily"), is it possible to recognize immediately that the statement is a fact or an inference or an evaluative judgment? Why? Or why not? Could it be different things to different people?

Demonstration options

1. Many organizations (businesses, governmental units, park boards, travel agencies, chambers of commerce, utility companies, educational institutions, etc.) print "fact booklets" or pamphlets and folders of various sorts. Try to find one such listing of facts. Report on one fact you would accept and say why. Or report on one you would not accept and say why.
2. Find a fact in a book or textbook on American history. Say why you believe it to be a fact, or why you are not sure it is one, or why you feel it is not a fact at all.
3. Scan the editorial page or pages of a newspaper or news magazine. *Underline* those sentences which you regard as inferences. *Circle* those words, phrases, or sentences which seem to you to represent value judgments. Team up with a classmate to exchange marked pages for a quick informal check of each other's choices in the two categories.
4. Find an inference somewhere, and be prepared to cite it and explain to the class exactly why you consider it an inference.
5. Do the same for a value judgment.

. . . .

This chapter opened with an appeal for our being more language-conscious by becoming more sensitive to the vagaries of (1) *context*, (2) *slanting*, (3) *allness*, (4) *labeling*, and (5) *self-qualification*. The next section offered some positive suggestions for increasing understanding through (1) appealing to the senses, (2) evoking word pictures, (3) relying on action words, (4) expressing feeling, and (5) adopting a "direct style." Then, a discussion of problems inherent in the processes of *abstraction, classification,* and *definition* was followed by a review of the language difficulties often encountered in the definition and use of the terms *fact, inference,* and *judgment*. The emphasis throughout was on greater precision in the conception of an idea, in the expression of it, and in the use of symbols believed to be within the knowledge of the person(s) with whom we are communicating—all these contribute directly to successful communication. A worthy objective in itself, that precision is prerequisite to accuracy in reasoning, the subject of the next chapter.

Whenever agreement or assent is arrived at in human affairs, . . . this agreement is reached by linguistic processes.

Benjamin Lee Whorf

3 / Common sense in reasoning

It is in the nature of man to flatter himself that he is logical. Further, each of us *wants* to reason with accuracy in the hope that his conclusions will be the "right" answers to problems. Unfortunately, what is logical to one may not be logical to another. Nonetheless, in our speaking and listening, in our "understanding and relating," it is helpful if we all follow the same general guidelines. Or if we do not follow the same rules, it is useful to know some of the common variations in them and some of the standard "diseases." Since knowing how a man reasons is helpful in understanding the man (and since most of us wish reason to become a stronger force in the lives of men), we should spend some time in review of the factors that man considers valuable in the communication of "the reasoned case." This chapter, then, is intended not only to sharpen your own ability to think logically but, more important, to help you meet the logical requirements of your listeners and adjust your reasoning to forces affecting how *they* think. "In argumentation the important thing is not knowing what the speaker regards as true or important but knowing the views of those he is addressing."[1]

Fundamental Concepts in Reasoning

The common premise. "... all argumentation," Perelman says, "depends for its premises—as indeed for its entire development—on that which is accepted; that which is acknowledged as true, as normal and probable, as valid."[2] The speaker should try to

---

1. Chaim Perelman and L. Olbrechts-Tyteca, *The New Rhetoric: A Treatise on Argumentation*, translated from the French by John Wilkinson and Purcell Weaver (Notre Dame, Ind.: University of Notre Dame Press, 1969), pp. 23–24. Reprinted by permission.

2. Chaim Perelman, *The Idea of Justice and the Problem of Argument*, translated by John Petrie (New York: Humanities Press, 1963), p. 156. Reprinted by permission. Framing argument with the help of common knowledge and common opinions is a principle as old as Aristotle; for two of many references, see his *Rhetoric* i. 1. and *Topics* i. 1. For a modern elaboration, see Holtzman, pp. 102–109.

link arguments whenever possible to positions generally held by an audience. Speaker and listener invariably share some views, desires, and values which can *serve as the base* upon which the audience-conscious speaker builds an audience-centered case. In 1970, when the United States and the Soviet Union initiated a series of talks on the limitation of arms, one or more of the following "common premises" could be said to be shared: "A lessening of U.S.–Soviet tensions is desirable." "The two superpowers have nothing to gain through a continuation of the arms race." "In the face of pressing internal problems, neither of the two countries can afford continuingly heavy expenditures on weaponry." It may be safely assumed that the first talks in the series included exchanges of views and statements of values to determine the common premises from which it would be possible to move to consideration of more narrowly specific objectives and the means to attain them.

Although some common premises or basic values[3] are transitory in nature, others are considered to have a long-lasting status. The abbreviated list which follows, for example, is part paraphrase and part quotation of the 1962 Steele-Redding enumeration of "relatively unchanging values shared by *most* Americans."

Acceptance of puritan and pioneer standards of morality

Recognition of the dignity of the individual

Admiration for "the self-made man"

Perennial optimism about the future

Adherence to the Christian ethic of the equality of man

Belief in equality of opportunity

Faith in the reward stemming from hard work

Emphasis on the merit of doing things efficiently and practically

Rejection of authority

Assumption that intelligent human beings can continually improve themselves

Concern for being outgoing and friendly on more than a superficial basis

Desire for material comforts

Equating of quantity (e.g., production of numbers of things) rather than quality with goodness

Compulsion to conform

Appreciation of poking fun as a "leveling influence"

Humanitarian generosity toward the afflicted

Pride in the American heritage coupled with loyalty to American patriotic ideals[4]

Now, not too many years later, the reader will agree that some of the 1962 values still endure, but others have been eroded in varying degrees. Nevertheless, most of them

---

3. From one point of view, these premises or values have a reasoned or logical force; from another, a motivational or psychological impact, especially when they are used as goals (see "Motivation and Goals," Chapter 4) or as attitudinal targets for change (Chapter 12).

4. Edward D. Steele and W. Charles Redding, "The American Value System: Premises for Persuasion," *Western Speech*, **26** (Spring 1962), pp. 83–91. Used by permission.

can still be used on a selective basis "as underpinning for persuasive, appealing argument . . . ,"[5] especially in communication with larger groups and audiences.

Still other values—those on the universal level, as differentiated from those common to Americans—are available as foundations for argument. We will not here go into the intricacies of the Perelman and Olbrechts-Tyteca distinction between abstract value (e.g., justice) and concrete value (e.g., one's country), but the following "virtues and forms of behavior" are universally associated with personal relations: ". . . obligation, fidelity, loyalty, solidarity, and discipline. . . . Likewise Confucius' five universally binding obligations—between rulers and ruled, father and son, husband and wife, older brother and younger brother, friend and friend. . . ."[6] It is easy to see that all or a part of an argument could have as its stated or unstated premise one or more of the above virtues or personal relationships. It is also self-evident that one or more of these values could take precedence over one or more other values in a kind of hierarchical structure.[7] Depending on the circumstances, for example, your listeners could be conceived of as believing that family obligations come first and that obligations to some fraternal organization come second. No matter what values people hold at a given point in time, some will be considered more important than others. The sensitive speaker-communicator tries to recognize those values held by his listeners and the order in which they hold them.

We see, then, that recognizing the common premise or premises is an important preliminary step in the construction of a series of ideas which will stimulate the listener to reason and respond affirmatively to what we have to say. A common premise is a *commonly accepted* opinion, view, value, belief, or attitude, but it is not an argument in or by itself; it is "the starting point ('if') from which listeners can be expected to move ('then') toward acceptance of an idea."[8] When such a premise is explicitly emphasized by a speaker, it normally appears in the course of introductory remarks; it is just as often omitted entirely, especially when the speaker knows that the premise is already well embedded in the minds of his listeners. For instance, it is unnecessary to remind a meeting of ecology experts that "pollution is bad." With common premise determined to the best of the speaker-planner's ability, he is then ready to work out details of his argument.

Argument. When a professor is describing a style of architecture, or when an athletic coach is outlining a defense maneuver, the exposition normally takes the simple form of a series of steps without emphasis on reason. No argument is necessary. In the more complex forms of speech-communication, those in which you attempt to modify or change the attitude of your listener(s), you similarly present related materials as a series of assertions, but in these instances, *some of the assertions are given as reasons for other assertions.* Under such circumstances, you are presenting an *argument.* If you offer information leading to inferences that the Egyptians are preparing for war, the Israelis are preparing for war, the Iranians are preparing for war, the Jordanians are preparing for war, etc., you can step up to the inference that the Middle East is about

---

5. Steele and Redding, p. 84.
6. Perelman and Olbrechts-Tyteca, p. 77. Reprinted by permission.
7. *Ibid.*, pp. 80–83.
8. Holtzman, p. 109.

to explode unless outside influences can be brought to bear on the situation. Implicit, then, in the concept of argument as an honest search for truth is *the establishing of reasonable connections and relationships between and among ideas.* Argument is the logical movement from fact to fact, from facts to inference, from inference to inference, and sometimes from inferences to judgments or conclusions on still higher levels. Conversely, argument is also the connecting and relating of what we believe we know (in the form of conclusions and accepted principles) to specific events and instances. It is this sensible and reciprocating movement from ideas on one level to ideas on another that argument is all about.

Induction. The word "induction" comes from the Latin *inducere*, meaning "to lead up to." If you collect, count, and weigh several hundred acorns from each section of your county, you will have enough data to lead up to the conclusion that, for the season in question, the acorns in your county had an average weight of so many grams. The method of induction requires the collection of data, which then permit the observer to lead himself up to an inference, generalization, or whatever else he chooses to call a conclusion of this kind. The data need not be all of one class as in the example above; you could study different kinds of details in the operation of your county government and, with all of the items of evidence in hand, discover that they lead up to the conclusion that your county government is inefficient. In this instance you would be observing a variety of facts and using them as the basis for the resulting inference. In induction, you first collect the evidence and then use it to arrive at a concluding statement. Since your evidence (facts, statistics, examples, etc.) is seldom, if ever, complete in the sense that it includes *all* available items, your conclusion represents only a *degree* of probability.

Deduction. If induction leads from one or more of the kinds of evidence *up to* a conclusion, it follows reasonably that deduction leads *down from* a conclusion (called, in this context, a *major premise*). In other words, the same conclusion can be, first, the product of the inductive process and, then, the base from which you reason in the deductive process. If the Mormons with whom you come in contact lead you inductively to believe that "Mormons are honest," that statement may become the major premise which you invoke deductively when you meet another Mormon. You have a broad, all-inclusive statement—which by now you should have learned to discount—and you make another observation placing the latest Mormon within its confines: "John is a Mormon." New conclusion: "John is (probably) honest." The only difficulty here is that such neatly constructed syllogisms are found only in textbooks. In conversations, conferences, and talks before audiences, deduction usually appears in the less easily recognizable form of the *enthymeme*, Aristotle's word for the adaptation of the formal syllogism to the informal probabilities of rhetoric. For example, "Richards will make a good mayor because he has experience in public office." If you wanted to take the time, such a statement could be reconstructed in a formal deductive syllogistic pattern, as follows:

Major premise: People who have experience in public office make good mayors.
Minor premise: Richards has experience in public office.
Conclusion: Richards will make a good mayor.

You will note that there is not a shred of evidence in this typical tripartite syllogism; acceptance of its conclusion depends entirely on agreement by all concerned (you and your listeners) on the "truth" or probability of the two premises. Speakers seldom attempt to use an enthymeme without following it up with evidence in support of one or both of the premises, a procedure which really converts the talk to one inductive in emphasis. Or the enthymeme is used in the conclusion of the talk; in this instance, it serves as a kind of summary for an otherwise inductively structured communication.

There are several kinds of formal syllogisms,[9] but what you need to remember about them is this: It is unlikely that you will ever hear or see one, except in a textbook. As demonstrated in the example above, syllogistic reasoning depends on (1) a broad statement that sets forth a generally-agreed-upon point about a classification or group, (2) placement of an individual or smaller group inside or outside that classification, and (3) the inevitable conclusion. Enthymemes or rhetorical syllogisms are especially useful if the foundation for their use has been previously established inductively, or if you have a partisan or uncritical audience composed of people who do not require evidence—or will not notice its absence. Again like syllogisms, enthymemes ordinarily move in the right direction "down the ladder" of inference, but they fail to go down far enough to reach "the bedrock of evidence."

Probability. This concept is included among the concepts in reasoning because probability is an inextricable part of every argument, no matter what that argument's particular structure happens to be. We assume, of course, that if some position can be shown to be absolutely true (as for some principles and laws of science), there is no need for argument; in fact, there can be no argument. At the other extreme, if it is not possible to find evidence to support a position, there can again be no argument. Attempts to influence attitudes take place between those extremes, and arguments typically range from the remotely possible to the highly probable.

Examples: A prosecuting attorney is not going to put himself in the position of pressing for an indictment unless he is convinced that he has enough direct and indirect evidence to make up a case. Probability cannot be demonstrated in a vacuum. Or let us suppose that a conclusion about the average weight of adult Italian-Americans is based on a study of 40 Italians of both sexes living in San Francisco; even the listener unfamiliar with statistics and the rules of "adequate sampling" will give that conclusion a very low rating in probability. Or if there is almost unanimous agreement that a candidate for mayor has relevant and successful experience in public office, the voters will assume there is a reasonable probability that, if elected, he will make a good mayor. When it is certain that something has happened, is happening, or will happen, argument is pointless. If it is raining, no meteorologist requires an argument to prove that fact; if he is forecasting rain, he is careful to give his reasons for believing that precipitation will occur, and he often states that probability in terms of percentages. When a group meets to wait for the end of the world at a specific time on a specific day, no one takes its warnings seriously because that probability is nonexistent. And sometimes a probability is simply so forced that it defies belief; Beardsley tells the apocryphal story of Lysenko, the Russian biologist "who put a flea on his desk and said, 'Jump!' Presently the flea jumped.

---

9. For a discussion of syllogisms, see Ewbank and Auer, pp. 138–143.

He then removed the flea's hind legs, and said, 'Jump!' again. This time the flea did not jump. 'Observe, gentlemen,' said Lysenko, 'This proves that when you remove the flea's hind legs, its hearing is impaired.'"[10] All arguments, then, must run the gantlet of the concept of probability. "The domain of argumentation is that of the credible, the plausible, the probable, to the degree that the latter eludes the certainty of calculations."[11] Efforts to persuade or to dissuade make sense only in the sphere of the uncertain; the speaker tries to present arguments having the highest possible degree of probability, and the listener attempts to assess that degree for himself.

Comprehension checks

What is a *common premise*? What does it have to do with speaker-listener relationships? What is its relation to argument? Does a speaker try to prepare and present an argument (or arguments) which seems reasonable to him? Or is he concerned primarily with preparing one which he hopes listeners will accept? Or does he prepare a line of thinking planned to make it possible for listeners to reason with him in let-us-reason-together fashion? What is the difference between an "argument" which you overhear and *argument* as a concept in reasoning? What is *induction*? Although conclusions arrived at inductively are said to "represent only a degree of probability," under what circumstances could an inductive conclusion be absolutely true? If a conclusion is inescapable, would it under *any* circumstances require argument? Give an example. How is the broad statement or major premise providing the foundation for a *deductive conclusion* originally arrived at? Of what importance in reasoning is the concept of *probability*? What do you think is meant by the statement "Probability cannot be demonstrated in a vacuum"?

Demonstration options

1. Cite a common premise which you believe is accepted by or acceptable to every one in the class. Explain why you consider it a common premise and why you assume that it is accepted or acceptable. What general argument or proposition could you build on that premise?
2. Find (or make up) what you consider a good or bad example of induction. Give your reasons for considering it good or bad. Include your estimate of the argument's probability from the standpoint of the listeners in the class.
3. Find (or make up) what you consider a good or bad example of deduction, defined very generally here as reaching a conclusion about an individual or thing because he or it can be placed within a classification covered by a broader conclusion. Include your estimate of the argument's probability from the standpoint of the listeners in the class.

---

10. Beardsley, p. 74.
11. Perelman and Olbrechts-Tyteca, p. 1. Reprinted by permission. See also Perelman, p. 134.

48 Common sense in reasoning

The Materials of Reasoning

The materials or items of evidence used to support an idea—as distinguished from reasoning processes utilizing those materials—may be considered to fall into the categories discussed in the following sections.

Facts and statistics. We have previously discussed facts in terms of happenings, acts, or states accepted as true by the people with whom you happen to be speaking. They are very much a part of the "common sense" in any speech. Statistics are facts in quantitative form, and they play an important role. Indeed, a speaker should use exact figures wherever they are reliable and pertinent.

In presenting numbers and in listening to them, remember that statistics can be selectively chosen or arranged to "prove" almost anything. A current text on evidence suggests these questions as possible tests of statistics: (1) Who wants to prove what? (2) What do the figures really represent? (3) What conclusions do the figures support?[12] An amusing but typical example of the need for such tests is the following account of a political campaign visit to Milwaukee.

> When Vice President Nixon stopped at the Milwaukee airport during the 1960 campaign, a Republican party official estimated the welcoming crowd at 12,000. The police put it at 8,000. A reporter said there were 5,000. *The Milwaukee Journal* enlarged a crowd picture and counted heads; the number turned out to be near 2,300.[13]

An example of the intentional misuse of a figure: In late 1970 there was considerable controversy in Congress about whether or not the Boeing supersonic transport (SST) should be subsidized with taxpayer money. It was initially argued without elaboration or qualification that failure to continue development of the plane would mean the loss of 150,000 jobs. After that total had been bandied about at great length, it finally became evident that *fewer than 20,000 jobs* were involved: approximately 5,000 at Boeing and about 14,000 in all subcontracting organizations. Included in the original figure were 50,000 additional jobs *in all involved companies by 1978* if the SST actually proved flyable and went into production. Based on the assumption of full production eventually, the 150,000 figure represented the total of all possible primary construction and secondary jobs *by 1980*. It pays to scrutinize figures, especially when they are being used in support of a case.

In the use of statistics, it is good practice to "round out" very large numbers, but adjectives and adverbs are obviously poor substitutes for accuracy. It is one thing to say that the number of American companies using personality tests is increasing; it is another to say, "Of 849 firms returning questionnaires, 27 percent were using such tests in 1958 and 38 percent were using them by 1963." Although

---

12. Robert P. Newman and Dale R. Newman, *Evidence* (Boston: Houghton Mifflin, 1969), p. 206. Adapted by permission.
13. Herbert A. Jacobs, "To Count a Crowd," *Columbia Journalism Review*, **6** (Spring 1967), p. 38. Reprinted by permission.

a talk consisting entirely of statistics has a high potential for boredom, no audience likes generalities when the figures are necessary and available.[14]

Examples. An example is "something selected to show the nature or character of the person or thing under discussion." It is a typical case or instance, sometimes real and sometimes imaginary, which serves to support, clarify, explain, elaborate on, describe, or illustrate the point being made. If you wanted to support the idea that the mayor of your city had failed to keep his campaign promises, the mere statement would be enough for people already opposed to him but would hardly influence uncommitted voters interested in "the evidence." To reach such voters, you would have to cite, as a matter of record and fact, each promise made and *typical instances* of his failure to keep it. Some of the instances cited might require fairly extended treatment; the mayor's original promise of better prisoner security at the local jail could be countered by a recitation of the increased number of jail breaks, and one or two of those breaks could be recounted in detail (*illustration*) to show how they were managed. *Anecdotes* about citizen reactions could be introduced; people talk about such affairs and some react humorously, some irately, to inept performances from public officials. *Case histories* of certain escapes could be introduced to show that happened or could happen as a result of the escapes. A *description* of the jail itself would contribute to a better understanding of the escape-prone institution. In other words, you would collect all the factual and supplementary information available in categories like those above.

Quotations. Since very little of what we know is within the realm of our own experience, we have to depend to a greater degree than we realize on what others say. Although we are indeed moving away from the oracles who tell us to do something "because they say so," we do listen to those who give us reasons for an action and to those who tell us what they believe they have discovered. The "knowledge explosion" of our times increases this dependency on the research and explorations of others and on the experts *as authorities in their respective fields.* This development, however necessary and inevitable, should also increase our caution about too ready an acceptance of this new breed of oracles. A general in the Quartermaster Corps may know the logistics of moving troops; his expertise in that area, however, does not qualify him to make pronouncements on our foreign policy. An atomic scientist who is an eminent authority on the dangers of fallout will not be consulted on the feasibility of building a bridge across the English Channel—though he may be asked how fallout could affect its use. When we quote someone, we should be as sure as we can be that (1) he is *currently* expert in the field involved; (2) he is in a position to know the problem at hand or others very much like it; (3) he has no vested interest in any proposed solution; (4) he has a reputation for being accurate and fair in his judgments; and (5) he has a good change of being accepted by the audience. James Hoffa could still be cited as an authority by a Teamsters Union officer in a talk before some of the members of that union; the advantage of using his name before other groups would be doubtful. A professor of economics may have

---

14. See Chapter 10 for further discussion of statistics and the handling of them in presentations.

a good reputation nationally as an expert on trends in the cost of living; he may not be so highly regarded by the local merchants with whom he does business.

You may also find it useful at times to quote one or more witnesses to some event and, though less often, a secondhand report, rumor, or "hearsay." However, the speaker who resorts to quotations from sources such as these does so at considerable risk. It is better to be in the position of exploding a rumor than repeating it, and witnesses should be used with extreme caution; at best their testimony is "inexpert."

. . . .

Comprehension checks

What are *statistics*? Assuming the accuracy of quoted statistics, does it make any difference who is doing the quoting? Is it true that figures in one form or another can be selectively chosen to prove almost anything? If 29 percent of the people want immediate end to a war, 32 percent want an early end to it, and 39 percent want a gradual end over a period of years, is it correct to say that the highest percentage of people want a gradual end? What does the citation of a few *examples* contribute to a talk? By themselves, do examples "prove anything"? Actors and actresses occasionally make public statements in support of candidates for political offices. On what bases would you consider such "stars" entitled to speak in support of a candidate? On what bases would you consider them *authorities* in a field other than their entertainment specialty? Do you know of any actors who are authorities in other fields?

Demonstration options

1. Try to obtain a pamphlet published by any national association or organization in any field. Examine the evidence (facts, statistics, etc.) in it. Underline those items of evidence which you accept; with pencil or crayon of a different color, underline those you do not accept. Report on your findings. For at least one specific item, give the reasons for your accepting or rejecting it.

2. In a newspaper or news magazine, find a quotation (or quoted passage) attributed to some subordinate officer in any organization—military, industrial, academic, business, professional, etc. Is it true that such people will almost always come up with statements and figures supporting the position of their superiors? Examine the quotation and comment on its reliability as a statement independent of any concern about "what the boss thinks."

. . . .

Practical Patterns in Reasoning

Although the division of reasoning processes into inductive and deductive categories offers a very neat and clear-cut dichotomy, such a separation is not so readily discernible in actual practice, and because the generalizations which provide the bases for deduction are, as already noted above, for the most part products of induction, modern theorists usually hold that induction is *the* fundamental reasoning process. The basis for this view, seen in the types of reasoning presented below, is that the "direction-of-reasoning-movement," almost without exception, is from evidence to conclusion or from a series of conclusions to a conclusion of a higher order. Except for reasoning by *classification*, treated last in this section, the patterns below move inductively from a study of evidence to a conclusion.

Reasoning by generalization. In the earlier discussion of evidence and the *materials* of communication in this chapter, your attention was called to the importance of collecting facts, statistics, and specific instances of all kinds for the bases which they provide for reaching inductive conclusions. A merchant who watches his business increase at the rate of 10 percent per year over a period of 10 years has some reason to conclude that, barring depression, war, pestilence, fire, or some other catastrophe, his business will probably increase at approximately the same rate in the eleventh year. If you note that your Representative in Congress finds it convenient to be absent whenever civil rights legislation comes up for a vote, you can infer with some accuracy that he will be absent the next time such legislation is voted on. When you see flags at half-mast, you assume that some dignitary has died. (The foregoing type of argument is often called *sign*, but the "signs" or "indications commonly associated with an act or event" are used cumulatively to arrive at inferences in exactly the same way as are other kinds of more direct evidence.) In argument by generalization, you move inductively toward what you consider a reasonable conclusion (i.e., generalization) by citing specific items of information, which may range from exact dollar figures in a budget to evidence of an admittedly circumstantial kind, such as the number of times you have seen a candidate for public office enter the home of a local gambler.

Reasoning by comparison. A comparison is a dicussion of the similarities between or among items in a class; as the word itself indicates, it is a bringing together of the "equalities." (Contrast is a type of comparison which suggests the ranging of items *against* each other to point up their differences.) For example, the prospective buyer of a compact car will want to *compare* the many cars in that class. If he should enter a Volkswagen agency, he will find the dealer more interested in *contrast* than in comparison; the Volkswagen will be described as markedly different from other cars in price, gas mileage, efficiency of design, etc. For another example, in comparing the cities of Columbus, Ohio, and Lexington, Kentucky, we could show that they have essentially the same traffic problems but that one city has a much better safety record than the other. We could study the problems of rearing a family in a major city and contrast them unfavorably with those in a western university town. Another kind of argument, "comparison in series," consists in the enumeration and elaboration of *parallel instances*, a reasoning process to which, for example, policemen and firemen sometimes resort as they plead their case for higher salaries. The argument goes something like this: "Our base salary is $9,000 while that in city A is $9,200; in city B, $9,800; in city C, $9,500; in city D, $9,600; etc. These cities are comparable to our own in per capita income, tax structure, and population. Our salaries are the lowest in the area for cities in this class. Therefore...."

Reasoning by analogy. A complex form of comparison, the analogy consists of a kind of inductive-deductive sequence through which an effort is made to show that, since two items have essentially the same attributes and since one of the two has an additional characteristic not definitely known to belong to the second, there is some possibility or probability that the second item also has the unknown attribute. In other words, if two items are alike in every known detail, they could be alike in still another detail known to be true of one but not of the other. For instance, an American supply vehicle, A, and a Russian supply vehicle, B, are known to have essentially the same general dimensions, the same total weights, motors of the same weight and horsepower, the same gear trains, the same suspension and shock absorber systems, and the same load capacities; they appear to be similar in every important detail of power and design. We know that vehicle A cruises efficiently at 50 miles an hour and has a top speed of 70 miles an hour. It is reasonable to conclude that its Russian counterpart has about the same cruising and top speeds. Another analogy (abbreviated): The United States and Great Britain are very much alike in many ways. The British system of drug regulation is apparently successful; if it works there, it should work in the United States.

Analogies may be literal, as above, or figurative, as in the comparison of the growth of a flower with that of a company. Figurative analogies are used more often in poetry than in serious speech-communication. (The trouble with analogies in general is that it is usually possible to point out as many differences as similarities, a built-in liability which causes many perceptive speakers to shy away from them entirely.)

Reasoning from causal relations. The writer once had a student with a peculiar orthographic blindspot who insisted on writing and talking about "casual relations." However, these relations *are* sometimes more "casual" than "causal," a fact which should be remembered by anyone attempting to use arguments from cause. The "laws of cause" are not laws at all but only reasonable expectations based on what has happened in the past, on what is happening now, or on what may happen in the future. These expectations are derived from our experiences and observations of results characteristically stemming from certain "sequential linkages."[15] If certain causes have produced certain effects in the past, we reason that the same connections, linkages, or relationships *may* again be operative between what we observe as a similar set of causes and their possible or probable effects. We also reason that observed effects *may* be the result of causes which produced the same effects in the past, or that causes producing observed effects normally accompanied by other (unobserved) effects *may* sometimes be assumed also to have produced these other effects.

"No one has ever seen a cause. ... Causality of any kind, partial or complete, is an *inference;* it cannot be proved."[16] Still, we have fire inspectors saying that "the cause of the fire was faulty wiring" (when it could have been wiring of poor quality, sudden surge in power, tampering, arson made to look like "faulty wiring," improper security, a tossed cigarette, work done by an electrician thinking about personal problems, failure of a building inspector to do his job, bribing of an inspector not to do his job, and so on). Once again, the subject-predicate structure of our

---

15. For a full discussion of causal laws and sequential linkages, see Dewey, pp. 445–458.
16. Weinberg, pp. 115, 118–119.

language makes it easy to say, in explaining the increase in juvenile delinquency, "*The* cause is a breakdown in family discipline," or in explaining the continuing power of the gangster fraternity to maintain illicit operations on a nationally organized basis, "*The* cause is the failure of police officers to enforce the law." There is no such thing as *the* cause, since it is possible in any given case to cite other possible causes, associated causes, contributing causes, near and remote causes, etc. With the idea of single causation rejected, in what ways can we use reasoning by causation?

First, on a *causes-to-effect basis*. We always have with us prophets of what the future will bring. For many years, a professor of political science in one of our major universities has been prophesying another revolution in Spain. He may be right ultimately, but over a long period his "causes" have been failing with extraordinary regularity to bring about the downfall of the present regime. This example serves only to highlight the difficulty of looking at a set of causes and trying to predict what is going to happen as a result of them. Quite obviously, some of the causes of the Spanish revolution of the late 1930's are not cooperating to bring about another one, or they are being counterbalanced by other forces strong enough to keep the present regime in power, or internal discontent is not at a high enough level to generate a revolt, or. . . . Again, this is not to say that, if we are careful enough in choosing causes which have in the past produced given results with a degree of dependability, we should refrain from trying to predict what is going to happen. At a hearing on some civic plan for improving opportunities for the underprivileged in a community, or in a formal or informal debate of any kind on a policy question, it is standard procedure for proponents of measures to make predictions about the results expected from the plan(s) proposed.

Second, on an *effect-to-causes* basis. When a high school principal notices that the combined grade-point average for all students has risen gradually from 3.3 to 3.7 over a three-year period, he may want to find out *why* (for this is the question that reasoning by causation attempts to answer). He appoints a statistician to study the grades earned; he checks the intelligence-quotient records (although he knows that the intelligence tests commonly administered do not measure intelligence); he attempts to determine what demographic shifts there may have been in the student population; he looks into teaching standards to find out whether they have changed; he examines the turnover in staff on the chance that the newer teachers are "easier markers." He does those things and many more, and if he decides on any *one* cause for the higher grade-point average, he will be wrong. If he decides to report a number of causes at various levels, he may be closer to the truth, but he can never be sure of the accuracy of his report. He could be "sure" only if he could go back three years and find a way to control all the factors and variables involved; we know, of course, that this would be impossible even if he were to start now to determine the causes of any changes in the next three years. Stating flatly that you have discovered *the* cause for any phenomenon is hazardous in the extreme; do not attempt it. By careful study and analysis, you can come to the conclusion that you have tentatively isolated *some* of the causes of a particular event or phenomenon. Once you have succeeded in isolating causes—and assuming that you can convince your listeners that you have done so—you are in a position to attack the causes, reinforce them, or introduce them into other situations; what you do will depend, of course, on your purpose in looking for them in the first place. So much, then, for an effect you observe for which you try to answer the question "Why?" by looking for its causes.

Third, on an *effect-to-effect* basis. During the Franklin D. Roosevelt administration, it was noted by many that a Harvard education was no handicap in securing a post with the federal government. Other causes were certainly operative (personal ability, available openings, etc.), but the Harvard background did for a time appear to be a salient factor. A young man could then reason with some validity that his aspiration to a post with, say, the State Department would be enhanced by his attending Harvard. He could look at a cause (Harvard) and at a result (government appointment) and decide that the same cause might be at least one important factor in producing the same result for him. Or he could look at an *effect* (government appointment) and at a cause (Harvard) and decide that the same cause might be a factor in producing *the same effect* in his case. This kind of reasoning is obviously a kind of combination of *effect-to-causes* argument with a *causes-to-effect* approach. Someone who notes that a companion of no greater ability has, through an education, succeeded in getting a good position will be encouraged to go the same route. He reasons from effect to what he sees to be an important cause for success, and he regards that cause as one which could also help him get ahead.

In all causal relationships of whatever variety, we must constantly be on guard against faulty inferences. Are other causes contributing to observed effects? Are the causes which we have discerned strong enough to produce the effects? If strong enough, were they operating within a set of peculiar conditions and circumstances which will never be duplicated? Do our predictions make sense in terms of past experience with a given set of causes? Will these causes, set in motion again, bring with them some undesirable "side effects"? Have we really succeeded in showing that causal relationships do exist in the situation under study?

Reasoning by classification. A part of many attacks on a particular system in any field of business, industry, government, social institutions, etc., depends on definition of a particular term, such as dictatorship, monopoly, socialism, or states' rights. The definition of such terms depends, in turn, on a listing of characteristics or criteria. Is the Democratic Party "the party of the common man"? Are Republicans too conservative? For another example, if you can successfully define or classify something or somebody as desirable or undesirable, you have engaged in reasoning by classification.

Here, too, we have some problems. A fundamental obstacle to our being "logical" in this type of reasoning is our Aristotelian proclivity to rigid classification, an inheritance embedded in the thinking and languages of the Western World. As we observed in Chapter 2, Aristotle made the classic error of considering classifications to be static in the things observed rather than in the minds of the observers. Without getting into all of the philosophical problems involved, let us resolve at this point to be "degree-minded." *For the sake of discussion,* we can assume that something remains constant so long as we recognize that it is changing constantly. (You are no longer the same person you were when you began reading this chapter.) *For the sake of discussion,* we can agree that a man is either a "liberal" or not a "liberal," so long as we realize that *we* are doing the defining and classifying. *For the sake of discussion,* we can take the position that one cannot be a "conservative" and *not* a "conservative" at the same time, but we must remember that *we* are doing the labeling.[17] Saying that

---

17. For a complete discussion of process versus static thinking, see Weinberg, pp. 77–95. See also pp. 35–36 in this text ("Classification").

something is so doesn't make it so; we must be wide awake to the logical problems stemming from the two-valued orientation (good-bad, white-black, right-wrong, for us—against us, etc.) that is a part of our Aristotelian heritage. Prerequisite, then, to intelligent argumentation in general and to classification in particular is the determination to think in terms of shades, degrees, gradations, and the middle-ground terms that are a mark of the mature thinker.

. . . .

Comprehension checks

What is a *generalization*? What is an *inference*? What is a *conclusion*? Are these different names for essentially the same thing? What is reasoning by *comparison*? By *contrast*? By *analogy*? What do these three terms have in common? In what ways are they different? Cite an original example of each of the foregoing three kinds of reasoning. What is meant by the statement "Causality . . . cannot be proved"? What are the kinds of reasoning by *causation*? Cite an example, real or imaginary, for each. How do you reason by *classification*? Why do we say that classification is a deductive pattern of reasoning? What are some of the handicaps inherent in reasoning by classification?

Demonstration options

1. Look in an editorial (or in a magazine article taking a position on some issue) for any inductive pattern of reasoning moving from some kind of evidence to a conclusion or stating the conclusion and presenting the evidence to back it up Summarize the argument and *identify the kind of reasoning*. If it is, in your opinion, an argument weak in appeal to listeners, say why you think so.
2. Look in the same kinds of sources for a deductive argument by *classification*. For example, the Ku Klux Klan has an unsavory reputation. If it can be stated flatly and accurately that someone is a member, his reputation would suffer in most circles. The entire argument need not be stated; for example, this single sentence is enough to carry the argument: "John Jones is a Ku Kluxer."

   State the partial or entire deductive argument. Add comment on whatever danger you see in argument by classification in this particular instance. *Note*: Proving that Jones is a member by citing evidence would be argument by inductive generalization; then that conclusion could be used deductively to place Mr. Jones in the larger undesirable category. The complete deductive argument may be cited as a syllogism; it seldom, if ever, appears in its fully complete and formal form. If it did, the argument in this instance could be as follows:

   The Ku Klux Klan is Un-American.
   John Jones is a Ku Kluxer.
   John Jones is Un-American.

. . . .

Checking Reasoning

Let us assume that you have collected evidence which, in your opinion, is (1) appropriate to the audience for which it is intended and (2) strong enough to lead its

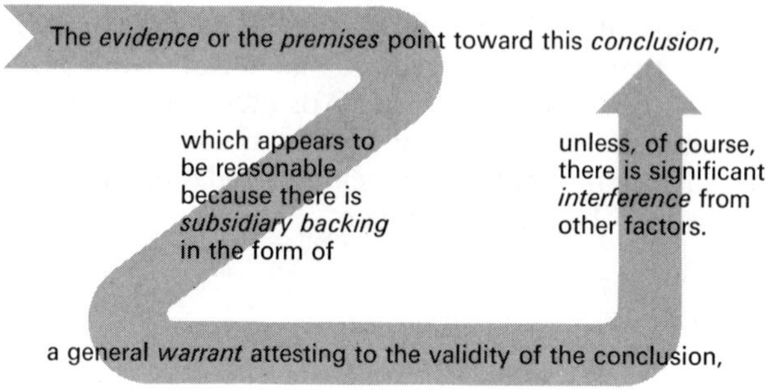

The *evidence* or the *premises* point toward this *conclusion*,

which appears to be reasonable because there is *subsidiary backing* in the form of

unless, of course, there is significant *interference* from other factors.

a general *warrant* attesting to the validity of the conclusion,

Figure 3.1

members to a particular inference. Or let us suppose that you are reading or listening to a particular "argumentative discourse." In either instance, whether you are producer or consumer, one or more of the approaches below will help you ask searching questions about both the evidence *and* the reasoning.

Analyze the arguments. This can be done in a number of ways, including the examination of or the reconstruction of a complete outline of "the case." A detailed outline enables you to evaluate the adequacy of evidence offered in support of any inference; it also makes possible the judgment that a given set of inferences or conclusions may or may not induce listeners to arrive at a higher-level conclusion.

If you are looking at the complete text of a talk, your own or someone else's, you may want to try working through it by using the following.

1. Underline all words and phrases seeming *to introduce the reasoned support* for conclusions; for example, *because, assuming that, may be concluded from, as shown by, for, since, in view of the fact that, as indicated by,* etc. You'll find that words and phrases of that kind draw attention to the evidence, facts, figures, examples, testimonials, and so on.

2. Then underline the words and phrases seeming *to call attention to the conclusions* themselves; for instance, *leads to the conclusion that, therefore, implies that, shows that, indicates that, permits the conclusion that, strongly suggests that, it follows that,* etc.

Once you know precisely what evidence is being advanced for what inference/conclusion, you are in a good position to evaluate both the evidence and the inference/conclusion. Going through this process for an entire talk or document will of course enable you to check the complete case for its total validity.

Or you may choose to check the elements of an argument against a model; an adaptation (Fig. 3.1) or the popular Toulmin model is useful for that purpose.[18]

---

18. Stephen Toulmin, *The Uses of Argument* (Cambridge, England: Cambridge University Press, 1958), Essay III. See also Mills, pp. 126–128; Ehninger and Brockriede, Chapter 10; and Freeley, pp. 139–143. Model in the present text is different from any others seen by this writer.

A "warrant" is a statement providing the general justification for going from the evidence or premises in the direction of a particular conclusion. For instance, we could say, "*Since higher prices for major investment items are usually followed by a rise in the cost-of-living index*, you have some justification or warrant for moving *from evidence* that the automobile companies have just raised their prices *to the conclusion* that the cost of living will soon go up; that is, you have justification to do so if there is no *significant interference* from other factors, such as a slump in food prices due to extraordinarily heavy crops or a subsequent decision by the car makers to lower prices." Presenting a warrant to an audience is the same as presenting a "certificate of entitlement" or "pass" to move from the evidence or premises to the conclusion. Without the "pass," you run the risk of someone's asking how you made the jump. Practically any form of reasoning can be fitted into the Toulmin pattern. Using it forces us to *justify* what we do in a particular reasoning mode and reminds us constantly to *beware of other interfering factors*.

Watch for common fallacies. Fallacies are "falsities" or mistakes in the reasoning processes; the two most common forms are *hasty generalization* and *after-this-therefore-because-of-this*.

In the first, one jumps to inferences and conclusions too broad to be supported by the available evidence. For the sake of example, let us call attention to the extreme in hasty generalization, the drawing of a conclusion from *one* instance. It doesn't happen? If your first visit to a particular restaurant is an unhappy experience, what conclusion do you ordinarily draw?

In the second, the *after-this-therefore-because-of-this* sequence, one assumes that because something happened before something else, the first happening is the cause of the second. For example, a company moves its offices and factory from the state of New York to Georgia, and the move is followed by an increase in business; therefore, the increase is due to the move to Georgia. By now we know that there is no such thing as *the* cause and that a thorough investigation into other factors should precede any conclusion that the move to Georgia had anything to do with the new success of the company. Another example: A doctor's wife served tuna salad at a social event and then fed some of the leftover salad to her cat. Later in the day she found the cat dead on the patio and hurriedly—and under the circumstances, commendably—telephoned all the guests to alert them to the danger of ptomaine poisoning. The next morning the milkman stopped to inquire into the state of the cat's health. "Why do you ask?" queried the doctor's wife. "Well," responded the milkman, "he scurried off all right after I ran over him yesterday, but then I began to wonder if he was hurt."

When a speaker "jumps to conclusions" or too readily assumes causal relationships, the modern audience arrives at a collective conclusion of its own, namely, that no great reliance should be placed on what he says. Confidence once lost is hard to regain, and this is doubly true if the listeners also have a suspicion, however faint, that it is a part of the speaker's "strategy" to be careless and/or deceptive in his handling of evidence and reasoning.

Learn to recognize "red herring" devices. Some speakers (and writers) intentionally try to divert listener attention from basic arguments and real issues. Such attempts are more often than not doomed to failure; unless an audience *wants* to be fooled, its members quickly detect "propaganda tools" and lose respect for the person resorting to them. Nevertheless, these devices are still used often enough to warrant a listing here.

1. *Bandwagon.* "Everybody's doing it." "These fabulous buys are going so fast—you'll have to hurry to get yours!"
2. *Card-stacking.* Deliberately concealing arguments against the speaker's position, i.e., "stacking the cards" in his favor.
3. *The folksy approach.* Attempting to gain support of listeners by taking on some of their characteristics, speech patterns, and actions.
5. *Name-dropping.* Referring to respected persons or organizations in such a way as to imply their support or approval.
6. *Name-calling.* Labeling, as already mentioned, here including the vicious practice of calling someone or something a name in order to avoid the necessity of meeting arguments. For example, if an opponent to a bill charges that it is supported by "Communist-sympathizers," that is all that is sometimes needed to kill the bill. Another variation on the same theme: "A certain proposition [which we shall call] *A* cannot be good unless it is formed by an honest man; I show that he who made this proposition is not honest, or that he was paid for doing it; thus I have shown that the proposition *A* is harmful to the country. This is absurd; and anyone who uses this reasoning has departed completely from the domain of reasonableness."[19]

The reader will note that the patterns summarized above have already appeared in one form or another in these pages; it is clear, of course, that many messages are going to include elements which could be called "propaganda" by the listener, depending on his evaluation of the speaker's purpose as being unselfish, or selfish, or both in combination. Among associated "propaganda tools" are the familiar attempts of unscrupulous speakers to find scapegoats, to resort to flattery, and to take advantage of the discontent and misfortunes of others. Brown takes the position that the power of all such techniques has been exaggerated; we "discover the character of another person from his actions and speech,"[20] and we are seldom fooled unless we want to be fooled.

....

Comprehension checks

What is a *fallacy*? When did you last jump too hastily to a conclusion? What were the circumstances in that "hasty generalization"? When did you last assume that, because one event preceded another, the first was necessarily the cause of the second? What do we call this kind of error in reasoning? If a man swears as he hits his thumb with the hammer, is the pain *the* cause of his swearing? What other causes could be

---

19. Perelman, pp. 180–181. Reprinted by permission. Interesting sidelight: In 1970 President Thieu of Vietnam disposed of a proposal by Madame Binh of North Vietnam by remarking, "Women should not be involved in political affairs."
20. R. Brown, *Words and Things*, p. 302.

operative? Do you ever use the "everybody's doing it" argument? What do we call that kind of device? Would a better term for *card-stacking* be *card-concealing*? Why? What are some of the other "red herring" devices? Why "red herring"? Do you consider the list given in this chapter to be exhaustive? A method of checking reasoning is to underline words-introducing-reasons and words-preceding-conclusions. How does it work?

Demonstration options

1. Find a statement listing the cause or the causes of a particular event, condition, phenomenon, etc. Histories and textbooks in the social sciences frequently include such statements, but others occur in newspapers, magazines, and journals of all kinds. Be prepared (1) to read the statement of cause or causes and (2) to discuss whether or not, in your opinion, the cause or causes are well stated, complete, etc.

2. Bring to class a statement for which you feel the evidence presented is inadequate. Before you contend that it is inadequate, be sure you know the audience for which the statement was prepared. (For that audience, the evidence may have been more than adequate.)

3. Bring to class an example of what you consider a "red herring" device. Include in your search speeches, editorials, and articles supporting various causes. If you find a "red herring," read it to the class along with your classification of its type.

4. Do you know a good way to analyze an argument or an outline of an argument? If you have a system you prefer to those suggested in this chapter, prepare a brief written description of it, and be prepared to present that description to the class.

. . . .

In this chapter, we first reviewed fundamental concepts in reasoning: *the common premise, argument, induction, deduction, and probability.* Then we listed and described in some detail the materials of reasoning, including such elements of support as *facts and statistics, examples,* and *quotations.* Typical patterns of reasoning were next discussed under the headings of *generalization, comparison, analogy, causal relations,* and *classification.* Finally, we noted various ways and means of *checking reasoning,* both as a means of checking our own capabilities for accuracy in reasoning and as a means of testing the reasoning of others.

Histories make men wise; poets, witty; the mathematics, subtile; natural philosophy, deep; morals, grave; logic and rhetoric, able to contend.

Bacon in Of Studies

4 / Perception, motivation, cues, and rapport

In Chapter 1 the focus is on recognition of the complexity of the speech-communication process; in Chapters 2 and 3 the emphasis is on attainment of expertise in the subtleties of language and elements of reasoning; in Chapter 4 interest is centered on an appreciation of psychological and physiological factors affecting speaker-listener perceptions and relationships in the general communicative scene.

Perception and Communication

Perception is the process by which man gives meaning to the objects and ideas he has become aware of through the senses. Another way to put it is to say that perception is "the process of making sense out of experience...."[1] Not a day passes without your receiving impressions from the senses of sight, sound, smell, touch, and taste; however, your total past life and experiences in large part determine the impressions to which you pay special attention. These selected impressions in turn play a part in creating, modifying, or changing your perceptions, your view of the world around you.

Impression selection can be readily demonstrated: If you are especially interested in fashions, what magazines immediately draw your attention when you pass or stop by a magazine rack? If your interest is foreign cars, what cars do you notice as you drive or walk down the street? In each case, the impressions you get are added to your "total store" on a particular subject and become a part of your perceptions in that area.

Your "view of the world," then, is based on your entire past experience: circumstances of birth, home environment, health, and education along with all the beliefs, attitudes, and prejudices that you have picked up over the years. As time goes on, your general view undergoes changes—new experiences beget new perceptions or

---

1. Haney, p. 51.

changes and modifications in old ones. And just as no two of us on this earth have exactly the same physical attributes, so no two of us have exactly the same perceptions for the very obvious reason that no two of us ever have the same life experiences.

Furthermore, only a part of your total past experience is going to have any bearing on a particular situation, and since memories are faulty, you may not always remember something that would be useful to you in that situation. In any event, specific situations call up certain "mind sets" or *predispositions to act in a certain way* to the exclusion of other ways.

Let us suppose that the "present you," a product of your total past experience, is walking down a hall to a class with two or three friends. Your "set" or predisposition, called up by past experience with a break between classes, is simple enjoyment of a few minutes of association with friends. That "set" prevents your seeing notices on a bulletin board, prevents your hearing what passing students are saying, prevents your noticing that you have picked up a spot of grease on a blouse or shirt, prevents your seeing a wave from an instructor, and operates against your doing anything but enjoying the walk down the hall. You have a certain "set" on this occasion, one which is called into play by the break between classes, and one which serves to exclude notice of things you would see and hear under a different mind set. In other words, *a selected part* of "your past" interacts with *a selected part* of "your present" to induce a certain kind of behavior—and another pleasant experience reinforces your perception of what happens when you meet a couple of friends under these circumstances.

To put it another way, you come to any communication scene with your *past* experiences and your *present* state of mind. Under the circumstances, it is easy to understand why people don't always speak and act in the ways we think they should speak and act—and understanding that fact is at least a part of relating successfully to others and getting them to behave according to our expectations.

In approaching communication, then, you will want to be *listener-oriented*. Asking yourself questions like these will help you achieve that goal:

1. In what ways is my listener's background the same as mine? In what ways is it different? What do we have in common? What stress should be placed on what we have in common?
2. Is his present state of mind or "mind set" favorable to me? Does he appear to "have a chip on his shoulder"? Is he interested or disinterested? Does he seem worried or preoccupied about other matters? What effort is necessary to get his complete attention? What effort is necessary to make him friendly and well-disposed to what I have to say?

. . . .

Comprehension checks

What do we mean when we say that "perception is the process of making sense out of experience"? Is it possible for each of two individuals to have "the same experience"? Is it possible for two individuals to react in the same way to "the same experience"? Does it make sense to you to use the word *set* for "predisposition to react in a certain way"? Explain.

Demonstration option[2]

You are a lawyer defending a client in his early twenties accused of murder. You must choose a jury of individuals whose backgrounds and predispositions are such that they are likely to react favorably, or at least impartially, to your client and to the evidence presented in the trial. Through questioning you elicit the information below. Decide whether each potential juror is acceptable or unacceptable to you.

Housewife—college graduate with two teen-age children; lives in high-income neighborhood; little experience with violence, but liberal in her views.

Army officer, retired—career officer who believes in disciplined life of the Army and to whom obedience is a rule of life.

Bearded young man, casually dressed—bachelor, self-employed; does not believe in capital punishment.

Businessman of 45—owns his own business; member of City Council; believes law and order must be maintained at all cost.

Chicly dressed secretary—high school graduate, aware of her personal attractiveness; has no convictions about moral issues.

Iron-worker in construction—has lived in city all his life; concerned about protecting his young family; thinks young people have it too easy these days.

Garage mechanic—high school dropout going to night school; has learned that it takes work to earn a living and get ahead.

Neatly dressed lady of 60—sympathetic to young people but alarmed by violence of modern times.

Be prepared to give reasons for your conclusions.

. . . .

Perception and the Self-Concept

When we communicate with others, it is also useful to keep in mind that the mental picture we have of ourselves is probably not the mental picture others have of us. And yet, the most significant part of a person's view of the world around him is his perception of himself, his self-concept. It is made up of all the things you feel you know about yourself. As Hayakawa says,

> The self-concept ... is the sum total of *the things we feel we know about ourselves,* including our past history, our present condition, status, and role, our ideals, our plans for the future, our estimates of our own relationships with others: "I am thin (or fat)," "I am a good mixer," "I pay my debts promptly," "I am poor at arithmetic," "I shall never be a millionaire," "I am beautiful," "Nobody loves me," "I have less money than Bill, but more brains," "I'm not that kind of girl," etc.[3]

---

2. I am indebted to Beatrice Schadle of Addison-Wesley (Menlo Park) for this option.
3. S. I. Hayakawa, "Conditions of Success in Communications" (italics mine), reprinted with permission from the *Bulletin of the Menninger Clinic,* vol. 26, pp. 227–228, copyright 1962 by the Menninger Foundation.

It is important to note that none of the following may coincide with reality: what you feel you know about yourself, your own evaluation of how you look, what you are capable of learning and doing, what you think is right and wrong. For example, a student may consider himself well liked because, in *his* opinion, he has a fine personality. However, if he is popular because he has money, or a car, or "good looks," or athletic ability, or some other attribute students like or admire, his personality could conceivably border on the obnoxious and he would still be "popular." In the latter case, his concept of himself as having a good personality would be the product of his mind and imagination only. Another student may have the ability to create cartoons for the campus paper but is hesitant about exercising his ability and, in general, fails to recognize his own talent. And so it goes. In some areas we underestimate ourselves, in others we overestimate ourselves, and in some (not too many) we "see ourselves as others see us." It is difficult to be completely objective about who and what we are, but that fact should not prevent us from trying.

In addition to the descriptive judgments we make about ourselves, our self-evaluations are affected to a considerable degree by the comparisons we make of our performances with those of others. For example, your opinion that your are a good dancer may be lessened, confirmed, or strengthened by your watching and dancing with others. Your belief that you are a good student is eroded, verified, or enhanced by the grade-point average which you establish in competition with other students over a given period. If you consistently win at chess, your opinion of yourself as a chess player blooms; if you lose regularly, it suffers.

The judgments we make about ourselves also depend heavily on the remarks, opinions, evaluations, and attitudes of others. When people react favorably to you, your self-esteem goes up; when they react unfavorably, it goes down. In either case, your self-concept undergoes some adjustment in the process.

Since our opinion of ourselves is affected by what other people think about us, we generally do what we can to present ourselves to them in a favorable light. If we want to be considered kind, generous, thoughtful, pleasant, etc., we try to act in ways that are kind, generous, etc. We do some "name-dropping" to impress others with the caliber of the company we keep or of the high-status people to whom we have access. We get more pleasure and satisfaction from passing on a rumor than from listening to one. We try to communicate a good impression nonverbally through our manners, the clothes we wear, the cars we drive, the educational level we attain, and the positions we hold. It's the old story of "putting the best foot forward" in the effort to generate a good opinion of ourselves in others; that good opinion, in turn, heightens our own self-esteem and brings us just a little closer to that unattainable ideal self which we all see in our dreams. In other words, what others say about us ordinarily leads us to enhance, adjust, defend, change, or even abandon (but not without a struggle) a favorite view of ourselves.

What does all this have to do with speech-communication? Through judgments about ourselves, through comparisons of our performances with those of others, and most of all, through talking and listening to others, we arrive at what we hope are realistic conclusions about ourselves, our problems, our hopes, our desires. We are constantly presenting ourselves to others in order to gain acceptance, in order to be liked, and in order to affect what others think and say. We depend heavily on verbal and nonverbal communication to indicate to people who and what we are. It is indeed possible over short periods to pretend to be someone we're not, but sooner or later the truth comes out. On the other hand, talking straightforwardly about ourselves and our problems leads to a self-concept more nearly based on the facts of who we are, what we are, and what it is sensible to expect of ourselves now and in the future. A reasonably accurate self-concept "fits comfortably" and makes it possible for one to communicate more readily and more directly. It is a vital step toward being accepted by others and living a more sane, satisfying, and productive life.

. . . .

Comprehension checks

What is one's *self-concept*? Why is it difficult for one really to "know himself"? What are the advantages of seeking to determine one's qualities, abilities, etc.? How can we go about obtaining such a determination? What is "happiness"? What does speech-communication have to do with the impressions we make on others? Or with the impressions they make on us? Is it possible to be anything but oneself over a period of time? Can you convince someone that you are tactful by saying, "I am tactful"? It is said that talking with someone about a problem may help solve it, even though the listener does not offer any specific advice. How do you account for this?

Demonstration options

1. In groups of four or five students, discuss one or more of these questions:
   Do you think it acceptable to talk about yourself? Do other people want to know how you feel about things? Is this a way to relate to others?
   Is it an advantage to belong to a group? A club? Can this help you arrive at a realistic self-concept?
   Is it bad taste to talk about your abilities? Must you always succeed in what you set out to do? Can you afford to fail at a project you have told others you will carry out successfully?

2. Prepare a short statement (about two minutes) using one of the following as a topic sentence:
   I have noticed changes in some of my attitudes over the past year. (If you prefer, discuss the changed attitudes of a friend, teacher, parent, or someone else).
   I believe (or do not believe) that all you need to be happy is money.
   Honesty is not always the best policy.
   There is something to be proud of in every man's background.
   We are (or are not) predestined to do certain things.
   A college educations is (or is not) essential to success.
   Students are (or are not) too young to involve themselves in community problems and politics.
   Adults as a group too often say one thing and do another.
   (Or use any other statement you can think of that is related to the self-concept and its development.)

. . . .

All we have is each other, and no one is strong enough to "go it alone" in all the situations of living.

James B. Macdonald

Person Perception

Perception, as we have seen, is the process through which man selects and organizes sensory stimuli into meaningful pictures of his world. Perception in the immediate context means the process through which we form impressions about people. When we meet someone for the first time, our direct information about him is limited to his physical appearance and his verbal and nonverbal behavior, "the way he handles himself."

Our reactions to those sources of information depend on such factors as prior information about or feelings toward the individual, the advantages or disadvantages we see as accruing from the present contact, the stereotyping to which we may be addicted, the concepts we have of our own worth in relation to the "stimulus person," our view or suspicions about his intent, and the general circumstances under which the meeting takes place. Then, as we go about rightly or wrongly ascribing certain traits to the individual, our "perceived whole" of the man comes into being. That total impression may be reasonably objective and accurate, or it may be unduly complimentary, or it may be unduly damaging.

The different modes of person perception may be summarized in the following ways:[4]

1. A person is described simply in terms of outward appearance or superficial characteristics; e.g., his body build, facial features, and mannerisms.
2. A person is described mainly in terms of a central trait and its immediate ramifications; e.g., a withdrawn person may be described by such closely related terms as *shy, quiet, retiring, ingratiating,* etc.
3. A person is described in terms of a cluster of *congruous* traits; i.e., traits which seem to belong together. For example, a large strong man may be described as having a powerful voice and as being aggressive, self-confident, and forceful.
4. A person is described in terms of a variety of traits, including some which are *incongruous,* i.e., traits which seem *not* to belong together. To illustrate, a person may be described as kind, thoughtful, dishonest, and unsociable.

The modes above are presented in the order of increasing complexity. The first is characteristically used by children and immature adults. The last is ordinarily used only by persons of intelligence and maturity. "Most adults probably use one of the less complex modes on some occasions...."[5]

How judgments about persons are actually arrived at is still in the area of "the unknown." We do know that perception of a particular characteristic is often

---

4. From *Social Psychology* by Paul F. Secord and Carl W. Backman, p. 54. Copyright 1964. Used with permission of McGraw-Hill Book Company.
5. *Ibid.,* p. 56.

projected over time. If in the first two times you meet a person he is walking rapidly, you may decide that he is an *energetic* type. We know also that there is a tendency to transfer attributes from one person to another; if we have a friend with known characteristics and we meet someone who appears to be like him in some way, we may "bestow" characteristics of the friend on the new acquaintance. We also resort to the time-saving device of rapid classification based on superficial observations; we look at individuals and, with or without conversations with them, infer that they are teachers, blue-collar workers, executives, farmers, clerks, housewives, etc. We also assume that certain traits (e.g., good judgment, understanding, patience) go with age and that other traits (exuberance, ambition, unpredictable behavior, etc.) go with youth. Inferences about physical characteristics are sometimes made from nonphysical attributes. For instance, we talk with someone over the phone and/or carry on correspondence with him; from that very limited evidence, we form a picture of the person and later express surprise if the real person doesn't fit our personally constructed image of him. Physical attributes are sometimes used as a base for conclusions drawn about other characteristics: "People who wear glasses do a lot of reading," "He looks like an intellectual," "You can't trust anybody who dresses like that," "He's obviously Irish; therefore...."

To examine this person-to-person reaction process at first hand, take a "good look" at the ushers in your church or at the members of any small group who are unknown to you. What impressions have you formed? Why? Make a point of talking with one or two of them. What adjustments have you made in your original "sight only" impressions? Why? How would you describe each person? Could you justify your description? However accurate you may try to be, you will find it difficult to avoid taking some "shortcuts." One gentleman may have a very stern countenance during your conversation with him, and you may assume that he is always "that way." Or you see him step into a Cadillac and assume that he is personally very successful; the fact may be that his wife inherited a fortune and that he cannot hold a job. Or he has a brisk, businesslike manner, and you arbitrarily assign to him a number of associated traits (honesty, efficiency, determination, stability, etc.). Or you follow another of the modes and ascribe to him characteristics associated with one of any number of convenient categories: foreigner, professor, salesman, doctor, and so on.[6]

What does person perception have to do with speech-communication? One answer: Since we know that our initial perceptions of other persons are highly subject to error, it is simple justice and good sense to reserve judgment until we have more information at hand. We have all had the experience of liking someone "on sight" and later finding out that the person in question had absolutely nothing in common with us. We also have made the mistake of deciding "at first sight" that we share no common ground with another person, only to discover to our later consternation that we do enjoy the same tastes, pleasures, hobbies, etc. Or we too quickly place a person in a particular category. For example, an individual sometimes successfully joins a

---

6. For a comprehensive discussion of person perception, see Secord and Backman, pp. 49–92. For comments on standards by which listeners measure a speaker-communicator, see Chapter 12 of this volume.

group or organization by simply assuming a role; in dress, customs, mannerisms, and speech, he tries to blend into the group and, if he is successful, is accepted by its members. Then, for some reason, the "cover" is broken, and the members of the group are instantaneously forced to change their classification of the masquerading individual. Similarly, it sometimes happens that an individual tries to gain entrance to a business by pretending experience he does not have or to some other organization by falsifying the record. You may have heard of an instance or two of persons without medical degrees successfully setting themselves up as "doctors." Sooner or later, exposure of the fraud is inevitable, and both townspeople and patients are astounded as they suddenly find it necessary to revise their original estimates and opinions.

As a speaker-listener you occasionally find yourself in something of the same situation. As Perelman points out, you—and all of us—occasionally have to revise an initially favorable reaction of someone because he later does something or says something which offends you or your "sensibilities."[7] Communicative relations cool, and you find it more difficult to carry on a conversation or any other kind of relationship with that individual. The need for reconstructing person perceptions can ordinarily—but not always—be avoided by taking plenty of time to arrive at conclusions about the people we meet.

While we are reserving judgment, there is nothing to prevent our "moving toward others with friendliness." Will Rogers, comedian of another era, used to say, "I've never met a man I didn't like." And if anyone who met Rogers didn't like him, that fact has been carefully hidden through the years. Rogers understood that there is something good in every human being, and his strong belief in the intrinsic worth of man always came through. If we concentrate—initially, at least—on finding something to like about every person we meet, we discover that communication is relatively easy. On the other hand, when we react unfavorably toward someone or when someone reacts unfavorably toward us, communication is handicapped from the start. Conclusion: People who make a habit of liking other people find it easier to communicate.

. . . .

Comprehension checks

What is meant by the phrase *person perception*? When you meet a person for the first time, is there much chance that your first impressions of him will match your impressions of him after a period of six months of frequent contact? Which of the four modes of person perception do you normally use? Or do you use more than one? Does a college education guarantee maturity? Does it help one to attain maturity? How? is there any sense in a statement like "I never met a man I didn't like"? Have you ever watched a person coming into a room in which he sees someone he likes? Someone he doesn't know? Someone he doesn't like? Does his expression change to fit each of the three situations? Have you ever watched someone pretend a liking he didn't really feel? Can it be done successfully?

---

7. Perelman, p. 176.

Demonstration options

1. From magazine clippings, portrait studios, or any other source, secure a half dozen or more stock photographs or portraits of unidentified and unidentifiable persons ranging widely in age, sex, apparent occupation, etc. If several students in the class are able to contribute a selection of such photos, choose a few for a class project in which each student jots down what he perceives as personality characteristics (e.g., kind, authoritarian, suspicious, friendly) in the subject of each photo. Then compare notes to point up the unreliability of determining personality characteristics in this way.

2. Arrange to have someone come into the class who is unknown to all or most of its members. Again, jot down individually the personality characteristics which you perceive in the subject standing before you. Compare notes again to provide a base for discussing similarities and differences in initial person perception. (For obvious reasons, this demonstration must be conducted in such a way as to avoid embarrassment to the person who agrees to act as subject.)

....

Motivation and Goals

Valuable as it is to know something of the variables affecting direct person-to-person impressions, we find that knowledge useful only in the context of the broader question of why people behave as they do. It is of course one thing to take cognizance of the personal commitments and values certain groups of men hold and to use them as common premises (described in Chapter 3) on which to build one's effort to engage in persuasive transactions with listeners. It is another to understand the general forces operating within all listeners and having the potential to cause them to decide to move from one position to another. We need that understanding before we can undertake to stimulate any change of behavior through speech-communication.

Psychologists agree that there is within each of us some kind of motivation for the things we do and for the communication we undertake. Moreover, we are never satisfied. As Maslow says, "Man is a wanting animal and rarely reaches a state of complete satisfaction except for a short time. As one desire is satisfied, another pops up to take its place."[8]

Berelson and Steiner describe a goal as the "object, condition, or activity... which will satisfy or reduce the striving."[9] A motive is considered to be "an inner state that energizes, activates,... or channels behavior toward goals,"[10] and motives fall into two categories: (1) physiological and (2) secondary, learned, social, or psychogenic motives. "By definition, the general result of motivation is purposive goal-directed behavior that leads to satisfaction."[11]

---

8. A. H. Maslow, *Motivation and Personality* (New York: Harper & Row, 1954), p. 69. Reprinted by permission.
9. Berelson and Steiner, p. 240.
10. *Ibid.*, p. 240.
11. *Ibid.*, p. 261.

Stated in a different way, motivation is the combination of a need-want-goal with recognition of one or more paths leading to that goal. If two or more behavioral paths are open, the alternative choices may also vary in the degree of satisfaction attained. The child trying to put a toy together may let his father come to the rescue, or he may insist on doing it himself for the added pleasure of independent action. Or a high school student may have a college education as a goal. Unless some avenue to that education opens up, college will be a dreamlike goal and nothing more. However, if he learns that a plan to work one's way through exists, or that a loan is readily available, or that some relative will help him, or that he can get some kind of scholarship, he is then *motivated* to take some action (behave in a certain way) to reach the goal. Again, there may be counterforces operating—he may not be to eager to leave home, or perhaps his potential earnings are necessary to help support the family. He must deal with all these push-and-pull forces in making up his mind to embark on a particular course at this time. A third example: Someone wanting to make a good impression on a group has that goal in mind. It is only when he sees a way to attain that objective that he is *motivated* or moved to action. The assumption is that he weighs pros and cons before he commits himself—he could decide to wait for a better and more dramatic opportunity. In the latter instance, the motivation would be said to be too weak to spur him to goal-attaining behavior at this time.

Another point of view appears in this statement by White: "There is widespread discontent with theories of motivation built upon primary drives."[12] White takes the position that the one central type of motivation is the desire for competence (i.e., mastery over the varied aspects of the individual's environment). To put it another way, everything the individual does he does with the objective of enhancing, maintaining, or defending his self-concept; that is his primary goal throughout life—all other goals are secondary. Maslow recognizes "that the individual is an integrated, organized whole"[13] and agrees that we "should give up the attempt once and for all to make atomistic lists of drives and needs."[14] However, he believes that there is some utility in describing *collections* of desires, needs, or goals, with the understanding that no mutual exclusiveness is implied. He calls his unified and goal-directed synthesis of earlier theories "a holistic-dynamic theory."[15] The discussion which follows is based primarily on Maslow (pp. 80–106).

Goals of basic security

It is ordinarily agreed that, in our society at least, physiological and safety needs are seldom of real consequence; a majority of Americans get a reasonable complement of food, rest, and shelter, and we are still in relatively little fear of violence. Others in this country are not so fortunate; some do live in squalor, misery, and danger. When an individual living in a slum is impelled to strike out or speak out against conditions there, he is demonstrating the urgency of the desire for security, and at the same time, he is using that urgent desire as a motivating factor in his appeal to listeners.

---

12. Robert W. White, "Motivation Reconsidered: The Concept of Competence" in Kuhlen, p. 81.
13. Maslow, p.63.
14. *Ibid.*, p. 70.
15. *Ibid.*, p. 80.

Goals of personal acceptance

There is a saying that "everyone wants to be loved." Indeed, many of our social ills are ascribed to the fact that too many youngsters grow up in an atmosphere totally devoid of family love and concern. Man is by nature gregarious. He wants to "belong," to be accepted by individuals and by groups. (If a group does not exist to which he can gain ready admittance, he is likely to organize one.) Unfortunately, some of us do not get a share of the varieties of belonging, so that we become fair game for the purveyors of procedures and potions "guaranteed" to make us socially acceptable and attractive to others. Whether or not we succumb to such overtures, we do derive satisfaction from acceptance as members in informal and formal organizations, and we do what we can to gain that acceptance.

Goals of special identity

Every man wants to gain a special regard for himself in the eyes of his fellows. He wants respect, an office or two in the organizations he has joined, success in his job or professional career; if others have a high regard for an individual, he will normally have a fairly high level of esteem for himself. Pure altruism is a rare virtue; people want to be recognized for what they do, even when they are working for "a good cause," such as a charity drive. Examples are readily seen in the many news stories containing endless lists of project-committee chairmen and members, lists serving no real purpose except to boost the egos of the persons involved.

Goals of potential-realization

Each of us is best satisfied when he is working and meeting challenges in a field which he likes and in which his potentialities can best be realized. The college graduate who finds it hard to get a position in the field for which he is trained, provided that the job market is good, is going to be frustrated. The talented artist who is forced to sell Fuller brushes in order to eat is going to be unhappy. The student interested in medicine but prevented from entering any medical school because of the shortage of such schools is going to be discouraged. However successful a man may be in achieving the goals represented by those listed earlier, his next goal is characteristically the attainment of what Goldstein, Maslow, Weinberg, and others call self-actualization, the drive to do what one is fitted for, coupled with the inner urge to reach the highest rung possible in one's chosen field. It is in man's nature to keep reaching out to meet the next challenge. If he fails to accept challenge, he has only himself to blame. If he is forced by circumstances to waste his life in an area not suited to his talents and his potential, the desire for personal achievement is tragically blunted, and the loss to society is equally severe. As Whittier said so incisively in *Maud Muller*,

> *For of all sad words of tongue and pen,*
> *The saddest are these: "It might have been!"*

Goals of education

Education, formal or informal, is the obvious path leading to many of the goals of life. In this age and society, education is so primary a path that any block standing in the way to one's training for a productive life is looked upon as a block to one or more of the basic aims. We see this "associated" goal emphasized almost every day in references to education as a prerequisite to success as an individual and as a citizen.

In final comment on goals . . .

Although points of view may differ on whether man's primary goal is always the preservation and enhancement of his self-concept or whether he is at times subject to separate goals or clusters of them, we do agree that man is subject to such fundamental needs; with or without his being aware of those needs, they lead him to communicate with his fellowman. "If you would know a man, determine his goals."[16] The communicator-listener's goals and purposes in life, stemming from the broad categories of goals noted above, are what largely determine which messages and parts of messages he will hear;[17] those goals should be kept in mind in the course of the communicator-speaker's message preparation and message sending.

Maslow agrees with other psychologists that needs or goals follow a kind of priority principle. *Goals of basic security* are dominant; when they are satisfied, other goals come to the fore in the general order of the classes listed.[18] In addition, the relative emphasis placed by individuals, groups, and audiences on the preceding collection of goals is going to shift and vary with the circumstances. When an all-day geological-study hike nears its end on a hot afternoon, the student geologists are going to be more interested in food and rest than in the instructor-leader's one last discourse on the features of outcropping number 99. Or when an entire nation works to reduce the illiteracy rate in its population, most of the citizens in it may be said place a high value on the goal of a basic education for all; on the other hand, if that kind of education is available to 99 percent of the populace, the literacy goal shrinks to near insignificance, although it may still be of paramount importance to some individuals. In other words, one of the tasks of the communicator is to be sensitive to the values his listeners place on goals *at the time he is trying to communicate with them.*

Since our goals to a large extent govern what we hear,[19] it is obvious that the speaker-communicator must take human goals into account when attempting to communicate. The listener who sees that attending to the speaker is going to help him reach a personal or group goal or help him avoid losing one already attained will have more interest in the proceedings than will the listener who sees no direct gain, loss, or avoidance of any kind.

. . . .

Comprehension checks

What is happening when you cannot quite make up your mind whether to study or go to a movie? Is it possible to be motivated when there is no way to achieve a particular goal? If so, in what direction? Give an example. Should a speaker provide

---

16. Brink and Kelley, p. 71.
17. For a discussion of selective perception, see Weaver and Strausbaugh, p. 234.
18. This idea of priorities in goals is akin to that of value hierarchies in argument. Compare discussion of the common premise in Chapter 3.
19. Brown and Van Riper, p. 54. See also footnote 17 immediately above.

motivation for reaching a goal? Or should he let a listener find the way or ways to achieve it? Does motivation occur anywhere else but *within* the listener? Paul D. Holtzmann says (p. 50) that man is "animal in his need for bodily comfort, human in his need for approval and achievement." Do you agree? Why? Why not? Do you sometimes react to what is being said in a way that you cannot help? Under what circumstances?

Are you ever concerned about basic security? In what way? Rod McKuen says that you can be a "loner" without being lonely. Does that view make any sense? Do you like to be noticed? Have you actively participated in any charitable enterprises? How? What motivated you to do so? What is your professional, business, or other goal in life? What is self-actualization? Are you attaining it now? What are your chances for attaining it? What is the difference between the common premises described in Chapter 3 and the goals outlined in this chapter? Is it a difference based on the purpose for which a particular idea is used?

Demonstration options

1. Try out on the class a statement which you believe to be a common premise for all the students in it. For example: "We are proud of our American heritage." Then cite the theme for a talk for which that premise could presumably be a base. For example: "A visit to Williamsburg, Virginia, is a fascinating lesson in history."
2. Cite a goal which you believe the members of the class would like to attain individually or collectively. For example: "Each of us would find it an enlightening educational experience to see his state legislature in action." Then, assuming that "motivation occurs when one sees a way to achieve a goal," outline one or more ways your listeners could reach that goal.

Cue Selection and Attention

Closely associated with the problems of properly assessing listener goals and maintaining interest through that avenue is the business of competing for the attention of the listener, for "more stimuli come to us than we are able to attend to."[20] Ordinarily, our general level of attention is relatively low until our senses apprehend some cue which "brings us to life" and encourages response to parts of the message connected with the cue. For example, you may be physically present in the classroom without paying much attention to a history lecture until the instructor mentions your hometown (cue!), whereupon you suddenly become alert to those parts of the message associated with the cue (e.g., details of an important conference which took place in the courthouse there). Then, as the lecture drones on, your interest wanes and you drift back into a state of semi-conscious "listening" and/or daydreaming up to the next cue. In a group or audience situation, naturally, the audience-wide cue is desirable; interest is normally quite high during political campaign speeches, but it is even higher when a *local problem* (cue) is the focus for some phase of the talk.

---

20. Schramm, *The Process and Effects of Mass Communication*, p. 29.

The speaker-communicator, then, is faced with the problem of planning and arranging cues to encourage the listener(s) to "tune in" and remain so for as much of the message as possible. He "therefore draws on all he knows about the listener, all that he can find out by feedback, in order to cue his message to the personal interests of the listener."[21]

In addition to being concerned about using cues keyed to listener needs, the speaker should also be in a position to take advantage of *universal factors* on which he may call to highlight or reinforce the listener's discrimination of the cues intended for him. Brief discussions of these factors follow.

Movement. It is a fact of life that the eye is drawn to moving persons or things. The animated speaker moves, gestures, points, and generally provides enough action to call added attention to cues and ideas he wishes to emphasize. If he does none of these things, a number of those present will soon be watching clouds, birds, or their neighbors in the audience.

Intensity. By this term we mean the amount of force or energy that provides stimuli affecting one or more individuals. Insofar as the listener is concerned, his attention is held more easily if the person attempting to communicate with him will vary the tone, rate, and volume of his voice and use that instrument as a kind of brush to highlight central cues and associated ideas.

If visual aids of any kind are being used, the "listener's" attention will be drawn to bold lettering and strong colors. The less intense colors and weak lettering will not only lose his attention but will frustrate him as well.

Size. The larger an object, the more easily it is seen. This is true for speakers themselves and for whatever devices, posters, or blowups they prepare as visual aids. We can do nothing about our height and little about our weight; however, we can do something about holding the listener's attention by adapting the "size" of bodily movement, gestures, and visual aids to the size of the audience. A very limited motion of the hand may be well suited to a small conference but totally unsuited for reaching several hundred people in a large hall. Similarly, a poster which can be readily seen in the classroom may be sadly ineffectual in the larger setting.

Proximity. The closer the listener is to the speaker, the more disposed he is to attend to what that individual is saying. Similarly, the closer the speaker is to his listener(s), the better chance he has of maintaining interest, and the more opportunity there is for a higher level of interpersonal interaction. If listeners are isolated from the speaker by unnecessary distance (e.g., 20 scattered listeners in an auditorium with a capacity of 200), the knowledgeable speaker either will ask the group to come together "down front" or will abandon the platform and take up a position near the group. Further, it sometimes happens that the stage or speaking platform is considerably higher than the level of the main floor where it abuts on the speaking area. Even if a small audience does come "down front" in such a situation, the speaker is still too far removed from the group and should consider stepping down to the level of the main floor. In a large flat-floored hall, it occasionally happens that those sitting toward the rear cannot see the speaker and he cannot see them; in such instances, the

---

21. *Ibid.,* p. 32.

speaker should resort to some kind of emergency platform, a desk top, table, or large and stable chair, for example. People find it very difficult to respond to cues coming from someone they cannot see.

Reference to the familiar. We feel more "at home" in association with familiar people and surroundings. Faced with new ideas and propositions, the listener appreciates having the "new" associated with persons, things, and movements within his own experience. Something of this reaction is seen in the ease with which sons of successful politicans win elections largely on the merits of reputations won by the fathers. Try to relate new ideas and things to familiar ideas and things.

Precision in language. Words like "car," "house," "street," "dog," "walk," "eat," "good," "beautiful," and "blue," are a part of everyone's vocabulary and serve useful functions. However, they could hardly be described as colorful, and they are of little help in developing an accurate "picture" for the listener. You increase his cue-sensitivity by substituting such terms as "Toronado," "Georgian mansion," "shaded lane," "wire-haired terrier," "saunter along," "have a leisurely dinner," "honest" (or any one of a hundred synonyms for "good"), "striking," or "soft shade of aquamarine." Work for accuracy in *specific* detail and, when appropriate, in *imaginative* detail.

Novelty and contrast. One hot summer day, the great Henry Ward Beecher is said to have opened an outdoor sermon on blasphemy with the words, "It's God-damn hot out here!" Presumably, that opening was both novel and attention-getting. The writer once heard a six-foot-three 250-pound male student present a process-talk on the baking of brownies. To simulate the equipment required, he used some miniature toy utensils and dishes in going through the motions of mixing the batter and putting it into the oven (a drawer of the desk). The incongruous sight of this very large man using the very small dishes was a study in both novelty and contrast; otherwise, the talk was a very straightforward exposition of the process involved. The point is that the listening students were fascinated by the novel approach to a relatively routine subject.

From the standpoint of the listener, contrast enlivens what could otherwise be a relatively dull exposition or description. It is possible to describe the plight of migrant workers with detail and accuracy. That plight is brought more vividly to mind if it is contrasted with the lives of a majority of Americans.

Conflict. "Practically everyone enjoys a good fight." That "truism" may not, in fact, be true; nevertheless, if you attack a particular organization, system, or condition, your listeners will be more readily attentive and interested than if your aim is simple description. If in response to a talk given by someone else, you take an opposite position, listeners will again be more concerned. Conflict is a part of life, and when it occurs, observers and listeners watch and listen with sharpened acuity.

. . . .

Comprehension checks

Are you conscious of the fact that your "ears perk up" when you hear something of interest to you? Or that, as you drive down a road with others, each person literally "sees" different things? Is there such a thing as an "odor cue"? Or a "touch cue"? Or a "taste cue"? Or a "kinetics cue"? As you watch a movie, play, or television drama, do you find yourself tense at some times and relaxed at others? When a speaker is intense and serious, do you have a tendency to be intense and serious? If he laughs and jokes, do you generally relax and enjoy the situation? Do you believe it is possible for a speaker to plan his cues in advance? Or to inject them into a communicative situation as they seem to be needed?

Do you know anyone who has a monotonous way of speaking? What is the problem? Is it tone? Volume? Rate? One gesture? Some or all of these? Have you heard yourself on a recorder of any kind? Do you believe that it is possible to become less monotonous in all kinds of communication through practice and exercises? Is there anything you can do to make yourself "bigger" in a large hall? Move nearer to the audience? Make broader and more sweeping gestures? Stand on a podium if the lectern is unusually large and high? Is there any need for any of these measures? Why? Why not?

Is it possible to be precise in language without really trying? Is vocabulary building a waste of time? Why? Why not? Or can it pay dividends? How? Why is it that some people of the same general background just naturally use more words and more appropriate words than others? Could it be a matter of one's having done more reading? Being more interested in words? Making frequent use of a dictionary? Pure accident?

Demonstration options

1. Illustrate cue selection by describing a situation in which a particular cue moved you from a state of relative inattention to a "state of temporary or continuing alert."
2. Read to the class a single paragraph from any source. The paragraph should demonstrate noteworthy use of precision in language, or it should be an example of routine, pedestrian language. Explain why you place it in the one category or the other.
3. Read to the class a paragraph which you consider lacking in language precision. Then read *your* improved version of the same paragraph.
4. Find the verbatim version of a speech in *Vital Speeches* or some other source. Read the first paragraph or two to the class. Then explain why you consider the opening lines lackluster or attention-compelling.

. . . .

Rapport

Rapport may be defined as the highly desirable sense of interrelated "oneness" which sometimes exists between one individual and another or among the members of groups ranging from a few persons sitting around a conference table to a mass meeting addressed by a single speaker. Interpersonal action-reaction, as we learned in Chapter 1, is integral and inescapable in the communicative process; with or without our consent, people react to us and we react to people. It follows that one of the prime objectives of those involved in communicative interaction should be the attainment of rapport at the highest possible level of interdependent response.

Rapport in one-to-one or in one-to-many relationships is occasionally "automatic" in that you immediately feel both completely at ease and totally immersed in the concerns and problems of the person or persons with whom you are attempting to communicate. More often, a real effort must be made to achieve that state. The highest level of rapport is empathy; it requires the temporary "losing" of one's own personality in the personality of another in order to understand him better; it calls for feeling for one's fellows but on a higher level than sympathy or simple compassion; it demands more than emotion, which is commonly defined as a self-centered feeling (love, hate, anger, etc.) moving out from oneself and sometimes moving others to a similar intensity. Whether or not a communicator is speaking or listening is a matter of no consequence; in either instance, he must be able to forget his own problems in a deep and sincere effort to see things through the eyes of his fellowman. You will be on the road to attaining rapport only if those listening to you find it possible to say, "He is really with us; he really understand us; he sees our problems from *our* point of view!"

"Feelings," of course, encompass every known variation in sentiment, expressions of sympathy, varied emotions, and the kinds of in-somebody-else's-place empathy described above. It is no news to anyone that "feelings" or emotions, self-centered or otherwise, play an important part in positions taken and decisions reached by man. A public relations expert participating in a television discussion of Madison Avenue promotion of candidates for public office: "More votes are decided on emotion than on logic. We base our management of campaigns on what really moves people rather than on what *should* move them." [22] A professor of marketing at a university in one of the middle Atlantic states: "People's beliefs are based on feelings and emotions."[23] William Simmons, founder of the "second" Ku Klux Klan (Atlanta, 1915): "All action comes from emotion, rather than from ratiocination."[24] If they were still alive, Hitler and Mussolini would be inclined to agree with Simmons and with the present-day observers. "People are persuaded by people, not by information," and "Belief is based on human relationships, not upon logical data."[25] And at least one study[26] brought the experimenter to the conclusion that audiences do not see any clear-cut differences between emotional and logical appeals.

At this point, if there is validity in the above viewpoints, you may be wondering why some considerable amount of time was spent on the previous chapter, with its emphasis on logical patterns in speech-communication. The reasons are (1) that the concept of the "thinking man" is coming back into vogue on the heels of cognition studies suggesting that each of us is impelled to be consistent in thought, feeling, and action, (2) that there are many conversational, conference, and audience situations in which the primary emphasis is on a nonemotional search for or exchange of information and inferences, (3) that thinking and feeling go on simultaneously and are mutually reinforcive, not mutually exclusive, and (4) that, while it is indeed possible on occasion to succeed in persuading without re-

---

22. Public Broadcast Laboratory program on evening of November 12, 1967.
23. Brink and Kelley, p. 150.
24. Arthur M. Schlesinger, Sr., *Saturday Review* (November 27, 1965), p. 24.
25. Brown and Van Riper, p. 85.
26. Randall C. Ruechelle, "An Experimental Study of Emotional and Intellectual Appeals in Persuasion," *Speech Monographs,* **25** (March 1958), pp. 49–58.

sorting to content or argument, the trained listener feels the need for *some* logic, and at one time or another, any listener requires logical ammunition for use in justifying what he may want to do for other reasons.

Except for convenience in a theoretical discussion, there is, as we have already noted, no way to separate one class of so-called "approaches to proof" (e.g., logical, emotional, or ethical) from another; the many messages which are being sent simultaneously by the "whole man" are so inextricably intertwined and interrelated that no one seriously undertakes to distinguish one from the others. Statements of causal relationships, for instance, may be heavily charged with affective appeals, and a speaker's "logical" conclusions may be threatening in the extreme. If you have a deep conviction that what you are saying is really worth saying, your *feeling will come through* as an integral part of the total message.

. . . .

Comprehension checks

What is rapport? Is it a *feeling*? What kind? Is it possible to have rapport with someone who doesn't give you an opportunity to say anything? Under what circumstances? As you speak, you sometimes see that your listener can hardly wait to break in with his comment or response. Is he listening to you? Can you have real rapport with him?

Why is it easier to establish rapport in one-to-one or small group conversations? Is it a matter of physical distance—proximity in conversations and greater separation in speaker-audience communication?

If you are anticipating criticism from someone, are you generally on the defensive, at least in the initial stages of the communicative transaction? If you don't quite understand why a particular person is taking the time to talk with you, are you going to be entirely open with him or just a little reserved or suspicious? Do you like people who seem always to be appraising you and awarding pluses for this and minuses for that? Do you get along well with people who phrase orders in command form rather than as requests? What do the questions in this paragraph have to do with rapport? Or with setting the stage for rapport?

According to Howell and Bormann (p. 227), "Humor can be used . . . to establish rapport, to control attention, and to improve retention." Why should humor be effective in those ways? Is it necessary to be a good joke and story teller in order to make use of humor? Do you like people "with a sense of humor"? Why? Do you feel more at ease with them? Why? Give an example of non-joke humor which was—or could be—used in communication. If a speaker is stiff, formal, and unbending, is the general atmosphere in the room affected? How? If an audience is stiff, formal, and unbending, is the speaker affected? How?

Demonstration options

1. In a short story or novel, find a short communicative excerpt (conversation, argument, or other type of speech-communication) in which close rapport is obviously lacking or clearly present. Read the passage to the class, and explain why you consider it an example of good or bad rapport.

2. Try to find an excerpt in which initial mistrust is displaced by trust. Read it and give your explanation of the shift.

3. Try to find an excerpt in which initial trust is replaced by suspicion or any other reaction. Read it and give your explanation of the shift.
4. If you have seen a speaker win the confidence of an antagonistic or noncommittal audience, give a short description of the circumstances, and explain how he went about establishing rapport.

. . . .

In summary

Although we still have much to learn about the phenomenon of perception and although there is little fundamental agreement on its components, what little we do know is of some help in learning more about ourselves, about others, and about communicative transactions.

Second, we are motivated to reach goals when we see a way to attain those goals without, at the same time, incurring penalties. In any event, we normally weigh pros and cons before taking action. It follows that communicator-speakers should make every effort to know the goals of communicator-listeners and the priorities in which they hold these goals. That kind of knowledge is a primary step toward successful communication.

Third, we attend to cues and the ideas associated with them. Some cues are personal; others catch the attention of all those present. In addition, certain related psychological and physiological factors affect the discrimination of cues and attention in general.

Finally, we expect others to "understand" us, and they expect us to "understand" them. Those participating in the give and take of the communicative experience find it comparatively easy to establish a feeling of rapport in conversations and smaller groups; rapport comes somewhat less easily in speaker-audience situations but it is still attainable and desirable.

Part 2 / Speech-communication in primary phases

5 / Acquiring initial experience

No matter what emphasis is placed on the theoretical importance of the role of the communicator-listener, it is safe to say that, initially at least, you are more concerned about your role as a communicator-speaker. Early activities in the basic course are therefore planned to initiate you into these practical realities of speech-communication: (1) The role of communicator-speaker is not so difficult as one may be inclined to imagine, and (2) the role of communicator-listener, although it may call for new habits of listening, is both pleasant and rewarding.

When one is approaching any new or relatively new endeavor, it is customary to "wade in slowly until one gets the feel of the water." You will discover that the first speaking-listening experiences offered to you are comparatively easy to handle. (Even at later stages in a basic course, opportunities for practical activities at essentially the same level are sometimes introduced to provide relaxation or variety from the normal routine.) It is relevant, then, to discuss at this point some of the more or less elementary forms of human interaction: the short introduction, interaction for mutual enjoyment, the impromptu talk, and presentation of one's point of view.

The Short Introduction

To give beginning students early practice with both listening and speaking roles (and to help them get acquainted), a round of introductions is frequently the order of the first day or two. Most of us would agree that an introduction is one of the easiest and most "natural" forms of human interaction; because it can also be mercifully short, it is a popular first project.

We are not here concerned with social introductions. We are talking about the kind of introduction in which a student says a few words about himself, or about some other student, or about some other person presumed to be—but not actually—present. The speaker tries to engage in the give and take of communication with his listeners, the other members of the class, in the effort to win a favorable reception for the individual being introduced.

Does it make sense to have you making introductions and listening to them? In this day of frequent meetings there is a reasonable chance that you will be called on at some time to introduce someone to an audience. Perhaps you've already had this experience. Perhaps you've introduced a representative from another school, college, or university. Or perhaps, you have attended some meeting at which the chairman, in the Ed Sullivan style, invited someone to "take a bow." In such situations, each introduction consists of a few well-chosen remarks followed by the individual's name. Here is an acceptable pattern for introducing *an individual*.

1. If there is a particular reason for the individual's presence (e.g., guest, substitute for an absentee, observer), mention what it is. "We have a visitor who is here because...."
2. Call attention to the individual's claim to special notice (reputation, position, honors, etc.).
3. Close with the individual's name as the signal for his standing up to acknowledge the introduction.

When you are asked to introduce *a speaker*, you will find this general pattern easy to follow.

1. Explain why the speaker's topic is important to the group.
2. Explain why the speaker is qualified to talk on the subject.
3. Close with something like this: "Our speaker on this timely and important topic is [name]."

What opportunities will you get to become acquainted with techniques of introduction in a speech-communication class? The first type, introducing an individual, is often a part of "opening ceremonies." Each student is sometimes asked to introduce himself. Or after a quick buzz session in which students exchange personal data (hometown, class, major or current academic interests, extracurricular interests or hobbies, etc.), you introduce to the class the student sitting next to you, and she reciprocates by introducing you; the same procedure is followed by succeeding pairs. Or on a round-robin basis, you introduce the student next to you, she introduces the next student, he introduces the next student, etc., and finally the last student gets back to telling the class about you. The only difficulty with these patterns is that students waiting to speak are inclined to concentrate on what they are going to say rather than on listening to what is being said. For this reason, it is wise from time to time to break the expected order by asking a student in another part of the class to repeat the introduction he has just heard, or repeat the second-last introduction, or third-last, etc. The student who knows that he may be called on at any time to introduce again someone who has already been presented to the class is going to be a better listener throughout the series, and he is also going to be better acquainted with everyone in the class.

The second type of introduction, that of presenting a speaker to a group (and listening to such a presentation), will come your way if the class schedule permits the appointment of chairmen for certain programs. As a chairman, your first task will be to find out in advance who the speakers are, on what topics they intend to speak, and what they have done (education, experience, interviews, or reading) to qualify themselves for talking on the subjects which they have determined to be of potential interest to the audience. Your second task, obviously, is to plan the introductions along the lines suggested earlier. On the other hand, whenever you are among the listeners, you have a chance to gain information not previously available to you, and you can also observe the chairman's handling of the introductions in order to improve your own facility in a skill that is commonly required in the world about you.

Not only because class time is limited, but because it is just generally good practice, a chairman should keep his remarks to a minimum. If you confine yourself to straightforward answers to the questions suggested above, you will never be accused of indulging in too much flattery or taking up time that should be allotted to a speaker. Outside the classroom, where the pressures of time are not so great, it is still advisable to say only what is necessary to set the stage properly for the speaker or speakers of the day. An example of a "real" introduction follows.

An introduction of a speaker

At a meeting in his New York home in March, 1968, Mr. Wyatt Cooper used the following words to introduce Senator Eugene McCarthy of Minnesota, then hoping to be the Democratic nominee for the Presidency.[1]

> Ladies and gentlemen:
>
> We live in a time of chaos, a time of change, a time of great confusion. Many of the old values do not hold. Certainly, the old slogans do not suffice. It is an age of skepticism, of cynicism, and of resignation. The world is so large and the individual so small that he shrugs his shoulders and says, "What's the use?"
>
> But there is a new spirit alive in this land. It is surely a sign of some kind of progress that less and less are we content to follow blindly, and more and more we ask the question, "Why?" When questions are asked, answers will be found. So long as men ask "Why?" we can live with hope. So long as men search for truth, we can believe in the possibility of a future.
>
> We have seen in the long march from our beginnings that great challenges have produced great champions. How fortunate we are, then, that our present crisis has brought forth a man for our times. How fortunate we are that a man has come forward who is not repelled by a spirit of inquiry. A man who dares to say "No" when others are saying "Yes." A man who dares speak out when others are silent. A man who dares take a stand when others play a waiting game. A man who says "Let us try," when others say "What good will it do?" A man who can be believed. A man who will talk sense to the American people.
>
> Ladies and gentlemen, Senator Eugene McCarthy.

---

1. Printed here in edited form with the permission of Mr. Cooper.

Introducing yourself

Speaking option

Introduce yourself in a way that might help us get acquainted with you. What experiences of yours might have been different from those of other students in the class? What about family experiences? What are your interests?

Listening option

What have you learned about the speaker from what he said? From what he didn't say? What questions would help you learn more about the experience or interest presented?

Introducing another student

Speaking options

1. Introduce another student as you would any "visitor to the class." Confine your remarks to mention of birthplace, current status as a student, major area(s) of study if known, hobbies, jobs, and notable experiences if any. Finish with the student's name, at which signal he or she should stand up.
2. The "visitor" can then respond with a very few comments to express appreciation of his welcome, his pleasure in visiting the class, etc., *or* ...
3. The "visitor" can in turn introduce either the student who has just finished speaking or another student in series. In other words, the introductions can be arranged in pairs, in round-robin groups, or on the domino plan, whereby one student introduces the second, who stands to acknowledge the introduction and then, in turn, introduces still another student, who ...

Listening options

1. What important question(s) seemed to have been left unanswered by one or more of the speakers of the day? Why do you consider the omission(s) important?
2. Was any of the information presented of *special* interest to you? Will it help you get better acquainted with someone in the group? Will the information be of any value to you now or later?

Introducing a speaker[2]

Speaking option

Suppose you have been invited to introduce a favorite author of yours as speaker at a dinner. Prepare to introduce him by giving the most important facts about his

---

2. Adapted from "Making the Most of Speaking-and-Listening Experiences," by Alexander Frazier, *The English Journal,* **46** (September 1957), p. 335. Reprinted with the permission of the National Council of Teachers of English and Alexander Frazier.

background and achievements. Withhold his name until the end of the introduction.

Listening options

Did this introduction make you want to know more about the author? How did these contribute to your interest: (1) selection of information on background; (2) information on achievements; (3) choice of wording; (4) way of speaking?

....

Interaction for Mutual Enjoyment

Another speaking-listening situation which is accompanied by very little if any stress is that of telling a personal anecdote, a brief account of something interesting that happened to you on campus, at home, at work, or anywhere else. *People like to hear about people;* that's why a story about yourself in relation to students, parents, professors, friends, employers, or others almost always holds listener attention. An anecdote practically "organizes itself." After a general statement about the happening (e.g., "Giving a girl a ring is not a good policy"), you name the members of "the cast" ("The people involved in this incident were...") and give the time and the place ("at 12:30 p.m. on a week night near the Administration Building"). Then you relate the details of the encounter with the girl in question—what she said, what you said. You close with the lesson learned from the experience: "The way to keep your independence is to keep from giving a girl any symbol she can interpret to her advantage."

Another age-old and sometimes rehearsed form of pleasurable speech-communication is the "re-creation" of literature by reading it aloud, an activity which is rapidly regaining popularity. In spite of the hectic pace of modern life and its sophisticated amusements, well-known actors continue to appear in solo performances of excerpts from plays, and amateur readers' groups are springing up everywhere. The reasons are easy to see: The spoken word brings the written word "to life," and reading aloud is universal in its appeal to people of all ages. Reading for others is not only an activity in which each of us has some measure of ability, but it is also one of the easiest ways by which to gain experience in speaker-audience situations.

One point to remember in undertaking "interpretative reading" is that it is a form of communication, not an exhibition. First, you look for a passage that you believe you could *enjoy reading* and that the listeners would *enjoy hearing*. Such a passage can be found in a novel, poem, epic, speech, short story, essay, editorial, or any other form of creative writing. After choosing the passage, you will want to read it very carefully in the attempt to understand as fully as possible what the writer was trying to say; you try to understand *his* ideas and *his* feelings. If you can with some accuracy and sensitivity interpret the "meanings" of the writer and bring them to life for your listeners, you can be sure that they will appreciate both what the author is saying and your own enjoyment and enthusiasm.

Communicating directly for pleasure

Speaking options

1. Present a personal experience you believe the class would enjoy hearing about.
2. Read to the class a very short story or passage from literature; try to choose one your listeners are not likely to have heard or read.

Listening options

1. Did the speaker succeed in the effort to interest and/or entertain you by sharing with you his choice of a personal experience or story?
2. What elements contributed to your enjoyment? The basic material? The way in which it was presented?
3. If you found it difficult to listen, what is your diagnosis of the problem?

The Impromptu Talk

Impromptu is usually interpreted to mean *without advance notice* and *without preparation*. In the sense that someone may unexpectedly call on you "for a few words," a talk may be truly impromptu. However, there are those who say that there is no such thing as an impromptu situation, because one's entire background really constitutes a general state of readiness for any talk, prepared or unprepared. Furthermore, the person with any background in speech-communication has closeted in his memory a few skeleton outlines which can be rattled on short notice to provide the base for the rapid "fleshing in" of a series of comments. Finally, there is usually *some* hint or warning, however belated, that one *may* be called on for his views or that one *may* want to present them in the course of a particular meeting.

However you choose to define *the impromptu talk*, it may be assumed to exist within the boundaries above. Although you will not want to be caught unprepared and unready in any speech-communication situation for which preparation is possible, the impromptu talk does have some virtues: (1) Experience with it helps you avoid panic when you are faced with the necessity for giving an "instant speech." (2) It forces you "to think on your feet." (3) It gives you practice in on-the-spot organization. (4) It encourages a greater degree of rapport with an audience than is sometimes possible with the speech that is thoroughly prepared. (5) It helps give you the confidence you need to speak up without fear when the unexpected happens in private and public meetings.

The following "idea organizers" for impromptu talks are suggested by James M. Lewis.[3]

---

3. "Spur-of-the-Moment Speeches," *Today's Speech*, **5** (September 1958), pp. 9–10. Reprinted by permission.

1. Who, what, when, where, why, how?
2. What is the problem; possible solutions, best solution?
3. Past, present, future
4. Theoretically, practically
5. Right way, wrong way
6. Necessary, beneficial, practical (and/or just)
7. Individual, the group
8. Local, state, national, international (or other similar divisions)
9. Employer, employee, general public
10. Mentally, morally, physically
11. What shall we do first? second? third?
12. The general principle involved (legal, moral, etc.) and relationship to topic
13. Probable results if we take this action; if we do not
14. What are advantages, disadvantages?

. . . .

Giving an impromptu talk

Speaking options[4]

1. On a small card, write a favorite quotation from literature or any maxim, motto, proverb, or saying that appeals to you. Put your signature at the bottom of the card, and give it to the instructor for use at his discretion at a later date. On any day that the schedule permits, he will be in a position to distribute the cards at random and, after a brief period of preparation, ask for volunteers to speak for two or three minutes "on the implications of the sayings."

2. Cut a picture from a magazine (photography magazines are excellent for this), sign it, and turn it in to the instructor for later distribution and use in the same way as for option 1. When called on to speak:

    a. Do not describe the picture.

    b. Speak on something the picture suggests to you—a vital issue, a tradition or value—or on something the picture reminds you of.

    c. Try to be creative and imaginative.

    d. Use the picture only as a visual aid *during* the speech at some point.

3. On a small card, write a serious *or* farfetched topic sentence or situation, sign the card, and turn it in to the instructor for later distribution and use as in the options above. Examples of the kind of topic you may want to submit:

    The voting age should be raised to 25.

    People over 65 should have two votes.

---

4. Adapted from *Purdue Basic Course Handbook*, 1970–71, pp. 151–152. Option 2 is adapted from a contribution by Valerie Knecht, Purdue Graduate Instructor. General editor for the *Handbook* was Sylvia Marks, Purdue Instructor, assisted by a staff of Graduate Instructors.

People should not marry before the age of 25.

What I would do if I found I had only two months to live.

You are going to live for two years in a remote lighthouse. You can bring three books, and you can receive two magazines by subscription. Defend your choices.

Listening options

1. What speaker in the program of the day was, in your opinion, most successful in adapting his impromptu topic to his audience? Write a one-paragraph nomination for the "best adaptation" award. Include your reasons for the nomination.

2. What speaker, in your opinion, appeared to have devised the best organizational structure for his talk? Write your one-paragraph nomination for the "most appropriate pattern" award.

3. What speaker appeared to generate the best rapport with his audience? Can you explain his success? Write a one-paragraph "best rapport" nomination.

4. On the basis of your observations of the total program of impromptu talks, what positive suggestions would you make to impromptu speakers in general. Write your list of suggestions (without identifying speakers) and turn it in to the instructor.

5. Was the audience a cooperative and active listening group? Was it cooperative sometimes and not at other times? What positive suggestions would you make to the audience? Write your list of suggestions and turn it in to the instructor.

Note: Either choose *one* of the selected listening options above, or adopt a plan, satisfactory to both students and instructor, for allocating to students selected options which will ensure the kind of coverage desired.

. . . .

Presenting One's Point of View

An early project in the basic course is often "a three-to-five-minute talk in which the student defends his viewpoint on an issue." Another is "an original three-to-five-minute speech based on a statement restricted in meaning and scope." These and other descriptions of a similar nature give the student an opportunity to take a stand and allow him, at the same time, considerable latitude in choice of topic.

One popular way to find a topic for such a project is to read an editorial and then present to the class a summary of it along with your reasons for opposing or agreeing with it. The reasons should consist of whatever conclusions you can draw from the kinds of support you are able to find in places other than the editorial itself: facts and statistics, examples, case histories, quotations, etc. Select an "idea organizer" from those cited in the preceding section for the impromptu talk as a framework for your remarks. Try to use two or three different kinds of support in the talk. As already suggested, you should not be satisfied simply to report what an editorial says and agree with it; your support should be *in addition to* any already appearing in it. (If you oppose the position taken, there will of course be no problem of simple repetition.)

The business of "taking a stand" brings with it some hazards. It is imperative that we recognize the need for expressing a viewpoint of any kind, controversial or non-controversial, *in a friendly manner* free of any hint of challenge. A speaker defending a viewpoint must remind himself (1) that almost never can he be 100 percent right, (2) that his views are not necessarily those of everyone in the room and may not be those of anyone there, (3) that seldom is any question divisible into "black" and "white," and (4) that self-qualification ("I may be wrong but . . . ," and "What I have read seems to indicate . . .") is a mark of maturity which audiences appreciate. If a talk of this kind is your first experience in taking a position on an issue, try to let your audience know that you are acutely aware of and respect the listener's right to a different or contrary opinion. The manner and tone of your presentation will ordinarily get this idea across without excessive emphasis.

. . . .

Reacting to an editorial

Speaking option

Read an editorial, a letter to the editor, or a magazine article, and present your reasons and evidence for agreement or opposition. Make a real effort to interact with your listeners as you present your ideas.

Listening options

1. What was your reaction to the speaker as a person holding a particular view on an issue? Did he seem to be open-minded? Willing to admit that he might not be right?
2. What was your own position on the issue? Did the speaker move you toward his direction of thinking? Were you repelled? Why?
3. Did you feel that he had good evidence in support of his stand?
4. At what times in the talk was rapport the strongest? Why? What was the general "atmosphere"? Friendly? Neutral? Argumentative? Why?

Opposing popular opinion

Speaking option

If you now hold a particular position which is the opposite of one generally held, state that position as if you were replying to an editorial affirming the popular view. Examples: The government should permit cigarette advertising on TV. The sale of alcoholic beverages should once again be prohibited. Communism is a result, not a cause.

Listening options

1. Did the speaker maintain poise and good humor in spite of the fact that he was running against "the majority view"? Did he communicate a sense of wanting to present some ideas for consideration by "the opposition"? Or did he give the impression of "wanting to pick a fight"?

2. Did his evidence support his position? Was it adequate? Why? Why not? Did the talk have any apparent organization? Did the organization help you understand the speaker, or did it get in the way?
3. How successfully did the speaker interact with his audience? How much effort did the audience make to interact with him? Did speaker and audience seem to respect the position of each other?
4. Did you personally interact with the speaker? Describe this interaction as best you can. Or try to explain why it was lacking. What was your overall reaction to the speaker and his message?

. . . .

The kinds of initial experiences described in this chapter require little or no advance preparation. Other speech-communication situations are more demanding in terms of the time needed for preparing to participate in them. For that reason, the next two chapters offer theoretical and practical suggestions for (1) keeping the listener in mind and interacting with him as you plan, organize, and present ideas, and (2) listening and interacting with the speaker when your role is that of listener.

6 / Planning with the listener in mind

Planning is a part of almost any communicating you do. In preparing to ask for a favor, you plan what you are going to say. Before asking for a job or assignment of any kind, you plan. When you're trying to get cooperation on a group project, you plan. *What am I going to say? In what order am I going to say it?* These are questions you have answered many times in the past; the suggestions in this chapter are intended to help you find better answers.

What Am I Going to Say?

Sometimes you don't have to concern yourself about a choice of subject. There's one waiting for you in the form of a topic everybody is talking about, or in the form of some specialty or hobby on which you have been asked to speak. Once in a while you do have to search for a topic. When that happens, the first question to ask is "Who will be the listeners?" Then, with the answer to that question as a guide, you can usually find some subject of interest to them either in your own experience or in newspapers, magazines, or radio-TV programs.

Review your own experiences. If your father is an insurance agent, it is far better to discuss some procedure in that business (steps in making a sale or in making a claim) than to go to the encyclopedia to find material for a talk on the fishing methods of the aborigines of Borneo. (If the encyclopedia is your only source of information on a particular subject, you should drop the subject; such a source should be used only as the beginning step in research or as a supplement to others you already have in hand.)

The writer was once confronted by a student who wanted to talk about the process of making and marketing beer, a subject about which he knew absolutely nothing. He had never done any reading on the subject, had never visited a brewery, and had no understanding whatever of the marketing problems involved. On the other hand, he had spent several summers working in a shoe factory and was well informed on shoe production, a topic which he dismissed as "uninteresting." Unfortunately, he insisted on giving the talk on beer; it was a failure because his basic ignorance showed through the thin screen of his "research." Posterity will never know whether or not the talk on shoes would have been successful; we do know that talking about a subject in which we have some experience gives us an automatic advantage. Furthermore, we know that there is no such thing as "an uninteresting subject." There are only uninteresting speakers.

Read editorials in newspapers and magazines. Once you've chosen a "live" topic, you can accumulate a file of materials on it at a fairly rapid pace. You may lack direct experience in a field, but if you prepare carefully enough, you will be able to convince your listeners that you do have a solid base for the position you take on an issue. You do not have to be a former prison inmate to talk on a particular prison or on our penal system; you don't have to be a black to make the attempt to understand and eliminate causes of the ghetto system; you don't have to "take a trip" to investigate the problem of drugs; and it is possible to talk sensibly about the tragedy of Appalachia without having been there. In the first three instances (prisons, ghettos, drugs), it would nevertheless be unwise to attempt a discussion or a talk without some firsthand investigating of the local situation.

It is always good practice, then, to begin with a subject you know something about and then expand it by collecting additional information from other sources. The "collecting" can be done from publications you have at home or from those in a library. Local experts on a subject also like to talk about it; sometimes you can find such an expert on the teaching staff, in an office, in a factory, or elsewhere. For instance, it may seem unreasonable that you had to pay a $2 speeding fine plus $20 in "court costs" for a trial which never took place, because you chose meekly to pay the full amount at the appropriate window at City Hall. Your effort to prepare a talk opposing payment for imaginary trials could take the form of (1) conversations with the city attorney, chief of police, traffic judge, and mayor; (2) attendance at sessions of the traffic court; and (3) checking of public records to determine the number of tickets issued, the number ignored, the number paid without argument, the number "fixed," the number contested, and the results in such cases.

On the other hand, direct on-the-scene research is not always possible. If you are one of the better students in a class in beginning geology, the professor may ask you to take over the class and lead a discussion on the "Pre-Cambrian Canadian Shield." Under these circumstances, *you may decide to bolster your book knowledge by talking with others,* e.g., professors and students who have been on field trips in Ontario, and you may also try to borrow slides, photographs, graphs, and any other visual aids available on that subject.

In the event that the subject at hand is one on which you are relatively uninformed, and knowledgeable friends, experts, and researchers are not readily available, you will be conducting the bulk of your research by mail and/or through libraries to which you have direct access, or through the library loan system. *Read selectively and critically.* Avoid the mistake of believing something because it is "in print."

Making a record of your conversations and reading is a problem which can be solved by you alone. Many students like to use small cards for this purpose. Each card should be large enough to hold a quotation, or a fact, or an idea, or the name of an expert in the field, or any other kind of item you consider useful. Cards have the advantage of being "easy to shuffle." The fact that they can be arranged, rearranged—even discarded, of course—often simplifies the process of organization. However, take your notes in any way that makes their later use easy for you.

Adopt a point of view. As your investigating and note-taking proceeds, you will be using the materials collected as a base for arriving at inferences and judgments which will eventually culminate in the central idea or point of view that you intend to present in your effort to communicate with one or more listeners. The details of organizing and outlining are the subject of the next chapter; at this stage, however, it is wise to remember that there are often more than "two sides to every question." And just as there may be many sides to a question, so there are many positions on a continuum. For example, there are intermediate stages between even the simplest of terms like "communist" and "capitalist"; there are shades between "white" and "black"; there are gradations between "believer" and "atheist," between "liberal" and "conservative," and between "patriotic" and "traitorous." The problem inherent in the *two-sides* or *black-or-white orientation* is that it causes us to overlook any other positions or middle ground.

On the other hand, if we condition ourselves always to look for additional degrees or graduated values in our assessment of ideas, things, or individuals, we develop the many-sided or multi-valued habit of mind. This *multi-valued orientation* is "the ability to see things in terms of more than two values...."[1] It increases our capability "of reacting *appropriately* to the many complex situations life presents."[2] The habit of reacting in a "degree-minded" way can and should be cultivated; the degree-minded person is more flexible in his judgments, less contentious in his relations with friends, associates, and opponents, and generally better able to understand another's point of view, because his own is not so deeply embedded in rock that a change is impossible. It is one thing to say flatly to another, "You're wrong." It is quite another to encourage him to explain his position more fully and, if necessary, to counter by saying, "There is some truth in what you say, but have you considered...?" There is also some value in assuming that, outside the world of science, very few statements of any kind are 100 percent true. Implicit in the democratic pattern of life and government is a respect for the views of others coupled with full recognition that a fellow human being is as much interested in "the truth" as we are. If we can envision statements as standing somewhere along a scale of truth rather than at one end (all true) or the other (completely false), the positions *we* take on any subject or issue will be carefully qualified, less vulnerable to attack, and more readily acceptable to those listening to us.

. . . .

Comprehension checks

Is it possible to prepare a talk on the basis of reading one article in *The Reader's Digest*? What are the advantages and disadvantages of that procedure? Do we owe anything to a writer or speaker we happen to be quoting? Is an encyclopedia a good

---

1. Hayakawa, p. 250.
2. *Ibid.*, p. 249.

source of information? *The National Geographic*? What are the advantages and disadvantages of quoting from those sources? Would the members of this class be very much interested in the fishing methods of the natives of Borneo? Why or why not? What are some of the favorite note-taking methods of the students in this class?

Demonstration options

1. Bring to class the names of three persons in the community who have special abilities which would qualify them as experts. List their names and fields on a card, and be prepared to give reasons why you feel the members of the class would be interested in what they have to say.
2. If you have had some experience in searching for information in the library, explain how you went about the job and how you did the necessary note-taking. Pass around a few samples of your notes.
3. Be prepared to demonstrate use of the *Readers' Guide to Periodical Literature*. Discuss using that work in tracking down specific recent articles on a subject of general interest.

. . . .

How Am I Going to Say It?

The *how* of what you are going to say involves both the verbal and the nonverbal dimensions first discussed in Chapter 1 and alluded to in Chapter 2 and elsewhere in this text. Randall Harrison, in reviewing the planning necessary for efficient communication, advises early attention to its nonverbal aspects. "Usually," he says, the relatively unskilled communicator "does not allow early enough for the incorporation of nonverbal communication into his strategy."[3] In other words, as you begin to put "the pieces" together, you will want to be making those decisions which can be made at this stage about such things as possible use of visual aids, appropriate supporting activity (gesture, etc.), and variations in vocal emphasis and tone. You should also be thinking about how close you are going to be or want to be to your listeners, what attention cues can be used to advantage, and what you can do about controlling the atmosphere and physical arrangements in the room. When you are preparing to communicate, it is a mistake to concentrate only on verbal composition, expecting to add all nonverbal components at a later time. If you do so, verbal and nonverbal "elements ... never quite mesh."[4] Keeping in mind, then, that nonverbal aspects should from the first be a part of the planning, let us consider the problems of organization and outlining.

There are differences of opinion on whether or not organization materially helps the listener. Although studies are continuing in the effort to determine the effects on listeners of ordered presentations, results have so far been generally inconclusive.[5]

---

3. Randall Harrison, "Nonverbal Communication: Explorations into Time, Space, Actions, and Object," in Campbell and Hepler, p. 271.
4. *Ibid.*
5. For a review of experimental research on "the order component of message organization," see Arlee Johnson, "A Preliminary Investigation of the Relationship between Message Organization and Listener Comprehension," *Central States Speech Journal*, **21** (Summer 1970), pp. 104–107.

There is some evidence that the later recall of *information* is not much affected by organization or the lack of it; on the other hand, the listener's *comprehension* seems to be somewhat greater if the message has some discernible structure. In an empirical study conducted by Arlee Johnson at Purdue University, results supported "textbook prescriptions concerning the importance of message organization, especially those prescriptions dealing with the concept of order."[6] So far as persuasion is concerned, the listener is apparently more susceptible to change in his views if the message calling for that kind of effect reaches him in an inductive pattern—presentation of evidence followed by inferences and conclusions which are either stated or left to the listener's intelligence; it seems to make no appreciable difference to the listener whether the most important point and its development comes first or last.

From the standpoint of the speaker, an organized structure provides a sequence which ordinarily makes it easier for him to remember key ideas, helps him decide whether or not he has enough evidence to help his audience reach a particular conclusion, and generally makes a good impression on listeners ("He's organized; he knows what he's doing; he must be a competent person"). In other words, organization can be useful to the speaker; whether or not it is always necessary to achieve the best possible effect on the listener is still a moot question, but we do know that "the organized speaker" normally makes a better impression than the speaker who rambles. We may reasonably assume, then, that organization does no harm, that in some instances it is useful to the listener, and that in most instances it is helpful to the speaker and contributes to his acceptance by an audience.

If you accept the foregoing rationale for organization, we are ready to discuss three common organizational patterns—*step*, *spatial*, and *topical*. These patterns can be used separately or in combination as a basis for organizing practically any subject.

Step pattern

We have already noted (Chapter 5) that some talks "organize themselves." Any speech covering a series of steps, one following the other, is in this category. If you have worked in a factory, your explanation of what goes on in it would begin with incoming materials and the steps required to produce whatever it is that the factory is making. If you enjoy amateur photography, you would find it easy to discuss preparing the camera for action, observing "rules" of photographic composition, and finally, developing the photos taken. The number of "build-it" or "fix-it" speech possibilities is endless. "How to Build a Model Plane," "How to take Care of and Ride a Motorcycle," and "How to Make a Chocolate Cake" are typical subjects offering *automatic*

---

6. *Ibid.*, p. 107.

organization in that the natural sequence of steps in the processes provides a framework for each talk.

Even if organization of your remarks is essentially automatic, some attention to structuring is still very much in order. For example, there may be 10 different and distinct operations in a valve-grinding operation or in any one of the other topics cited. No audience can readily remember 10 points; it is the speaker's responsibility to *reorganize the subject matter under two or three major headings* which can be absorbed by the audience. One way to do so is to examine the available information to see if some of it can be covered in the introduction to speech; another is to try to relegate some elements to the conclusion. The remaining core items can then be organized under fewer headings. Let's look at this approach in practice.

Photography

Basic Steps	*Simplification 1*
1. Choice of camera	1. Initial choices
2. Choice of lens	
3. Choice of film	
4. Exposure of film	2. Taking the pictures
5. Fixation of film	3. Developing the film
6. Washing of film	
7. Drying of film	
8. Printing	4. Making the print
9. Fixation of print	
10. Washing of print	
11. Drying of print	
12. Finishing touches	5. Finishing touches

We see that it is possible to talk about photography (or wood-pulp production, or cookie-making, etc.) in a series of steps; we see also that, for the benefit of the audience—and the speaker—the number of topics could, in this instance, be easily reduced to five. It is then clear to anyone looking closely at the new list that still further simplification is possible. For example, the discussion of initial choices could be handled in introductory remarks. "Taking the pictures" is clearly a very important part of the process, but the next three items could be handled under the one heading of "Making the prints." So now we have only two major listings (this time with the Roman numerals generally used to indicate main points in outlines).

Simplification 2

I. Taking the pictures
II. Making the prints

Continuing with our example on photography, the main elements of a basic outline might be as shown below.

Purpose: To give the members of the audience a better understanding of the process of photography.

INTRODUCTION

Opening sentence(s): As some of you may have noticed, several of the "candid photos" appearing in recent issues of the campus paper were taken by me.

Personal competence: Ever since high school days I have been a "shutter bug." Of course, the fact that my father is a free-lance photographer has had a lot to do with my interest.

Purpose and subject: Photography is all around us today. Each of us should know something about this important process.

Reason(s) to listen: It seems to me—and I hope you agree—that a basic knowledge of the process of photography is fascinating in itself. Maybe some of you will join me in this hobby. Perhaps others will later take it up professionally.

BODY

I. "Taking the pictures" is the first step in photography.
   (Transition: After you have exposed all the frames in a roll of film . . . ,)
II. "Making the prints" is the second major step.

CONCLUSION

Summary: You now know that there is more to photography than just aiming the camera; good pictures depend on attention to details—first, in taking the pictures, and second, in developing the prints.

Concluding sentence(s): There is a steady demand for portrait, commercial, and industrial photographers. Who knows? Maybe one of us will make a name for himself in this field!

. . . .

Comprehension checks

The word "chronological" (indicating a series of events in time) is often used interchangeably with "step" to describe patterns for talks. Could the outline immediately above be described as "chronological"? Even in its very abbreviated form, the outline seems to be repetitious. Is there more reason for repetition in a talk than in something printed or written? Why? Why not?

Demonstration option

Bring to class a list of steps in some process or procedure. The list must have in it at least five steps in one column with your reduction to two or three items in a second column. Be prepared to put both lists on the board to defend your restructuring. (Remember that one or more items may sometimes be moved to the introduction or conclusion.)

. . . .

Spatial pattern

Another standard organizational pattern is called spatial. In describing a zoo, for example, it is possible to "begin at the gate" and give the audience an account of sights and sounds in the spatial order in which you encountered them on the grounds; the same order could be employed for describing the "high spots" of a vacation from the time you left home until you returned. The spatial order can be likened to a string of beads—experiences, events, sights, and sounds are strung along "in space" in the order in which they were encountered.

New Harmony, Indiana, was the scene in the early nineteenth century of two fascinating social experiments. A group of German immigrants, called "Rappites" after their leader, George Rapp, established a cooperative, joint-property colony there in 1814 and sold out in 1824 to a universal-happiness-through-universal-education group called the "Owenites" after their Scottish philanthropist sponsor, Robert Owen. A visitor to newly restored New Harmony would have no difficulty in preparing an absorbing talk on that community. The main points and subpoints of a spatially oriented outline could be:

I. Let's explore the center of town.
   A. The innovative Rappite School is our first stop.
   B. The Owenite Free Library is across the street.
   C. The Owenite Opera House is close by to the east.

II. A cluster of Rappite homes is only a quarter-mile to the north.
   A. The Barrett-Gate House was the first built in New Harmony.
   B. The adjacent "Poet's House" (1816) was restored in 1960.
   C. The "Frame House," two "doors" north, was a typical Rappite home.

III. Two other landmarks are a short walk to the west.
   A. The Rappite granary also served as an Owenite laboratory.
   B. The nearby cemetery marks the uniform graves of 230 Rappites.

If the "tour guide" for such a talk is reasonably competent, you can visualize yourself accompanying him from place to place. (Enlarged photographs or drawings of maps and of building exteriors and interiors would be especially appropriate as visual aids in commenting on detail.)

. . . .

Comprehension checks

The word "spatial" is often used interchangeably with "step" and "chronological" in describing patterns. How do you account for this? Could the step pattern which you tried to restructure also be called a spatial pattern? Why? Why not? Could a certain process or procedure be organized under a pattern we could call "step-chronological-spatial"? Name one.

Have you ever been bored by someone's long-winded day-by-day account of some trip he took? What would you have done to make the account more interesting?

Demonstration option

Prepare two or three *main points* which could serve as effective spatial-pattern leads into an account of some trip, walk, or hike (real or imaginary). Either exchange main-point lists with another student and discuss with him the improvements possible in both approaches, or give the instructor your list for comment or use in a general class discussion.

. . . .

Topical pattern

When the step or spatial patterns cannot be used, a pattern dealing with *topics* is appropriate. It is somewhat more difficult than the other two kinds of organization because the order of ideas is no longer automatic—it must be determined by you. If you are presenting information designed to let people know how much (or how little) help your community is giving to the needy, you are going to have to decide what comes first, second, third, etc. You might want to establish this topical order:

I. Our town gives *practically no help* to the individual needy family.
II. We give *some help* to organized community projects.
III. We give *considerable help* to organizations hardly classed as needy.

After looking at that order and at your available evidence (facts, figures, statements, etc.), you could reasonably change the order completely. Or you might put the second and third topics together and say, "Instead, we give help to organized community projects and to organizations." The point to be stressed is that a topical pattern is one *you* work out to fit your audience and the situation. You experiment with different orders of ideas until you find one that you believe will make sense to your listeners. A topical pattern is a *planned* order—when you finish working it out, the sequence of ideas should be clear and sensible.

. . . .

Comprehension checks

Why bother with outlines, organization of ideas, etc.? Does outlining have any real advantages? Does it call attention to statements for which you have little or no information or backing? In other words, can outlining point up gaps in your information?

What are the advantages, if any, of working with an outline rather than a complete word-for-word manuscript? Can an outline help you eliminate ideas which really don't fit into a talk very well? Isn't it just as easy to write out a talk without trying to put the ideas in any kind of order? Should a talk sound memorized? If it isn't memorized, does some kind of order of ideas help the speaker? Is order of any help to listeners? Is there only one way to organize a given set of ideas in a topical pattern? Or many ways? Is the first outline you work out going to be entirely satisfactory? Or does it make sense to experiment with a number of different possibilities? Why? Or why not?

Demonstration options

1. When you are phrasing the points of a talk, it is considered a good idea to aim at making them *short, simple,* and generally *similar* in structure. Assuming that those qualities make the phrasing of main points easier for both you and the audience to remember, examine the three main points in the help-for-the-needy topical pattern above; try to rewrite them to make them shorter, etc. Compare your "improved version" with those written by other students in the class.
2. Rewrite the main points of the outline on "mental boobytraps" at the end of Chapter 10. Compare your version with those of other students.
3. Rewrite any set of two subpoints (A and B) in that Chapter 10 outline. In what ways are they now shorter, simpler, and more similar? Explain to the class why you do or do not believe that your new version of these subpoints would be helpful to listeners.

. . . .

Transitions

In any conversation, discussion, or other form of speech-communication, transitions provide the signals which tell our listeners that we are moving from one major idea or topic to another. Even in a relatively simple talk, it is good practice to plan—and include in the outline—transitions between main points and, when they seem to be necessary, between subpoints.

Perhaps you noticed the transition between the main points in the step outline of the talk on photography. In the spatial outline on New Harmony, moving from main point to main point could be handled in a similar way. If you were giving the talk, you would readily see that the jump from a description of the Opera House (last subpoint under I) to the second main point would be too abrupt for listeners. To help them understand where you are going next, you would probably say something like this: "Now that we have explored three landmarks in the center of town, our second focus of interest is a cluster of Rappite homes, a quarter-mile to the north." In the speech on the airplane flight (Chapter 10), note the transitions between the first and second main points. Such transitions tell the audience that the speaker has finished with the first main part of the talk and is now moving on to the second.

In practically any talk you will also find signpost words and phrases that lead into a succession of subpoints: *another major concern, then, after, in any event, another method, while, in addition, furthermore, not only, also, besides, too,* and other transition indicators of movement through time and space and from topic to topic. Such indicators are preferable to numbers for introducing subpoints. Listeners become confused if you use numbers (e.g., first, second, third, etc.) to introduce both main points *and* their subdivisions.

As you already know, word or phrase transitions may be reinforced by gestures, facial expressions, changes in stance, and other forms of nonverbal communication. For example, if you move physically as you refer to moving on to another main area of the talk, the verbal transition gains emphasis, and listeners receive that much additional notice of your intentions.

No matter how well prepared a talk may be, the work should not be considered finished until suitable transitions have been planned; they are the station signs which tell listeners *where you are* at any given point in the speech. They help any speaker stay "on the track" and help listeners understand and follow what he has to say.

Comprehension checks

Do we use transitions in everyday conversations? What forms do these transitions take? Can you cite a few? When someone says "I didn't notice but you seem to have changed the subject," is he also saying "If you had given me warning of a change in subject, I would be in a better position to understand you"? Is "That reminds me of a story" a transition? "To come to the point"? Have you noted any nonverbal reinforcement of transitions? Or transitions that were entirely nonverbal?

Demonstration options

1. Listen to a conversation and take mental note of the verbal/nonverbal transitions used. Afterward, jot them down and bring them to class for inclusion in a composite class list of "conversational transitions."
2. Bring to class a list of at least ten transitions you found in a magazine article or story.
3. Bring to class a list of at least ten transitions you found in a speech or an editorial.

Introductions and Conclusions

You've heard unorganized speakers who somehow became "stalled" in their introductory remarks and never did have time to deal properly with the subject at hand. You've also heard some who didn't seem to know how to bring a talk to an end. These people were in trouble because they did not recognize the need to plan opening and closing remarks. The planning can take place at a relatively late stage in the preparation of the talk, but it should not be omitted by the speaker who wants to avoid possible embarrassment.

In the introduction of a talk, your purposes are (1) to get the attention of your listeners, (2) to convince them that you know something about the subject, (3) to let them know what you are trying to accomplish, and (4) to point out why it is in their interests to listen to you. If attention is already at a high level (e.g., the second speaker in a public debate normally has the attention of the audience), the first step may be a waste of time. The second can be left out if you are known to be knowledgeable in the field. The fourth step is unnecessary if possible benefit to the listeners is too obvious to require comment. In other words, you use the four purposes as a kind of check list to be sure that your introduction has in it those elements required by the listeners you face in a given situation.

How do you get attention? Five different ways are suggested below and others will occur to you.

1. Recount an incident, example, illustration, or anecdote. Be sure that the relation to your subject is direct.
2. Tell a story or joke bearing directly on the subject. (This technique, if well executed, also helps to put an audience at ease.)
3. State a startling or shocking fact.
4. Make some remarks about the occasion which brings the listeners and you together.
5. Quote some authority or expert who has said something noteworthy about the subject.

A look at some of the outlines and parts of outlines in this book will help you plan details of an introduction. Whatever you decide to say in opening a talk, a good "rule of thumb" is to aim at an introduction requiring no more than about *a fifth of the total time available* to you.

The conclusion of a talk can also be left to a late stage in the preparation process. It usually consists of (1) a summary of the main point leading up to a restatement of the main idea of the speech and/or (2) a final statement or appeal in accord with the purpose for which the talk was given. Depending on the circumstances, either of those two elements is sometimes left out. In any event, the *conclusion should be short.*

. . . .

Comprehension checks

Why does a speaker sometimes begin a talk with a joke? Do you remember any such instance? Why should the joke be related to the subject under discussion? Wouldn't an unrelated joke also help to win over and relax an audience? Is everyone equally able to tell a joke? Are you good at telling jokes? How well do you tell short stories or anecdotes? If the introduction comes first in a talk, why not prepare it first? This book recommends that you spend no more than a minute on the introduction to a five-minute talk. Does that recommendation seem reasonable to you? Why? Why not? If in doubt what elements to include, should you play it safe and include all four? Or take a chance and leave one or more out? Under what circumstances do you think the summary could be left out of a conclusion?

Demonstration options

1. Bring to class the introduction to a speech, an editorial, or an article from any source. Be prepared to read it aloud and point out what you consider its good and bad qualities.
2. Do the same with a conclusion drawn from the same kinds of sources.

. . . .

In final comment . . .

Carefully planned talks take time, and planning pays dividends. However, the perceptive speaker considers it a part of his planning to make sure that he does not become so involved in mechanics and machinery that he blocks his need and obligation to interact with his listeners. Organizing and outlining serve useful purposes, including some insurance of efficiency in covering topics and materials; they should not be permitted to become a kind of introspective shell within which the speaker labors to remember each and every item and seems to forget that the listeners exist. As a detailed straitjacket, an outline can be a veritable abomination; as a general guide, it is often indispensable.

Whatever your views on organization and outlining may be, it is still true that following a planned pattern—including attention to transitions, introductions, and conclusions—can add to your reputation for being "organized," can make almost any subject easier for you to handle, and can make it easier for your listeners to under stand and act upon your messages.

7 / Earning listener confidence

When you listen to a speaker-communicator in a one-to-one or one-to-many situation, you may very quickly come to conclusions like these: "*He* doesn't seem too sure of his ground; how can *I* be sure?" "His lack of control over his material makes me uncomfortable; how can I concentrate on what he is saying?" "He spouts words but shows little understanding of the problem." On the other hand: "I'm inclined to have confidence in him; he seems to know exactly where he's going and how to get there."

Providing a base for listener confidence is a major key to success in any speech-communication effort. This chapter deals with advanced phases of preparation for informal talks or formal speeches, phases which rank close to planning in winning listener acceptance of you as a reliable source of information and ideas. In fact, it is axiomatic in speech-communication that "people really listen only to those whom they trust." As we have already seen, planning what one is going to say is a part of earning that trust; another is carrying the saying through later stages to final interaction.

The Dry-Run Stage

You are ready for the "dry-run" stage as soon as you have finished planning and organizing your remarks. Your work on an outline will already have made you familiar with your materials and the best order for them. Simply "run through" the talk a few times. If you have chosen the ideas and materials well, they will soon lead easily from one to the other, and you will begin to feel comfortable with the overall design. As recommended in Chapter 6, your plan should include transitions to make it "flow."

Word-for-word memorization is a waste of time. Even if you succeed in the feat of memorization, the audience will quickly sense that it is listening to a robot instead of a human being. As you practice, you will never give the speech twice in exactly the same words; when you give the speech before the audience for which it is intended, you will again communicate your ideas in a way different from that of any practice period. Become reconciled to the fact that you will never give a talk exactly as you planned it. You will forget an item or two on one occasion and forget a few different items on another occasion. Accept some hesitations and pauses as inevitable; if you cannot finish a sentence, simply abandon it and start another. Assume that these kinds of things are going to happen; absolute fluency is a myth and should not be a goal. *Aim only at communicating.* If you prepare carefully, you will find it impossible to forget the main theme or objective of your talk, and you will also find it impossible to forget main ideas. If you want to do some memorizing, confine your efforts in that direction to the opening sentence (it's always comforting to be sure about how you are going to begin), the subject sentence, the main points, and the concluding sentence (it's similarly comforting to have a planned ending). With those elements of the talk under control, the subordinate arguments and evidence fall into place with no great difficulty—and if you do forget an idea or example here and there, who's the wiser?

Once you have a general sequence of ideas in mind, you may want to write a key-word outline—two or three words leading into each major block of the talk—on one side of a small card, which can serve as a "prompter." It isn't large enough to get in the way, and it does help you remember the main points or areas which you hope to cover.

. . . .

Comprehension checks

Assuming that we agree on the advisability of avoiding word-for-word memorizing, are there any segments of a talk for which memorization would be a good idea? What would be the advantages or disadvantages of memorizing those elements? Is there any particular merit in giving a talk—in practice or at any other time—in exactly the same way twice? Is it possible to be concentrating on "what comes next" and, at the same time, on communicating with listeners?

Demonstration option

As evidence for deciding whether "to memorize or not to memorize," volunteer if you can to "recite" a short passage which you have in your memory bank. It could be an excerpt from a play, speech, poem, short story, novel, etc. Concentrate on *communicating* with your audience. Immediately after reciting the memorized passage, explain *in your own words* what it was all about. Let the class decide which of the two "performances" is the more communicative.

. . . .

The On-Your-Feet Stage

When you are able to "run through" your materials without overlooking anything of real consequence, you are ready to simulate—privately or in the presence of a friend or two—conditions you will face in the presence of your intended listeners. Some of the more obvious nonverbal aspects of language now come into play, and you have an opportunity to try to control them in such a way that they lend support to what you have to say.

Voice

Experimentation with tone will help you "say more" with the same words and avoid monotony at the same time. As for rhythm, most of us speak rhythmically by nature, but unfortunately, some of us never vary the rate. Yet some ideas are more important than others and should be given some additional emphasis. Other ideas are in the "throw-away" category—they are not really essential to the talk; their delivery can be "speeded along." Vary your timing to fit the importance of whatever you happen to be saying at any one time. On the subject of volume, those sitting in the last row of the room must always be easily able to hear you. In addition, you may want to employ variations in volume to give emphasis to central ideas. Do not leave pitch, rhythm, and volume to chance. Do some experimenting and try to *bring the voice into play to your advantage.*

Gestures

Attention to the use of gestures goes hand in hand with management of the voice. "Gesture" here means use of the hands and arms in support of your remarks. In addition to whatever way you may wish to gesture in order to reinforce transition (e.g., use of the forefinger to indicate a first main point or area), gestures are ordinarily employed (1) to direct attention to persons or things, (2) to describe persons or things, and (3) to emphasize or strengthen ideas.

Directing attention. Gesturing for this purpose "comes naturally." For example, you hang a large and well-designed poster where it is readily visible to the members of your audience. Then, as you proceed with the talk, you point to items and labels on the poster. Or if you are using an actual piece of equipment (or a mock-up of it), you lift it into sight and point to the various sections as required.

Caution: When using posters or charts, face the audience and do the necessary pointing with the arm nearer the poster/chart.

Describing. We all use our hands to outline objects for the benefit of listeners. We tell a contractor that we want a window of "this approximate size" in the top of the kitchen door; we indicate "this size" by space between the hands to show both height and width. Pilots demonstrate aerial maneuvers by sweeping the hands in ways simulating the paths traced by planes. A witness to an automobile accident will demonstrate with his hands how a car tumbled or twisted through a number of gyrations until it came to rest. Each of us has on many an occasion heard someone describe another with accompanying gestures to outline details of dress and physical attributes. We use the hands and arms to encompass squares, circles, pyramids, cubes, rectangles, and endless varieties of "outer boundaries" for various shapes. (Try to describe a ride in an amusement park without using your hands.) Next to gestures for pointing at something, descriptive gestures are the easiest to use—they practically force themselves on us.

Emphasizing ideas. You have certainly seen a speaker pound a table to add emphasis to a statement. You have also seen one raise both arms in a gesture that conveys ignorance of what to do. With hands extended palm down, the speaker could be saying, "Let's keep the lid on this situation." The key to the development of gestures for emphasis is to do what comes naturally as well as to watch other speakers. Adopt those patterns with which you can become comfortable.

Bodily action

In general, try to "look alive" and aim at being a responsive human being. A stance which many people find comfortable calls for keeping the feet fairly close together with one foot slightly ahead of the other. This placement helps you stand erect, makes you look alert, and provides for easy movement in practically any direction. Try to avoid aimless pacing, but don't hesitate to move whenever you feel that movement would help you in your "transaction" with the audience. For instance, while you are saying "Let's move on to . . . ," taking one or more steps to right or left gives emphasis to the transition.

You will not want to stand behind a lectern for any length of time unless there is good reason to do so. One such reason, of course, may be that only from that position can you be heard over a public address system. Or you might need the lectern for reading from a manuscript (more on this subject later in this chapter).

Handling of notes

In preparing for a platform presentation, handle your notes as you expect to handle them before an audience. If you have decided to use a small card as a prompter, hold it in one hand, but don't hesitate to gesture with the same hand. Unless you are continually glancing at the card, the audience will scarcely be aware of its existence. If you have a sheaf of notes or cards, it is best to place them on a lectern or table. In the ordinary course of events, the well-prepared speaker finds a sheaf of notes unnecessary. We've all had the uncomfortable experience of watching a speaker move from one side of a lectern to the other with his eyes glued to notes on the stand in the middle.

Other speakers bend over to scan a sheaf of notes lying on a table or hold them in both hands like a bouquet. A speaker who is well enough prepared to talk from a "key-word prompter" never has to face the problem of notes coming between him and the listeners with whom he is trying to communicate.

Timing

If you are supposed to be talking for five minutes, you should practice often enough to be reasonably sure of finishing within 30 seconds over or under the limit. It is not easy to say something worthwhile in five minutes or in any very limited time; *you have to work at it.* One way to get the job done is to keep cutting down on the breadth of the subject until you are sure it is manageable in the time available. For the sake of example, let's assume that you are a student in civil engineering and that the subject of "highway construction" is your original choice for an informational talk. However, you quickly sense that the topic cannot be covered in five minutes, so you move progressively from "highway construction" to "street-paving in cities" to "asphalt street-paving" to "emulsified asphalt street-paving" to "emulsified-asphalt hot-mixture street-paving." Practically any subject can be limited once and then again and again. If you find that the time limitation will not permit your saying everything you had planned, make "cuts." Conversely, if you don't have enough material to fill out the time, add some.

There is more to timing, of course, than just finishing on time. As already noted, some ideas can be handled in an offhand fashion; others call for a very deliberate tempo. Varying your rate of speaking can help listeners understand what you consider to be the relative importance of the material being covered at any one point in the communicative transaction.

Speaking from a manuscript

The educated person occasionally finds himself in the position of having to read in public. For instance, he reads "minutes" at a meeting, reads a proposal to the city council, reads a radio or television appeal for funds in support of a community project, reads a part of the service in his church, reads a quotation as a part of a talk, reads a paper at a convention, or reads a statement to the press. In other words, reading aloud is a form of speech-communication which is required often enough so that we should know how to do it effectively.

The procedure is to prepare the talk in exactly the same way that you would prepare any other, but instead of planning to give it extemporaneously, you write it out and practice reading it word-for-word (or nearly so). The following suggestions will help you escape from "the prison of the manuscript" in delivering this kind of talk.

1. *Try to write in your oral style.* Test phrases, clauses, and sentences for *sound*. Remember that it is not an essay that you are writing; picture yourself as actually giving an extemporaneous talk, and frame the language accordingly.

2. Once the talk is written to your satisfaction—as with outlining, the first draft is seldom the final draft—you may want to add markings or symbols of some kind to help you make the talk "come alive" through variety in emphasis, timing, and expression. The "typed" text below demonstrates *one* way to accomplish those ends. Slash bars have been used to suggest where very brief hesitancies (/) and more definite

pauses (//) could be inserted to advantage. Words deserving stress or special interpretation are underlined once; those calling for stronger emphasis are underlined twice.

In the environment of language / the <u>color</u> of a man's <u>skin</u>, for example, // is <u>tied</u> to <u>plus-or-minus</u> words / that <u>influence</u> human attitudes. The words "<u>black</u>" and "<u>white</u>," / as defined in Western culture, / are <u>heavily</u> <u>loaded</u>. "<u>Black</u>" has all sorts of <u>unfavorable</u> connotations; // "<u>white</u>" is almost <u>all favorable</u>. Consult your favorite dictionary or <u>Roget's Thesaurus</u>, / and you will see what I mean. No less <u>mind-conditioning</u> than <u>black</u> / are some of the words / associated with the color <u>yellow</u>: <u>coward</u>, / <u>fear</u>, / <u>soft</u>, / <u>sneak</u>, / and so on. We cannot easily <u>doctor</u> the <u>dictionaries</u>, // but people in Western cultures / should come to <u>realize</u> / the <u>extent</u> to which their <u>racial attitudes</u> / have been <u>conditioned</u> / since <u>early</u> childhood / by the <u>power of words</u> to <u>ennoble</u> or <u>condemn</u>, to <u>glorify</u> or <u>detract</u>. What is needed / is not so much a change in language / as <u>an awareness of the power of words</u> / to <u>condition</u> attitudes. If we can <u>at least</u> <u>recognize</u> the <u>foundations</u> of prejudice, // we may be in a position / <u>to deal</u> with the effects.[1]

---

1. Passage is a paraphrase (with some direct quotation) of a section in a *Saturday Review* editorial by Norman Cousins, April 8, 1967, p. 36. Copyright 1967, Saturday Review, Inc. Used by permission.

3. After you have attached whatever types of notations or symbols you consider useful as appropriate cues for delivery, you are ready to *practice the oral reading of the talk*. Read it aloud a few times at a fairly slow pace in order to give yourself an opportunity to become completely familiar with the general sequence of ideas and with the kinds of interpretation you want to give them. Then *check the timing*. If the talk is too long, do some editing; if too short, amplify some of the ideas. Concentrate on interacting with your audience—at this point imaginary, unless you can enlist a friend or two to listen. You should also be well enough acquainted with the manuscript to use it only *to pick up cues for the beginning of paragraphs or sentences*.

4. Plan to handle actual presentation in much the same way as that recommended for extemporaneous speeches. If your manuscript has become "dog-eared," have it retyped (or rewritten by hand) and resymboled. Use only one side of a soft, noncrackling paper. When you finish with a page, move it to the "bottom of the pack," set it aside on a stand, or put it down on a table. Finally, remember that *the "reader" shouldn't do much reading* in the audience situation; the manuscript should at this stage be a set of cues and nothing more.

. . . .

Comprehension checks

Do you know anyone who talks "with his mouth closed"? Or someone who seldom varies his tone? Or someone who, in your opinion, speaks too rapidly? Or too slowly? Do you enjoy listening to the sound of a particular person's voice? Why?

Have you ever been conscious of a speaker's gestures? If you are conscious of them, are they good gestures? Do you use your hands in conversations with friends? Do your hands help you communicate? What about your eyes? Face? Is it possible to plan gestures in advance? Why or why not? Any dangers in doing so? Can they be overcome? Are there some listeners who might react negatively to active gesturing during a talk? Who? Do you tailor gestures to the audience? How?

Some very successful speakers prowl the platform like caged tigers. If moving without a good speech-connected reason is bad policy, how do you explain the success of the prowlers, leaners, sitters, and other unconventional types? What are some of the advantages, if any, of the one-side-of-one-card note system over the multi-page sheaf-of-notes system?

Sometimes you hear this alibi: "I just couldn't do a good job on that subject in the time available." What do you think of it? If a person is reading effectively and communicating with his listeners, is he really reading? Or is he using a "cue sheet"? Should the reader of a manuscript be looking at you most of the time or at his manuscript most of the time?

Demonstration options

1. If you know someone in the class or in the student body (or among the professors) who has a characteristic gesture which may be recognized by other students, have members of the class guess the identity of that person as you perform the gesture.
2. Read a short passage from any source, using appropriate gestures as you do so.

3. Copy a 150- to 200-word passage from any source. Use the system in this text or one of your own to help you in your expressive reading of it. Prepare to "read" it in class.

. . . .

The Day-Arrives Stage

Confidence-generating "presence"

You have seen and heard enough speakers to know that the business of winning audience confidence begins with the first sight of the speaker. If he dresses in a slovenly way, you are unlikely to be impressed. If he drifts or slouches his way to the lectern, your impression will not improve. Another speaker may give you the impression that he is well mannered and competent—all this *before* he addresses a word to the audience. Similarly, a part of the impression that you make on your classmates or on any audience will depend *on how you look to them.* Your interaction with them begins as soon as they see you.

Confidence-generating "tension"

People seem to have more confidence in a speaker who appears "in a state of readiness" than in one who is super-suave and nonchalant. Even your appearing to be somewhat tense can be an asset—at least, the listeners know you are not taking them for granted. You can keep tension under more than adequate control by following three simple procedures:

First of all, *switch your attention to the chairman or the speaker of the moment.* If you can successfully concentrate on what he is saying, you will be doing both him and yourself a favor.

Second, *remember that everyone is tense to some degree* in addressing a new audience on any subject or in addressing any audience on a new and possibly controversial subject. You cannot avoid some measure of tension, but you can reduce the impact of that uneasiness by reminding yourself (1) that you are well prepared for the occasion and (2) that "the world will little know nor long remember" the communicating you do in this class or anywhere else. In fact, what you say on any one occasion will frequently be forgotten by the beginning of the next. Don't fight apprehension; learn to function in spite of it.

Third, *breathe deeply and regularly*, a process guaranteed to slow the rate of heartbeat. Man reacts "as a whole" to conditions of stress; if we can reduce physiological reactions, we can reduce the anxieties which give rise to them.

Confidence-generating "control"

When a speaker has been conscientious about adequate preparation, his actual appearance before an audience is often a pleasant and exhilarating experience. The speaker *knows* he is fully prepared, and the audience quickly *senses* that he is. When you are announced as "the next speaker," wait until any bustle or conversation has subsided. If there is a chairman on hand for the occasion, begin by saying, "Mr. Chairman." If there is none, begin by directly addressing the listening group.

As you speak, you can further win audience recognition of your competence by your command over the materials of the message you have chosen to present. If you have this command and control over message contents, you will not only feel competent, you will *sound competent*.

Confidence-generating "character"

The possession of varying degrees of "presence," "tension," and "control" will avail you little unless your listeners feel that you have "character" and trust you as a person. That a man must be of good character to be successful in speech-communication has long been a pervasive view in rhetorical theory.[2] Modern studies corroborate that view.[3] For the moment, however, it is enough to say that, if you thoroughly study problems and take honest and ethical positions, audiences will respect you, even when they disagree. On the other hand, once listeners sense that you are not sincere in what you say, or that your position is one of expediency, or that you are trying to mislead them, their confidence in you will vanish—permanently, as far as that particular group is concerned.

. . . .

Comprehension checks

Do you believe that the way you "look" on a particular day has something to do with the impression you make on people? Do you glance about you in any public place and draw some conclusions about individuals you see there? As you watch a speaker waiting to be introduced at some campus event, can you just about "hear" him before he begins to talk?

---

2. For typical early observations, see Isocrates *Antidosis* 97, Aristotle *Rhetoric* ii, and Quintilian xii. 2. 1.

3. The subject of *ethos* or "source credibility" is discussed in some detail in Chapter 12.

Is it really true that you can do some things better under tension than in a relaxed state? Is it true of speaking before a group? What is the best insurance against being *too* tense in that situation?

Can you tell by the way a speaker performs whether or not he *wants* to talk with the group or whether he is just "performing a duty"? In which man do you have more confidence? Is it possible to tell whether or not the speaker is well prepared to talk on a particular subject? If he isn't, what is your reaction? What does the word *ethos* mean? What does it have to do with speech-communication? Some speakers are sincere, others are not. How can you tell the difference? Are there other ways (not mentioned in this chapter) of winning the confidence of the listener?

Demonstration options

1. Volunteer to play the role of some visiting lecturer *waiting to be introduced*. The "lecturer" can be someone whom you actually saw in this situation or some product of your imagination. This pantomime need last only a minute or so. When it is over, ask for comments on the *prespeech* confidence-generating impact of the person you are imitating.
2. Describe as briefly as you can an incident in which a speaker won your confidence (or lost it). What did he do or not do? If he lost your trust, was he able to regain any part of it before the talk came to an an end? How?

. . . .

It is indeed possible to go a long way toward earning listener confidence through the measures suggested in this chapter. Following them will contribute to your success but will not guarantee it. The point has already been made several times in this book that speech-communication is a complex process and that one of its most important elements is interaction with your listeners. *Make a real effort to think and feel with them.* Listeners in general are notoriously sympathetic; they will have confidence *in you* as long as they believe that you are showing an honest and responsible interest *in them*.

8 / Listening: modes and methods

This cuff was but to knock at your ear,
and beseech listening.
                                Shakespeare

Some of us are so entranced by the sounds of our own voices that it practically takes "a cuff" to bring our talking to a halt and gain our listening attention. In *Taming of the Shrew*, Petruchio realized that the only way to gain the floor from Katharina was to take some direct action. His particular approach, however effective, is not currently in vogue; to bring about improvement in listening, we rely instead on increased understanding of the importance of that vital function.

In Chapter 1, on the process of speech-communication, the *communicator-listener* was described as one who, as he listens, is communicating with the *communicator-speaker*. His listening is in itself communication, with or without any other accompanying words or signs. We intend in this chapter, by elaborating on listening as an integral part of the two-way transactional process of communication, to provide added detail on common listening modes (listening *actively, self-defensively,* and *analytically*) and on methods suggested as appropriate for each mode.

Listening Actively

Since speech-communication is the primary means we have of relating to others, the more people with whom we talk and listen, the more outgoing we are likely to become. Every time you talk-listen with someone, it contributes to your growth and development as a person; the more you learn to talk sensitively and sensibly with others, the better chance you have of solving the problems and questions that come up in daily life. And usually, the person who develops his ability to talk and listen, who works at establishing friendly relations with others, is better-adjusted, more satisfied, and more successful in his human relationships. We don't always think of listening as a way to grow, or as a way to get to know others. Yet, through listening, a person can absorb information, examine and test his beliefs and attitudes, and even influence others.

Listening is not simply hearing. As we have seen, listening carries with it the idea of active cooperation with a speaker. It is easy to label a speaker (student, instructor, acquaintance, etc.) uninteresting. The next time you are tempted to tag a speaker with that label, decide instead to listen *actively.* As you listen, concentrate on the total message. What an individual says is only part of the story—how he says it is important, too. How does he feel about his message? Try to understand fully the meaning that the speaker is trying to convey with his particular choices of words and other signs.

When you give someone active attention, you are telling him that you believe he has something worthwhile to say, that you recognize his right to present his ideas, and that you accept him as he is and respect him as a person. Since it is a physiological fact that you can think much faster than anyone can present ideas, try using the extra time to ask yourself such questions as "How can I put this information to use?" "Where does it fit into my world?"

What do you gain from this kind of *active listening*? For one thing, you can gain satisfaction from simply listening as a human being. To mention just a few of the humanitarian aspects of listening: Lonely people, particularly the elderly, like to talk. People with problems of any kind appreciate "good listeners." Children look forward to communication with someone who will really listen to them. And listening encourages troubled individuals to unburden themselves. In these and similar situations, the following advice is appropriate.

1. Take time to listen.
2. Be attentive.
3. Employ three kinds of verbal reactions only:
    As the talker proceeds, encourage him with "Hmmm," "Uh-huh," "Oh," "I see," and so forth.
    If he pauses, nod understanding and encouragement but *remain silent.*
    If he wanders, restate what has just been said. For example, "You really think that all middlemen are dishonest?"
4. Never probe for additional facts.
5. Never evaluate what has been said; avoid giving advice.
6. Never lose faith in the ability of the talker to solve his own problems. All he may really need is a chance to talk about them.[1]

Further, as Nichols and Stevens point out, "Listening is the best way for improving language facility."[2] Intentionally or unintentionally, we imitate. Your use of language is affected by your total past as well as by your continuing present—the literature you read, the plays you attend, the readings and speeches you hear, the people with whom

---

1. An abbreviated version of material in *Are You Listening* by Ralph G. Nichols and Leonard A. Stevens (New York: McGraw-Hill, 1957), pp 53–54. Adapted by permission.
2. *Ibid.,* p. 30.

you associate, the radio and television programs you listen to. Your language patterns are affected by the written and spoken communication with which you come in contact; they are affected more selectively and in greater degree if you become "communication-conscious."

Then, too, the chances of your learning something useful are good. For example, everyone with whom you carry on a conversation knows a number of things which you don't. If you are a member of a discussion group, your opportunity to gain additional knowledge is multiplied in proportion to the number of individuals in the group. And listening carefully to a speaker, however dull and repetitious he may be, can pay dividends in added information or, at least, in your observations of what to do or what not to do.

Finally, in almost any situation, the following guideline questions can help you become a better listener.

1. What are the speaker's central ideas?
2. What new information does he offer?
3. How does the speaker seem to feel about his topic?
4. Do I fully understand his meaning? Do I see the problem as he sees it?
5. Does my listening attitude seem to encourage the speaker?

. . . .

Comprehension checks

Do you consider the distinction between listening and hearing to be realistic? How would you define *"listening"*? *"Hearing"*? If there is a clear-cut distinction between the two, is there any particular need for using the word *actively* with *listening*? What function does *actively* perform?

Do you know any "good listeners"? Are there any qualities which you would attribute to these people as a group?

Are you "a good listener"? Have you ever listened out of courtesy rather than out of any interest in what was being said? Did you get anything from the encounter? Could you get something from a similar encounter today?

Do students ever pretend attention in a class or lecture? Admitting that some classes and lectures leave something to be desired in contents and mode of presentation, do you believe there is any merit in looking upon such occasions as chances to improve your language facility and/or pick up some information and ideas? Have you ever tried these approaches? Should all students in a speech-communication class listen, or as one student is speaking, should the others scheduled to speak spend their time silently going over their speeches? Should an instructor concentrate his attention on what the speaker is doing or on what is going on *between* the speaker and his listeners?

Demonstration options

1. In conversation with a friend or with anyone else of your choice, try following the Nichols and Stevens suggestions on page 115. Report (1) the effects which you thought you observed on the other person and (2) your own reactions to this kind of listening experience.

2. Report on a class lecture which you regarded as generally dull but to which you decided to listen actively for (1) additions to information and/or (2) improvement in your speaking ability and handling of language. Cite any personal gains you noted. Cite any effects your demonstration of interest had on the instructor or on other students in the class.
3. If a particular class you attend is relatively small and sometimes dull, try to reach an agreement with all or most of the other students in it to react with complete and total interest to everything said by the instructor within a given class period. Report on the "contagion of interest within the group" and on whatever effect the active, collective interest seemed to have on the instructor.

. . . .

Listening Self-defensively

Listening *actively*, sympathetically, empathically, and helpfully is a way of communicating in which we cooperate with each other in the name of humanity as well as for mutual benefit.

Listening *self-defensively* helps us to cope with the steadily rising flood of "communications" which daily threatens to engulf modern man. From morn till night, we struggle through successive waves of information, indoctrination, "small talk," exhortation, defamation, propaganda, flattery, intimidation, accounts from "informed sources," insinuations, justifications, direct and indirect suggestions, accurate and inaccurate descriptions, official proclamations, and unofficial assessments, reports, statements, and explanations. Battered by streams of messages in the mass media of radio, television, film, and newspapers, assailed by crosscurrents of views in editorials, pamphlets, and books, buffeted by the conflicting views of relatives, friends, neighbors, and associates, we too often abandon the effort to row toward "truth" and simply ride along on the tide of tacit assent or apathy.

The pressure to ride along in assent is especially strong in face-to-face situations. It is patently easier to say "No" over the telephone than in the physical presence of the magazine salesman; it is easier to tell a friend what you are going to tell a low-grading professor than it is to say the same things directly to the professor; and it is easier to refrain from taking a specific position when you find yourself in a group known to have one diametrically and rabidly opposite. You know that the bargaining position of someone standing in front of you is stronger than that of the person who writes you a letter. You know, too, that some accidental meetings are not so accidental; they are contrived in order to serve the particular purposes of the contrivers. In any event, the listener should be aware that, in face-to-face situations, the talker-promoter-salesman of things or of ideas has a built-in advantage stemming from the mere fact of his on-the-scene presence—to say nothing of his opportunity to adjust his messages to the feedback described in Chapter 1.

Less easily pressured and more discriminating in his choices and evaluations of messages, a person trained in the art of listening self-defensively is better able to screen fact from fiction, appraisal from libel, argument from fallacy, idealism from opportunism; in short, he is better able to contend with the modern world and to contribute at the same time to his own well-being and that of the people around him. Listening in self-defense is not a retreat from the active listening position advocated in the preceding section of this chapter; rather, it is recognition that there are times, no matter how cooperatively you are listening, when you should "have your guard up." In this context, we interpret self-defense to mean (1) prudent questioning of "sales messages" and (2) prudent questioning of "idea messages." The purpose of the questioning is obvious: to protect ourselves in the marketplace of materials and ideas.

Questioning of sales messages. Whenever someone is trying to sell you something, that is a good time for prudent questioning. Unfortunately, the seller usually "holds the best cards." For almost every instance of a seller's "showing his hand" and truthfully communicating reasons for doing business with him, there is another instance of near or total misrepresentation.

For example, listen with questions in mind when the hero or heroine in sports or on the screen is endorsing cereal or any other product. We sometimes forget that *celebrities recommend products only when they are paid to do so.* It often happens that the "testimonials" are not the honest opinions of the speakers or writers.[3] Sales announced by local stores are usually the efforts of reputable businessmen to clear shelves of worn or dated stock, but some "sales" give you the privilege of paying higher rather than lower prices. Be wary of the "only-a-few-left" line and "Hurry! This is positively the last day of this gigantic sell-out!" You may be the one who is "sold out." Some television commercials are done in good taste, and they accurately describe the product; others not only exhibit bad taste but also assume that the watcher-listener has no sense at all. If the encyclopedia salesman says, "You have been chosen as the lucky person in this area to receive a *free* set," remember to ask him how much you pay during the next ten years to cover the annual supplements mentioned in fine print on the "gift receipt." If you rush down to the photo shop for the *free* picture awarded to you in the "random promotional drawing," you may discover that the only thing free in that situation is your walking through the door of the shop. Some salesmen want only to step in the door of your home to give you your "free sample"; then they become quite upset if you don't buy anything.

The point to remember is that the seller ordinarily has the advantage and that, in selling consumer goods at least, he may be inclined to let fiction displace fact. For example,

> ... an advertising writer cannot permit a cake of soap to remain a cake of soap and "nothing more." Whatever the object for sale is, the copywriter, like the poet, must invest it with significance so that it becomes symbolic of something beyond itself—symbolic of domestic happiness (like Van Camp's pork and beans), of aristocratic elegance (like Chanel No. 5), of rugged masculinity (like Marlboros), or of solid, traditional American virtues (like Log Cabin syrup). Whether he writes about toothpaste or tires, convertibles or colas, the task of the copywriter is *the poeticizing of consumer goods.*[4]

Poet or pragmatist, the seller knows the quality of the product and he knows its real value, at least in terms of cost to him. If he is honest, he will avoid exaggerated

---

3. For specific instances, see Brink and Kelley, pp. 320–328.
4. S. I. Hayakawa, *Language in Thought and Action* (New York: Harcourt Brace Jovanovich, 1964), p. 263. Reprinted by permission.

claims and distortions of value; he will also be glad to answer *all* your questions. If he is dishonest, all your questions will be little enough protection.

Questioning of idea messages. Listen just as critically when someone is making a public statement or trying to sell you an idea. In the fall of 1969, charges of misconduct against several military officers were dismissed when the Central Intelligence Agency would not permit its personnel to present testimony in the case. On a Monday, the President's press secretary answered "No," when newsmen asked if the President had made the decision not to prosecute. On Tuesday, when the question was repeated, the answer became, "No—not to my knowledge." On Wednesday, when the question was repeated, the answer was, "The President *approved* the decision." We are not here questioning whether the decision was right or wrong. We are pointing out that the answer was "No" on Monday, "I don't think so" on Tuesday, and essentially "Yes" on Wednesday. Examination of the political record of any administration at almost any level will disclose similar variations and shifts in the handling of information. It is this kind of handling, of course, which leads to "credibility gaps."

If a representative of some radical group appears on or near your campus, he may make some startling statements. When he pauses for breath, questions like these are reasonable: *"What is your evidence* for that statement?" *"Can you cite any facts* to back up that conclusion?" "Isn't that statement only your *opinion?"* You will discover that the right question at the right time will often bring such people up short. If they have little or no basis for what they are saying, you will be doing yourself and other listeners a favor by uncovering that fact.

When you move to a more formal public-speaking situation, the occasion normally calls for silent questioning, especially since it is sometimes impossible, impolite, or even unwise to question the speaker directly. Under such circumstances, you may find self-defense questions such as these useful:

1. *What is the speaker trying to accomplish?* Does he give us any good reason to listen to him?
2. *To what wants or goals of the audience does he appeal?* Or does he seem to recognize only goals of his own? What objectives does he hold out as desirable for all of us? Are they reasonable and justified? Are they within reach?
3. *What are his specific arguments?* Is he well informed? Does he have facts and figures at his command? Does he recognize the existence of any contrary evidence and argument? Is he resorting to any "red herring" devices? Does he slant, quote out of context, etc.? Does he admit the possibility that he does not know all the answers? Does his total argument make good sense?
4. *Does he really care about his listeners?* Does he seem to understand us? Does he feel strongly that he can help us in any way? Or is this occasion a kind of self-promotion opportunity to him?

In other words, use all the questions you can think of—including some in the next section of this chapter—to measure the honesty and effectiveness of a speaker's interaction with you and the other members of an audience. Many of your questions will be inspired by your own background as well as by your reading of other parts of this text, particularly Chapters 2, 3, and 4. (As you gain experience in framing questions, a by-product will be improvement in your own speaking; when you are doing the speaking, you will try a little harder to anticipate the questions occurring to individuals, groups, and audiences.)

In closing this discussion of listening self-defensively, we can agree that many sellers of things and of ideas respect your ability to think; others assume that, if they "play their cards right," you will forget to think. The person who never believes anyone or anything leads an uncomfortable and needlessly troubled life. The person who believes everyone and everything is the gullible "easy mark." To protect yourself in this world, you have to learn to walk the middle road—it is not asking too much to expect people to give good reasons for the products they ask you to buy and for the positions they ask you to take.

. . . .

Comprehension checks

Have you ever heard a salesman recommend that you buy a competitive product at another store? Have you had a salesman try to switch you from one product to that produced by another manufacturer? Did it occur to you to ask "Why?"

Under what circumstances do merchants look out for the welfare of the consumer? What protection does the consumer have? Does he have to look out for himself or are there any government agencies to help him? What kind of help? How effective? When you see a television commercial "proving" that one soap is superior to "Brand X," what is your reaction? Do the "scientific tests" impress you?

This section of the chapter suggests a series of model questions aimed at helping us protect ourselves in the marketplace of materials and ideas. What questions would you personally want to add to the series? What is the advantage, if any, of having some kind of plan for your approach to a materials-or-ideas salesman and what he has to say? If you recognize that always to be suspicious is an unhappy, if not dangerous, state of mind, what do you consider to be "the golden mean" in this seller-buyer relationship? Is *prudent questioning* a possible statement of that mean? Would you suggest a more appropriate phrase?

Demonstration options

1. Bring to class a one-page description of a radio or television commercial which you nominate as the least convincing of those you sampled. Try to include time, date, station, general sales line, etc.
2. Bring to class a one-page description of the radio or television commercial you found most convincing. Give details about the commercial and your reasons for the high evaluation.
3. Visit the offices of a local credit bureau to ask the manager what services the bureau performs. Find out what it does (1) for the businessmen of the community and (2) for the consumers. Report your findings to the class.
4. Visit the local Chamber of Commerce. Ask the same questions and report.

5. Attend a meeting to be addressed by a speaker presenting *an informational talk.* Use the questions suggested in this chapter (or make up your own) as the basis for preparing an "off-the-cuff" 5–6 minute reaction to what you heard. Or prepare a 5–6 minute written manuscript on your reaction and read it to the class. Or prepare the same manuscript to be handed to your instructor in partial fulfillment of the requirements of the course.
6. Attend a meeting to be addressed by a speaker presenting *a persuasive talk,* either controversial or noncontroversial. Supplement the questions in this chapter with any others you wish to formulate. Handle your reaction to the talk in any one of the three ways outlined above, subject of course to the recommendation of your instructor.

. . . .

Listening Analytically[5]

The preceding sections of this chapter call for your listening *actively* and for listening *self-defensively.* In such instances, you are the target toward which the message is directed, and you respond in varying ways. In the suggestion that you should sometimes listen *analytically,* the subject of the present section, there is no implication that you should not listen in an analytical way at the other levels. The only assumption is that you will sometimes want to listen primarily *as an analyst interested in what you can learn about the process of speech-communication* through a careful study of what goes on in a particular speech-communication event. You move from the two earlier positions in which you are, in a sense, a speech-communication "consumer" to one in which you are primarily a speech-communication "observer."

Given some degree of natural aptitude, you can become a reasonably good speaker-communicator-listener through (1) a study of principles and (2) practice in applying them. You can become an even better communicator if you have an opportunity to use the same principles and your experience as bases for the analysis of one or more speech-communication events. The time and energy you spend in becoming a responsible analyst will give you the extra measure of perception and appreciation of speech-communication which can be acquired in no other way. *Analyst* is used here in the sense of one who (1) collects all possible or selected data associated with a given speech-communication event or series of events, (2) measures what happened against relevant criteria and choices made by a speaker, and (3) attempts to make evaluative judgments about the interactive process observed.

A preliminary step in the process of becoming an expert speech-communication analyst, however, is that of following the ancient counsel, "Know thyself." Each of us represents a special, unique, and intricate synthesis of natural and acquired attributes, complicated by a goodly share of prejudices, quirks, and outright idio-

---

5. Because of some of the less desirable connotations of *critic* and *critically,* the words *analyst* and *analytically* are generally used in this section as constructive and positive equivalents.

syncracies. Before you attempt responsible analysis and evaluation, you owe it to yourself to try to avoid "contaminating the results." You can do so, at least in part, by realistically assessing your own capabilities for the task and by recognizing personal beliefs, attitudes, biases, and foibles which may interfere with it. Another factor, that of your position in relation to the person speaking (e.g., inferior, equal, superior; friend, neutral, opponent), may easily color your views as an analyst. Finally, in excessive attention to faults, there is sometimes a tendency to overlook positive and praiseworthy aspects of a communicative situation.

With the advantages and cautions of the foregoing paragraphs in mind, what is the function of the speech-communication analyst? He tries to reach *a judgment on how well the speaker succeeds* in interacting with listeners in a given situation. He uses the key concept of *adaptation to the audience* as the vantage point from which to attempt a kind of "stop-action" examination of the more obvious elements in the process. He notes and records as objectively as possible (1) the facts of the communication setting, (2) the events and interactions of the ongoing communication process, and (3) any postcommunication "results" and phenomena. If a copy of the speech is available before, during, or after the event, the analyst includes it in his collection of basic materials; a tape recording is even more valuable, and a videotape of the delivery of a talk is of course priceless.

Once the analyst knows to the best of his ability all the circumstances included in and surrounding the speaking situation, *he is ready to scrutinize the choices made by the speaker* when preparing for and presenting a particular set of views or arguments to this particular audience. In other words, the analyst tries to measure effectiveness primarily in terms of how well the speaker exercised the faculty of creative choice in determining what to say and how to say it. One who undertakes this task of listening analytically will find that, in his opinion, some of the choices were apt in varying degrees, some were inept, some were unintentionally overlooked, some were purposely omitted, some were adroitly handled, and some were mishandled. *Always in terms of adaptation to the audience*, the analyst looks at what the speaker was trying to accomplish, at what actually happened, at what was possible creatively under the circumstances.

Then, subject to his own biases and background and admittedly with the advantage of hindsight, he comes to the conclusion that the speaker approached perfection in dealing with this audience or that he deserved a rating somewhere else along the continuum between perfection and abject failure. (As a part of his final evaluation, the analyst *may* include some comment on the effects of the speech *if* any can be discerned and *if* any can be attributed with some degree of certainty to the speech.)

The following outline will help you visualize steps common to the critical analysis of a speech.

I. Recording of information and observations
   A. The communication setting
      1. The occasion and events leading up to it
      2. The complexion, attitudes, and expectations of the audience
      3. The reputation and other attributes of the speaker
   B. The ongoing communication process
      1. Initial audience reaction to the speaker

2. Audience reactions to the purpose and development of the speech
3. Terminal audience reaction
C. Postcommunication phenomena, including any apparent "results"

II. Evaluation of choices made by the speaker
A. From the standpoint of *purpose* and this audience
B. From the standpoint of *motivation* and this audience
C. From the standpoint of *language* and this audience
D. From the standpoint of *reasoning* and this audience
E. From the standpoint of *rapport* and this audience
F. From the standpoint of any other considerations worth noting in this speech

III. Overall judgment on the relative merit of the speech
A. Summation of major accomplishments in adaptation
B. Summation of primary failures in adaptation
C. Final critical estimate of worth

As a part of the basic course in speech-communication, the student is sometimes required to prepare a report on speech-communication heard outside the classroom. The project may call for a report on any kind of speech; more frequently a course syllabus is specific in prescribing analysis of an informative speech, a persuasive speech, or a group-process meeting of the democracy-in-action type.

Let us suppose that you decide to hear a speech to be given by one of the candidates for some office in your state. In accordance with the pattern for analysis outlined above, your first problem is the "recording of information and observations." Obtaining the facts about the candidate's background, education, experience, and reputation should be relatively easy in this instance; a letter to him or to his campaign office should get a prompt reply on the first three, and you could check his reputation in other ways. Let us assume further that the particular occasion in this fictional instance is described in the newspapers as "the fifth in a series of campaign speeches delivered in the major cities of the state." If two or three of the speeches have already been given, writing to the newspapers of the cities involved would provide information on what the candidate had said in those instances. (You may find out that he is giving exactly the same speech in every city on the tour.) The occasion for the meeting will be simply that of the typical political rally, but there may be other noteworthy factors. For example, your city may be the candidate's home town, or perhaps the event is scheduled for some historically significant hall or outdoor meeting place. Are there special conditions (like a strike in progress or a very high level of unemployment) which could have a bearing on attendance or atmosphere? What is it possible to predict subject to checking on the scene at the time of the speech, about the composition of the audience? Primarily factory workers? The "country club set"? Students, professors, intellectuals? Complete cross-section of the community? Will the atmosphere be serious? Festive? Explosive? Will there be any social, racial, or religious undertones? If we assume that your prediction of audience or audience-mix turns out to be fairly accurate, what is likely to be its collective mood?

If you find out in advance as much as you can about the occasion, audience, and speaker, the evening of the event will find you well enough informed to make rapid corrections of your predictions, if that is necessary, and then to detect and interpret nuances of audience feeling and reaction before the talk starts, while it is going on, and after it is over.

The analyst should be very cautious in his observation of postcommunication effects. Results of a speech are difficult, if not impossible, to determine with assurance. If a man asks for votes in a community and 80 percent of the votes are cast in his favor, that result is not necessarily a result of the speech. The local party organization may be strong enough to deliver 80 percent of the vote for *any* candidate endorsed by the party. Further, the vote may be one *against* the opposing candidate. It is also a fact of political life that the people who go to hear a political speech are like students at a pep rally. Nothing intelligent need be said—anything is vigorously cheered. Nevertheless, it sometimes happens that a speaker does affect results, so the analyst should be aware that this can happen and try to recognize it when it does. Helpful in this assessment of results will be interviews with some members of the audience, as well as the later collection of news media reviews and comments. *Carefully qualified speculation on results* of a speech is justified, but it should be avoided unless the signs are quite clear.

After you have recorded and observed everything there is to know about a speech situation, you have the materials in hand for the next step, *an evaluation of the choices made by the speaker.*

Begin with his purpose and your estimate of the purpose of the audience in coming to hear him. Are the two the same? What do the listeners expect the speaker's purpose to be on this occasion? Is there a common premise or set of values shared by the listeners and possibly by the speaker? Does the speaker seem aware of that premise or those values? Is he making use of them as a foundation on which to build his case? What do the listeners know about the subject? Does the speaker appear to know what they know? And to take advantage of their knowledge? What would you say are the opinions, beliefs, and attitudes of the listeners on the topic under consideration? What are the sources of those opinions, beliefs, and attitudes? Does knowledge of the sources provide any explanation of the causes of those views?

If listeners expect a speaker to deal with hard-core unemployment, but he chooses to deliver a eulogy of his party, the listeners are going to be bored and you will know it. If something like the foregoing happens, the speaker has failed to adapt his purpose to the audience; you may also be able to ferret out *why* he did not or decided not to come to grips with matters of local interest. Then, in similar fashion, you check (below) what the speaker actually did in relation to what he could have chosen to do in order to achieve the best possible transaction with his audience.

Did he make reasonable choices in his attempts to motivate his listeners? What kinds of listener *goals* or *satisfactions* did he seem to recognize? What objectives did he hold out as desirable for the audience and for himself? Did they seem "within reach"? Or the concoctions of a "dreamer"? Did he content himself with generalities and support of "mother, home, and country"? Did he appear to have any understanding of listener attitudes? Was he trying to change listener attitudes? How did he go about it? Did he seem to know anything about factors affecting attitude change? Did he introduce any ideas inconsistent with those known to be held by a majority of his listeners? Did he try to reduce any existing inconsistencies? How? Was the emphasis on tension-increasing, on tension-relieving, or on a combination of both? Did he introduce any overt or suggested threats? Did he anger his listeners at any time? Was he able to polarize individuals and groups in such a way that the audience "became one with him"? In general, how successful was he in setting up rationales which the audience seemed to accept as justification for changing, intensifying, diminishing, or discarding attitudes?

Did he use words and signs in ways keyed to his audience? Were "his" words "their" words? What nonverbal forms of expression did you detect? Were the listeners puzzled at any time? What appeared to be the problem? Was he careful in his inferences, accurate in his classifications, and precise in his definitions? Were his forms of expression clear? Colorful? Dull? To what extent were they forms common to his listeners? Did his words and/or signs get in the way of the messages? In what ways did he use words and/or signs that were especially well suited to his audience? What mistakes did he make in choice of words and/or signs for these listeners?

Was his reasoning suited to this audience? What stated or implied "common premise" provided a starting point for the presentation of the speaker's case? Was his case as strongly constructed as possible in relation to this set of listeners? Did he have a case? Did he appear to know the difference between fact and inference? Was he well informed? Did he quote out of context, distort facts, resort inordinately to the unqualified use of "all"? Did he do any name-calling or "mud-slinging"? What was the audience's reaction if he did? Did he consider himself to be the final authority on the problems of the state? Or did he admit that the possibility of his not knowing all the answers did exist? When he drew a conclusion, did the audience seem skeptical or convinced? Or totally uncritical of anything he said? Did he use comparison? How effectively? Analogy? How effectively? How careful or careless was he in his analysis of causal relationships? Did the audience seem to accept his "arguments"? Or did its members seem ready and able to find flaws? Did he try to anticipate audience resistance to an idea? Did he present only one side, or did he admit there was another side and discuss it? (See Chapter 12.) How successful or unsuccessful was he in his attempt to win belief?

To what extent did the speaker generate rapport with the audience? To what extent did the audience respond? Did the speaker "strike the right chords"? Were his listeners emotionally moved at any time during the speech? What were the circumstances? Did he appear at any point or points to be adjusting his remarks to audience feedback? Did the audience appear to trust the speaker? Did the audience accept him as "sincere"? As really concerned about their problems? As self-interested? As fair-minded? As a "trickster"? Why? Did he succeed in arousing enthusiastic support? How was it manifested? What was the state of his rapport with his listeners throughout the speech as well as at specific stages of it?

From the standpoint of other considerations, did he conduct himself appropriately? If one or more special qualities of the man or the speech stood out as making a deep impression on the audience, what were they? Was he "chained" to a prepared text? If he had a text, was he able to depart from it or adjust it in any way? What obvious blunders (like referring to the wrong city or mispronouncing the name of local politicians) did he make?[6]

---

6. The list of questions is intended only to suggest typical approaches to areas which could be investigated. Obviously, not all questions and not all areas can be profitably examined for every speech-communication event.

Finally, after you have exhausted all resources in determining the efficiency of the speaker's choice-making in relation to a particular audience, you should be in a position to summarize the speaker's accomplishments and failures in adaptation to his listeners, and then you may compose a short evaluative judgment on the relative merit of the entire speech. (It is here that you may also include comments on "results" if it appears reasonable to do so in connection with a final estimate of the speaker's ability to communicate effectively under the circumstances described.)

. . . .

Comprehension checks

What is a speech-communication analyst? In what way is he different from a speech-communication critic? Isn't this just another instance of an attempt to find a better-sounding word for a particular activity? Is "analyst" a better word in your opinion? Why? Why not?

The text makes the statement that each of us is biased in some ways? Are you biased? In what ways? If a particular newspaper has taken a strong editorial position against any kind of welfare program, is it likely that you will find in it a favorable review of a book supporting such a program? If you are strongly opposed to the position taken by a speaker on a controversial issue, can you be completely objective in your analysis of his talk? In such an instance, what can you do to place your analysis in perspective?

If ten students of widely different backgrounds approach analysis of the same speech-communication event, will they come up with essentially the same evaluations? In what respect will their reports be essentially the same? In what respects different?

A speech is a speech. Why is so much emphasis placed on events leading up to and following it? Why not just analyze a talk from the standpoints of what happened during it rather than from choices made by the speaker before and during it? When the President of the United States makes a major speech, it is sometimes followed by "instant analysis" by well-known commentators and news analysts. Is this kind of activity in the national interest? Why? Why not? Is instant analysis possible? Under what circumstances?

Demonstration options

1. Attend a meeting addressed by a speaker *presenting information.*
   A. Use the material in this chapter and the discussion in Chapter 10 as bases for preparing a 5—6 minute extemporaneous analysis.
   B. Prepare a 5—6 minute analysis for reading to the class in manuscript form (see Chapter 7).
   C. Prepare a 4—6 page analysis, preferably typewritten, to be turned in to your instructor in partial fulfillment of the requirements of the course.
2. Attend a meeting addressed by a speaker presenting a *persuasive talk*, either controversial or noncontroversial. Follow instructions for option 1, using in A the material in this chapter and the discussion in Chapter 12.

3. Analyze a *discussion*, formal or informal, unstructured or parliamentary. Try especially to attend any special or regularly scheduled group-process meeting to which you can gain admittance as "an interested citizen." (Attending a meeting of an organization to which you belong should be ruled unacceptable for this assignment.) In this context, meetings such as these would be appropriate: school boards, city councils, town meetings, township boards, county boards, commission hearings, governmental legislative sessions at the state or national level, and public meetings of almost any kind on social, political, or economic problems. The purpose of this option is to encourage students to observe and report on "democracy in action." (A meeting called to give a particular speaker an opportunity to present his views is not a "discussion meeting," even though there may be discussion afterwards.) Follow instructions for option 1, using in A Chapters 11 and 14 as bases for preparing an extemporaneous analysis of "democracy in action."

Comment on the options above: Unless some controls are exercised, the difficulty with a general class assignment to report on speech-communication events is that most of the critical analyses are based on the one or two events scheduled just before the reports are due. When oral analyses are required of all students in the class, it becomes progressively harder under these circumstances for "analysts" to hold listener attention as the series continues. One answer to the problem is to have students turn in typewritten analyses which give the instructor an opportunity to assess levels of analytical ability; oral reporting can be omitted entirely or restricted to a few leading papers or excerpts from them.

Of the three options, the third meets with increasing favor because *practically no students have ever seen one of our governmental units in operation*, and very few have any experience whatever with speech-communication in "legislating" and other forms of "due process." Reporting on a meeting is more complex and arduous than reporting on a single communication event, but any serious student can do it well. There will, again, be a tendency for groups of students to attend the same meetings; as suggested above, only the best analytical reports—or excerpts from them—need be chosen for any special comment or hearing. We are governed by decisions reached in official and semiofficial hearings and meetings of many kinds; students of speech-communication should see for themselves how these decisions are reached and how their interests as citizens are at stake. They should see for themselves what opportunities the citizen has to affect such decisions.

. . . .

Whether or not you agree with the designation of three kinds of listening (active, self-defensive, and analytical) described in this chapter, we hope that the emphasis given to the subject will help you recognize that "lending one's ears" is just as important a part of speech-communication as the attempt on the part of a speaker to adapt his messages to an audience of one, several, or many. Students interested in doing further reading on listening will find excellent discussions in Irving J. Lee's *How to Talk with People* (New York: Harper and Row, 1952); Ralph G. Nichols and Leonard A. Stevens' *Are You Listening?* (New York: McGraw-Hill, 1957); and Paul D. Holtzman's *The Psychology of Speakers' Audiences* (Glenview, Ill.: Scott, Foresman, 1970).

Part 3 / Speech-communication in action

9 / Interacting person-to-person

In Ernest Gann's *Song of the Sirens*, the author describes a sailor who "... had a magic facility for making bosom friends of total strangers in ports all over the world." Not too many of us are endowed by nature with the gift of instantaneously making friends—perhaps it's the veneer of "civilization" that gets in the way. However, if we work at it, we can learn to be less evaluative and more human. It is especially important that we do so in order to communicate successfully in what we call one-to-one, face-to-face, person-to-person, twosome, or (if you want to be technical) dyadic situations.

Definitions and types

Characteristically, you communicate with one other person either in an informal conversational setting or in a more or less formal interview. In the first, the pattern of interaction is primarily social; typical examples would be exchanging pleasantries with a friend, trading comments about a party with someone, or comforting somebody in distress. There may be elements of "hidden agenda" or ulterior motives in any conversation, but in general the two communicators are talking simply because one or both enjoy chatting together or find the conversation necessary to satisfy certain social amenities.

The interview, on the other hand, carries with it the implication that two individuals are meeting by appointment to discuss a specific subject that one or the other or both have decided on in advance. They may begin by talking conversationally about the weather, about mutual friends, or about some event in the news of the day, but then they move into the interview proper to take up the business that has brought them together.

Interviews are ordinarily considered to fall into two broad categories, (1) those in which the primary emphasis is on giving, getting, or exchanging *information* and (2) those in which the objective is *persuasion*, the effort to cause someone to modify his views and/or his actions. In practice, the distinction is not always clear to the observer (although the interviewer usually knows what he is doing) for the reason that persuasion often appears in the guise of information. The ancients believed that if you give a man enough information, he will come to the desired conclusions without any overt persuasive effort; it is true that the intelligent and perceptive individual finds information more acceptable—and more complimentary—than outright efforts to move him to think and act in certain ways. In the main, however, the information/persuasion dichotomy is useful only if we think of it in terms of the immediate purpose which one or both participants have in mind for a given interview.

Immediate purposes

The primary distinction between the conversation and the interview has already been noted. Within those classifications, the following purposes may be discerned.[1]

1. One or both individuals may simply find satisfaction and/or pleasure in the companionship of two-person interaction, e.g., two students talking about their job experiences during the past summer.
2. One individual may be trying to change the emotional state of another, e.g., a mother consoling son or daughter after some personal disappointment.
3. One individual may be trying to convey knowledge, information, or understanding to another, e.g., a foreman instructing a new employee on the handling of a particular lathe.
4. One individual may be seeking knowledge, information, or understanding from another, e.g., a young person looking for advice.
5. Both may be cooperatively exchanging knowledge, information, or understanding, e.g., two students preparing for the same examination.
6. One individual may be trying to change the attitudes, beliefs, or behaviors of another, e.g., the salesman trying to shift a confirmed Chevrolet buyer to a Ford product.

The first purpose above would, more often than not, fall into the province of the casual conversation. The example given for the second is also clearly conversational; however, if it's a psychiatrist who is trying to change someone's emotional state, the event is an interview. The last four purposes would also be in the interview category.

Characteristics

Insofar as typical characteristics of two-person interaction are concerned, Argyle notes the following three regular sequences of verbal communication.[2]

Topic. If A makes a remark about a particular topic, B will probably reply by speaking on the same topic. If he does not, and fails to explain why not ("to change

---

1. See Argyle, p. 181, for a discussion of specific purposes on which the distinctions in this text are based. For a discussion of general human goals, see Chapter 4.
2. Michael Argyle, *Social Interaction* (New York: Atherton, 1969), pp. 169–170. Reprinted by permission of Methuen and Company (London), original publishers.

the subject...."), there will be a discontinuity of interaction, and indeed social interaction will have broken down.

Type of utterance. If A asks a question, B will probably answer it; if A gives orders or instructions, B will probably carry them out or explain why not. If A asks open-ended questions on a specific topic, B will give longer replies, and this is one way of getting a person to talk more.

Timing of speech. People have characteristic styles of speech..., but also adjust to one another. For example, an interruption virtually forces a person to stop speaking. There are also strong elements of imitation involved; for example, if A interrupts B, B will interrupt A.

On the part that questions and answers play in our lives, few of us realize that we spend a high percentage of our speaking day in "asking and being asked, answering and being answered, taking in and giving out by means of the spoken word bits of information without counting."[3] Questions vary widely in form from those calling for a simple "Yes" or "No" ("Is there a pollution problem in your community?") to open-ended patterns ("What is the nature of the pollution problem in your community?"). Many "questions" are less interrogative than they are statements of encouragement to say more. For example: "You feel that he doesn't really understand you?" or "This is hard on you?" or "You feel that's not right?"[4] In whatever way they are phrased, questions and statements of encouragement play an important part in the ordinary conversation and are normally the core of an interview.

Motivation

Motivation in the two-person communicative situation is defined in the same way as for all other types of human communication. One of the prospective participants sees a goal which can be attained through this kind of one-to-one transaction, or both of the potential participants see the same or different goals and the mutual advantage to be gained through conversation or interview. If the primary motivation for the encounter is present in the first of two persons and not in the other (as in attempts at door-to-door selling), the second person "is very likely to spend some of his attention and energy on trying to evaluate [the communication] in terms of the possible motives of the sender or of its adaptability to his own needs, including his need to make a certain impression."[5] The first communicator doesn't have much chance of success until he can break through the second communicator's initial state of wariness. In any event, individuals are generally motivated to take part in face-to-face discussion because they see it as the means to an end, attainment of a particular goal or goals.

---

3. Robert L. Kahn and Charles F. Cannell, *The Dynamics of Interviewing* (New York: Wiley, 1957), p. 5. Reprinted by permission.

4. *Ibid.*, p. 71.

5. *Ibid.*, p. 7. For a review of motivation and other general dimensions of speech-communication, see Part 1 of this text.

The extent to which cooperation develops in the one-to-one communicative situation depends on the general atmosphere in which it takes place and on the gains or penalties which each participant envisions for himself. A warm and friendly interviewer is, under normal circumstances, going to generate warmth and friendliness on the part of the respondent or person answering the questions, and a good personal relationship between the two commonly augurs well for the interview. As you well know, the satisfaction derived from simple association with someone you like and/or respect is often reward enough for a person-to-person encounter. On the other hand, in some instances of a routine nature—for example, answering the questions of a census taker or of someone conducting a political or consumer survey—we cooperate from a sense of duty or commitment. Other situations are more difficult and delicate; when you are "called on the carpet," the person issuing the reprimand also has a problem. Nevertheless, whatever happens in any kind of interview, it is essential that every effort be made to encourage the respondent to be really free in presenting his point of view and feelings on the subject at hand.

A close-up of the communication process

A special advantage of studying any kind of two-person interaction is that this kind of transactional pattern provides a close-up of the communication process. If you are close enough to a person to see a small freckle on his chin, you are close enough to experience human communication in some of its varied and microscopic detail. And if you become adept at two-person interaction, you will discover other forms of communication to be much easier and more satisfying.

If, for example, the idea of the simultaneous existence of several message channels has been confusing, you can now see them being used. Let us say that you are a girl sitting alone at a twelve-chair table in the library. It would probably surprise you to have a total stranger take the chair immediately to your left or right; in our culture, if he sat at the same table at all, you would expect him to sit some distance away—unless his silent message is that he'd like to get acquainted. Under the same circumstances, if a friend came into the room and did *not* sit near by or stop to pass the time of day, you would rightly or wrongly get some message or messages from his failure to meet normal expectations in this instance. Watch any two persons in conversation. You can draw fairly accurate conclusions about their interpersonal relationships by observing where they are standing or sitting in relation to each other, what changes in facial expressions are in evidence, what tones of voice they are using, whether the rate of speech for one or both is rapid or hesitant, what kinds of gestures come into play, etc.

As an observer, you can also see something of the extent to which feedback is being used to modify behavior and the messages which are a part of that behavior. When one of the principals looks puzzled, does the other seem to react with additional explanation? If one of them looks at the ceiling in boredom, does the other take some step or employ some cue to recover his interest? When one appears to be getting angry, does the other change his tactics and try to mollify him? Does one of the participants seem to be oblivious of feedback and the advantages which adjustment to it offer? Without actually hearing a single word, you can draw meaning and interpretations from the many channels operative in any speech-communication situation; a conversation or interview enables you to see this multichanneled process of communication at close hand.

Interaction in Conversations

In days gone by, those who aspired to be "genteel conversationalists" were always advised to avoid the subjects of sex, religion, and politics. Practically no subject is now taboo, a fact which many applaud but which also accounts for an increase in "confrontations" and occasionally some mayhem. For example, the story is told about the solid citizen who had just succeeded in bribing a building inspector to overlook a section of the local building code. Shortly thereafter, he stopped a casual acquaintance on the street and said, "All building inspectors are dishonest." As luck would have it, his listener had once been such an inspector, and he immediately retorted, "All building inspectors are *not* dishonest." A heated argument began, continued for some time, and ended in an angry draw. The moral is one all of us eventually learn: You can win more arguments by listening and by questioning—to be sure you understand—than by jumping into the fray and "proving" you are right. When you take sides on an issue, you know that you have good reasons to do so; you can be sure the person who takes an opposing view has his good reasons too.

You need no particular training to talk about the weather and the news of the day. However, some conversational skills do not come so easily "by nature." For purposes of demonstration, then, it is helpful at this stage in the study of speech-communication to keep in mind the advantage a degree-minded person enjoys over the individual with an "all right or all wrong" two-valued attitude. The first is usually successful in keeping open the channels of communication; the second's claim that his is *the* only right position clogs the channels if it doesn't block them entirely. Let us look into the practical differences between the two-valued and multi-valued approaches.

. . . .

Participation options

1. Pair off with another student in the class and find some issue on which the two of you are at opposite poles. (If you have difficulty finding such an issue, change partners or simply adopt opposite points of view for the purpose of this conversation.) For instance, one of you could take the stand that a college education is the right of every American high school graduate; the other would take the contrary

position. In demonstrating the two-valued approach, neither of you monopolizes the conversation, but each sticks to his position and doesn't "give an inch" in the ensuing word battle of five to seven minutes (or shorter) in length.
2. Pair off in the same way as above with the understanding that one of you will continue to maintain a two-valued stance and the other will become a multi-valued "sympathetic listener." The listener withholds any objections and limits his comments to such remarks as "You really feel . . .," "Very interesting; tell me more about that," "I've never heard that before," "You may be right," "There is something to what you say," etc. If the listener has the opportunity, he can suggest an occasional qualification or less sweeping statement, but he should avoid all argument.

Listening options

1. As you observe the principals in a two-valued exchange, you may see that one has a clear advantage in his reasons and his evidence. What is likely to be the attitude of the "loser"? Join the "winner"? Continue to oppose him? Oppose him more strongly than ever? Write a paragraph on the effect that taking an early and specific stand seems to have on any communicator. Does he feel a compulsion to stand his ground and stick by his commitment? Or is he as free to change his mind as the man who has yet taken a positive position?
2. From your observation of one or more interviews, do you agree that it is possible to make a speaker less sure of his position by encouraging him to talk and by avoiding any direct contradiction of what he had to say? Did this approach seem to block communication, or did it appear to open it up? Do you know anyone who prides himself on his ability "to argue"? Anyone who habitually reacts in a multi-valued way? Which of the two seems to you to be the better communicator? Explain why in a paragraph.

. . . .

Interaction in Interviews

In contrast to conversations in which topics and the discussion of them are seldom planned, the interview, as already defined, is a speech-communication event in which two people meet by appointment to discuss a specific topic known to one or both of the principals. For instance, if you get a message reading, "Professor Smith would like to talk with you in his office," you may be able to make some "educated guesses" about the subject he wants to take up with you, but only he knows exactly what it is. When you get there, Professor Smith will be in control of the conversation and in a position to direct it into whatever channels he has chosen in advance. On the other hand, if you want to see Professor Smith on some subject, and a particular time is arranged for the meeting, you will be the planner and director of the discussion which takes place.

A second possibility is the interview in which both individuals know what the subject is going to be, and both have an opportunity to prepare for the meeting. Thus both are essentially on equal terms. For example, when you decide to apply for a part-time job advertised in a local newspaper, the prospective employer knows what information he wants, and you know what qualifications and concerns you want to discuss.

Either as interviewer or as interviewee, if you know what the topic of an interview is going to be, you should be able to touch some of the following "bases" in advance.

1. *Determine your purpose.* Perhaps you want to be excused from a regulation, to get a job, to obtain information, etc.
2. *Work out a discussion plan.* List in some reasonable order the points and evidence which you feel support your purpose. Since questions play a heavy role in most interviews, plan carefully the questions you will ask and the order in which you will ask them. When making your plans, ask yourself some of the following questions.

   How should I begin the meeting to develop rapport and create a climate in which the work of the interview can get underway? How is the other person likely to respond to the main objective I have for the meeting? What resistance can I anticipate? Do we have common ground that can serve as a starting place? What do I know about his personality, his motivations, his knowledge, interests, attitudes, habits? What major points do I hope to make? What is the best order in which to take up the main topics? What follow-ups should be planned during the meeting? How can the conference best be concluded?[6]
3. *Arrange "favorable circumstances."* It is sometimes possible for you to set the time for meeting; people normally feel "fresher" and more favorably disposed in the morning. And if the person you are waiting to see is engaged in a violent argument just before your turn comes around, it is just as well to slip away unless a specific appointment is involved.

During the interview itself, certain elements appear regularly and form a pattern. For example, almost every interview begins with self-introductions or greetings and some "small talk."

In the "working period," one of the individuals, normally the one who asked for the meeting, begins with the questions and/or statements he has worked out in advance. From this point forward, the individual who arranged the meeting has primary responsibility for conducting it. If he understand the interview process, he makes a special effort to note and take advantage of feedback; if he is learning the process, he discovers that an interview is the perfect opportunity to become "feedback conscious."

When the business that brought the participants together is finished, the interview is customarily brought to a close with expressions of appreciation, if appropriate, the usual goodbyes, etc.

---

6. Adapted from *Presentational Speaking for Business and the Professions* by William S. Howell and Ernest G. Bormann (New York: Harper and Row, 1971), p. 57. Used by permission.

In conclusion...

Unless you are a hermit by choice, scarcely a day goes by without your engaging in a number of conversations and interviews. A person-to-person encounter doesn't have to be labeled an "interview" to be one. Sometimes a student makes an appointment with a professor (or simply stands by after a class) to discuss delay of a term paper because the student is leaving campus for a few days to take part in a job interview; this kind of discussion is really an interview, in this instance an effort to obtain a concession. On the way out of the building, the student meets his class president, whom he hardly knows; nevertheless, he stops to discuss nothing in particular because he thinks it wise to maintain good relations with someone in that position, and besides, it enhances his personal status to be seen chatting on intimate terms with him. The meeting with the professor was a planned interview; the meeting with the class president is an accidental conversation. Both require skill in the communication process, especially in those aspects of it associated with the special problems of person-to-person interaction. How well you engage in these unplanned and planned encounters depends in part on your understanding of the interpersonal relationships involved and on your interest in participating as successfully as possible each time.

. . . .

Participation options

1. Try to recall an instance in which someone in authority (parent, adviser, counselor, dean) attempted to talk you into a course of action which you resisted. Coach another student to present the authority's line of argument. Then try with him to re-create for the class the give-and-take of the original interview.
2. Imagine that you are the manager of a local gas station. Prepare the general line of questioning which you would direct to an applicant for a job, and include statements of information describing the duties, hours, policies, etc. Have another student in the class make application for the "opening."
3. Play the role of the manager of a department of your choice in a store, real or fictitious. One of the clerks "lacks initiative" and confidence in approaching prospective customers. Have a talk with this clerk and conclude it by using him or her as the customer in a demonstration of how to approach a prospect and sell an item.
4. With another student in the class, set up an interview situation in which you are either the interviewer or the respondent. The "scene" can be information-seeking, job-seeking, telling someone how to do something, conducting a questionnaire, suggesting improvement in someone's actions or attitudes, asking someone about his hobbies or special interests, etc. In whatever type of interview you choose to engage, remember that planning and tact have much to do with its success or failure.
5. With another student, plan an interview in which one of the participants breaks "every interviewing rule in the book."
6. Arrange an interview with another student who is preparing some other class project (e.g., informational talk, discussion, persuasive speech). Have him give

you in advance (two or three days) an outline of the talk he intends to give or of the discussion area on which he is supposed to contribute materials and ideas. Use that outline as the basis for asking him tactful questions about what he intends to do, how he intends to do it, how adequate his materials are, etc.

Listening options

1. Focus your attention on the interviewer in any one interview or in any interview specified by the instructor. Did he establish a good atmosphere in his opening comments or questions? If not, why not?
2. Did the interviewer in a designated interview seem to be following a *planned series of questions* and observations? Were you satisfied with his planning? What suggestions would you make for improving it?
3. Did the interviewer in a designated interview bring the interview to a reasonable and fitting close? How did he accomplish this? Would you have handled concluding remarks in the same way? Differently? How?
4. Focusing your attention on the respondent of your choice (or on one assigned), what observations would you make about his answers to questions, general cooperation, and understanding of interviewing? What comments would you make about learning through interviewing? Advantages and disadvantages as compared to reading?
5. If any pair of students attempts the fifth participation option above, write a short paragraph in which you explain how you, as interviewer or respondent, would have coped with the rule-breaking participant?
6. Of what advantage to the interviewer is asking someone questions about a particular subject if the interviewer does not intend to make use of the answers in some practical way? In the sixth participation option above, what benefit can the student being interviewed gain from this experience? If you learn that someone is breeding alligators in his basement, are you inclined to ask him questions if an appropriate occasion arises? Why? What does the alligator breeder get out of the encounter?

. . . .

10 / Presenting information

Anyone attempting the communication of information may be said to be trying to stimulate learning. Although "learning" is a word we use rather freely, "... a universally acceptable theory of how humans learn (i.e., the laws of learning) has not been stated."[1] Or from another point of view, "It is as difficult for psychologists to agree about learning as it is for a group of theologians to agree on a definition of sin."[2] In spite of the fact that psychologists disagree on how learning comes about, their theories on that subject fall into two broad classes, *association* (or stimulus-response) theory and *field* theory. The first emphasizes motivation and "the response made to a set of stimulating conditions."[3] The second emphasizes the individual and the impact on him of the total setting, including the influence of hereditary factors. Both overlap. To whatever schools of thought psychologists belong, they do agree that "learning refers to the effects of experience, either direct or symbolic, on subsequent behavior."[4] (This means that, provided there is some attention and a degree of effective communication on your part, those listening to your presentation of information will never be the same again.) Some psychologists believe that when one learns, "he builds on what is already there, just as a bricklayer adds courses of bricks to change the wall."[5] Others support the position that in the process of learning, one modifies earlier learning in its entirety rather than adding to it.

Whatever the differences in theories, there is general agreement that we accumulate learning through (1) *experiment* ("I don't know what brand of shaving cream to use; I'll try them all to see which one appears to be the best."), (2) *experience* ("My

---

1. Edwards and Scannell, p. 255.
2. Miller, p. 160.
3. Edwards and Scannell, p. 258.
4. Berelson and Steiner, p. 135.
5. Brink and Kelley, p. 130.

experience with Fords has been good; I need a new car; I'll buy a Ford."), and (3) *insight*, the sudden realization of new relationships ("I had been thinking about this problem for some time when the solution suddenly came to me like a bolt out of the blue.").

In an informational talk, as in any other, it is good practice to begin "where the listener is" and try to "lead him where you want him to go." As suggested above, this goal can be reached through the conducting of an *experiment* or through demonstrating a process or law; this kind of approach is familiar to all of us, especially through its use in science classes everywhere. The goal can also be reached through vicarious *experience*; the listener may never have been to Mexico City, but if you are skillful in describing your experiences there, they become his. Finally, the listener will absorb information if you help him attain an *insight* which simply has not occurred to him before; if, in discussing the concept of prejudice, you explain the ways in which people do not recognize prejudice in themselves, some of your listeners will for the first time appreciate how prejudiced they are.

How much learning actually occurs in a given situation will depend in part on listener reaction to you as a person, on how well you understand listener goals and provide reasons to listen which are in line with those goals, and on how successful you are in gaining and retaining attention. (A review of Chapter 4 will be helpful here.) Certain additional factors or "laws" of learning are known to be especially relevant from the standpoint of intensifying or augmenting listener reaction to speakers presenting information—as well as to speakers attempting persuasion or debating issues.

Immediate reward

When you show that a particular process or craft (e.g., making leather products) can be quickly mastered, the reward for learning is immediate. By nature, people want their satisfactions *now*, and they learn faster if the reward is not delayed.

Comparative reward

The rate of learning is ordinarily in proportion to the strength of the reward stimulus. When you are choosing the subject for an informational talk, it is wise to consider the possible choices from the vantage point of "size of reward." If, in your opinion, the listeners will get *more* personal satisfaction from information on "how to study" than from a talk on "how to raise chinchillas," the first subject will be the better choice.

Reasoned sequence

Listeners find it easier to learn and absorb materials which are presented in reasoned sequence. This kind of "natural order" is relatively easy to achieve in discussing a process which can be described in a series of steps. It is more difficult to provide a pattern of progression in talking about a concept like "society," but it can be done.

Listener-related experience

When you undertake to talk about some aspect of statistical method, your listeners will lose interest unless you relate what you are talking about to *their* experience. The examples chosen for illustrations should be within the range of their familiar areas of knowledge. For instance, if you are one of a group of "laymen" listening to an expert on atomic physics, you will learn little if anything—and probably remember nothing—from the talk unless the speaker makes a successful effort to find explanations and specific instances meaningful to you and others like you.

Sensory stimulation

The sense organs of sight, sound, touch, smell, and taste are powerful receivers of "sensations" which help man interpret his world. When we undertake speech-communication, we do depend to a great extent on the spoken word as a primary medium for carrying out our purpose. We should also recognize that learning may be significantly accelerated if we can show an object to our listeners, if we let them see, hear, touch, smell, or taste it. Showing a large drawing of a gear assembly —or better still, a large model of one—to a group makes the explanation of the gear principle a relatively easy project; having listeners feel the texture of a rug gives them a more accurate knowledge of that quality than does the mere description of it; offering listeners a taste of a new cheese will give them taste and smell sensations which they could experience in no other way.

Planned redundancy

Each of us has been bored at one time or another by a speaker who "says everything five times." Nevertheless, since listeners don't always grasp an idea the first time it is presented to them, *some* repetition helps guarantee understanding and contributes to retention of learning as well. Planned redundancy leads to learning for those who, for some reason, fail to absorb the meaning of a message the first time it is heard; redundancy can also provide "incremental learning" for those who do hear the initial message. Listeners—and readers—usually appreciate added explanation of the "in-other-words" type; carefully devised and differently worded repetition does serve a very useful function in the learning process.

Strain toward completion

"The direction of behavior is toward an end-situation which brings closure with it."[6] People like to finish what they have started in a learning situation, and they expect a speaker to help himself and them to finish whatever project they have jointly begun. In speech-communication, a speaker can and should set up certain audience expectations, and by the time he finishes communicating, those expectations should be more or less fulfilled. If you say that you are going to explain the principle of capillary attraction, your audience is conditioned, however temporarily, to expect you to accomplish that objective for their benefit and satisfaction. The strain to finish a job begun is a universal trait; the speech-communicator often finds it possible to capitalize on this aid to learning.

The Informational Talk

With some understanding of learning theory and factors affecting listener absorption of what we have to say, we may now examine some of the details involved in the laying of the "courses of bricks" to change the information wall.

---

6. Hilgard and Bower, p. 235.

The "informational talk" is one in which the student undertakes to describe or explain a concept, process, technique, procedure, principle, design, operation, or some other function or idea. In his discussion of the practical aspects of a topic, the speaker may tell the audience how to make something or how it is being made, how to do something or how it has been done. Whether working with explanations and descriptions or with ideas and abstractions, the speaker's primary aim is simply *to create or increase audience understanding*.

Some examples of topics (in subject-sentence form) appropriate to that aim follow.

Group 1: explanations and descriptions

Process   When you open a can of peas, do you sometimes wonder how they got that way?

Technique   Do you know how to take a good outdoor photograph?

Product   The ordinary chair is made in some unusual and glamorous forms; let's look at some of them.

Procedure   We'll soon have to fill out income tax forms; we may as well learn how to do it now.

Design   Some pottery designs are marvels of creative art.

Function   Metabolism is an important function in living organisms.

Group 2: ideas and abstractions

Concept   Social stratification is a part of "life in America." What is it? What are its implications?

Theory   The theory of evolution is still not too well understood.

Law   What kind of "law" is operative on the high seas, and how does its interpretation affect you?

Principle   An understanding of the principle of racial equality is vitally important to every American.

Doctrine   Have you ever heard of the "doctrine of diminishing returns"?

Report   What provisions have the major cities made to control street riots?

Structure   The Eli Lilly Company is a large, complex, and efficient organization.

The categorical listing above is not intended to be complete; it does indicate *topical bases* for the communication of information. Other terms could serve equally well to suggest talks contributing to understanding; further, a term serving as a base for topic suggestion could, in different contexts, appear in both groups (e.g., the "principle" of jet propulsion would properly fit into Group 1). However, the topic possibilities are set up in two groups because, in many basic-course plans, the students prepare and present two speeches of information, one on the plane of practical applications and the second on the challenging level of the world of ideas. It is one thing to talk on the sights and sounds of Bourbon Street in New Orleans; it is quite another to explain Plato's "Forms of Souls." Yet some of the best student speeches are explanations of such concepts as imperialism, exploitation, emotional maturity, the liberal arts, existentialism, faith, free enterprise, and so on.

The importance of the "speech of information" cannot be easily exaggerated. Because it is relatively simple in content and sometimes elementary in its step-by-step organization, there is a tendency to overlook the fact that this kind of talk is probably the one type which the student will most often encounter, both as speaker and as listener, in his business or professional life. The good "salesman of ideas" is almost always a good "demonstration speaker." In Chapter 1, we noted that Aristotle considered the general objective of speeches to be primarily persuasion and that George Campbell (*The Philosophy of Rhetoric*, 1776) is given credit for broadening the classical doctrine of speech purposes to include that of "enlightening the understanding."[7] Actually, we need not be too much concerned about who decided to give separate status to information as a primary purpose in certain communication situations. The fact is that the informational talk does enjoy special attention in the majority of modern texts. Nevertheless, informational discourse is like other types in that additional objectives (to persuade, to amuse and entertain, to attack past practices in explaining new ones, etc.) may be woven into the speech fabric. For instance, the plant superintendent who is explaining the care and feeding of some new and very expensive equipment is simultaneously persuading his foremen that it is in their collective best interests to see that their men handle the equipment properly. The county agent explaining a new and improved method for preventing insect damage to field corn is at the same time hoping that his farmer audience will be persuaded to adopt the method.

Because of the relative simplicity of the informational talk, there is sometimes an inclination on the part of the student to assume that practically any subject on which he is reasonably well informed will be acceptable. However, here as in any approach to speech-communication, you must be careful in estimating what your audience knows and what it does not know about your proposed topic. Explaining some elementary principle of engineering to a class composed largely of engineers is going to be a boring experience for everyone in the room. The administrative organization of your college or university will be known to a majority of the students enrolled; discussing it would be a waste of time. If you are in doubt about the extent of general student knowledge in an area on which you would like to speak, a quick informal questioning of a number of students should give you some idea of the current state of information on that topic.

When you are planning the development of a topic, it is wise to begin on "familiar ground" and then move to the kind of reporting or explaining you have in mind. For example, if you want to describe the political system operative in Nicaragua (or in some other country in the news at the time of your speaking), beginning with similarities between governmental units of the United States and of Nicaragua would provide a base from which to branch out into a full exposition.

The need for adaptation to your specific audience, always a crucial requirement, is more easily overlooked in the informational talk than in others. Steps in a process are clearly steps in a process, and you cannot change them; however, with care and some ingenuity, you can relate discussion of them to listeners. The principle of racial equality can be covered in theory only, or it can be brought home more directly

---

7. New York edition of 1851, p. 23.

through the inclusion of examples affecting the people sitting in front of you. If you are discussing the general impact of environment on personality, remember that *some of the differences between you and the other students are totally social in origin*; look for real or hypothetical examples drawn from your own experience and that of the other people in the room. Quoting examples about the differences between two tribes in New Guinea may be appropriate but somewhat far removed from the immediate scene.

In summary, (1) choose a topic which you *already know* reasonably well, (2) try to assess the collective "state of knowledge" of your listeners on that topic, (3) plan to work from what they know to what they don't know, and (4) constantly and conscientiously adapt your development and examples to those listeners.

Visual Aids

There are two reasons why informational projects are usually among the first speaker-audience assignments in the basic course in speech-communication. First, as we have previously noted, this type of talk is relatively easy to prepare, and second, the use of visual aids in conjunction with it gives the student an easy and more or less automatic entrée into the world of gesture and bodily movement. (Visual aids may be used, of course, in any speech-communication situation in which they will contribute to understanding.)

The types of visual aids most readily available or most easily prepared are (1) actual objects of a size permitting convenient handling and display, (2) models or mock-ups of such objects, (3) drawings, (4) diagrams, and (5) graphs. Items in the first two classifications can usually be borrowed; for example, if you want to explain how a carburetor works, it should not be too difficult to get one for a few days from a local garage or car dealer, and people in business often have lightweight models or mock-ups of various kinds which they are willing to lend on a short-term basis in return for the free advertising obtained through a demonstration. Drawings or tracings of drawings, diagrams, and graphs can be made by any student willing to spend a little time on the preparation of posters or charts. (Sometimes these units, too, can be borrowed.)

146 *Presenting information*

Fig. 10.1 Student calling attention to parts of a camera.

Fig. 10.2 Student explaining air flow over wing.

Fig. 10.3 Student showing function of gears in power transmission.

Fig. 10.4 Student describing forces that affect rocket in flight.

Actual objects

The student in Fig. 10.1 is discussing the parts of a camera and, at the moment, happens to be pointing to the lens. This "object" is light enough to hold up before an audience; its parts are also large enough to be seen without difficulty in the average classroom. Actual objects can be used to good effect in a talk if you remember that such display units must be big enough to see and either self-supporting (e.g., camera on tripod) or not too heavy to handle easily.

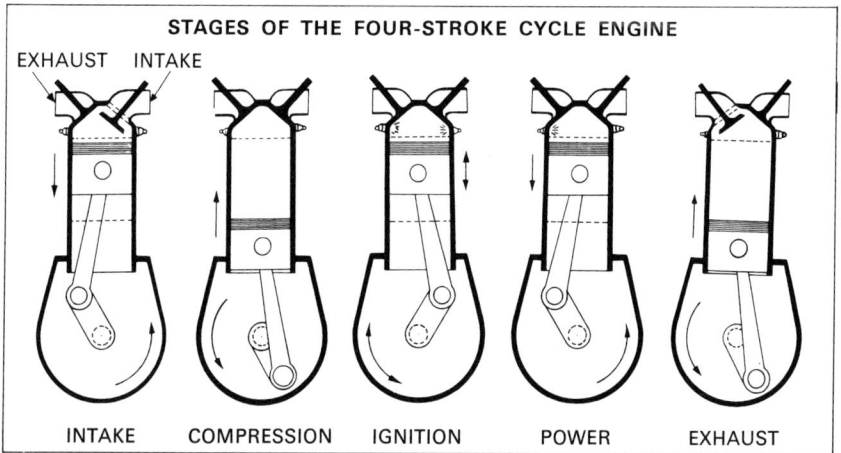

Fig. 10.5 Drawings reproduced through the courtesy of the Institute of Aviation, University of Illinois, Urbana, Illinois.

Models or mock-ups

In Fig. 10.2 the student is explaining the forces affecting a plane in flight. With model in hand, he can demonstrate factors of lift, gravity, thrust, and drag. (If he were to attempt discussion of aircraft controls, his audience would be handicapped because control details would be hard to see.)

The student in Fig. 10.3 is holding a cutaway mock-up of a differential gear assembly. He is explaining (1) how power is transmitted to the rear wheels of an automobile and (2) how this assembly permits the wheels to turn at different rates as the car goes around a curve or corner.

In Fig. 10.4 the student is discussing the conformation of a rocket, how it is powered, and the forces which act upon it in flight. In each of the four instances, you will note that the object, model, or mock-up is light enough in weight to be held with ease and still large enough to be seen easily by the members of a class or relatively small audience. (The same visual aids would be of little use in an auditorium.)

Drawings

The poster on the stages of an engine (Fig. 10.5) shows the five-stage sequence of events which take place in each cylinder of a reciprocating gasoline-powered motor. Although these drawings are professional in appearance, a student could draw reasonable facsimiles suitable for use in a classroom or small-audience talk on that subject. Similarly, if a student wished to give a talk on "Classical Greek Temples," he could roughly draw a series of illustrations on flip-chart pages. The first chart could represent the general proportions of the Parthenon, the second could show the ground plan for a typical temple, the third the Doric order of columns, the fourth the Ionic, and the fifth the Corinthian. The student could find basic illustrations in any encyclopedia, and he could draw rough enlargements freehand.

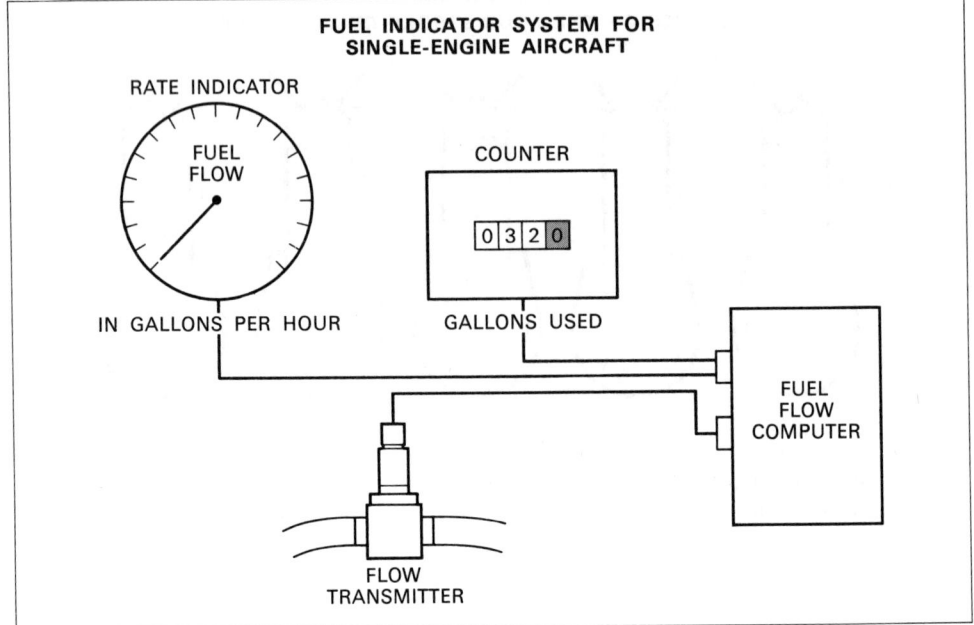

Figure 10.6

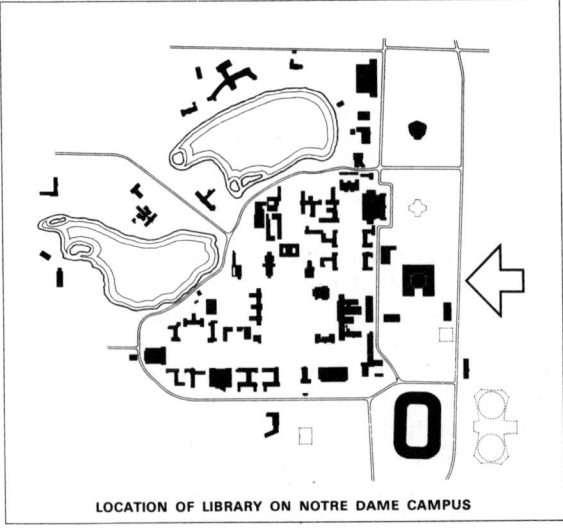

Figure 10.7

Visual aids 149

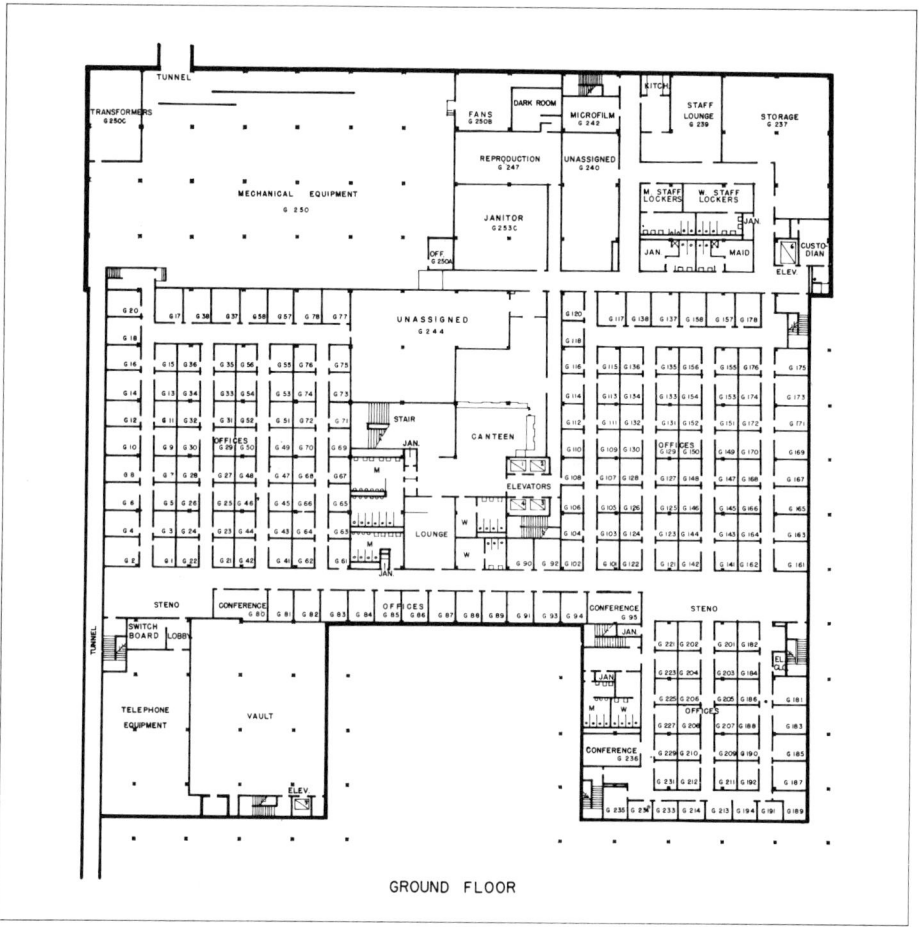

Fig. 10.8 Example of too much detail in a poster.

Diagrams

As you move away from accuracy in detail to more general representations, you move from drawings to diagrams. For example, the poster on the aircraft fuel indicator system (Fig. 10.6) shows no details of physical appearance; it simply indicates units and their function. Note that the captions appear *next to* or *on* the elements to which they refer.

The poster shown in Fig. 10.7 indicates the location of structures on the campus of Notre Dame University. The arrow points to the Memorial Library; this particular poster would be useful as the first in a series of charts or other visual aids on that building. The floor plan diagram (Fig. 10.8) is a good example of what not to attempt in a poster; there is too much detail, and not even the people in the first rows of an audience would be able to make out the captions or the items shown.

150 *Presenting information*

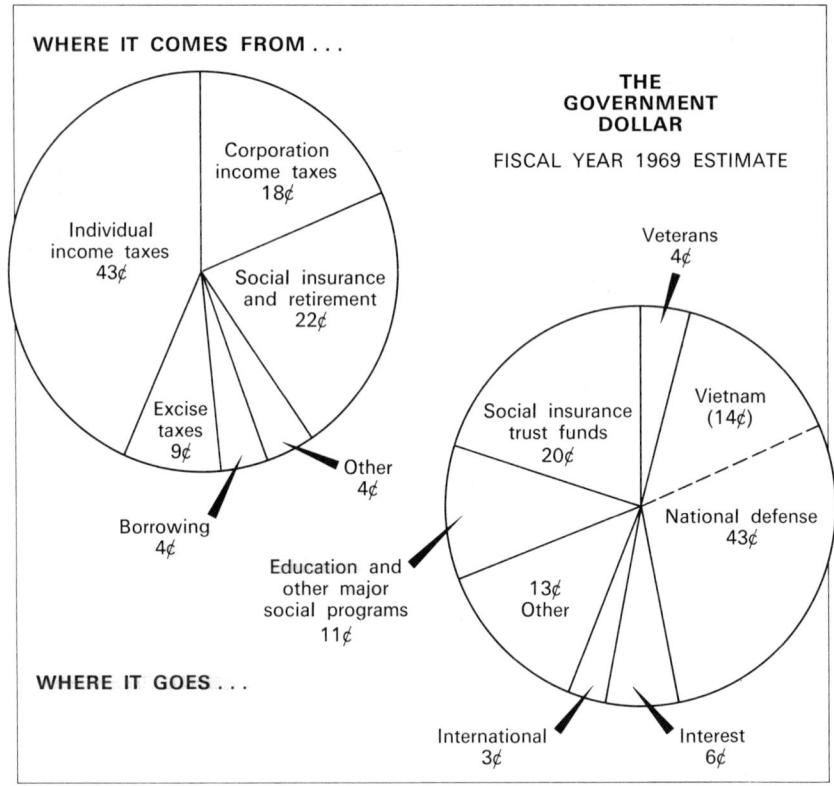

Figure 10.9

You have often seen "pieces-of-pie" diagrams. The two shown in Fig. 10.9 will remind you that they are frequently and efficiently used to show "income" and "out-go." They can also be used to illustrate certain kinds of batching in the mixing of various grades of concrete, ingredients in livestock feed, and in any situation for which *proportioning* can be appropriately indicated by this method.

Graphs

At various times in the past, you have used facts or data in numerical form to present information on a subject or to make a point. Through the use of graphs it is often possible to make such statistics more interesting and to dramatize them as well. Although this is not the place to go into a detailed description of statistical method,[8] an under-

---

8. For details of statistical method, see Frederick Williams, *Reasoning with Statistics* (New York: Holt, Rinehart and Winston, 1968). For a useful review of the technique of setting up tables and for a thorough discussion of "statistical forms of support," see Howell and Bormann, pp. 134–167.

standing of the following basic terms is useful in deciding how to construct a graph and properly designate the numbers appearing in it.

Average (mean). The result of dividing a distribution of quantities (scores or values) by the total number of the quantities involved. For example, if the ages of five people in a group are 25, 32, 18, 28, and 87, the average or mean age is 38. You can readily see that the figure 87 throws the average in this group out of line and that, to be meaningful, the average or mean must be used with care. If the fifth number were 22, the average would then be a more typical 25.

Median. The quantity that is in the middle of a series, with half the quantities above it and half below. The graph showing ages of congressional committee chairmen in 1970 (see Fig. 10.11) could have been drawn more simply to show that the chairmen's median age was 69 in the House and 67 in the Senate. In the first series of five ages presented under average (paragraph above), the median age is 28, a figure much more representative of that group than the average of 38.

Mode. The score or value that occurs most often in a given distribution. For instance, manufacturers of a cash register may want to know what particular button or bar is pressed most often in a typical supermarket day. Several machines are wired to record this data, and after a reasonable period of time, the designers know what button or bar gets the most wear. The number of times that unit was pressed is the mode. The results of the test could be easily shown in a bar graph showing the number of tallies for each button or bar.

A graph is really a kind of picture which the communicator-speaker designs to help him present his statistical material in an accurate and undistorted way. Sometimes averages are reliable indicators of typical instances or trends; at other times the median or mode will better serve the purpose at hand. Whatever the source of our figures, if we do not have a complete record of all the units under consideration, that fact should be made clear in the presentation. On a national election day, television commentators depend on the computer to detect trends, and on the basis of incomplete evidence, they predict the winners long before the polls are closed. The final evidence is not in until all the votes are counted and certified. As the commentators make clear, their predictions are not on the same level of credibility as the certifications to come.

The more common types of graphs are *bar* and *line* graphs. The bar graph in Fig. 10.10 is constructed on a vertical plan; that in Fig. 10.11 is handled horizontally. In these instances, the plan is of no great consequence; in others, you may find that one or the other better fits your particular set of statistics. The graph in Fig. 10.12 achieves a striking effect through the use of human figures as symbols. If a subject permits and you are artistically inclined, a symbolized graph is especially interesting to the average audience.

Line graphs are more versatile indicators of variations and variables. For instance, the line graph on the poster in Fig. 10.13 shows the widening gap between black and white family income between 1947 and 1965. It would be difficult, if not impossible, to make this point as effectively with a bar graph. Figure 10.14 is a very simple curve type of graph showing a striking increase in enrollment; the impact of the change in trend (from a slowly increasing rate to a rapidly increasing one) would be lost in a

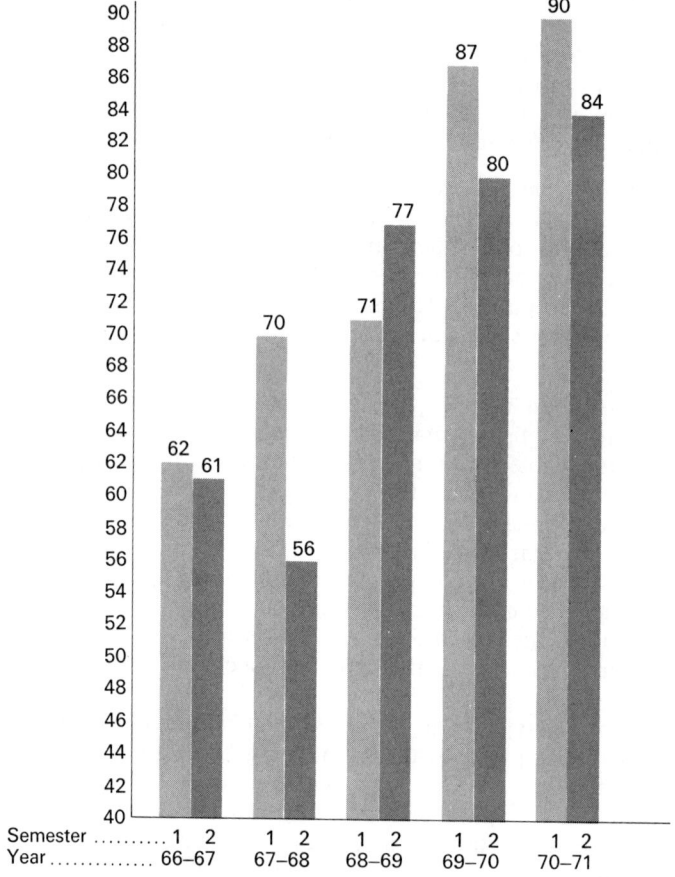

Fig. 10.10 Example of vertical bar graph.

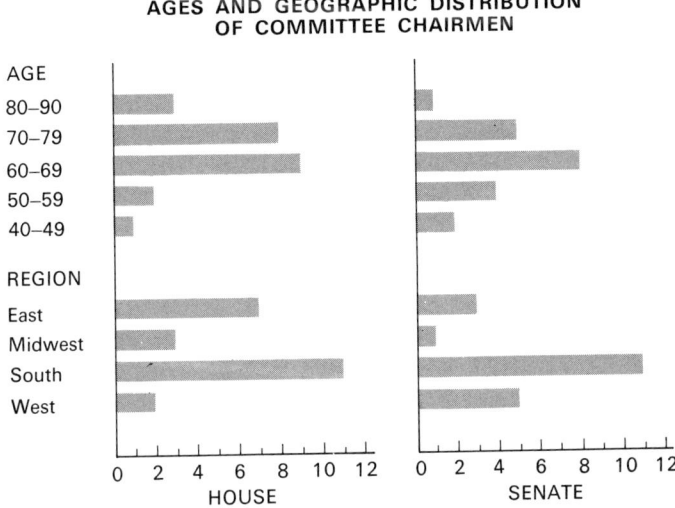

Fig. 10.11 Example of horizontal bar graph. From *Common Cause Report from Washington* (December 1970). Used by permission.

DEPENDENCY: THE CITIES' NEW MATH
The proportion of welfare recipients to the population in America's major cities* varies dramatically. Some examples:

	Atlanta	Baltimore	Boston	Chicago	Cleveland
Proportion of recipients to population	1 in 10	1 in 7	1 in 5	1 in 12	1 in 13

	Dallas	Detroit	Los Angeles	Miami	New York City
Proportion of recipients to population	1 in 23	1 in 8	1 in 8	1 in 25	1 in 7

	Philadelphia	Pittsburgh	St. Louis	San Francisco	Washington, D.C.
Proportion of recipients to population	1 in 8	1 in 14	1 in 7	1 in 7	1 in 11

*In some cases, calculations are based on the population figures for the county in which the city is located.

Fig. 10.12 Graph using human figures as symbols. From *Newsweek*, **77** (February 8, 1971), p. 23. Used by permission of Fenga and Berkovitz, Inc.

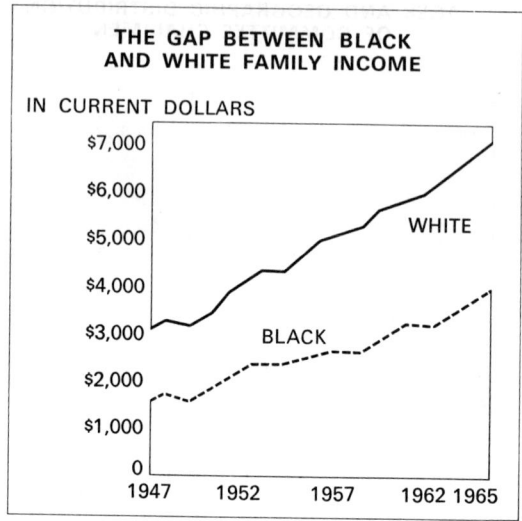

Figure 10.13

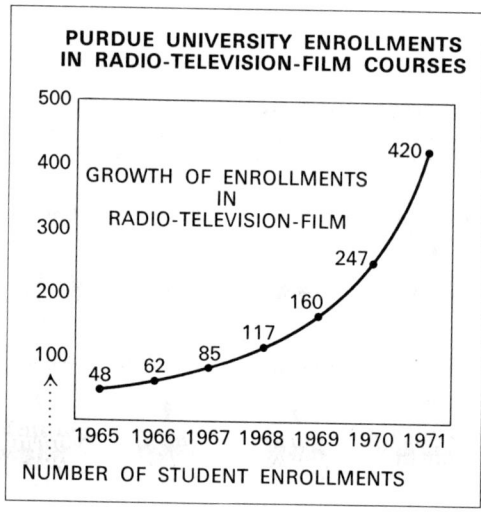

Figure 10.14

bar graph. The graph in Fig. 10.15, based on Department of Labor statistics, indicates the number of young people reaching the age of 18 between the years 1950 and 1970. Note that key figures are placed *in* the graph. If you plan to use graphs, it is sometimes wise to experiment with both bar and line types in order to find the one which best illustrates the point(s) you want to make.

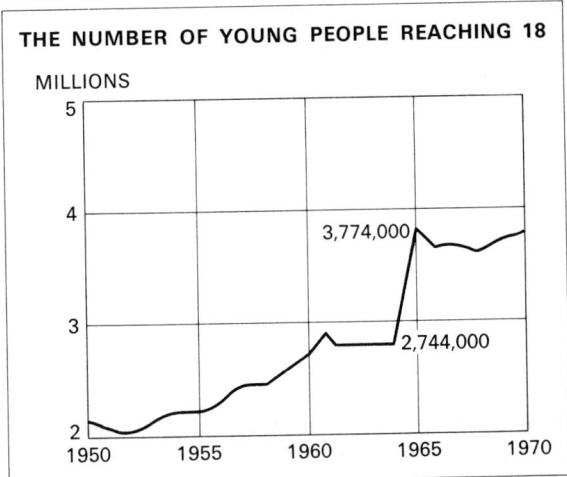

Figure 10.15

The projection of visual aids is not discussed in this volume[9] because projectors (slide, overhead, opaque, motion-picture), closed-circuit television, and other kinds of equipment are seldom available to students in beginning classes. (However, if you are faced with the need to use visual aids suitable for a large audience, consult an audiovisual expert; at least one such person is on the staff of the smallest college. Some colleges and universities have special courses in the communication of technical and/or industrial information; students interested in the more sophisticated methods for illustrated reporting and lecturing may find such a course available.) Finally, although visual aids are described in this chapter, which is concerned primarily with the informational talk, *they should be used in any speech-communication situation to which they can contribute interest and clarity.*

A few do's

1. If you plan to use objects or models—
    a. *They must be large enough to be easily seen.* Trying to show an audience the details of tooth construction in a gear would be close to impossible, even if the gear itself was easily visible. (A supplementary poster drawing of tooth detail could serve this purpose.)
    b. *They must be light enough in weight* to suspend from available hangers or to hold up in the hands for as long as necessary. A casting so heavy that it must remain on a desk or table throughout the talk is not going to be of much use. A mock-

---

9. Those interested in the projection of slides will find a fine example of that technique in Edward Stasheff's "What Will The Satellites Say?" in *On Speech and Speakers,* an anthology edited by H. Bruce Kendall and Charles J. Stewart (New York: Holt, Rinehart and Winston, 1968), pp. 262–273. For a first-rate guide to all kinds of visual aids and methods for projection, see Wilcox, pp. 144–207.

up made of plastic, cardboard, or other lightweight materials is occasionally available. Such a demonstration unit can be a completely satisfactory substitute for the real three-dimensional item.
2. If you plan to use posters—
   a. *Make them big.* For use in the average classroom, a poster should measure at least $2\frac{1}{2} \times 3$ feet. Sometimes one poster will suffice; if you need more than two or three, use standard "tablets" of chart paper of approximately the same size or larger. As you finish with a page of the chart, tear it off or turn it over to show the next page.
   b. *Use bold diagrams and lettering.* Thin-line drawing and lettering cannot be easily seen and often cannot be seen at all from the rear of the room. Use *dark* inks, crayons, paints, or pencils on light backgrounds. (Unless you are an art student, the reverse—light colors on dark backgrounds—is seldom successful.) Plastic lettering and drawing aids are inexpensive; their use almost guarantees the neat appearance of a poster or chart.
   c. *Keep them simple.* Cluttering posters with detail makes them more difficult to see and understand. Complicated designs and elaborate artistic drawings do little to clarify a talk and can have the opposite effect. Place your labels directly on, next to, or connected by arrows to the diagrammed elements involved.
   d. *Plan the display system.* Is a stand available for posters and/or charts? (Trying to hold poster or chart in hand is tiring and awkward.) Are any hooks or clasps available from which you can suspend your visual aids? You will ordinarily find that "standing" them in the chalk rail of a blackboard is impractical; such rails are usually too low, and even when they are high enough, posters seem to delight in bending and falling from them. Masking tape can be used to attach certain kinds of poster materials to a blackboard or wall. Do some preliminary prospecting in the room for which the aids are planned. The effect of good visuals is easily lost if they are not high enough to be seen.
   e. *Test the effect in advance.* Take your visual aids to the room in which they are going to be used, and between classes or at some other time, set them up and check them for easy viewing and reading from a seated position in the back row of the room.

A few don'ts

1. If you use a blackboard at all, plan to do the necessary drawing or writing *during the talk*. It takes some experience to use a blackboard well, and unless you have opportunities to practice with one, forget it. If you do use one, keep the use of it to a minimum and keep talking as you write or draw.
2. Remember that shades of red and yellow make fine poster backgrounds but that these colors present problems if used for drawing or lettering. Under ordinary circumstances, they cannot be readily seen or easily deciphered by students in the middle rows, let alone those in the back of the room.

3. If your talk is as well organized as it should be, you will not need a poster for the purpose of displaying your main points. Visual aids should be used to provide supplementary detail and to clarify ideas, not to present them. If the only thing you can think of is a poster of main points, you may as well abandon the idea of using visual aids.
4. Standard-size photographs, prints, pictures, newspaper clippings, copies of magazines, and small objects of any kind are virtually useless. Don't waste your time and that of the audience by holding up something which cannot be seen clearly and definitely by the students sitting in the last row.
5. Avoid bringing materials to be passed out to the students. This takes time, too valuable a commodity to be used in this way in a speech-communication class. If papers or models are passed out in advance, they distract the students from the speech; the handicap is intensified if they are handed out during the talk.

. . . .

Demonstration options

1. Bring to class in the form of broad topic sentences two or three subjects which you feel you could discuss well enough to hold the interest of the class. Examples: "Do you know how to photograph a landscape?" "Some Indian totem poles are good genealogy charts." Read your sentences to the class and ask for reactions on the topic of most interest.
2. Bring to class a facsimile (your version) of a visual aid you have seen in a demonstration (e.g., "Down with Pollution!"). Comment on its effectiveness.
3. Bring to class your very rough crayon or pencil enlargement of a diagram or graph you have seen recently in a magazine or newspaper. Comment on whether or not it contributes to understanding. Could it just as well have been omitted?
4. Bring to class a full-page advertisement from one of the larger-sized popular magazines. Comment on whether the illustration contributes to or detracts from the message.
5. Open a dictionary at random and list the abstract-idea words which you can find in from four to six pages. Stop looking when your list reaches ten items. Mark with a check two or three concepts you might like to investigate and present to the group. Then read your entire list of ten items to the class to give its members a chance to indicate those topics which seem to offer promise of an interesting-to-the-listener talk. Compare the class choices with those you checked.

Speaking options

1. Choose an informational topic *with which you have had some direct experience* and which you feel would be of interest to the members of the class. Prepare a 4–6 minute explanation and/or description along the lines suggested under Group 1 in this chapter. (If you have any planning or organizing problems, consult Chapter

6.) Plan and use visual aids to the extent that they can help you create or increase audience understanding. Among the subjects you may wish to consider are the following.[10]

   a. *Charities*, e.g., Goodwill Industries, United Fund, Mental Health Association.
   b. *Religions*, e.g., Mennonites, Church of Jesus Christ of Latter-Day Saints, Buddhists. (Avoid talking about your own religion; there is a tendency to be too subjective about it.)
   c. *Guarantees*, e.g., on paint, hosiery, appliances, etc.
   d. *Occupations*, e.g., orthodontist, waitress, sales engineer, summer-camp counselor, circulation manager, etc.
   e. *Foreign countries*, e.g., France, Thailand, Nigeria, Columbia, Australia. Discuss one country from one angle (e.g., political system) or from a number of them, including climate, topography, natives, industries, tourism, etc.
   f. Any process, technique, procedure, operation, or function with which you are familiar.

2. Prepare a 4–6 minute talk in which you explain an abstract idea or concept of the kind found in Group 2. It is usually possible to find a professor who is an expert in the particular field within which your topic lies. For example, some professor of philosophy can contribute to your understanding of a philosophical concept, and you will be better able, in turn, to explain it to a group. (Visual aids are still possible in this type of informational talk, but it will take some care to adapt them to the subject you have chosen. This talk is sometimes undertaken as a manuscript speech, with emphasis on proper handling of this kind of "speaking aid.")

3. If the class has set up a number of committees, each with responsibility for investigating a certain subject area, you will be endeavoring to find and report facts and other kinds of evidence on the area of particular interest to you and your committee. For example, you could decide to present a 4–6 minute report on "the extent of the unemployment problem in the United States." Remember that you need not and should not take any specific persuasive or controversial position in this talk; your aim is simply to add to your own learning and that of the class. If you use visual aids, prepare them well in advance, and practice before trying to use them in the audience situation. If you are planning to use a manuscript, follow the suggestions given in Chapter 7.

Listening options

1. On one page, list the three informational talks you considered the most interesting given in your class. Under each listing, add two or three sentences of comment on *why* the talks appealed to you. Try to be specific. Avoid such general comment as "It was interesting."

---

10. Topics adapted primarily from Paul D. Brandes, "II. The Common Materials Approach to the Teaching of Speech," *The Speech Teacher*, **16** (November 1967), p. 266. Used by permission.

2. Prepare one page of comment on the talk accompanied by, in your opinion, the most appropriate visual aid. Tell *why* the visual aid was appropriate.
3. In your opinion, what speaker seemed to be doing the best job of adapting his material to you and the other members of the class? Did he give you some good reasons for listening? Did he point out any advantages to you for doing so? Was he "friendly" or "detached"? Did he use a conversational style? Prepare a one-page description of the ways in which he made direct contact with his listeners.
4. Which of the speakers in this series took a topic you knew absolutely nothing about and succeeded in explaining it in a satisfying and attention-holding way? Write a note of specific comment and thanks addressed to that speaker; give it to the instructor for transmission to the speaker at the instructor's discretion.
5. If a particular talk left you "hanging in air" with one or more questions unanswered, write your question or questions on a sheet of paper and give it to the instructor for transmission to the student at the instructor's discretion.
6. If the speaker used a complete manuscript in his presentation, did he succeed in maintaining contact with you? Did the manuscript "get in the way"? Write a note to the manuscript speaker who, in your opinion, did the best job in the series. Tell him what he did well and, if you wish, where there was room for improvement. Give the note to the instructor for passing on to the student at the instructor's discretion.

. . . .

Example of Skeleton Outline on Explanation of a Concept[11]

Purpose: To explain the common "mental boobytraps" which we encounter.

INTRODUCTION

Opening sentence(s): In basic training, a new soldier learns that he must always be alert because a battlefield is filled with boobytraps.

Personal competence: My experiences have led me to belive that various types of boobytraps exist in everyday life.

Purpose and subject: The boobytraps to which I refer are those of false reasoning. I am going to describe five common types of "mental boobytraps."

Reason(s) to listen: As students interested in thinking logically, we should be anxious to avoid these types.

BODY

I. One of these mental boobytraps is called *hasty generalization*. Hasty generalization occurs when we draw a conclusion from too few instances. (Examples)

---

11. Written by Dr. Robert E. Davis of Arizona State University and reprinted with his permission. For elements of an outline on a *process*, see Chapter 6.

II. A second kind of common boobytrap is the *after-this-therefore-because-of-this* mistake. This is the assumption that because one event precedes another in time, the first event is the cause of the second.
(Examples)

III. A third common boobytrap is *attacking the person* instead of his argument.
(Examples)

IV. Another mental error is the *appeal to authority*. This is the assumption that, since an authority has been quoted, the question is automatically settled.
(Examples)

V. The last common fallacy we are considering today is the *two-valued orientation*. This is the assumption that there are only two sides or values in every case.
(Examples)

CONCLUSION

Summary: For each of us the "lesson" should be this: (1) Don't jump too fast to conclusions; (2) don't assume that one thing is the cause of another just because the one precedes the other; (3) don't stoop to attacking a man's reputation because you can't refute his argument; (4) respect but don't worship authority—anyone can be wrong, including the experts; and (5) do everything you can to look at things in terms of values and degrees—nothing is ever all black or all white.

Concluding sentence(s): Think for yourself, think carefully, and by all means, avoid those mental boobytraps!

Representative Informational Speech

The talk which appears below is an example of the relatively simple informational approach, in which the nature of the material determines the order of ideas. The only organizational problem lies in being careful to provide a good opening, give the audience some idea of personal experience with the subject, state the topic clearly, provide some reasons to listen, include reasonable transitions between major areas of the subject, and close with a short summary.

The speaker used one visual aid, a sectional map of the Indiana-Illinois area with a heavy black line indicating the route from Lafayette to Chicago. Mounted on heavy cardboard, it was hung from a standard portable screen before the talk began, and the speaker made references to it as required. For your convenience, a number of checkpoints appear in the margin of the recorded script.

Cross-country flying[12]

By Jeanne M. Nadeau, *Purdue University student*
Presented at a hobby club meeting
Lafayette, Indiana, October 7, 1970

Purpose: To try to give listeners a better idea of the problems involved in planning and carrying out an airplane flight.

Opening sentence(s)	Some of you, perhaps most of you, have had the experience of boarding an airliner which moved out near the end of the runway and then simply sat there for 10 or 15 minutes, while you wondered what was going on. I may be able to "shed a little light" on that problem.
Personal competence	I have done some commercial flying, and I have also done considerable flying in small one-engine planes. My dad is a private pilot, and we have taken numerous trips, including vacation flights, ranging up to a thousand miles in distance and up to seven or eight hours in time. On many of these occasions, I've been called upon to act as copilot or navigator, and I've come to know planes fairly well.
Purpose and subject	Few nonflyers know what steps are involved in preparing for a flight—you can't just hop in a plane and sail off into the "wild blue yonder"—and, secondly, very few know what steps are involved in making the actual flight. Therefore, I'm going to talk about how to plan and fly a typical flight, say from Lafayette, Indiana, to Meigs Field on the lake front in Chicago.
Reason(s) to listen	If you will go with us, our intrepid pilot will be Meredith Meriweather, that daring devil of the skies, and I'll go along as navigator. You will, I hope, find the trip instructive.
First main point	First, the pilot carefully plans his flight. A major concern is the *weather*. Instead of relying on reports in newspapers or on radio and TV, Meredith calls the local Flight Service Station for the complete weather forecast over his intended route. If the weather looks good for the time of the flight, Meredith immediately files a Flight Plan. Good weather means clouds no lower than about 2000 feet over the ground, winds no stronger than about 20 miles an hour, and visibility no less than about five miles in any direction.

---

12. Reprinted by permission of the speaker.

Another major concern is the *route* of the flight. It occasionally depends on the weather report because, when you fly, it is sometimes possible to fly around or to one side or to the other of a storm or some other unfavorable condition. In any case, our heroic pilot is watching an aerial map of the area as he listens to the weather report. Then, in filing his Flight Plan, he provides the following information: point of departure, intended time of departure, destination, exact route of flight, intended cruising altitude, cruising speed, estimated time in flight, amount of fuel on board, number of "souls" on board, name of pilot, registration number and description of the plane (type and colors). This information is relayed to the destination, so that the Flight Service Station at or near that point will know when to expect the plane to arrive.

Transition

With all his planning completed, Mr. Meriweather collects or meets his passengers—you and me—at the airport. He has already arranged to have the plane hauled out of the hanger, and it is waiting for us on the ramp. We are now ready for phase two, the flight itself.

Second main point

Meredith unlocks the doors to let us in. He then checks the plane to be sure that the propeller is firmly attached, that no birds have built a nest in the motor, that the wing bolts are tight, and that there's enough gas to get us to our destination. I always insist on helping him with that last item.

Our brave airman then enters the plane and runs through another check list, which goes something like this: doors locked, seat belts fastened, switches off, both fuel tanks on, mixture in, carburetor heat off, controls free, master switch on, ignition switch on, clear propeller—see that nobody's standing in the way—and start engine. Of course, it's a bit more complicated than this, but you get the general idea. Incidentally, the "steering wheel" is similar to the one in your car, except that the pilot also moves it in and out, forward to go down and back to go up. He also controls altitude, or height over the ground, by adding power to climb and decreasing it to descend.

After the check-list routine, the motor is now buzzing away up front and it is safe—and necessary—to turn on the radios. Meredith calls the Lafayette Flight Service Station and reports that he is ready to taxi. The man he's talking to gives him wind velocity and direction, barometer reading, number of the active runway, and makes other useful observations on other planes Meredith should look out for, both on the ground and in the air. Meredith taxis without running into anything and then stops where we started this talk, near the end of the active runway. There he turns into the wind and goes through the ceremony of checking again to see that everything works. That chore finished, he moves up to a yellow line short of the runway and calls the Station to say he is ready to take off. Unless he is told that there is a plane or two coming in for a landing, he moves out on the active runway and adds full power to begin the take-off roll. If planes are coming in, he has to wait until the landings have taken place. What causes longer delays in the case of airliners is that they are usually waiting for instrument-flying clearances—such clearances take longer because every mile and flying level of the entire flight must be cleared in advance of takeoff. The ordinary flight does not require this kind of advance reservation of flying space. It's the calling back and forth to arrange that space that takes time and often delays planes for no reason that is apparent to the passengers.

In any event, we're now rolling down the runway at full throttle, and the plane lifts off—with a little help from Meredith—at about 70 miles an hour. We climb out at about 100 miles an hour until we reach an altitude of 4500 feet. Since we're going in a northwesterly direction, we're required to fly at even thousands plus 500 feet. Going in an easterly direction, we'd be flying at odd thousands plus 500. When we reach 4500 feet, we level off, and Meredith does several things in the cockpit to set us up for "cruise." We're now moving at 150 miles an hour but, as most of you know, there is no sensation of speed—you simply hang there and move slowly over the landscape.

Since there aren't any road signs in sight, you have to learn to navigate by other means. That's my job on this trip. The easiest method is to use the "omni" or radio-signal stations located at intervals of from 50 to 100 miles on the ground. Each station has its own frequency and call letters. You tune in on the frequency of the next station up the line, and an instrument in the cockpit indicates the exact direction to that station; the instrument also tells you whether or not you are exactly on course and, if you're off course, in what direction to go to get back on it. On this flight, we first tune in on a station 15 miles northwest of Lafayette, then to a station about 20 miles south of Chicago. It is possible to "track out" of stations as well as "track to" them, so we have no trouble staying exactly on course. These stations are also reporting stations; as we go over each one, fearless Meredith reports his altitude and receives adjusted altimeter readings, latest weather, and so on.

Another method of navigation—which I don't recommend—is by landmarks. Navigation by this method adds interest to a trip, especially when you aren't sure just where you are. When this happens, everyone in the plane has a different name for that small town way down there. The hard part is trying to distinguish one small lake from another small lake, but somehow we manage it—at least, up to now we have.

Well, while we've been screaming here over the roar of the motor, our faithful pilot has reduced power and started his descent toward Meigs Field. He has called Meigs Tower, an agency similar to a Flight Service Station but with more authority, and he has announced his approach from 15 miles south at 1400 feet. This is no surprise to the Tower; they have been expecting this call because the time of takeoff had been relayed to them by the Station at Lafayette. Meredith is given instructions as he approaches the field, is told in what direction to land, etc. He is careful to land in the first third of the runway, so he won't run the risk of going off the end of it. At Meigs this is pretty important because Meigs is right out in the lake and you wouldn't want to run off the end into "the drink."

After landing, our pilot is instructed where to park the plane, and after asking the Tower to close the Flight Plan, he goes through another check list in the process of shutting down.

Summary

Well, there you have it. You've seen the process of planning a flight and the process of flying it.

Concluding sentence(s)

You will be glad to know that, if we had had an accident on the trip—gulp—there would have been an air-rescue search for us within an hour of our being overdue at a particular station. The Flight Plan would tell the searchers where to look. However, flying in a well-equipped plane with a competent pilot is a very safe and convenient way to travel. If you haven't flown, you've missed something. If you have, you already know how interesting and exciting it is to be "flying through the air with the greatest of ease."

11 / Planning and participating in discussion

News item: "Senate and House leaders have proposed a newly revised civil rights bill; the details were worked out in a joint Senate-House committee appointed to resolve differences and effect compromises between proponents and opponents of the original bill." You may not be now and may never be an elected official, but you do know that the average business man or woman may attend as many as two or three luncheon or evening meetings a week, in addition to engaging in many conferences during regular working hours. "To anyone familiar with business and industry it hardly seems necessary to point out the amazing amounts of time that are spent in meetings."[1] Your own experience should corroborate that view; if you are at all active in social or extracurricular activities, you regularly attend a number of formal and informal meetings. In other words, much of our problem-solving and decision-making today takes place at a table around which several individuals discuss a problem which seems to be more susceptible to cooperative attack by a number of people than to attack by one person or by a number of persons working separately.

Preliminary Distinctions

Definition and objectives

Discussion, then, is here interpreted to mean the small-group process (preferably no fewer than five members in a group and no more than seven, with a practical maximum of nine or ten)[2] through which people *work together* in the effort to add to their learning or to solve part of a problem or all of it. Sometimes the discussion is limited to the members of the group participating in it; sometimes it takes place before an

---

1. Barnlund and Haiman, p. 3.
2. According to Berelson and Steiner (p. 360), "The personally most satisfying size seems to be five...."

audience whose members may or may not be invited at some point to take part in the proceedings. In the latter instance, the discussion objective may be really one of trying to arouse popular interest in a current problem rather than to arrive at any solutions to it.

Types of discussion questions: fact, value, and policy

Problem questions susceptible to discussion may sometimes be solved through study by an individual, through informal and formal debate, through parliamentary procedure, and through other methods, including feeding data to a computer. However, if the problem is one on which the *shared* experience and judgment of a small number of people can be brought to bear on a relatively informal basis, discussion may be the best of several possible approaches.

When the discussion group is trying to determine what happened and/or what is happening in connection with a particular problem, the question is said to be one of *fact*. Example: "What is the present role of the United States in world affairs?" Here the members of the group would be looking for facts, figures, examples, and opinions about that role. They would be trying to arrive at consensus on an accurate *description* of the part presently played on the world scene by the United States.

If the group goes a step further in the attempt to evaluate our role as well as to describe it, the question is said to be one of *value*. Examples: "Is the present world role of the United States *justified*?" "Is Communism a *monolithic international conspiracy*?" "Is drug regulation *a failure* in the United States?" In each of these questions, the group would be attempting not only to find out what is going on but to discover whether or not a particular evaluation of the situation seems to be accurate.

A question of *policy* asks what *should* be done. Examples: "*Should* the U.S. recognize Mainland China?" "What *should* be the place of women in the professions, business, industry, and government?" The assumption is that a group looking into either of those questions would first collect available information on the subject, would attempt to determine evaluatively whether or not the status quo warranted action of any kind, and if the answer seemed to be in the affirmative, would then try to choose the best way to correct the wrong or wrongs observed.

Approaches to discussion

Although discussion questions are said to fall into the categories of fact, value, and policy, they may be approached from a number of different angles, as already suggested.

The learning approach. When the objective of the group is simply to find and/or share information of a certain type or, for another example, to discover what someone was trying to accomplish in a book or play, the purpose of the discussion is obvious: in the first instance, to add to collective and individual knowledge in a certain area; in the second, to arrive at some understanding and interpretation of a literary work. This approach is essentially the same as that used in attacking questions of fact. The only problem to be solved here is the gaining of control over a certain body of knowledge through collective action. To extend the examples cited, if a group of students is working together to find out what five different experts have to say about the goal of education, each student is likely to learn more about that subject than if he were to work alone. The pooling of ideas on a story (theme, plot, relationships of character, significance of setting) usually has the same result: more insight and better understanding on the part of everyone in the group in contrast to what could be accomplished by the same individuals working separately.

The case approach. Students very quickly see the advantages of shared views—and gain interpersonal experience at the same time—when the facts of a particular case are given to them and they are asked to find a solution. Although the construction of cases requires ingenuity (sometimes a complicated riddle serves as well), little or no advance preparation is required. One source of cases is to be found in the letters on personal problems written to popular syndicated columnists. A selected problem-letter case may then be presented to the members of one or more discussion groups; they study the case and then recommend what they consider to be desirable courses of action. In case studies generally, there is no search for the facts; they are provided. However, value judgments do come into play, certain choices have to be made, and sometimes solutions are called for.

The complete-problem approach. Full-scale studies of complex questions, especially those in the policy category, make the greatest demands on groups and on the individuals in them. Not only do they require skill in group attack on the problems themselves, but they also call for greater sophistication in the handling of the personal relationships among the people in the group. How to attack such problems and handle such relationships is the subject of the greater part of this chapter.[3]

Informal and formal discussion patterns

The common seating arrangement for a small informal group of five to ten persons is one in which all sit in a circle or around a table. The chairman is typically a participating member of the group; his duties and those of the other participants are described later in this chapter. If the discussion is taking place before an audience, the seating plan is modified so that no member of the group has his back to the listeners. Ordinarily, this requirement is met by having the members seated behind and along the sides of a rectangular or square table (see Fig. 11.1). This kind of structure—a small group participating in a discussion before an audience—is often called a *panel discussion*. A *forum discussion* takes place under similar circumstances, but the members of the audience may ask questions and are sometimes permitted to make short statements. A number of television shows are based on the forum format, i.e., a preliminary discussion followed by questions or comments from the studio audience as well as from individuals who telephone in. The *symposium* normally consists of a group of experts whose prepared and uninterrupted statements before an audience provide the take-off point for the general discussion which follows. Ordinarily the discussion takes the form of audience questions that are answered by the experts. The closer a discussion gets to the more formal and public situation, the more likely it is that a "moderator"

---

3. Any complete problem may of course be divided into segments, each of which may be an end in itself. For example, a group may use the so-called brainstorming technique to stimulate the rapid and uncritical generation of solutions. Advertising and public relations agencies use brainstorming to come up with a variety of promotional ideas in a short time.

Figure 11.1

will supersede the chairman. A moderator performs many of the same functions but ordinarily does not participate directly in the discussion except to keep it on track. He makes the initial introductions of the participants, gets the discussion started, provides the running summaries, and handles the audience participation which follows.

Advantages to the student

Since discussion can help us learn and help us solve problems of many kinds, and since we frequently participate in discussion, it follows that at least a part of one's personal future depends on his becoming acquainted with the theory of discussion and on his having an opportunity for some practice in putting it into effect. It has been amply demonstrated through the centuries that people can profit from study of relevant principles and from practice in communicating in speaker-audience relationships; it is no less true that "people can stand some coaching in the arts of talking together."[4] Hayakawa says, "It would seem that, in training students to become citizens in a democracy, practice in being members of committees of inquiry would be more suitable than debating, after the fashion of medieval schoolmen, for 'victory.'"[5] And, commenting on the importance of discussion in modern life, Phillips observes, "No educated person in a responsible position can avoid participation; for this reason, understanding of the small group is essential."[6]

---

4. Lee, p. 171.
5. Hayakawa, p. 253.
6. Phillips, p. 5.

The Task Environment

The task or problem environment[7] encompasses "all stimuli, obstacles, rewards, and 'things' except the behavior of other group members."[8] In other words, elements such as the following would be a part of the task-problem environment: any phase of learning activity aimed at gaining group control over a specific subject area, any exchange of information or reasoning in connection with the effort to solve a problem presented by the facts of "a case," any presentation of materials and ideas with the objective of arousing interest in a problem area, and any work on one or more phases of the study of a complete problem. For an example with a narrower focus, difficulties encountered by a group in finding and interpreting facts are task or problem difficulties; if finding facts is difficult because members of the group object to working together, that factor is a part of the interpersonal or people environment (discussed in the next section of this chapter).

The first step in "getting to know" a thing, a task, or a problem is analysis. When you bump into a chair in a dark room, you first recognize only that "something is in the way"; second, your senses of touch and proportion will support your subsequent definition of the object as a chair; third, a careful examination (still in the dark) will enable you tentatively to identify the chair as a Duncan Phyfe design; fourth, you will note its general location in the room in order not to bump into it again as you search for the light switch. What you do under these circumstances may be described as *an analysis of matter.*

Although man may not have been very bright in earlier periods of the Pleistocene epoch, he has for many eons since been going through the above analytical sequence, and by the time of the ancient Greeks, he was already identifying these steps in the analysis of physical material: (1) recognition of the existence of an unidentified mass, (2) definition of its essential qualities, (3) identification of its nonessential qualities, and (4) determination of its relation to other things and/or beings. He was also clever enough by that time to extend the analytical method in the world of physical science to that of the world of intellectual inquiry and speculation. He perceived that in the world of ideas, too, man (1) notes the existence of a problem, (2) tries to define it, (3) studies its qualities, and (4) studies its relationship to other entities and ideas of varying kinds. Like us, in other words, the citizen of ancient Athens asked these questions: Is there a problem? What is the exact problem? What are the solutions, and are they necessary, possible, etc.? What related considerations should be taken into account?[9]

The "scientific method" was rediscovered in the Renaissance, and with appropriate and continuing refinements, it is of course the way to solve problems susceptible to scientific methodology. In 1910, John Dewey published his adaptation of the scientific

---

7. The terminology in this chapter appears in (or is adapted from) Collins and Guetzkow; Shepherd; Berelson and Steiner; and Secord and Backman. The words "task" and "problem" are used interchangeably and sometimes together, as in "task-problem."

8. Collins and Guetzkow, p. 70.

9. For a discussion of early physical approaches to the analysis of matter as compared with a system for the analysis of problems, see Ray Nadeau, "Hermogenes on Stases," *Speech Monographs,* **31** (November 1964), pp. 369–373.

method to the world of ideas.[10] First, according to Dewey, man experiences a felt difficulty; then, sometimes in orderly succession and sometimes not, he analyzes the problem, looks for solutions, checks and compares them against criteria, and makes a choice of one or a combination of the best features of a number of them. Whether you follow the reflective thinking pattern of the ancients or Dewey, the five groups of questions below provide fundamental guidelines for the discussion of a specified part of a problem or of a problem in its entirety.

I. *How can we best phrase the felt-difficulty problem* in the form of an open-ended question that is neither too broad nor too narrow? (An open-ended question is one which does not restrict the number of choices to two. "Should trading stamps be abolished?" offers only two alternatives, and therefore it is not a good question for open-ended discussion. However, a question may also be so wide open that it, too, handicaps productive investigation. "How can the administration of justice be improved in the traffic courts of the city of Omaha?" is obviously specific enough to provide focus, at least for people living in that city, and open-ended enough to allow approach to the problem from a number of different angles.)

Do we agree on the meanings of the terms used in the question? Are there other associated terms which should be clarified at the outset, so that all of us will be using them in the same way? Should we now rephrase the question by incorporating in it terms and phrases which will add to its clarity?

II. *What is the extent of the problem?*
   A. What are the *facts*? Available statistics? Opinions of experts? Similar situations elsewhere? How are they being handled? How serious is the problem?
   B. What are the *causes* of the problem? How directly can they be traced? Other peripheral or contributing causes? What is the relative impact of each cause?
   C. What are the *criteria*, standards, or goals against which we should measure any solutions proposed?

III. *What can we do about the problem?* What are some of the possible approaches to solution? Should we modify the present system? How? Undertake some entirely new attacks on it? Such as?

IV. *How does each solution meet the criteria previously agreed upon?* Any other criteria applicable? Cost? Disadvantages? Chances of success? Possible effects of failure?

V. *Can we agree upon one of the solutions proposed,* either as it stands or as we may now amend it? Or upon some combination of solutions?

You have already participated in many an informal or formal discussion session and you will take part in many more. You know that few attempts to solve problems by "group process" follow the very regular and orderly series of steps outlined above.

---

10. John Dewey, *How We Think* (Boston: D. C. Heath, 1910), p. 72. It is almost impossible to pick up a modern treatment on problem analysis without running into Dewey. Typical examples: Phillips, pp. 10–13; Barnlund and Haiman, pp. 84. ff.

Nevertheless, through whatever labyrinth the group threads its way, the topics represented by the outlined steps are normally touched upon, and groups seriously interested in problem-solving through discussion characteristically try to follow an "orderly plan of attack." However, this does not mean that such a group moves mechanically and rigidly from point to point to point. In a study reported under the title "Idea Development in Small Discussion Groups,"[11] Scheidel and Crowell show that the interaction process of the small group is characterized by "the progressive modification of ideas":

> An idea is introduced spontaneously by one of the participants. Another in the group suggests an extension, a different emphasis, an example, a substitution, et cetera, or perhaps merely expresses his affirmation or rejection of the point. Others volunteer similarly. Thus there is an idea-in-the-making, a preliminary idea changed by the work of the group through oral modification until it represents more or less well their cumulative, developing, mutual point of view.[12]

In other words, instead of moving more or less steadily in lock-step progression toward whatever goal the group wishes to attain, the Scheidel-Crowell study points up the "spiraling" or "circular course" which a group follows in arriving at various levels of group consensus.[13]

Whether or not a group will "spiral" through all steps will depend on the "charge" or objective given to the "committee" when it is formed. For example, some discussion groups are asked only to *report on the facts*. In the early months of 1968, many citizens of Chicago were in active opposition to a plan for transporting specified numbers of elementary and secondary school pupils from district to district in order to achieve better proportions in the racial mix for each school. The Chicago Board of Education appointed a committee of its members to study the problem, and the chairman of this committee was later asked by a reporter, "Since you are about to make your report, what will be the recommendation of your committee?" Answer: "We won't be making any recommendation; ours is a fact-finding committee."

Committees are sometimes asked to go beyond the fact-finding stage but to conclude their deliberations with *an evaluation of the situation*. For instance, the Chicago fact-finding committee could have been given the added task of evaluating conditions from the standpoint of a collective judgment on the causes of certain parent attitudes which were discovered to exist and on an evaluation of the relative strength of opposition to the plan. Thus, without being required to go as far as searching for possible solutions to a problem, the members of a committee or discussion group may be asked (1) only to find the facts, or (2) to find the facts and attempt to interpret them, or (3) to interpret facts presented to them, or (4) to find the facts, interpret them, and try to evaluate the gravity of the situation, or (5) to evaluate the situation on the basis of

---

11. Thomas M. Scheidel and Laura Crowell, *Quarterly Journal of Speech*, **50** (April 1964), pp. 140–145.
12. *Ibid.*, p. 141. Reprinted by permission.
13. The Scheidel-Crowell study is based on an analytical system devised by the authors for rapid organization of logical "thought-units" along five dimensions. See pp. 141–142 in the article cited.

previously assembled facts and interpretations of them, or (6) to do any other necessary job, such as editing a report or rewriting a set of goals, etc.

A group working together to facilitate learning would normally undertake the second of the projects listed above. A group attacking a case problem would undertake all or part of the fifth project as preamble to suggesting a solution to the problem posed. When the group has full responsibility for coming up with a report of the facts, interpretation of them, evaluation of the situation, and prescriptions for solution of the problem, its members move through all the major steps on problem-solving. (It could happen—but seldom does—that such a committee would also be charged with putting a proposed plan into effect.) The point of the foregoing paragraphs is that a discussion group or committee tries to reach only those objectives, narrowly restrictive or broadly general, which are indicated in its "charge."

We see, then, that certain behaviors of members in a group will obviously stem from the particular task-problems or parts of task-problems posed to the group or voluntarily undertaken by it. We now move from a consideration of the task environment to a study of the interpersonal environment, or what goes on between and among the individual members of the group.

The Interpersonal Environment

"It is inevitable that when people engage in discussion they will respond not only to each other's *ideas*, but also to each other as *people*."[14] The fact that a group is engaged in examining facets of a problem does not suspend the "rules" of interpersonal relationships; it accentuates them. Instead of the public-address, single-speaker focus of attention, the focus in group process is constantly shifting from one person to another. Individuals invariably have an influence on the behavior of other individuals in any face-to-face situation, and this acceleration of person-with-person interaction greatly affects the efficiency and productivity of the group.

To put it another way, when you are asked to work with a group of students on some project, isn't one of your first concerns this question: "Who are the other members of the group?" Contributions made to a discussion by an individual obviously depend on how well he relates to the others in the group as well as on how much he knows about the problem at hand.

Over and above the obvious need for a spirit of interpersonal cooperation, other factors affecting interaction in discussion should be noted by anyone who aspires to understanding and skill in this problem-solving activity.

Leadership. The leadership in the small group, whether it is centered in one individual or shared by more than one or by all, is important to the reaching of agreements and often responsible for failures to do so. Studies[15] indicate that the democratic approach is more effective than dictatorial leadership in molding the group into a cohesive work-accomplishing unit. Too much permissiveness, on the other hand, leads to time-

---

14. Barnlund and Haiman, p. 186.
15. See Berelson and Steiner, pp. 325–360, and Collins and Goetzkow for summaries of findings in the field of group processes.

wasting and needless digressions. The leadership of the group must keep the goals of the discussion constantly in mind and should try, however diplomatically, to maintain "forward motion."

A good reason for the formal or informal sharing of leadership responsibility is the fact that small groups are faced with the need both for task-related ideas and for interpersonally related talents for generating understanding and harmony. These qualities are not too often found in one person.

Status. When no one member of the group possesses a special status which, for some reason, sets him apart from the other members of the group, communication between the members of the group may be nearly equal; each member is likely to initiate and receive roughly the same number of messages. If one or two individuals of higher status are members of the group, communications will normally take place between equals or from an individual of higher status to those in a lower rank. Those in the lower ranks less frequently initiate communications to those higher than themselves. Differences in status are of course due to such factors as age, education, popularity, position, reputation, etc. Higher-status individuals normally communicate more freely and more often than those individuals at a lower level.

Group cohesion. As the members of a group associate with one another "under conditions of equality," they progressively arrive at a sharing of norms and values and at a greater liking for one another. Experimental findings aside, it is common knowledge that individuals have a tendency to agree with people they like and that they believe those people to be in agreement with them. As any group grows in cohesiveness, interaction between individuals in it increases and leads to a still higher degree of cohesion. The number of interactions directed to any one member is usually in proportion to the number of interactions initiated by him; the higher the number of interactions initiated, the higher the number received.

Model of Factors Affecting Group Behavior

The performance or productivity of groups will naturally depend on the task and interpersonal environments within which they operate. The diagram in Fig. 11.2 is presented here as a model of the factors affecting group behavior and as the base for a summary of the interrelationships existing between both environments.

The two sets of obstacles, those stemming from the task environment and those arising from the interpersonal environment, serve to remind us of the two kinds of basic hurdles which must be surmounted in discussion by a group. Not only must the people involved overcome the difficulties inherent in the task of problem-solving itself, but they must also face the challenge of working with one another, a situation which encompasses interpersonal difficulties the individual does not encounter when he works alone.

As the members of the group analyze the problem, determine its extent, look for solution, etc., they may spend too much time talking about points agreed upon; if so, they are engaging in inefficient task-related behavior. Too rapid an agreement on points not thoroughly discussed could also be a behavior resulting from procedural or task-related problems (or it could be a behavior stemming from too great an eagerness

174 *Planning and participating in discussion*

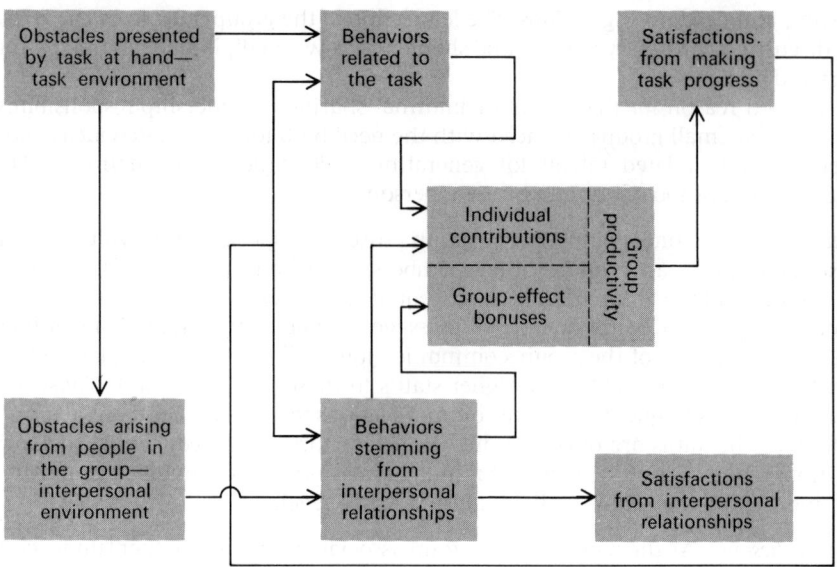

Fig. 11.2 From *A Social Psychology of Group Processes for Decision-Making* by Barry E. Collins and Harold Goetzkow (New York: Wiley, 1964), p. 81. Diagram reproduced and adapted by permission of the publisher.

of the members of the group to agree with one another for interpersonal reasons). Interpersonal obstacles, inherent in any grouping of individuals, arise from the need to adjust to one another and to the group as a whole in establishing a cooperative personal relationship. If two students in a group of five refuse to cooperate for personal reasons, that unfortunate circumstance is an undesirable behavior resulting from an "interpersonal obstacle." Similarly, the following interpersonal behaviors can arise from the fact that the members of the group, however well disposed, are working together on a discussion question: distractions of one participant due to personal interests in or aversions to another participant, defensive attitude due to an imagined or real slight, resentment of a chairman's tight control of the proceedings, etc.

In other words, "behaviors related to the task" are those activities in which the group members actually engage in their efforts to solve the problems posed by the task. You will note that task-related behavior is affected both by the task obstacles posed and by the extent to which the people in the group are disposed to work with one another. Five intelligent and congenial friends should be able to get a task done faster and more efficiently than five people who do not get along well together. Conversely, working at the task has a bearing on the ways in which the individuals interact personally; they may get into a time-wasting argument about some minor procedural matter. It is also obvious that some of the ways in which the individuals interact will have nothing at all to do with the task; this factor is represented in Fig. 11.2 by the path from the box for interpersonal-environment obstacles to that for "behaviors stemming from interpersonal relationships." If a boy is in a discussion group that also includes a girl he particularly likes, some of his behaviors (and some of hers) will have nothing to do with the task—except, possibly, to interfere with it.

The contributions of any one individual in the group will depend both on how efficiently he works at the task and on how well he relates to the other people in the group. He could have a very fine analytical mind but not be able to work well with others; his contribution would be limited by the degree to which the others would be willing to listen to him. On the other hand, people working together can often accomplish more than the same number of individuals working separately on the same problem; this phenomenon may be called "group-effect bonus." Group productivity is clearly the result of individual contributions plus the "bonus" or special advantages accruing from members working together, as suggested by the center box in the diagram.

Further, when people are attacking a discussion problem, the members of the group are going to gain a series of satisfactions from task-related achievements at various stages, and as they continue relating to one another as persons, they are also going to derive some satisfactions in the interpersonal area (e.g., a compliment that bolsters one's self-concept, some act of consideration that relieves tension, a smile of appreciation, a bit of humorous self-depreciation, etc.). Interpersonal rewards also come simply from associating with people we like and who like us, or from being recognized by the group for some special quality of leadership or special knowledge in an area.

Finally, in the course of the discussion process or during any group decision-making (including parliamentary deliberations), rewards or losses—satisfactions or dissatisfactions—continually feed back into the system at the behavioral level where they favorably or unfavorably affect both task and interpersonal behaviors. For example, you may not at first be much interested in the proceedings; then someone in the group compliments you in some way with the result that you begin doing your share in attacking the task-related problem.

Finesse in Discussion

Since a class in the basic course ordinarily consists of approximately 20 students, the number of committees or discussion groups which it can efficiently support is normally three or four (from five to seven students in each group). Let us assume, then, that we have in one group five students who have expressed an interest in applying the discussion process to such a problem as "What should be the role of American college students in determining policies of their institutions?"[16] What are the five students supposed to do with that question—or any other?

They must first choose one of their number who, as chairman for at least one class period, will assume responsibility for keeping the discussion "on the track." (The responsibility can be rotated, so that more than one member of the group gains experience in this particular role.) A second student can be designated by the group

---

16. Topic of the student discussion which appears in transcript form at the end of this chapter.

as a "reminder," whose job it is to help the leader keep the group's attention centered on the problem at hand.

Task finesse

The chairman obviously has "official" responsibility for getting the discussion started and for bringing it to a close. In the area of "task environment," he sets the stage by stating or restating the problem at hand and by defining or calling for definition of the major terms involved. Then, with the help and cooperation of the other members of the group, the chairman plays the role of "tour guide" at the same time that he participates as actively as he can as one of the deliberating members of the group. For instance, he tries to ensure that the problem is reasonably well described and evaluated (how serious, etc.?) before the discussion moves to the volunteering of solutions. Whatever solutions are suggested, he and the other "leaders" within the group then see to it that they are matched against the needs discovered in earlier phases and that other relevant criteria (such as cost, practicality, and the consequence of failure of any one solution) are not overlooked.

The emphasis throughout the discussion, for which about five hours of class time should be set aside, should be on *cooperation* and *compromise*. The leader does not attempt to "tell the others what to do or how to think...."[17] His function is to ask leading questions and make suggestions which will provide reinforcement and help guide the group through the steps described earlier in this chapter. Some examples follow.

> We have the question before us. Let's first talk about the meanings of the terms in it.
>
> Let's move on now to a review of what we know about this problem.
>
> Do we have enough information? Should each of us take on some responsibility for finding additional information before the next class?
>
> We now seem to have the facts at hand; are we ready to try determining the causes which brought this matter to a head?
>
> How do you feel about this?
>
> That sounds like a reasonable proposal, but are we ready for proposals at this time?
>
> Do you agree that we've talked about this topic long enough? If so, let's move on.
>
> Is this line of thought relevant?
>
> How does this look to you?
>
> Let's summarize what we have accomplished so far.
>
> The last time we met, we agreed that....
>
> Would you like to add a comment on that statement?
>
> Are these ideas directly related to the subject? Are we going in the right direction?

The comments and the questions above are not only diplomatically worded; they do not at any time *require* any one student to make a statement. (Asking a member of

---

17. Lee, p. 7.

the group if he has *something to add* is not asking him to volunteer a fact or state an opinion.) In a small group operation, the leader for the day should be *thinking along with the group* in addition to meeting his "regulatory responsibility." Furthermore, this responsibility for progress toward a goal should be regarded as belonging to the group as a whole; any one of the members, in addition to the leader and the "reminder," should feel free to call the attention of the group to omissions or errors of a logical or procedural nature. Just as the leader must not regard himself as a chairman who sits aloof from the proceedings, so each of the members should assume a share of the burden of the "collective leadership" implicit in the basic idea of *group* process.

Interpersonal finesse

It goes without saying that the generating of a satisfying and productive "interpersonal environment" is equally difficult to and somewhat more demanding than the handling of the ideational mechanics of the "task environment." The chairman and those accepting a share of responsibility for the success of the discussion should try to develop the habit of addressing remarks to *all* members of the group and of listening sympathetically to any and all ideas proposed. As all of us know, there is no faster way to stifle contributions of ideas and modifications of them than to have someone ever ready to place "tags" of approval or of disapproval on each idea as it is brought up. An alert chairman can diplomatically suggest or insist, if necessary, that immediate assessment of the value of an individual's contribution serves no useful purpose.

Point-blank contradiction is another pattern of behavior that the leadership in the group should discourage. The sane and sensible alternative is simply to ask an individual member to state his *reasons* for holding particular views. The question gives him an opportunity to elaborate and also gives others in the group chances to call attention to different evidence, other possible inferences from his evidence, and so on, as the "progressive modification of ideas" proceeds. Once the all-ideas-are-welcome atmosphere is solidly established, a shy or inhibited member of the group finds himself participating in the discussion without stopping in advance to worry about being rebuffed or contradicted.

If two members become enmeshed in an argument, another (not necessarily the leader) should ask each to give the reasons for his conviction on a particular point. Not too many direct clashes will develop if everyone has the attitude that there is *some truth* in any statement and that everyone has *some reason* for his belief. On the other hand, it often happens that an individual member may be reluctant to take a personal position or say what he personally thinks during some phase of the deliberations. In such instances, someone in the group could ask the reticent member what he has heard *others* (outside the group) say about the subject. (Anyone talks more freely about what he has heard "others" say.)

The above observations should not be taken to mean that, as a member of a committee or discussion group, you must accept everything that is said. Although belligerent controversy is out of place in a small group *working together* to solve a problem (and should be out of place elsewhere), you should not hesitate to question any "fact" or "opinion" about which you have reservations. However, it *is* possible to conduct such questioning without arousing resentment, and it *is* possible to have some healthy differences of opinion within the group so long as the members in it have an honest mutual regard for each other as human beings and as co-workers. The success of group process is based on the principle that *everyone* in the group should be encouraged to make contributions and that *everyone* has contributions worth making.

The biggest problems of our times are essentially world problems. War and peace is a world problem. Famine is a world problem. Population pressure is a world problem. Pollution of air and water is a world problem. Racial violence is a world problem.

Norman Cousins

Planning the Discussion Series

How many class periods should be set aside for discussions? The number will vary with the kind of discussion and with the objectives of this activity in any one course. For example, elements of interpersonal interaction in discussion can be rather quickly demonstrated in one class session devoted to small-group attack on "a case." A learning discussion, on the other hand, requires some advance preparation and, sometimes, more than one class session to bring it to a satisfying and satisfactory conclusion. The learning discussion demonstrates the advantages of pooling knowledge and perceptions; like the case discussion, it also helps students gain understanding of the interpersonal relationships involved.

The case discussion requires no preparation whatever; the learning discussion requires some; the attack on a complete problem requires out-of-class digging for facts and information and, unless the "charge" is strictly limited, a number of in-class sessions. The number of these sessions will naturally depend on the length of the periods; the usual allowance is from five to six periods up to an hour in length or four to five periods of longer duration. A common plan is one which calls for an "introduction to the question" period; it is held two or three class meetings before the actual discussions are scheduled to start. In this period, the class is divided into groups before or after the students have had an opportunity to express a preference for a particular topic or topics. The suitability of various questions is discussed by the instructor and/or the students. By the end of the class, each group will have made at least a tentative choice of a discussion question, will have made some progress toward a defining of terms, and will have decided who of their number is to be the chairman for the next active discussion on the nature and extent of the problem. The initial period, then, is primarily one in which some kind of organizational pattern is set up for the discussion periods to come.

The next two or three class periods are normally devoted to a study of discussion theory and practice. At the same time, the students are collecting materials and ideas for later use. We have already discussed the advisability of constructing an outline in preparation for a speaker-audience situation. Similarly, the writing of a discussion outline provides insurance that the materials collected constitute a reasonable base for profitable examination, that no important considerations will be overlooked, and that the steps in the process will follow each other in logical progression. The discussion for which each participating member has done the necessary "spadework" and for which each has prepared an outline guide normally moves along smoothly with a minimum of wasted time and erratic wandering from the subject. The outlines should not be regarded as straitjackets governing what is to be said; they are attempts to facilitate cooperative thinking through a listing of topics which, in the judgment of the participants, *may* be discussed. The efficiency of the small-group approach to problem solution depends in large part on anticipation of possible areas for discussion. (If the preparation for discussion consists of searching for answers to the fundamental questions posed in the section above on the task environment, a participant is generally ready to do his part as a productive member of the group.)

In the next period, the first devoted to active discussion of the problems decided on in the earlier meeting, each group of students convenes in a particular area of the room, and after introductory remarks by the chairman for the day, the discussion is centered on the nature and extent of the problem. This is primarily a contribution-of-facts session along with an examination of the scope of the problem. In this meeting, the "reminder" (also chosen or appointed in the organizational period) helps the chairman keep the comments "on the track" at the same time that he jots down a few observations on the techniques of discussion as he sees them in operation.

Approximately ten minutes before the end of the class, some kind of time-for-summaries signal is given by the instructor. Each chairman then presents a very brief summary of the progress made and the agreements reached. Thereupon, with the "reminder" taking over as chairman pro tem, the students quickly move on to self- and group-evaluations of successes and failures in the period of discussion just past. (A group of five students participating in five discussion periods can rotate the chairmanship and "reminder" responsibilities so that each has one opportunity in each role. In larger groups, the plan should include at least one such assignment for each student in the group.)

In the second discussion period, the chairman for the day begins with a quick review of the earlier discussion to set the stage for any additional comments on the nature of the problem and for an emphasis now on a determination of causes and, if there is time, criteria for solutions. The period then ends with the "reminder" of the day again serving as chairman for an evaluation of successes and failures in the group process.

The third period begins with a review of causes and of criteria against which to measure possible suggestions for solutions. Thereupon, the students move on to solutions to the problem under consideration. Each proposal is checked against criteria agreed upon, the objective of this particular meeting being to try to arrive at a consensus on a solution or combination of solutions. If the students are to prepare a written resolution or "statement of sentiment," a part of the time may be spent in phrasing the reasons for it and the specific action proposed.

If additional periods are allotted to this series, they are used (1) for finishing the discussion; (2) for writing or polishing the draft of the resolution; (3) for a full-scale review of the discussions, including final evaluations of individual and group performances; or (4) for any combination of the foregoing activities.

In the paragraph concerned with activities of the third period of discussion, reference was made to the *resolution* as a possible end product of the problem-solving small-group process. Resolutions are commonly adopted by organizations wanting *to go on record* on a particular issue; they are also prepared by informally organized groups wanting *to present a certain point of view* to a school board, park board, country board, city council, state commission, college or university board of trustees, a state governor, the President, or any individual or group having some policy-making responsibility. Since resolutions (similar to and often identical with *bills* presented to state and national legislative bodies) are an increasingly common mode for presenting and making known formal "statements of sentiment," knowing how to put one together is a very useful kind of expertise for students and citizens everywhere. You will see from the resolutions (pages 206–208) that the word *Whereas* (because) is used to introduce each of the major arguments cited as reasons for the actual resolution, which is introduced by the phrase *Therefore, be it resolved.* (Sometimes the prefatory reasons are omitted, and sometimes a resolution contains a succession of subsidiary sections, each beginning with *Be it further resolved.*) The degree of formality in language will depend on the body or public for which it is intended. However, the general structure is invariably (1) a reason or series of reasons leading into (2) a resolution taking a certain position, which frequently includes a specific solution recommended for the situation cited.

Evaluating Discussion

Various forms and check lists have been devised for evaluating the performance of individuals and groups engaged in small-group process.[18] Some students and instructors prefer the more flexible approach of free "discussion of the discussion." The latter is advocated here, partially because a less structured mode of self-criticism and evaluation is in keeping with the concept of total involvement of every member of the group in the leadership of it. The tone of the self-examination should again be "cooperative." The primary questions should be: (1) How efficiently did we work in the task environment to solve the problem or handle the "charge" given us? (2) How well did we work in the interpersonal environment to interact productively as human beings? These two questions should be the base for a short daily review on the subject of "let's look at how we worked together." They can also serve as broad questions for a final evaluation after the entire discussion of several days has been finished.

Subordinate evaluative questions will readily occur to the students reading this chapter and participating in active discussion. Those below provide typical guidelines for evaluation and may, in turn, suggest related lines of inquiry.

On task environment

Was the problem clearly stated, defined, understood?

Did *all* members of the group provide information on various aspects of the problem? Enough information to guarantee a good grasp of the subject by the group? Were sources adequately identified? Were cited authorities automatically accepted as qualified? Or was their competence questioned? Did the evidence pre-

---

18. Appendix B, pp. 387–406, in Barnlund and Haiman is devoted entirely to "evaluating discussion" and, so far as this writer knows, is the best single source on this subject.

sented support the inferences drawn by individuals? By the group? Was there any "jumping to conclusions"? If so, was the "jumping" detected?

Were causal relationships properly established? Reasonably defended? Were all possible causes explored? Was the reasoning, here and elsewhere in the course of the discussion, entirely logical? Were there any errors in the reasoning processes of individuals? Of the group? Were individuals and the group able to avoid common fallacies (such as those described in Chapter 3)?

Were criteria for a solution related directly to the needs evident in the causes? Were any essential criteria omitted?

Were solutions of a routine and obvious nature? Did any really creative and innovative thinking take place? Were solutions checked against the criteria agreed upon? Were any additional criteria considered (e.g., cost) in relation to the solution chosen? Should they have been? If a formal resolution was framed, was it in acceptable form?[19] Were ideas clearly stated?

In general, did the group operate efficiently in the problem-solving effort? Did it become bogged down at any point? Waste time on matters of no consequence? Move too fast and superficially at any point? Was adequate time given to thorough analysis of the problem? How systematic was the approach? Were summaries and transitions handled in such a way as to keep everyone informed on progress and on the next task at hand? Were "all the bases touched"?

On interpersonal environment

Was the general atmosphere of the discussion friendly and pleasant? Were the individuals in the group considerate, courteous, tactful? Was there any hostility—or did any develop—between individuals in the group? Between subgroups? What was the apparent reason or reasons for the existence or development of antagonism? What, if anything, was done to "smooth feathers"? Was the atmosphere at the end of the discussion the same as at the beginning of it? Worse? Better? Why?

Was any member unduly talkative? Was anything done to bring his excessive zeal under control? By the chairman or by one of the members? How well was the situation handled? Was any member reluctant to speak? Was he given encouragement to contribute facts or ideas? How? Did he respond?

Was any member able to win over others in the group after receiving no initial support for an idea? How did he accomplish the change in attitudes? Was there a general willingness on the part of members to compromise, especially on minor issues? If a minority of two or three was unable to agree with the majority on either the gravity of the problem or a plan to solve it, was it possible to have this "split" without unfavorable personal reactions?

Did the group as a whole exercise leadership functions? Or did it depend excessively on the chairman for guidance, summations, transitions, etc.? Was mutual

---

19. Any of the examples of resolutions at the end of this chapter could have been prepared by three or four students; two or three others from the same committee could have prepared a "minority resolution."

respect an obvious characteristic of the session(s)? If not, why not? Did the group members feel that participating in discussion contributed to their understanding of "man"? In what ways?

. . . .

Demonstration options

1. Check the transcript of the model discussion that appears later in this chapter in order to find any failure to handle the task-problem in an adequate way. Use the five general questions cited in the section on the task environment as your check list. Report your finding to the class.
2. Find in some novel or short story an incident in which one character, by making a thoughtless or snide remark, causes another to feel insecure or unhappy. Read the passage to the class and comment on it.
3. Find an incident from the same kinds of sources in which one person sincerely compliments another with good results—at least in immediate reaction. Read to the class and comment.
4. Check the discussion transcript in this chapter for evidence of interpersonal consideration or the lack of it. Read and comment.

Discussion options

1. Take part in a "learning discussion" with four or more other students; talk about the theory of discussion or about some segment of that theory (e.g., the interpersonal environment). Objectives are to become better acquainted with the subject and to thresh out any hard-to-understand details. The group can engage in this discussion for the benefit of the class as a whole.
2. Join four other students in a symposium in which the five of you (a moderator and four "experts") undertake to present four short statements on four different parts of this chapter—or on four different parts of any body of subject matter—for the benefit of the members of the class. The presentations can be followed by questions from the audience.
3. Engage in a "learning discussion" with four or more other students, exchanging ideas and views on a particular book or story (fiction) that all of you have read. The objective is a better understanding of general theme, specific plot, setting, characters, etc.
4. Engage in a "learning discussion" with or more other students, exchanging ideas and views on a limited collection of nonfiction books or articles dealing with the same central subject. The primary objective is to become well informed on that subject.
5. Participate in a "case discussion" with four or more other students. Discuss the facts presented to you, and try to arrive at some conclusion on what ought to be done. As suggested earlier in the chapter, a newspaper letter to the editor or to a columnist specializing in advice can be the "problem." In addition, the newspapers and news magazines often carry the report of someone's going to the

courts to protect his civil liberties under the Constitution; a discussion on how the court should rule can easily follow a statement of the facts as reported by the news media.[20] A case like that of the ten people marooned on a desert island (below) is relatively easy to construct through the substitution of different circumstances; one variation is to have the survivors of a plane crash deciding what supplies of those available to them should be taken along in the effort to get out of the middle of the Sahara Desert.

The Case of the Five Saved and Five Doomed:[21] The following people are on a desert island, and only five of the ten can be saved. A helicopter will be arriving to take five individuals to safety. Discuss this problem within your group, and come to a collective decision on the five who should be saved.

Army captain	Well-known nuclear scientist
Minister, rabbi, or priest	Small boy
Society matron	Governor of your state
Miss America (current)	High school principal
All-American football player	You

6. Organize or join a group to discuss any open-ended question (see list of typical questions below) along lines suggested in this chapter. (If members of the class wish to work in "committee" groups, the discussion may deal with any open-ended question within the limits of concern with urban affairs, interior affairs, foreign policy, armed services, etc.)
7. If discussion groups in the class wish to carry their deliberations through to the preparation of a written "statement of sentiment," called a *resolution*, they may follow the examples of resolutions which appear at the end of this chapter.

Listening options

1. Attend any special or regularly scheduled group-process meeting to which you can gain admittance as "an interested citizen." Meetings such as these would be appropriate: school boards, city councils, town meetings, township boards, county board, commission hearings, governmental legislative sessions at the state or national level, and public meetings of almost any kind on social, political, or economic problems. The purpose of this option is to encourage students to observe and report on "democracy in action."

   a. Use the section on "evaluating discussion" in this chapter as the base for preparing a 5–6 minute informal oral report on your observations of "democracy in action." Concentrate on either the problem environment or the interpersonal environment.

---

20. The facts from other legal cases can be cited from collections of case studies in such works as Harry. P. Kerr's *Opinion and Evidence* (New York: Harcourt, Brace and World, 1962). Similarly, books on interviewing and business management frequently cite cases which can be used as bases for discussion.
21. Contributed by Professor William B. Cash, Jr., Eastern Illinois University, Charleston, Illinois. Original source unknown.

b. Following the guidelines in (a), prepare a 5—6 minute manuscript report for reading to the class or for turning in to your instructor in partial fulfillment of the requirements of the course.
2. Use the section on "evaluating discussion" as the base for preparing a 5—6 minute oral or written report on either the problem environment or the interpersonal environment as you saw it during a discussion in which you participated.
3. Prepare a report as indicated in (b), drawing on a discussion which you observed.

. . . .

Typical Open-ended Discussion Questions[22]

What are the prospects for a world of permanent order and peace?

What are the major causes of world hunger? What should we do about them?

What is Africa's role in the increasingly interdependent and universal civilization?

What are the problems and prospects of the Alliance for Progress?

How can we cope with the gold drain?

What impact does dissent in America have on the formation of propaganda in other countries?

To what extent does propaganda from other countries influence dissent in America?

What are the trends in the world of religious beliefs and ideas?

What is the future of graduate education in the United States?

Why has the United States ratified only one of the nine Human Rights Conventions proposed by the United Nations?

What are the goals, problems, and dynamics of the Atlantic Community?

What should be our approach to combating dental disease in children?

Why would it not be possible to bring *all* international struggles before the United Nations?

What are the overall causes of urban decay? Which problems should be met now and in what order? Who *can* and who *should* take the lead and bear the financial burden?

Whence will come the food we need both now and in the future?

What are the prospects for a Latin American Common Market?

What can be done to win the "war of ideas" in the struggle against Communism?

What are the roles of the individual, industry, and the government in the control and eventual elimination of air pollution?

What can be done to provide better nursing care for the aged?

---

22. Adapted primarily from press releases of the Radio-TV Georgetown University Forum.

In this age of science, are the humanities being forgotten?
What can be done to bring stability and peace to the Middle East?
What do we owe the developing nations?
Collective bargaining: Is it dead?
Why must we have inflation? What are its advantages? Disadvantages?
What is India's role in Asia?
Whose problem is that of the hard-core unemployed? How can it be solved?
How can American unions help labor abroad?
What is the extent of the population problem? Can it be solved?
What is the impact of motion pictures on the generation of ideas?
How can we eliminate race and income as bars to higher learning in [your state]?
What should be the role of students in college or university policy formation?
To what extent is the study of foreign languages important to the student of today?
How can we encourage the appointment of instructors and professors from "minority" races?
How can we encourage the appointment of women as instructors and professors?
Who should we approach and handle the problem of welfare payments?
Is every able-bodied citizen entitled to government guarantee of employment?
How can we control unauthorized electronic surveillance and monitoring of private oral conversations?
Is a college education worth the time, trouble, and expense?
Now that we have won the race to the moon, how much of the national effort should continue to be channeled into space exploration?
What should college and university students do about the drug problem?
Does talent invariably have a chance to exhibit itself in our society?
Is democracy endangered by open discussion of such ideologies as communism, socialism, facism, etc.?
Should we give up some of our national sovereignty in the interests of coordinated world effort to achieve a better world?

Example of Learning Discussion Guide[23]

The Old Man and the Sea by Ernest Hemingway
    I. *Introduction* by the chairman.
        A. Brief summary of the book.
        B. What will the group touch upon (plot, characters, theme, setting, etc.)?

---

23. Contributed by David R. Harris, at the time (1969–1970) a Purdue University student.

C. What does our group hope to learn through our discussion?
   1. What is the book about?
   2. How can we apply this book to our lives?
II. What is involved in the *plot*?
   A. What is the significance of the big fish and the long fight to catch him?
   B. What is the significance of the sharks?
   C. What is the significance of the bird landing on the boat?
   D. Is there any significance in the fact that the man was certain he would catch a big fish on the eighy-fifth day?
III. What part do the *characters* play in the story?
   A. What is the relationship of the boy and the old man?
   B. What type of person is the old man? The boy?
   C. What type of relationship develops between the old man and the fish?
IV. What part does the *setting* play in the story?
   A. Why has Hemingway picked the sea for the story?
   B. Why does he give few clues to the exact location of the setting?
   C. What part does the village play in the story? The rundown shack?
V. What is the *theme* of the story? And why do you feel this way?
   A. Why has Hemingway chosen this theme?
   B. Do you agree with this theme?
VI. What influence does the story have on our lives?
   A. How can we identify with the old man, the boy, or the fish?
   B. What message is Hemingway trying to impress on us? Do you agree with this message?
   C. What do you think were his reasons for writing this book?
   D. Did this book have any bearing on your way of thinking? If so, how?
VII. *Conclusion:* Summary of what has been said in the discussion.

Example of Problem-Solving Discussion Guide[24]

Question: How can we deal with the problems of civil disorders in the United States?

I. *Definition and limitations*: Do we agree on the meanings of the terms used in the question?
   A. How shall we define the terms in the question?
      1. How shall we define *we*?
      2. How shall be define *deal*?
      3. How shall we define *civil disorders*?
      4. How shall we define *problems*?
      5. Are there other terms which should be defined?
      6. Are there any terms implied by the question which should be defined?
      7. Would rephrasing of the question add to its clarity?

---

24. Contributed by Marilyn Mathias, Instructor at Wisconsin State University (La Crosse); originally written under supervision of Professor Henry C. Vander Heyden, Bradley University, Peoria, Illinois.

B. What limitations should be considered?
  1. Should we consider civil disorders which grow out of civil disobedience?
  2. Should we consider civil disorders which are brought on by racial tensions?
  3. Should we consider only those civil disorders occurring in our major cities?
  4. Should we consider those civil disorders which require local police involvement.
  5. Should we consider those civil disorders which require the involvement of the National Guard?
  6. What other limitations should be agreed upon?

II. *Analysis*: What is the extent of the problem?
  A. What are the facts of the situation?
    1. What has been the history of civil disorders in the United States?
    2. What is the current status of civil disorders in the United States?
    3. Why is dealing with civil disorders considered important now?
      a. What were the conclusions and recommendations of the President's riots commission?
      b. What have been the conclusions and recommendations of other commissions investigating civil disorders?
      c. What impact have the statements of the presidential candidates and other political figures made on investigations of civil disorders?
  B. What are the underlying causes of civil disorders?
    1. Is racial unrest a cause of civil disorders?
    2. Are the problems of our cities causes of civil disorders?
    3. What is the role of the protest movement in civil disorders?
    4. Is distrust of government and police officials a cause of civil disorders?
    5. Do participants in civil disorders feel that they obtain results from civil disorders?
    6. What effect does nationwide television, radio, and press coverage have on civil disorders?
  C. What standards or criteria must be met by a solution to deal with the problems of civil disorders in the United States?
    1. Should the solution be in the best interest of all concerned?
    2. Should the solution improve relationships between the races?
    3. Should the solution improve the conditions of life in our cities' ghetto areas?
    4. Should the solution improve relationships between citizens and authorities?
    5. If the solution is to include the initiation of programs, should the following be considered as criteria?
      a. Cost
      b. Feasibility
      c. Efficiency
    6. Should the solution protect the rights of the individual?
    7. What other criteria should be met by the solution?

III. *Possible solutions:* What can we do about the problems of civil disorders in the United States?

A. Should municipal, state, and/or federal government take action to eliminate those elements in society which lead to civil disorders?
   1. Should educational opportunities be improved and equalized for ghetto-dwellers?
   2. Should employment practices and opportunities be improved and equalized for ghetto-dwellers?
   3. Should housing be improved for urban ghetto-dwellers?
   4. Should welfare programs be reevaluated and improved?
   5. Should laws be made more stringent concerning riot and agitation conspiracies?
   6. Should police-community relations be improved?
B. What can be done by institutions and organizations other than those provided for by local, state, or federal government?
C. What can be done by the mass communications media?
D. What should be done concerning the recommendations of commissions which investigate the causes of civil disorders?
E. Should the problems of civil disorders be dealt with morally and socially as well as legally?
F. What other solutions should be considered?

IV. *Appraisal of proposed solutions*: How does each solution meet the criteria previously agreed upon?
   A. Do all of the solutions meet the criteria agreed upon?
   B. Does one solution seem to have particular merit?
   C. What are the advantages and disadvantages of the solutions?
   D. What are the relative merits of the solutions?

V. *Choice of solution*: Can we agree upon one of the solutions proposed, either as it stands or as we may now amend it?
   A. What can be done to test the hypothesis or solution concluded to be the best?
   B. What practice situation can be devised to test the hypothesis concluded to be the best?
   C. On policy, what steps would need to be taken to put the hypothesis or solution into operation?
   D. What steps are needed to test theory and conduct scientific observation?
   E. How can we get backing for our program?

Model Student Discussion

The transcript below (slightly edited) was made from the taped recording of a discussion which took place at Purdue University under the direction of John Pacilio, Jr., a Purdue University doctoral candidate at the time, now Assistant Professor at the University of Arizona. The students involved were from Indiana: Stephen (Steve) P. Schnautz, Evansville, who acted as chairman of the group; Paul D. Brink, Indianapolis; William (Bill) G. Nigh, Greenfield; Geoffrey (Jeff) A. Emerson, West Lafayette; and Dale R. Pitzer, Veedersburg. The "perfect" discussion does not exist, but this transcript does provide an abbreviated model of small-group process.

The comments in the right column are restricted to the task environment. The text of the discussion itself offers some evidence of interaction in the interpersonal environment. (The latter is, of course, difficult to reconstruct from a script.)

Transcript

Steve: A statement printed this summer in the Plainville, Kansas, evening paper read: "The school board is composed of seven men elected to resent you in school affairs."—obviously a misprint. The statement does reflect an attitude apparently held by many students on American college campuses across the nation today, the feeling that administrators and, in some cases, faculty members are mistreating them, putting them in a situation where they have no real, formal role in determining the educational process. They're being denied their rights and privileges. It is for that reason that we have gathered together to discuss the question, "What should be the role of American college students in determining the policies of their institutions?" The members of our panel are myself, Steve Schnautz, a junior, political science.

Paul: Paul Brink, a senior, mechanical engineering.

Bill: Bill Nigh, a freshman, political science.

Jeff: Jeff Emerson, a freshman, biophysics.

Dale: Dale Pitzer, a junior, speech education.

Steve: In an earlier meeting, we defined "role" to mean "a position of power and/or influence," and we defined "policies" to mean "rules and regulations governing student behavior." Incorporating these definitions in the question, it reads: "What should be the position of power and/or influence held by American students in determining rules and regula-

Commentary

The function of the opening statement, here as in a talk or formal speech, is to set the scene for the ensuing discussion by introducing the question in an interesting way.

Since this particular discussion was, in effect, a kind of "radio program," each student introduced himself. This is good standard practice, unless the members of the group know each other very well.

I. *Phrasing of the problem*

Problems of definition and clarification had been taken care of prior to this meeting. Note that the definitions agreed upon are worked into a lengthened and more exact version of the original question.

Transcript	Commentary
tions governing student behavior at their institutions?"	
(All agree.)	
Steve: Are there, then, any indications of a problem with respect to the present position of student power or to student influence in institutional policy-making? In essence, how does the problem show itself?	II. *Extent of the problem* With agreement from all on the new wording of the question, *the chairman provides an opening for contributions on the extent of the problem.*
Jeff: I think the first indication, Steve, is the student demonstrations which have erupted throughout the country, such as the Berkeley "free speech" riot of October 1964.	A. *What are the facts?* *All four* of the participants provide specific information on demonstrations indicative of student protests.
Paul: Right. Or, for example, the demonstrations at Ohio State supporting the service employees in October of this year.	
Dale: Or at City College of New York where there were protests over the buildings.	
Bill: And even the Vietnam demonstrations like those at Harvard, Columbia, Purdue, Oberlin, and Kent State.	
Jeff: But aren't these Vietnam demonstrations more or less a matter of demonstrating against a national issue rather than the college issue?	Jeff suggests that the Vietnam demonstrations do not really have anything to do with the problem of institutional policy. Bill *agrees* but adds that such demonstrations may, under certain circumstances, be relevant.
Bill: Well, this is right, Jeff, but they also have the objective of demonstrating against certain institutional policies which allow recruiting by armed service groups and industries supporting the war.	
Paul: Right. I agree with Bill.	
Steve: OK, we've shown some dramatic and obvious indications of student unrest and desire to change institutional policy. Are there other significant manifestations of a problem which are not quite so obvious?	The chairman suggests (and this suggestion could have been made by anyone) that attention should also be given to some of the less dramatic evidences of student unrest. Advance preparation again enables every participant to bring up examples.

Transcript

Paul: There seems to be a lot of more "quiet" student reform activities, Steve. Examples are possible "Bills of Rights" that are being talked about in many universities today.

Bill: Or election reform candidates, such as at Iowa—

Paul: —Iowa University.

Dale: And we also find the development of this student-run instructor-and-course-evaluation program.

Bill: Like those at Harvard and Purdue.

Jeff: Or the expansion of student-government activities, for example. Our Bruce Cordingly, student body Vice President at Purdue University, told the members of the Student Senate of their changing role when he pointed out that several years ago student government had been concerned 75 percent with problems outside the area of student government. Today the situation is just reversed.

Paul: Today students are much more involved with important questions than with the old line of parties and dances that take so much time.

(All agree.)

Dale: We might also look at the reform activities of the Associated Student Government and the National Student Association organizations.

Bill: Yes, and also at the underground newspapers that have been sponsored by many student groups throughout the nation.

Jeff: But aren't there also underground newspapers sponsored by nonstudents, Bill?

Commentary

Continuing the search for facts, Jeff introduces the idea of nonstudent support, and the chairman follows up shortly by asking for comment on other areas of nonstudent interest.

Transcript

Bill: Yes.

Steve: Are there other areas in which nonstudents are also showing interest in the problem?

Paul: Yes, very much so, Steve. For example, university professors seem to be quite involved here. In a statement on the academic freedom of students, the American Association of University Professors has taken the following position: "Free inquiry and free expression are essential attributes of the community of scholars. As members of that community, students should be encouraged to develop the capacity for critical judgment and to engage in a sustained and independent search for the truth."

Bill: Also, Paul, the American Civil Liberties Union has done extensive work in this area. For example, in November 1961 a pamphlet was published concerning student rights and student government.

Steve: All right then, we've shown that there are a lot of examples, but does this indicate that the problem is widespread or pretty well localized?

Jeff: I think the problem is widespread, Steve, at least in terms of area. *U.S. News and World Report* of November 13, 1967, stated that incidents flared at campuses large and small in every region of the country.

Dale: We might also look at this problem in an aspect of time, such as was stated by Dr. James F. Ross, Chairman of the Department of Philosophy at the University of Pennsylvania. He said, "In the beginning universities in Paris, about 1200 students formed a body and demanded their rights."

Commentary

Paul has done his "homework." He is ready to quote directly from an AAUP statement.

Bill has time to note a pamphlet published by the American Civil Liberties Union before the chairman brings the citation of examples to a halt (prematurely?) by asking another question on whether or not the problem is widespread.

Transcript

Bill: The *New York Times Magazine* recently had an article which included this statement: "The stormiest era in the history of American colleges was from 1880 to 1895 when strikes, demonstrations, violence, and resignations erupted across the nation." I think from this, along with our other points, that it is definitely a widespread problem.

Paul: No question about that.

(All agree.)

Steve: OK, then, we've shown that the problem shows itself in three basic areas, two of which are student-directed. One is the obvious publicity-grabbing, headline-grabbing idea of riots and demonstrations. A second, less obvious but possibly more persuasive to the university communities at large, is the idea of students being involved in such things as bills of rights, increasing student-government activity outside student government per se, Associated Student Government and National Student Association reform movements. The problem is also seen in a third group outside the students themselves; in this third group would be, in many cases, faculty, as the *AAUP Bulletin* has indicated, or the American Civil Liberties Union and other pressure groups like that throughout the country. We've also shown that the problem is not isolated, but is, rather, a widespread problem both in terms of time—since the late nineteenth century in our own country—and in terms of space—reaching from coast to coast and from northern border to southern border.

(All agree.)

Steve: It would seem, then, that if the problem exists in the areas we have

Commentary

B. *What are the causes?*

At this point, *the chairman summarizes what has been said about factual manifestations of the problem in three areas.* When all agree on his summary of the evidence of unrest, the group is ready to go on to the "why" of unrest, an examination of the causes of student protest.

Interjection of the goal at this point is intended to keep attention focused on the

Transcript

pointed out, our purpose might be to establish an appropriate student policy-making role.

Jeff: I think that would be a good goal.

Dale: Yes, that would be.

Steve: OK, with this goal in mind, let's begin to examine the reasons *why* students are dissatisfied with their present policy-making position. What are some of these reasons?

Jeff: I think one, Steve, is that students perceive that student-government organizations and other student activities are more or less what they call "Mickey Mouse" organizations.

Bill: Insignificant or insufficient.

Paul: Students feel that they only have the power of "recommendation" on what you would call important issues.

Dale: And I also think that sometimes the students are more or less after the fact unless—what I mean is that they really don't know about these issues until after they have already been determined.

Jeff: For example, at Purdue University, the Faculty Senate has almost passed a bill prohibiting student parking on campus before the students are even aware of the possibility of such a bill being passed.

Bill: I think from all of this that students seem to feel like second-class citizens.

Jeff: Well, don't you think the reason they feel they are second-class citizens is because *they are*. I mean, legally students are minors so that, under society, they are protected as second-class citizens.

Commentary

primary discussion question. (Many experts would consider the goal statement premature at this juncture. It assumes that students should have more to say about policy. Dissatisfaction with policy is, of course, not ipso facto evidence that those affected should automatically have something to say about what it should be.)

The *search for causes* moves along, with all of the students engaged in a free exchange of ideas on various possibilities. There is considerable speculation here, and we should expect it because the group is drawing inferences from the evidence previously presented. As students, they are also qualified to say what they personally "feel" are some of the causes. However, the general emphasis throughout a discussion should be on the "facts" and on inferences which appear to follow validly from them. "Opinions" should be scrutinized with extreme care.

The idea that students are restless because they are minors and because they are, as a consequence (?), treated in a certain way is not, of course, "the whole problem."

Transcript

Dale: Right. I think that's the whole problem, Bill.

Bill: Because they are under the age of 21 and things of this nature.

(All agree.)

Steve: Are there other reasons why students feel that they are being mistreated, other than the below-legal-age point?

Dale: Well, I think that sometimes a student, in the present role that he has, seems to be at odds with the educational objectives which he perceives.

Jeff: How do students perceive their educational objectives?

Paul: It seems to me that maybe you might say that the educational objectives are to train students to fit into a democratic society.

Jeff: The National Student Association is an example of this movement to determine student powers. It is designed to gain for students their full rights as citizens, their rights to democratically control their nonacademic lives. I think that this is showing that the National Student Association believes that students should be prepared to fit into a democratic society.

(All agree.)

Bill: —and is learning by doing this type of operation.

Steve: Is this attitude confined to the students themselves, or is there support for it from groups outside student groups?

Paul: As I showed before in the statement by the AAUP, there is talk here of a community of scholars, which definitely

Commentary

Note how the chairman promptly attempts to counteract this simplistic approach with a question which invites discussion of "other reasons."

Jeff is not the chairman, but he very properly uses Dale's remark as the stimulus for an open question addressed to the others. This is a common and valuable technique which can be used for this purpose by any member of a group. Note its continuing occurrence as this discussion progresses.

Transcript

implies a democratic society in the University, I think.

Jeff: Right. Also, Nicholas Ginnet in his Ph.D. thesis on student freedom, which was later published in *School and Society* magazine, stated that the power structure, faculty and administration, doesn't disagree that students should have more freedom. I think it can be concluded that not only do students perceive their educational objectives as preparation for living in a democratic society, but the faculty and administration tend to agree with them.

Bill: Theoretically.

Jeff: Well, yes, at least theoretically.

Steve: Well, you raise an interesting point. If they agree in theory, why don't the administrators give the students more policy-making power? Why doesn't it carry over to practical implementation?

Dale: It seems as if the administration feels that it is threatened in some way.

Bill: Yes, they can't—because of this threat, they can't delegate responsibility to the students.

Jeff: Don't you think the threat perhaps arises from the pressures placed on them by the fact that students are minors and are protected by society?

Bill: Yes, but I also think that it is because of the pressure from outside society, such as when Clark Kerr was fired in California.

Jeff: So administrators fear for their jobs, more or less, or feel the threat to themselves as individuals.

Paul: The administrators perceive some kind of responsibility they cannot dele-

Commentary

A qualification readily accepted by Jeff. Discussion participants should stand ready to qualify (and accept qualifying) statements made by others in the group. The careful interjection of acceptable modifiers and qualifications is a part of the "spiral" road to consensus.

Transcript

gate to act in place of the parents when students are still minors.

Jeff: Isn't this what we call in loco parentis or acting in place of the parent?

All: Yes, definitely so.

Jeff: And it's a responsibility felt by the administration.

(All agree.)

Steve: OK, then, apparently the largest cause of the problem, as we defined it, is that students perceive a disparity between the goals of their education as students see it and as faculty and administrators see it on a theoretical level. The practical implementation of those educational goals is hindered by the concept of in loco parentis, which has much to do with preventing students from holding an effective policy-making role.

All: Right, Steve.

Paul: You can't train for a democratic society and live in an environment of in loco parentis. The two just don't—

Bill: Right, Paul. The students are learning something in the classroom that's completely different from what they're actually practicing.

Steve: OK, then, with the problem defined and the basic cause for it analyzed, can we look for criteria which would allow us to develop a solution to alleviate the problem?

Dale: The one criterion I think we should use as a guide to our solution is that of relieving the threat which the administration feels that they have upon them.

Jeff: And if this threat arises from the doctrine of in loco parentis, maybe we should try to get rid of this doctrine.

Commentary

The chairman brings the discussion of causes to a close with an emphasis on the primary cause (differences on educational goals) of the problem and on a secondary cause (concept of in loco parentis). Paul and Bill throw in gratuitous comments on that concept before Steve asks the group to move on to *criteria for solution*.

C. *What are the criteria for solution?*

Since one of the major causes is thought to be the concept of in loco parentis, any solution should somehow be aimed at it. Dale and the others agree on this point.

Transcript

Paul: Right, just do away with in loco parentis.

Bill: —try to attack this responsibility and threat in some way.

Dale: Well, then, could we state as our first criterion that it would be to relieve administrators of the in loco parentis responsibility and threat?

All: Yes. Good idea. Fine. (etc.)

Paul: We talked also about student policy-making roles and educational goals. I think a criterion also should be that we should try to align these two.

Jeff: This alignment is needed if, as we have stated, there is a disparity between the educational objectives and student policy-making roles.

Steve: Then let's look for a possible solution or a group of solutions which would meet these criteria and, in turn, alleviate the problem that we outlined.

Paul: One solution that I think is very feasible, Steve, is to try to set up a university structure that is patterned after the national government.

Dale: You mean by this, Paul, that there would be three branches within the university?

Paul: Right—legislative, judicial, and executive.

Jeff: I can see, Paul, that the executive branch would probably be the administration, and the legislative branch would probably be the student senate or faculty senate, but who would be in the judicial branch?

Paul: A fairly equitable approach to this, I think, Jeff, might be to set it up

Commentary

The other cause, *differences on educational goals*, is somewhat garbled here, but the members of the group do agree that any solution should have as an aim an attack on the disparity between "educational objectives" and "student policy-making roles."

III. *Solution(s)*

After the disposition of the business of setting up *two* criteria to attack the two causes discerned, Steve now moves quickly to the proposal of solutions. Paul then proposes a governmental structure analogous to that of the U.S. system of three branches. The pros and cons of this plan are discussed at some length.

Transcript

with equal representation from students, faculty, and administration.

Dale: Yes, but is this feasible—to consider the students equal with the faculty and administration?

Jeff: I don't really think that the faculty or administration would ever accept the students as equals simply because, as I mentioned before, legally they are not.

Dale: Right. The students are considered minors so, therefore, it just doesn't sound feasible.

Bill: Well, maybe we could arrange it this way: Have some type of an apportionment, maybe have 30 percent student involvement and 70 percent faculty/administration involvement.

Dale: Yes, Bill, but speaking of the educational objectives that we were talking of earlier in connection with the democratic society, this apportionment arrangement would not have the equality which we would assume in a democratic society.

Bill: A good point, Dale.

Jeff: Right. The students would—it is definitely not democratic living if the students have only 30 percent of the vote.

(All agree.)

Jeff: Well, perhaps what we should turn to, then, is this doctrine of in loco parentis. If this place—if this is the reason that the faculty and the administration won't accept the students as equals, namely, because they feel that this doctrine places a responsibility upon them, perhaps we could go about getting rid of this doctrine.

Transcript

Bill: Yes, kind of attacking the roots of the problem, then.

Paul: OK, if we are going to try to get away with it, maybe the first step would be to change the laws.

Bill: Yes, but what do you mean? For instance?

Paul: Well, for example, change the age of majority, the voting age, to 18 instead of 21.

Dale: Well, this might change the legal aspect, but what will it do with the morals? I mean, we still have other areas within the in loco parentis idea which we need to consider.

Jeff: Don't you think, Paul, that laws are more or less a representation of how the people feel. I mean, if the people don't want this doctrine changed, there is no sense in just sort of arbitrarily deciding that it should be. I think, rather than having a kind of law decide the morality aspect, perhaps we ought to work it the other way around. Do the people want this sort of law?

Paul: Very good point, Jeff, and in the last issue of *Playboy*, February of this year, Senator Javits quoted the recent Gallup Poll which showed that 64 percent of the voting population would be in favor of this kind of change.

Jeff: Then the moral aspect is already undergoing change.

Paul: I think so. Another analogy might be the civil-rights movement, where you have change in laws, and with change in laws comes eventually change in feelings—but not immediately.

Jeff: Then the legal aspect would more or less give rise to a law lowering our age

Transcript

of majority, and this would, in turn, affect the moral aspect.

Paul: Right, I think most people would be in favor of a change anyway, and those who weren't, after the law was changed, would eventually come around.

Jeff: OK, fine.

Dale: What about the delegation of the responsibilities that we mentioned earlier. Also, would this change in the laws help in this area?

Jeff: Do you really think that the faculty and administration would still allow the students to be equals with them?

Paul: Not entirely. There's still the problem of academic matters. Students are in no way equals with the faculty when it comes to academics.

Jeff: Right. The students are more or less just educationally inferior to the faculty members and, therefore, cannot assume the responsibility.

Paul: They wouldn't be here in school if they weren't.

Bill: Maybe we could exclude student participation in such areas as hiring and firing faculty or something along this line.

Jeff: But don't you think the students should still have a recommendatory power in these areas? Or at least have the right to be heard?

Paul: Well, surely there's no reason in the world why students shouldn't be able to be heard in everything. The question is, I think, whether students should have a decision-making role, a power role.

Dale: —applied in areas which they really don't understand, are not familiar with.

Transcript

Jeff: So, it should just be influence in—

Paul: Yes.

Jeff: Just kind of recommendatory.

Paul: It makes sense to me that you might say that students should have a power role, an equal power role, with faculty in everything except academics, hiring and firing of staff, and maybe the administration of physical facilities.

(All agree.)

Steve: This is certainly in line with our original definition (the one we agreed upon at the beginning of this discussion) of what the position of college students should be. We've apparently eliminated or, at least, greatly overcome many of the drawbacks that were originally proposed when Paul suggested his plan and basically set up a structure by which the *in loco parentis* concept could be gradually phased out of our society. Once this is accomplished, might we then develop Paul's idea (or some other ideas) and make it into a workable position which can be implemented with some practicality?

Paul: Yes, I think so, Steve. It's got a lot of potential. When you do away with in loco parentis and you put people on an equal basis, there's a lot of advantages.

Jeff: I can see, Paul, that, once we had both a student senate and a faculty senate, the student senate would operate having a decision-making vote on nonacademic matters and only an influential vote on academic matters. But exactly how would a bill, perhaps, go through student and faculty and on to the administration?

Commentary

When all seem to be in general agreement that the plan could conceivably work, at least in theory, Steve steps in once more with a preliminary summary of the plan, along with some comment on the relation of it to the criteria it was intended to meet. Then he brings up the question of "practical implementation."

Transcript

Paul: OK, good question! Suppose a bill was started in the student senate on matters that we have considered that faculty and students have an equal vote on. If the bill was passed in student senate, it would then go on to faculty senate. If passed there, it would go on to the administration to be signed into the code or vetoed, as the case may be. If the bill was vetoed, it would go back to the legislative branch, and if the student and faculty senates still wanted the law with a two-thirds majority as in the national system, it would become a part of the code in spite of the administration veto.

Bill: Then all laws passed would also be subject to judicial review.

Jeff: Could it also work the other way around, Paul? Could a bill start in faculty senate and go on to student?

Paul: Yes, just as in the national system. The only distinction here, I think, should be that in matters of academic concern, and with the other restrictions we've mentioned, the bill would have to start in faculty senate and go to student senate only for a *recommendation* before going to the administration.

Bill: And the administration would take the role of the executive department, and it would carry out and execute the plans that were approved by the legislature.

Paul: Yes. This would really go back to the way universities were all started, I think, where you would have a group of students and a group of faculty getting together for the mutual purpose of learning and teaching, and where you would have these people sitting down and solving their problems together.

Transcript

Dale: I think this plan also meets the criteria which we have set up.

Bill: Yes. I think it also kind of carries out this idea we talked about earlier, about learning by doing and preparing for this democratic society we will be entering.

Jeff: Furthermore, it gets rid of the threat upon the administration. If the faculty senate and student senate pass a proposal and the administration vetoes it, and if it goes back and the student and faculty senates pass it over the veto of the administration, I don't see how the administration can be held responsible.

Bill: So the entire university family, you might say, actually is benefited.

Steve: I take it, then, we're very definitely satisfied with the proposal as it has been modified.

(All agree.)

Steve: OK, then, we started out by rephrasing our question to incorporate definitions so that it would read: "What should be the position of power and/or influence held by American college students in determining the rules and regulations governing student behavior at their institutions?" We then went on to show that the problem manifests itself in three basic areas, two of which are primarily student-concerned. The first is the obvious, well-publicized area of demonstrations and riots over a wide variety of problems ranging from free speech to support for employees striking for higher wages to issues subordinate to the real issue of Vietnam. We also pointed out that students are less obviously involved, though perhaps more actively in a subtle way, in such areas as creating bills of rights which attempt to codify the student position, support for reform candidates for offices, development of course and instructor evaluation, and reform activities of the Associated Student Government and the National Student Association. We also showed that there was a third area of input in the problem, that of professors and organizations like the Civil Liberties Union, which have distributed statements in support of many

Commentary

IV. *Solution(s) meet criteria?*

With discussion of the practical aspects concluded, the final reference to criteria is somewhat perfunctory here, although, as often happens, criteria are kept in mind and referred to at various times in direct relation to proposals as they are made.

V. *Final agreement*

Steve enters again to bring the discussion to a close with a thorough final summation of the entire process. Such a summary can rarely be handled without reference to notes taken during the discussion.

of the things which students are criticizing. We then pointed out that the problem is not small, but rather widespread in terms of both time and space, and we decided that our goal was to establish an appropriate student policy-making role. Moving from there, we pointed out that the cause of student unrest was varied but generally fell into dissatisfaction with student roles, which the students felt should be in line with educational objectives, and that, in fact, the decision-making role was hampered and restricted by the concept of in loco parentis. In an attempt to solve the problem, we established two criteria: (1) to relieve administrators of in loco parentis responsibility and threat; and (2) to align the student policy-making role with the educational goals as perceived by students and, on a theoretical level, by administrators and faculty. To meet those criteria, we suggested a three-part structure, patterned much after our national government, in which the faculty and students would be equally represented in separate houses of a legislative branch; the executive function would be exercised by the administration; and there would be a judicial branch composed of all three groups with equal representation for each of the three. We pointed out that the biggest drawback to this solution was that it didn't really do away with the idea of in loco parentis, and we then decided that the best way to approach that area was to lower the age of majority to 18. This would mean that almost all students, graduate and undergraduate, would be, by the time they went into college, of the age of majority. This decision on the age of majority was made in the hope that it would, in fact, take care of the more than 30 percent of the people that apparently, according to the Gallup Poll, don't already feel that students should have the age of majority at 18. In other words, if students were of legal age upon entering the university, people would not expect the university to take on the "parent responsibility." Then, a second part of the proposal was that there should be a three-part organization giving students an equal role in those areas which are nonacademic and in those areas which do not involve employment or staff relations with the university.

It is our hope, I think, that in the event that such a proposal could be adopted—and I think we have shown that it is feasible—we could avoid the type of attitude which makes the statement in the Plainville, Kansas, paper (even though a misprint) fairly accurate in terms of what students are thinking. Students would then feel that they had reached their full status in the university community, the community of scholars. No longer would a statement like "The school board is composed of seven members elected to resent you in school affairs" be anything other than a misprint.

The attention of readers of the above discussion (and commentary) should be called to the fact that it took place within the framework of certain specified ground rules. Discussions in the real world seldom follow progressive steps in so tidy a fashion, but there is merit in learning to follow some reasonable pattern to ensure efficiency in the discussion process. The one major change recommended for discussion situations in general: *The chairman and the members of the group should, if possible, participate more equally in all functions of the process.* The chairman should feel free to make substantive and conceptual contributions; the members should be more free to ask directive questions and to summarize at various stages. The line between "leader" and "led" should be less distinct.

Examples of Resolutions[25]

A resolution prepared by a "committee on urban affairs"

A RESOLUTION PROPOSING INCREASED FEDERAL CONTROL OVER THE PURCHASE OF FIREARMS IN ORDER TO FACILITATE LAW ENFORCEMENT

WHEREAS, easy accessibility of firearms is a significant factor in the crimes committed in the United States, and

WHEREAS, in a great number of the homicides committed in the United States, the weapon is a mail-ordered and mail-delivered firearm, and

WHEREAS, far too many recipients of mail-ordered firearms have previously displayed criminal tendencies, and

WHEREAS, knowledge of the sale and distribution of firearms would aid law enforcement officials in crime detection; therefore:

Section 1. BE IT RESOLVED that the purchase and transfer of firearms by way of mail shall be prohibited except when the exchange is between a manufacturer and a licensed dealer.

Section 2. The importation into this country of military surplus firearms and certain other firearms be restricted.

Section 3. The over-the-counter sale of concealable firearms to persons not residents of the state in which the licensee conducts his business be banned.

Section 4. Special regulations be placed on the acquisition of other "destructive devices" (military-type firearms, such as bazookas, machine guns, mortars, and antitank guns).

Section 5. The sale of firearms to certain categories of persons, such as habitual drunkards, drug addicts, mental incompetents, and persons convicted of certain offenses be prohibited.

Section 6. Immediately upon purchasing a firearm, the buyer shall have his name submitted to an agency of the state government and registered along with the results of a ballistics test of the weapon and the fingerprints of the buyer.

Section 7. Violation of the provisions above shall be deemed a felony, and upon conviction, said person or persons shall be fined not less than a sum of seventy-five dollars ($75) and not more than one thousand dollars ($1,000), to which may be added imprisonment of one (1) month to five (5) years in a federal penitentiary.

A resolution prepared by a "committee on interior affairs"

A RESOLUTION FAVORING GUARANTEED EMPLOYMENT FOR UNITED STATES CITIZENS

WHEREAS, there are numerous overlapping welfare programs, and

---

25. With minor editing by the writer, the three examples in this volume appear through the courtesy of Professor Charles Stewart of the Purdue Department of Communication. Professor Stewart is the Director of a student conference and legislative assembly which is convened annually on the Purdue campus.

WHEREAS, this society measures a man's worth in accordance with his ability to work, and

WHEREAS, this present welfare system gives a man no feeling of "worth" and further contributes to society's breakdown, and

WHEREAS, there is a resulting reservoir of hatred, causing civil disturbances which threaten the basic social fabric of this nation; therefore:

Section 1. BE IT RESOLVED that there be a reevaluation of the criteria for granting welfare.

Section 2. There shall be an elimination of duplication of welfare programs.

Section 3. A system of guaranteed employment shall be enacted with the following provisions:

a. Employment offices shall be set up in poverty-stricken areas.
b. If a job is not forthcoming for an applicant within three weeks of application, a job shall be created which is meaningful. This job shall be created by the federal government and/or private enterprise.
c. In cases where a job is created by private enterprise in cooperation with the federal government, the company shall pay one-third of the salary, and the government shall pay two-thirds, with the individual company increasing its responsibility for the original salary by one-third each year.
d. The employee shall be paid on an equal basis with other employees of the company who perform equal service.
e. No company shall have more than five percent of its employees under this plan.
f. On-the-job training shall be provided where it is needed, with the government and private enterprise paying the cost in the same ratio as in part (c).

A resolution prepared by a "committee on foreign policy"

A RESOLUTION FAVORING THE WITHDRAWAL OF THE UNITED STATES FROM THE SOUTHEAST ASIA TREATY ORGANIZATION (SEATO)

WHEREAS, SEATO was drawn up to stop Communist aggression in Southeast Asia and has proved to be inadequate, and

WHEREAS, three of the member nations are Western powers who oppose non-Asian interference in Asian affairs, and

WHEREAS, some member nations have refused to abide by the agreements of the treaty, and

WHEREAS, several Asian countries have been unwilling to participate in SEATO, leaving the scope of the organization limited, and

WHEREAS, SEATO has no standing armed forces and, therefore, must depend upon the cooperation of its members, leaving the United States to bear much of the military burden, and

WHEREAS, the United States would provide military and economic aid to Southeast Asia regardless of membership in SEATO, therefore:

Section 1. BE IT RESOLVED that the United States withdraw as soon as possible within the provisions of the SEATO Charter from the Southeast Asia Treaty Organization.

Note: The separate lines for each section of a resolution are usually numbered in sequence along the left margin in order to facilitate reference to specific parts of the resolution. For example, in the course of preparation of the resolution immediately above or in later debate on it by the members of a large group, one could "move that the word 'immediately' be substituted for the words 'as soon as possible' in lines 1 and 2 of Section 1."

12 / Changing listener attitudes

Faced with problems, man sometimes works alone to analyze and solve them or, at times, he works in cooperation with others, as described in the previous chapter on discussion. Having arrived at what seems to be a reasonable analysis of the problem, or at a reasonable solution for a recognized problem, or at a reasonable analysis-and-solution, one often finds that nothing will be accepted or accomplished unless others can bring themselves to the point of accepting one's views.

This chapter, then, is an extension of earlier comment (primarily in Chapters 1 and 4) on the motivations and forces which operate within listeners to cause them "to decide to move from one position to another." To put it another way, we are here dealing with factors leading listeners to conclude that they should adopt, strengthen, abandon, or in some other way change their attitudes. The change, if any, occurs within the listener, and the only part played by the speaker in the process is the selecting and providing of what he considers to be stimuli appropriate to his purpose. He does this with the full knowledge that a host of other internal and external stimuli may be also operating to facilitate and/or block listener reception and acceptance.

The chapter opens with a general discussion of attitudes, beliefs, and opinions. A section on the communication process with specific reference to attitude-changing then leads into a three-part discussion of factors affecting listener attitudes toward the message, toward the speaker, and toward the situation. A diagram (p. 214) serves as a basis for the development of the chapter and as a guide for concluding remarks on listener response and observable effects. A related section on the analysis of listeners and their attitudes brings the chapter to a close.

Attitudes, Beliefs, and Opinions

By way of introduction to the problems posed by listener attitudes, we begin with definitions and distinctions. and follow with a discussion of attitudinal bases and functions.

Definitions and distinctions

What is an attitude? In paraphrase of McGuire and Allport (as quoted by McGuire), an attitude is a state of readiness to respond to a stimulus; it appears to be organized in the sense that it is based on a series of related components or beliefs; it comes to us through experience in the broadest interpretation of that word; and it exerts "a directive and/or dynamic influence on behavior."[1] It is directive in that it channels energy "into one kind of behavioral outlet rather than another, or toward one target rather than another," and it is dynamic in that it may also *produce* behavior.[2] For example, an antipolluter's attitude directs some energy against polluters; it may also add to one's *general* hostility toward other groups. Turning the coin to its other side, McGuire suggests that we can reduce an individual's "total level of hostility" by reducing his hostility toward a specific group.

Approached from another angle, an attitude may find expression as *an overall evaluative response*. It becomes apparent through one's verbalizing the view that an object or class of objects is good or bad, favorable or unfavorable, superior or inferior, admirable or detestable, etc. For example, if you say, "Materialism is bad," your statement may be considered an attitude on materialism; it is your "learned predisposition to respond to an object or class in a favorable or unfavorable way."[3]

Although the distinction between belief and attitude is one which not all writers make, it was introduced in Chapter 1, and it is presented more fully here as an aid to precision and focus in the persuasive effort. ". . . the term belief refers only to the 'probability' or 'improbability' that a particular object (belief in) or a particular relationship (belief about) exists."[4] An example of *belief in*: "There is a Communist conspiracy." Of *belief about*: "The Communist conspiracy is a myth." The first example is a statement about belief in the *existence* of the object; the second says something about the object *in relation to* some other "object, concept, value, or goal"[5] (in this instance, the concept of *myth*). If you were to say, "The Communist conspiracy should be exposed," you would again be saying something about the "object" in relating it, this time to a goal of some specific action as distinguished from simple cognition of the nature of the "object." There are clearly evaluative elements in many a belief statement, but by itself, such a statement falls short of attitude status in that it does not indicate the individual's *overall* or *general* evaluation of the object or class of objects under consideration.

If an attitude is a high-level predisposition to react to a stimulus object or class in a certain way, and if a belief is a statement that something exists or is related to something else, what is an opinion? According to this writer, an opinion may be regarded as a kind of lower-level belief; in its present popular connotation, at least, it seems to be in the class of incidental observation, impression, or guess, to which the individual feels no great commitment. The average individual is seldom discriminating

---

1. McGuire, p. 142.
2. *Ibid.*, p. 147.
3. Steiner and Fishbein, p. 107.
4. Martin Fishbein, "A Consideration of Beliefs, Attitudes, and Their Relationships," in *Current Studies in Social Psychology*, edited by Ivan D. Steiner and Martin Fishbein. Holt, Rinehart and Winston, 1965, p. 111. Reprinted by permission.
5. *Ibid.*

in his use of "in my opinion." When you hear that phrase, it may precede an opinion ("That horse is too heavily loaded"), a belief ("The Scotch are thrifty"), or an attitude ("War is immoral"). After initially defining opinions, attitudes, and beliefs, Berelson and Steiner lump them together in their treatment of what they call OAB's.[6] McGuire holds no brief for excessively detailed distinctions but seems to prefer placing opinion-beliefs (called beliefs in the present text) in one classification and attitude-beliefs (called attitudes in the present text) in another.[7]

The distinctions above may seem reasonable enough, but the situation is complicated by the fact that, when you make a statement about an object, you are actually relating one object toward which you have an attitude to a second object toward which you also have an attitude. For instance, let us suppose that someone has heard you say, "Easterners are suave." It could be one of a number of "belief" sentences which, taken together, would provide a basis for an observer's determining your attitude on Easterners. The word "suave" is one toward which you may also have an attitude; its meaning may be positive (complimentary), neutral, or negative, depending on your evaluative response to *that* term. In other words, belief statements, in tying objects to other objects, concepts, etc., which we regard positively, neutrally, or negatively, are not attitudes, but they are the *indicators* of attitudes. If we discover that you consistently attach positively oriented terms (in *your* frame of reference) to Easterners, we can reasonably assume that your attitude is: "Easterners are fine people." If you express both positive and negative views, your attitude is obviously ambivalent. If your views are predominantly neutral, you have no strongly based attitude on Easterners. The more information we have on an individual's beliefs about what we call "the stimulus object," the better position we are in to use all of the responses in his total "belief system" as a key to his attitude. No one "belief" statement is likely to be a sure indicator of attitude; however, if we correctly interpret the statement and its strength[8] as an *indicator* of some kind of evaluative response, and if we know a person's beliefs, we can with some degree of accuracy predict his attitude. Conversely, if we know a person's attitude, we may be able to make some "educated guesses" about his beliefs. Finally, if we know what a man believes about an "object" *and* how he evaluates it, we have the best possible basis for accurately assessing his attitude. Stated another way, a man's attitude toward an "object" is best indicated by what he believes about it *and* how he feels about it.

At this point, you may be wondering about the difference between the common or value premises discussed in Chapter 3 and the attitudes or value statements under consideration in this chapter. In the first instance, the speaker is looking at an

---

6. Berelson and Steiner (p. 558) list opinions, attitudes, and beliefs in that ascending hierarchical order. Opinions are "short-run judgments," attitudes are "more enduring and inclusive" judgments, and "beliefs are more basic still, having to do with the central values of life."

7. For a review of studies distinguishing attitudes from opinions and from beliefs, etc., see McGuire, pp. 150–153.

8. "The strongest beliefs about an object that an individual holds are those that serve to define and describe the object for him, i.e., descriptive beliefs." Martin Fishbein, "An Investigation of the Relationships Between Beliefs About an Object and the Attitude Toward That Object," *Human Relations*, **16** (August 1963), p. 234.

audience-held value premise, stated or unstated, *as a base for his argument*. In the second instance, the speaker is looking at what could be the same audience-held value position or attitude *as a target for change*. The distinctions are more or less arbitrary, but they do have some utility as descriptions of two quite different approaches to the same basic idea.

Bases and functions

How do we accumulate our attitudes and the complex of perceptions, beliefs, feelings, and action directives that go to make them up? As earlier noted, especially in Chapters 1 and 4, we come to be as we are through our total past experience and the numberless perceptions underlying that experience. We assimilate some attitudes from those with whom we associate over the years—parents, friends, instructors, advisers, clergymen, businessmen, *et al.*; others we arrive at independently through personal observations and the conclusions drawn from them.[9]

McGuire enumerates other bases—genetic, physiological, environmental, and nonverbal—which may play a part in determining attitudes.[10] He cites studies which seem to indicate that there are, for instance, hereditary components in levels of aggressiveness, and he describes hypothetical situations in which the process of evolution could genetically produce perennially hostile groups or, on the other hand, could bring about a society of meek individuals. The fact that aging and illness affect attitudes has long been known. We also recognize that one's environment, to the extent that it determines the stimuli that an individual will receive, "programs" some of his attitudes. And in the nonverbal sphere, the mother who, without saying anything, telegraphs anxiety under stress to her children presumably engenders attitudes of anxiety which will be a part of the children's makeup for some time to come if not permanently.

Moving from some of the bases or sources underlying our attitudes, what personal needs do attitudes satisfy? Or phrasing the question another way, why do we cling to our attitudes? They perform a number of functions, sometimes separate and sometimes overlapping, in relation to man's efforts to attain his goals.[11] For example, an attitude may be useful to us in gaining personal acceptance by a particular group. Young people have been known to adopt an attitude of acceptance toward drugs and drug users in order to win admission to what they considered an "in" group. Or people trying to climb the social ladder will often take on, as their own, attitudes known to be characteristic of those on the next rungs of the ladder.

Attitudes also help us adjust to the complexities of the modern world. We pro-

---

9. Except for initial emphasis on Steiner and Fishbein, this chapter is based primarily on the following works: Berelson and Steiner, *Human Behavior*; Cohen, *Attitude Change and Social Influence*; Hovland, *The Order of Presentation in Persuasion*; Hovland and Janis, *Personality and Persuasibility*; Hovland, Janis, and Kelley, *Communication and Persuasion*; Karlins and Abelson, *Persuasion*; Kiesler, Collins, and Miller, *Attitude Change*; McGuire, "The Nature of Attitudes and Attitude Change"; Rosenberg *et al.*, *Attitude Organization and Change*; Sherif, Sherif, and Nebergall, *Attitude and Attitude Change*; and Schramm, *The Science of Human Communication*. For complete publication data on these and related works, see the Bibliography.
10. McGuire, pp. 161–171.
11. See Chapter 4 for a review of the general goals common to man. The discussion in the present chapter is based on McGuire, pp. 157–160.

cess the information streaming at us from a multitude of sources and fit that information somewhere into the pyramidal base of the relevant attitude. In other words, an attitude helps us simplify and make sense of the knowledge we acquire. If you oppose government investigation into the organizational affiliations of private citizens, you have a convenient repository for incoming information on that subject. If you favor active participation of all citizens in political campaigns, you have a ready place for storing information of that kind. Attitudes based primarily on information may be regarded as mental sponges, ever ready to absorb facts, figures, and ideas which serve to bolster or modify the attitudes concerned.

Attitudes may also help us attain goals of special identity and potential-realization. We want to be known by others and to be respected by them. The woman executive who has made a local charity almost a one-woman show is certainly interested in charity and apparently has the attitude that work of this kind is highly necessary and desirable. This activity may also be her "thing," through which she gets local recognition, praise, satisfaction, emotional release, etc. Sometimes people working at frustrating jobs find that off-the-job activities provide their only opportunity to show themselves and others what they can do. They do public good and solve the problem of some of their inner conflicts at the same time; they become known as individuals having a fine attitude toward community service, and the ego blows suffered at work are counterbalanced by the ego inflation won away from it.

Attitudes, then, may exercise a central, subsidiary, or parallel function in helping us reach our basic goals—or preventing us from doing so.

Attitude-Changing and the Communication Process

You will remember that there was considerable emphasis in Chapter 1, on the streams of stimuli simultaneously and continuously passing between speaker and listener. You will recall, too, that these streams were envisioned as passing through the respective personal screens of the speaker and the listener. The diagram in Fig. 12.1 is at one and the same time an expansion and a distortion of Fig. 1.3 in that it provides more detail but represents stimuli as moving in one direction only, from the total communication situation to the listener. With that advantage and deficiency in mind, you will find that this diagram provides perspective for continuing the discussion of attitudes.

By this time, you are generally familiar with the "observable stimuli" of a communication situation. Among them are (1) the characteristics of the message—*content-based stimuli*, such as the topic under discussion, the goals and arguments to which the speaker resorts, and the kind of language he uses, (2) the characteristics of the speaker—*speaker-based stimuli*, such as the overall impression he makes on the audience, the interests he appears to be serving, the integrity he appears to have or to lack, and (3) the characteristics of the situation—*situation-based stimuli*, such as the occasion, the place, the time, supporting and interfering "noises," and all other factors and influences arising from the situation over and above those arising from the speaker and from the verbal and nonverbal aspects of the message. Thus we see the total communication situation as the source of stimuli stemming from the characteristics of the message, from the characteristics of the speaker, and from those characteristics of the situation not included in message or speaker.

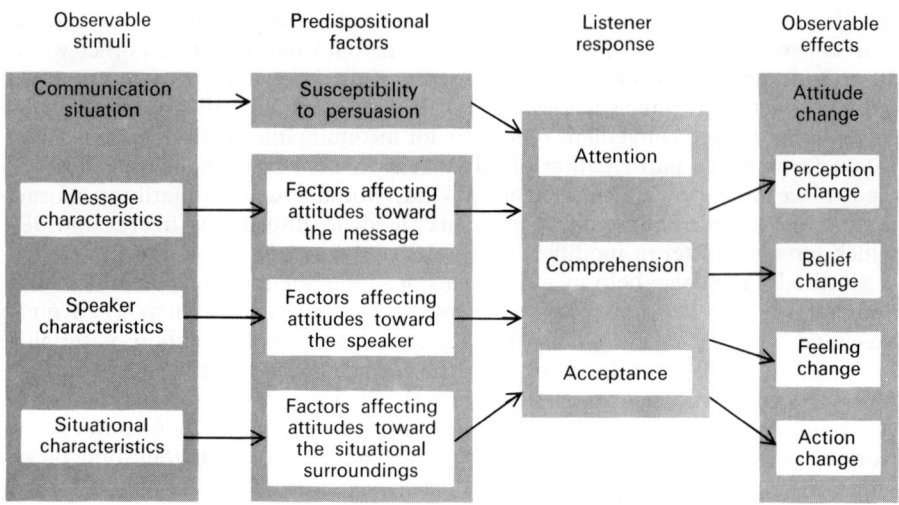

Fig. 12.1 Factors affecting listener readiness to accept a given point of view.[12]

The listener sees the "observable stimuli" of the communication situation through the personality wrappings of his own special cocoon or personal screen (described in Chapter 1). The screen consists, first, of the individual's general susceptibility to persuasion of any kind from any source; it consists, second, of the listener's attitudes toward a specific message, a specific speaker, and attendant situational surroundings. However, we are not now expanding on what was said in Chapter 1 about the screen of the listener's total past experience and resulting attitudes. We are here concerned with *factors affecting those attitudes,* factors which the speaker should recognize and over some of which he can exert control.

In the top box of the second column in Fig. 12.1, then, we are reminded that individuals vary by nature and conditioning in their susceptibility to persuasion. Some people are easily persuaded, no matter how weak or inconsistent the case may be. "Women are more persuasible than men,"[13] and children are more persuasible than adults. The elderly are more easily bilked out of their savings by confidence men, and the uneducated are more readily a prey of here-today-gone-tomorrow salesmen. You know some people who can be talked into anything and others who can be talked into nothing. So it is that some listeners are persuasion-prone, some are almost

---

12. This diagram (as well as many of the terms used here and in the remainder of the chapter) is adapted from the more complex and complete form in *Personality and Persuasibility,* edited by Carl I. Hovland and Irving L. Janis (New Haven: Yale University Press, 1959), p. 4. Used by permission.
13. Karlins and Abelson, p. 89. McGuire suggests (p. 251) that "the greater influenceability of the females may be due to their more effective message reception rather than to their greater yielding...."

persuasion-proof, and others represent degrees of susceptibility between those extremes. In other words, there is in every listener some predisposition to persuasion which is operative regardless of the characteristics of a given communication situation.

The remaining boxes in the second column identify three groups of factors affecting the attitudes of the listener toward the immediate communication situation. To help you understand how a speaker may cope with and change attitudes toward his message, toward himself, and toward the situational surroundings, each group is discussed separately.

Incidental comments on attitudes[14]

Lauren Bacall, actress, on prospect of going back into films: "Yes, but only in films of a level I feel I've earned. That's a new attitude of mine [in contrast to taking any offer and being grateful for it]."

Marilyn Biehl, lecturer in a training school for waitresses: "Management recognizes that waitresses should be trained, especially in attitude." To waitresses: "The most important point ... is that you feel pride in your job."

Tulsa woman returning to college: "The most surprising thing, however, has been the attitude of the professors. They seem to harbor a very ill-concealed contempt for the over-40 student."

Factors Affecting Attitudes Toward the Message[15]

Message strategy

We know, of course, that a traditional approach to composition of "a persuasive message" has for centuries been that of showing that a problem is serious enough to require doing something about it (often called *need for a change*) and then suggesting a plan to solve it. An example of this threat-and-resolution technique is seen in the efforts of a Cancer Society speaker to convince his audience that the threat of the disease can be minimized by regular checkups. A second approach to persuasion depends on calling man's attention to one or more of his *basic goals* (described in Chapter 4); here no direct threat is involved, but the individual is made very much aware of his "wants" and, second, of ways to achieve them. The used-car salesman uses such a technique in (1) arousing desire for a particular bargain and (2) demonstrating how easy it is to enjoy "ownership" through time payments. Desire or threat-oriented tensions may be based, of course, on any block thrown in the way of man's reaching the goals outlined in Chapter 4; they may also be aroused through appeals to any emotion or combination of emotions appropriately invoked in a given situation

---

14. From *Indianapolis Star*, March 7, 1971.
15. One of the best summaries of empirical findings affecting attitudes is the 1970 edition of Karlins and Abelson.

—envy of the affluent, sympathy for the unfortunate and afflicted, anger at those responsible for injustice, indignation growing out of insults to a respected individual or group, etc. Emphasis on emotions of distress and deprivation stimulates tensions. Release from the tensions comes in the form of satisfactions arising from a speaker's suggesting that the need he has described has been, is now, or will be met through some reassuring avenue for release (e.g., suggested plan, resolution, or action).

However necessary the arousal of some form of need-tension may be, the persuader must be careful not to "overplay his hand." *People believe what they want to believe, hear what they want to hear,* and generally ignore any threat which, if believed, would create *too intense* an anxiety. It is the view of many that the reason we have so few private bomb shelters is that people are unwilling to believe that a nuclear war could occur. They don't want to think about it, and nothing is accomplished by telling them that a single megaton explosion over their city of one million would destroy 40 percent of the population and 60 percent of the city itself. In fact, if a speaker were to persist in describing in vivid and gory detail exactly what would happen to him and his audience under atomic attack, the audience could be expected not only to reject the possibility of attack but also to become covertly aggressive or even openly hostile to the speaker. (We are assuming, of course, that this hypothetical audience is not made up of atomic experts or Civilian Defense personnel.) Each of us has a kind of built-in threat resistance factor; if we are suddenly and unexpectedly confronted by an overpowering threat of any kind, we try to shrug it off as being too fantastic to believe, especially if the release or escape provided by the speaker is inadequate. One of the keys to successful persuasion is to be sure that the "cure" is strong enough to handle the "disease" for which it is prescribed.[16]

Another key to message strategy is the decision on the extent to which the speaker should weave suggestion into the message. In Chapters 6 and 7, the point is made that you can win listener confidence through careful preparation followed by effective interaction with the audience. Knowing a subject and being able to communicate sensibly about it are subtle forms of suggestion. So are being diplomatic in language and avoiding the "command syndrome" by phrasing directives in the form of requests. An older speaker of some reputation is relatively safe in giving direct and positive advice, especially when he is addressing a younger group; a younger speaker is better advised, especially in addressing senior citizens, to offer a number of options for changes in thinking or action. He may know what option he wants to stress and he can go about stressing it. However, again in the spirit of friendly suggestion, it is important that he avoid giving the impression of being "another of those smart kid know-it-alls" with his personal panacea for the ills of the world.

Comment on message strategy would not be complete without emphasis on the fact that information, by itself, "almost never changes attitude."[17] In theory, if you give someone information which is both relevant and accurate, he should be able to arrive at the same conclusion you have drawn from that information. It

---

16. For a discussion of the intricacies of "appeal by threat," see Hovland, Janis, and Kelley, pp. 56–91; and Cohen, pp. 16–22.
17. Karlins and Abelson, p. 33.

seldom works that way for reasons still under investigation. In practice, it is considered advisable to use whatever logical and emotional appeals seem to fit the situation and not to hesitate stating the conclusion you would like to have your listeners accept. There is consensus that the more change requested, the more will be achieved[18] (something like asking for more money than you need as a hedge against getting less), but there is no consensus on the effectiveness of emotional appeals[19] as distinguished from results obtained by emphasis on the facts and formal argument; dependence on feeling works well with some audiences and fails completely with others. The speaker still has to rely on "sensing" whether or not introducing emotion will be appropriate in a given situation.

Finally, although humor is clearly helpful in relieving tension and establishing speaker-audience rapport, especially in the course of introductory remarks, there is some evidence that it is "not an effective persuasive technique."[20]

Message structure

Just as empirical research has led us to conclude that audiences characteristically reject tension-arousing appeals for which the speaker provides little or no relief, so it has also led to a number of hypotheses on the subject of the arrangement or order[21] of ideas:

1. *It is best to present both sides* of a controversial issue
   a. when the audience is composed of people who are well educated, and/or
   b. when you are talking to people who are opposed to your point of view, and/or
   c. when you know that the audience will later be subjected to opposing arguments. (In this instance, you are really trying "to inoculate the audience" against the contrary position.)

   And if you do present both sides, *it is best to present first the arguments in favor of your position* and then follow with the arguments against it.

2. *It is best to present only one side* of a controversial issue
   a. when the members of the audience are not well educated, and/or
   b. when you are talking to people who favor your point of view.

3. *The overall case should have some obvious structure.* Further, it is advisable to
   a. present the strongest arguments first if the audience appears uninterested or inattentive, and
   b. present the arguments that you especially want the audience to remember at the beginning and/or the end of your case—arguments presented in the middle are not so easily remembered—and
   c. use a point-by-point treatment unless the listeners are clearly intelligent enough to do their own organizing as you proceed.

---

18. *Ibid.*, p. 126.
19. *Ibid.*, p. 35.
20. *Ibid.*, p. 36.
21. For reports of hypotheses and experiments on order, consult Hovland, Janis, and Kelley, pp. 99–122; Hovland, pp. 130–138; and Cohen, pp. 6–16.

4. *Conclusions to arguments should be explicitly stated*, especially
   a. if the arguments are quite complicated, or
   b. if the audience is low in intellectual ability.

When to state the conclusions is a subject on which views differ. There is some agreement that it is safe to state your positions first and follow them with support if there is no strong argument and feeling against them. However, if the audience is known to be strongly opposed to your positions, it is generally advisable to begin with support for an idea and then state the conclusion which you hope the audience has reached at the same time. In other words, an inductive massing of evidence followed by a conclusion is, under certain circumstances, preferable to the bald statement of a "conclusion" followed by the evidence supporting it. In the inductive pattern, as an alternative to stating the point first, it is an easy matter to suggest an examination of the evidence in a certain area in order to "see where it leads us." (In general, the purpose or central idea of a persuasive talk is a statement of the attitude or attitudes which the speaker hopes the listeners will come to accept. The main points and some of the subpoints are usually in the belief or opinion categories.)

Message consistency

Consistency is a concept which, as Brown says, "seems always to have existed,"[22] although formal studies and experiments in the area apparently date from Freud in the first decade of this century.

Plato (and many others since his time) held the view that the "thinking man" will see "the good" and, to the extent that he recognizes it, will see to it that his actions are in concert with that recognition. He further believed that doing what is "right" and avoiding what is inconsistent with that right makes men happy; the corollary is that men are unhappy in doing something inconsistent with reasonable action as they perceive it.[23] Over the centuries, rhetorical theorists without number have suggested that the first concern of speakers should be the establishing of a "need for a change" from the *status quo*, for early writers felt intuitively and learned from observation what we have now determined scientifically, namely, that it is in the nature of man to resist change and oppose any disturbance of his equilibrium, i.e., any idea inconsistent with his present state of mind.[24] Modern discussions of consistency generally center on such terms as congruity, equilibrium, consonance, balance, symmetry, and their opposites. For our purposes—and again at the risk of oversimplification—we can say that man is so constituted by nature that, when confronted by an effort to change his beliefs and attitudes, he will either (1) modify them to resolve the conflict with the new ideas presented, (2) try in some way to resolve the difficulty by finding justification for the old beliefs and attitudes, or (3) try to avoid, distort, or attack the incoming information and argument. Let us examine through a

---

22. Brown, *Social Psychology*, p. 604.
23. See Plato's *Republic, Protagoras,* and *Gorgias,* available in many translations. These dialogues concentrate attention on ethical and political problems.
24. One of the best general reviews of the development of the consistency principle and of modern approaches to it is to be found in Brown, *Social Psychology*, pp. 549–609.

few examples what man's "consistency compulsion" means to the persuader-communicator.

For one thing, *a communication can be made persuasive by introducing an idea inconsistent with one the hearer already possesses and, then, by suggesting how the inconsistency can be eliminated.* A father who is well satisfied with the *status quo* in the amount of life-insurance security he has provided for his family is made to feel less secure by a trusted agent who analyzes the family's needs and shows the father that his program is actually deficient. The agent then gives the father an opportunity to purchase additional insurance and thereby resolve the inconsistency between what he has and what he now feels that he should have. Government savings bonds are usually sold by inducing the potential buyer to follow this line of reasoning: "I have bought few, if any, bonds. The patriotic citizen, regardless of his views on these bonds as an investment, should support the government at this time. Therefore, I will buy some bonds." Thus a new belief creates an inconsistency by being arrayed against the old; either the attitude changes and bonds are bought, or the attitude doesn't change and is justified on available grounds or prejudices.

Second, *a communication can be made persuasive by helping listeners reduce an existing inconsistency.* "Cognitive dissonance" is the term made popular by Festinger[25] for the kind of situation in which the individual acts in a way contrary to what he apparently thinks or believes. He knows better but he does something discordant and incongruous with the knowledge in his possession. For instance, the sale of cigarettes is still heavy in the face of substantial evidence that smoking them is at least one major cause of lung cancer. The average smoker enjoys smoking, and in spite of the fact that he knows it may be "hazardous to health," he looks around for some way to reduce his fears and his tensions. He tells himself (intrapersonal communication) that smoking helps him relax and contributes to his success in business and social relationships, that the new filters are extraordinarily effective, etc. He reduces the inconsistency between what he is doing and what he knows through a self-deceiving exercise in rationalization. Convincing such a person that he should stop smoking is well-nigh impossible, but it is possible by careful campaigning to induce a smoker to curtail the number of cigarettes he smokes, thereby making him "happier" through a reduction in this particular inconsistency. Another example: Suppose that you have done nothing at all about the racial inequalities existing in this country, and suppose that you are also convinced that every good citizen should become directly involved in some way. You know that you should do something but you have done nothing; ergo, a state of cognitive dissonance exists. Under these circumstances, a communication asking you to make a contribution to the Negro College Fund would probably be successful, because it would enable you to reduce your dissonance in a relatively comfortable and painless way. However, if you were asked to take part in a demonstration of community solidarity on the issue, you might find this action too wide a departure from your past inactivity, and such a communication would probably fail.

---

25. See Leon Festinger, *A Theory of Cognitive Dissonance* (New York: Row, Peterson, 1957). For a review of studies on this subject, see Brehm and Cohen.

Each of us, then, has a built-in aversion to any form of inconsistency; one who wishes to persuade should aim at the elimination or reduction of a newly introduced inconsistency or of an inconsistency already existing. One's beliefs and attitudes are changed to the extent that the persuader is successful in those aims.

Factors Affecting Attitudes Toward the Speaker

Who says something is as important as *what* is said in understanding the effect of a communication of an attitude. How the listener perceives the communicator can affect attitude change in numerous ways: the vividness of his personality, his status, the expertise attributed to him, the stake he has in the issue—all of these may make a difference. Many attitudes can underlie the effects: affection and admiration for the communicator, fear and awe of him, trust and confidence in his sincerity, fairness, and credibility.[26]

Students today have little of the placid, I'm-sitting-here-you-teach-me attitude. This age is scientifically and experimentally oriented; young and old accept the view that what is "true" today may not be "true" tomorrow; the day of the pat answer from anyone, including professors, is long past; this is the era of the probing question, the searching analysis, the careful investigation, the *tentative* conclusion. References to authority (parental, academic, ecclesiastical, governmental, etc.) are regarded with something less than enthusiasm, and a quotation from some great figure out of the past no longer lends as much support to a case as it did in the more credulous and reverent past. Although some speakers still try to gain credence for their views by aligning themselves with Marcus Aurelius, Bacon, Simon Bolivar, and President Kennedy, the listeners of today expect something additional in the way of argument. The same listeners consciously, subconsciously, or unconsciously react not only to the speaker's messages but also *to him personally*. In other words, although reluctant to accept quotations of authority as reasons for doing something or not doing it, present-day audiences from one to thousands stand ready to confer "ethical appeal" or "source credibility" on a speaker thought worthy of that consideration.

Nevertheless, in a course in basic speech-communication, it is not uncommon for students to attempt to talk on subjects for which they have inadequate background. A student from a prosperous farm community tries to describe conditions in the slums (without his ever having seen one), and one from the city endeavors to discuss irrigation projects in the Southwest (without his ever having been there); another attacks the United Nations (without a single direct contact with the organization or its activities); another expatiates on the evils of drug addiction (depending almost entirely on an article he has read in *Life* or the *Readers Digest* for information as well as point of view). Students in such a class, except for those silently rehearsing their own speeches or preparing for their next classes, are quick to sense that "he doesn't know what he is talking about," and they quickly lose confidence in the speaker's "right to speak." In fact, in his next appearance before the class, the speaker

---

26. From *Attitude Change and Social Influence* by Arthur R. Cohen (New York: Basic Books, 1964), p. 23. (Opening paragraph in chapter entitled "Characteristics of the Communicator.") Reprinted by permission.

must turn in an outstanding performance simply to regain audience confidence lost on the previous occasion. It is possible, of course, to prepare oneself to take a position on a very deep and complicated problem. However, this process takes time and cannot be accomplished in the week or two normally devoted to the preparation of a speaking engagement. To earn the confidence of an audience, you must appear to be "worth believing." One advantage which the student speaker enjoys is the fact that the other students in the group ordinarily perceive him as one of themselves; any speaker is more persuasive when he is accepted as one of the group.[27] Thorough preparation, real interest in the topic, and a strong desire to communicate information or a point of view—all these are essential if you are to win trust.

Over and above knowing what you are talking about and being interested in communicating it in a way acceptable to the audience, a strong factor in winning over an audience is your acceptance of ethical responsibility for what you say. If you believe strongly that the right to open housing is one every citizen should enjoy, it is irresponsible to go along with a majority opposing legislation to guarantee that right. If you believe that pollution of waterways should be vigorously opposed, it is unethical of you to caution others that "the biggest industry in town will move out if we make too much fuss about pollution." If you are formally or informally participating in a debate on any issue, it does you no honor to take sides on a basis of friendship rather than on the merits of the case. The real point of this discussion, however, is the good sense inherent in every audience. Insincerity and a lack of conviction are just as hard to hide as a lack of study and background. "A message will be credible, a recommendation to action will be persuasive, to the degree that the source of the message is thought to be trustworthy."[28] Note your own reactions as speakers go to the platform for their performances in the course; you will discover that you have already decided whether or not a particular student is going to be worth listening to. By the time of the last speech, each classmate has earned your respect through prior performances and participation in discussion—or he has lost it. The point to remember is that your credibility as a source of accurate information and of views honestly arrived at is a tremendously valuable asset—once lost, the regaining of it can be accomplished, if at all, only by a long and difficult struggle.

In Aristotle's *Rhetoric* and in other theoretical and practical communication manuals of his time and later centuries, a speaker's reputation (*ethos*) was ranked with reason and emotional appeal as one of the three "constituents of proof." The popular term for ethical appeal is now "source credibility," and through relatively recent studies, we do know a little more about it than did the Greeks and the Romans. In 1951, for instance, Carl Hovland and Walter Weiss had two groups of students read a series of identical articles taking positions on issues of the day. The first group of students was told that the sources of the articles were notables and experts in whom they had some confidence. The second group was told that articles originated from *Pravda* and other "less trustworthy" sources. The directors of the investigation discovered, as you would expect, that the more highly credible sources were more

---

27. Karlins and Abelson, p. 128.
28. Roger Brown, *Words and Things* (New York: Free Press, 1958), p. 317. Reprinted by permission.

influential in causing changes in attitude toward the goals advocated; interestingly enough, they also learned that the students absorbed about the same amount of information, no matter what the source. The inference drawn from this study and later investigations is that the credibility of the source appears to affect acceptance of ideas but it does not seem to have any appreciable effect on learning.

From the standpoint of pure technique, note that the effectiveness of a speaker is "increased if he initially expresses some views that are also held by his audience."[29] It is also true that one's persuasiveness can be enhanced by arguing, however temporarily, against one's own best interests. Karlins and Abelson cite a study in which a U.S. general is alleged (for the sake of the study) to have said that the number of U.S. casualties in the Vietnam war far exceeded the number reported in the press. The credibility of this imaginary general was judged to be greater than that of an anonymous source to whom the same report was attributed.[30]

Evidence also seems to indicate that, when a highly respected speaker presents a viewpoint or case which we do not like to hear, the resulting state of tension is usually "resolved in any of three ways: (1) changes in attitude toward the communication (which would include either accepting it or reinterpreting it), (2) change in attitudes toward the communicator and (3) change in perception of the communicator's role in originating the communication."[31] In other words, we are temporarily thrown off balance by listening to a "disliked communication" from a favored source, and we try to restore the balance by modifications in our attitudes. To illustrate: The Vice President of the United States may be a person for whom we have the highest respect (in spite of the ever-recurring jokes about the office he holds). Let us suppose that he gives a major speech in which he advocates no military draft deferments of any kind under any circumstances for college and university students. Let us assume further that you are in good health and of military age. How will you react? You can accept the communication, or you can decide that "he means in time of war" or that "he must say what he is told to say by the President." Second, you can revise your evaluation of the speaker and conclude that he is not so astute a statesman as you had imagined. Third, you can try to overlook the speaker's position on the ground that "the ideas seem to be his, but *in this particular instance*, he is ill-advised; after further consideration, he will change his views."

Human nature being what it is, there are other standards by which listeners "take the measure" of a speaker. Bettinghaus cites unpublished research by Berlo, Lemert, and Mertz in which factors of *safety, qualification*, and *dynamism* were identified as guides used by audiences in evaluating speakers.[32] The first two are not unlike the factors of competency and trustworthiness already described in foregoing paragraphs. The third dimension, dynamism, is apparently somewhat less important but still significant. "A source rated high on the dynamism factor would be described as aggressive, emphatic, frank, forceful, bold, active, energetic, and fast. A com-

---

29. Karlins and Abelson, p. 120.
30. *Ibid.*, p. 117.
31. Carl I. Hovland, Irving L. Janis, and Harold H. Kelly, *Communication and Persuasion* (New Haven: Yale University Press, 1957), p. 43. Reprinted by permission.
32. Bettinghaus, pp. 105–109.

municator rated as low ... would be ... meek, hesitant, reserved, forceless, timid, passive, tired, and slow."[33] Most of us are aware that there is a natural inclination to accept ideas from a forceful, dynamic speaker when we might disregard or reject the same ideas presented by a meek, reserved type. We are also aware that some political figures, movie stars, football coaches, and other notables are said to have "charisma," magnetic appeal, "presence," and similar hard-to-explain powers for enthralling listeners. People may not remember what they say, and what they say doesn't really have to make sense. In these instances, at least, dynamism *is* a primary weapon in the hands of the communicator.

Although there are later studies that could be reviewed in detail,[34] it is enough for our present purposes to emphasize the fact that empirical evidence (1) confirms the insistence of the ancients on the importance of the speaker's reputation and performance in influencing attitudes and (2) continues to provide supplementary data which can be helpful to us, both as communicators and as listeners.

Factors Affecting Attitudes Toward the Situational Surroundings

Group consensus

Some of the ways in which people react in a communication situation have nothing to do with the message and nothing to do with the speaker. For example, if the collective view of the members of your speech-communication class has come to be that the meetings take place in order to give the individual student a chance to perform before an instructor-critic, your attempts to communicate will be handicapped. But if the collective view is that students are real people who can be drawn into real communicative transactions, your attempts to communicate will be bolstered by this supportive class attitude.[35] In the first instance, you would have to work extraordinarily hard to cope with an understandable lack of interest on the part of other members of the class; in the second, the potential for interest would be there if you were ready to take advantage of it.

There are other kinds of group-held views which either support or work against persuasive effort. Among the stronger bases for such attitudes are the "institutions" to which one belongs or to which one professes allegiance. Parents bring up their children in a certain faith, and more often than not, the children so brought up are conditioned permanently to react in a particular way whenever that faith becomes the focus of a conversation or issue. There are still many families in which for several generations the voting members have always voted either Republican or Democrat; and, sadly, there are others in which the adult members have never voted at all. Students go to a university for the first time and never consider the possibility of joining any but the

---

33. Erwin P. Bettinghaus, *Persuasive Communication* (New York: Holt, Rinehart, and Winston, 1968), p. 107. Reprinted by permission.
34. For two such reviews, see Hovland, Janis, and Kelley, pp. 19–48; and Cohen, pp. 23–36.
35. See Holtzman, pp. 116–117, for an elaboration of the argument that the "only effective practice of communication comes from preparing for and engaging in real communication transactions."

same fraternities, sororities, and other organizations to which their parents belonged. Such institutionally based attitudes provide a certain emotional safety, and it is characteristic of many people not to want to examine alternatives.

Group pressure

One's "opinions and attitudes are strongly influenced by the groups to which he belongs and wants to belong,"[36] and as a corollary," one is rewarded for conforming to group standards and punished for deviations."[37] Speakers seldom have to be reminded of the fact that whether or not listeners are persuaded to accept a message depends in part on the approval or disapproval which those listeners anticipate from their immediate friends and associates. Convention dictates much of what we think and do; group pressures are ever-present forces in our daily life. There is no one of us who has not, for instance, found himself in a situation in which he overtly agreed with someone but privately and silently disagreed with him; each of us has contributed to public collections with which he was not in sympathy; we participate in rituals of many kinds while at the same time regretting that we have to do so. It is a part of a communicator's task to recognize such pressures and take cognizance of what we have come to know about ways to use them or overcome them.

In this context, a key concept is *awareness* of membership.[38] If you were planning to assail the evils of alcohol before a group of students belonging to the Wesleyan Foundation, you could reasonably use a part of the introduction to heighten their pride in Methodism and what it has accomplished in the lives of men, partially through a traditional emphasis on sobriety. If you wished to take the position that drinking in moderation is a social asset, your chances of success would be enhanced by finding a heterogeneous student group in which group pressure would not be a factor; the members would not be aware of a mutually reinforced attitude expected of them. In other words, you can heighten awareness of membership in a group to increase group pressure and achieve a persuasive end, or, depending on your purpose, you can either ignore or minimize the implications of such membership, or you can look for a situation in which membership in a particular group will have no particular strength. The student in the classroom is different from the same student in a chapel, from the one at a pep rally, from the one at a meeting of the student government, and from the one at a local snack bar. A Puerto Rican—American is one person in the ghetto and another at his place of employment. The officer of a labor union is not the same man in his bowling league that he is in the union hall. The body and mind may be the same, but an individual's persuasibility varies with the topics and the places.

Although group-anchored attitudes are very strong, especially when membership in the group is emphasized, they can be changed. Cohen reports a 1956 experiment[39] in which a group of students at a "progressive teachers' college" listened to the recording of a speech advocating a return to traditional teaching methods. In the recording, the speech was interrupted at intervals by applause. One group listening to the record-

---

36. Karlins and Abelson, p. 49.
37. *Ibid.*, p. 53.
38. See Hovland, Janis, and Kelley, pp. 157—160.
39. Cohen, p. 40.

ing was told that the applauders were other members of their own "progressive" circle; another was told that the applauders were "outsiders." A questionnaire then determined that those exposed to applause by members of their own group showed a greater degree of change toward the objective of the speech than those who were exposed to applause from nongroup members. The conclusion of the experimenters was that one way to effect change in group-anchored attitudes would be to convince the members of a group that others in the same group have already changed their views.

Group leadership

Another significant hypothesis in any discussion of predispositions and susceptibilities is that of the "two-step flow of communication."[40] For example, the farm publication *Prairie Farmer* sponsors a show of farm methods and equipment which takes place one year in Illinois and the next in Indiana. The location of the show is *always* the farm of one of the most influential and enterprising farmers in a given area. The theory is that influence to adopt new methods and equipment moves from leaders in any field to their associates and to those of lower status but that influence seldom spreads upward from those of lower status. A farm agent follows this principle when, in the effort to gain acceptance for himself or an idea, he begins the campaign by trying to win over the farmer in the area who is most highly regarded by his fellows. Once again, people are persuaded by people. Furthermore, it is sound practice to try to win the approval of those known to exert influence in any group; their approval will reach others of influence and more readily filter down to the less influential members. If you can "polarize" the audience and arouse the leaders in it to react favorably through obvious interest or applause, the followers will usually fall into line. (It is also interesting to note that persons of relatively high status in a group feel freer to ignore group pressure, since they do not normally place as high a value on membership as do persons of lower status and self-esteem.)[41] An intriguing example of the influence of a person highly regarded in a community: In 1965 Marlowe Hartung abandoned a demanding commercial job in Seattle, Washington, to achieve the independence of running his own "visual arts center" in sculpture, painting, architecture, and graphic design. For a location he chose Doebay, a cove in one of the San Juan Islands of Puget Sound. Getting the project started was no easy matter, and among early difficulties was the rumor that he was setting up a nudist colony; this idea was dispelled only when one of the students spread the word that the operation was indeed a bona fide school for artists. The student was Jean Benson, *the wife of the Episcopal vicar* on the island.

Group participation

There is no faster way to enliven the proceedings in the speaker-audience situation than to make provision for some kind of active participation on the part of listeners. In addition to the gain in interest, another gain is often achieved: many a "lost cause" has been rescued by a question-and-answer period or by some other device offering

---

40. See "The Diffusion of New Ideas and Practices" by Elihu Katz in Schramm, *The Science of Human Communication*, pp. 77–91.
41. Hovland, Janis, and Kelley, p. 151.

active involvement to those present (e.g., having the audience move into a number of small discussion groups). In any event, "audience participation . . . helps to overcome resistance"[42] to a persuasive appeal, and there is some evidence that it also renders any opinion change more long-lasting.[43]

Somewhat less easy to demonstrate—in the classroom at least—is the observation that "persuasive appeals become more powerful when presented in conjunction with moderately distracting stimuli which positively reinforce the individual."[44] However, if you want to pass out mildly distracting coke and peanuts (as was done in a Yale study), it is possible that this kind of "audience participation" will cause your listeners to listen more favorably to your persuasive message. All of us are aware of the business practice of taking the client out to lunch, and we know that political rallies and meetings of other kinds are often accompanied by "free food and drink."

In review, we may observe that situational attitudes are frequently based (1) on group consensus, (2) on group pressure, (3) on group leadership, and (4) on group participation. In some situations you will want to enhance and highlight the association of a person or persons with a particular institution, group, or leader, and in others you will want to minimize or ignore such an association. Second, you will note that, no matter how strong group-anchored attitudes may be, change can be effected through introducing evidence that others in the group have already changed their views in the direction advocated. Third, you will recognize that the influential member or members of a group should, under certain circumstances, be the prime targets of the persuasive message because of the influence they exert on other members of the group. Finally, you will be aware that there are some inherent advantages in fostering audience participation, either directly as in providing for questioning, or indirectly as in making provision for light and pleasant distraction.

Listener Response and Observable Effects

The preceding discussion of "observable stimuli" and "predispositional factors" brings us to the third column in Fig. 12.1, in which we consider the listener response (via attention, comprehension, and acceptance) to those stimuli as screened or affected by listener susceptibility to persuasion and by the message, speaker, and situational factors affecting the listener's attitudes. Where education stops and persuasion begins has been a troublesome question in the history and theory of attitude distinction. McGuire points out a possible difference when he says that "we are 'educating' when the recipient of the communication has no initial stand on the issue and we are persuading when he does have an initial stand."[45] Again according to McGuire, any change occurring "with respect to attention and comprehension" is educational; to the extent that there is "yielding to what is comprehended," the situation is persuasion. He cites as example the change effected by the physics professor whose lecture would be listened to and comprehended (rather than yielded to) in con-

---

42. Karlins and Abelson, p. 62.
43. *Ibid.*, p. 78.
44. *Ibid.*, p. 16.
45. McGuire, pp. 150–51.

trast to the change in one's own judgment about certain paintings brought about by hearing fellow students express varying opinions on them. In the latter instance, the response components of attention, comprehension, and acceptance are *all* operative, a condition which is deemed characteristic of persuasion.[46]

Finally, we reach the goal of "observable effects" or "observable changes in attitude." If an attitude is some kind of amalgamation or fusion of perceptions, beliefs, feelings, and predispositions to speak or behave in set ways, it follows that pure education—attention and comprehension—can bring about observable change in one's attitude. Programs of black studies would fall into this category; students who learn more and more about black history, sociology, etc., are going to find their attitude changing in one way or another. The changes could occur in one or more of the constituent elements of an attitude. It also follows that persuasion—attention, comprehension, *and* acceptance—has as its objective a change in one or more of the same elements. When you see, as the result of education/information or as the result of persuasion, that a person is making statements and taking positions different from those he has made or taken in the past and/or that his behavior is changed in some other way, you are observing that, unless he is dissembling, a change in his attitude has taken place.

Analyzing Listeners and Their Attitudes

At this point in the course, it is assumed that you have developed an awareness of the complexity of communicative transactions, of the powers and pitfalls inherent in the manipulation of language, of the common value premises and argumentative forms on which good reasoning is based, and of the roles played by perception, motivation, cues, and rapport in affecting behavior. It is further assumed that you have acquired additional experience in interacting sensibly and sensitively with the other human beings around you. With that background in the theory of communication and with some practice in various forms of it, you now approach the task of trying to persuade individuals to accept a point of view and, possibly, to take some kind of action or change behavior in some way. Whether or not you succeed will depend heavily on the accuracy of your audience analysis and on the extent to which you use it intelligently.

What is analysis in this context? It is the attempt to learn as much as possible (1) about the general persuasibility of the listeners, (2) about their specific attitudes on the question at hand, (3) about those predispositional factors which could affect listener attitudes in this instance, and (4) about the ways in which the collected attitudinal information could be used as a part of the preparation for the intended communicative event.

STEP 1: Analysis from the Standpoint of
         General Listener Persuasibility

In this step, the prospective persuader makes the attempt to determine the persuasibility of an individual listener or the collective susceptibility-to-persuasion of a

---

46. *Ibid.*, p. 151.

group. He tries to answer this question: What are the general characteristics of this listener or of this audience? In an early session of some speech-communication courses, each student is asked to fill out a personal data blank which is intended to provide information on date of birth, home address, previous education, current academic majors and minors, career objectives, extracurricular activities, work experience, hobbies, etc. With that class directory in hand, for example, you would have a valuable knowledge bank for use in talking with any one student or with all of them in any setting, including a persuasive one. You would also be able to set up a kind of composite image of the class as a whole, its variety or its homogeneity in terms of social, religious, economic, political, and occupational categories, its common premises and collective values, its shared goals and motivations, and sometimes its prejudices and idiosyncracies. With or without detailed information on the exact makeup of an audience, it is always possible—and necessary—to do some careful conjecturing about audience composition and characteristics.

STEP 2: Analysis from the Standpoint of
    Specific Listener Attitudes

In the course of trying to determine the general composition of the audience and its susceptibility to persuasion, the analyst normally comes to recognize or suspect its prevailing attitudes, especially those having a bearing on his persuasive goal. Attitudes seeming to be irrelevant should not be too readily set aside. For example, your knowing that a particular audience strongly favors world government would not ordinarily help you win support for restructuring the procedural rules in Congress; however, you might be able to show that the restructuring proposed would increase the influence of younger senators and representatives who favor world government.

    In seeking to discover an audience's attitudes, some will become apparent through your understanding of "who will be there." Sometimes there is no way to pursue the matter further. Occasionally, however, you will be very well acquainted with the group itself or with the types of people who are drawn to a certain kind of meeting (e.g., a local political rally or a lecture on social problems). In the latter instance, you may be close enough to the situation to know the collection of beliefs leading to an attitude as well as the attitude itself. In any event, as indicated earlier in this chapter, if we can change a person's perceptions, beliefs, feelings, or behavior toward people or things, his attitude is likely to be changed one way or another in line with the changes achieved. Further, if a person's attitude undergoes or is made to undergo a change for any reason, there is ordinarily a corresponding modification of perceptions, beliefs, feelings, or behavior to accommodate the new attitude. It follows that audience analysis should not only include speculation about the attitudes which prospective listeners hold but should also encompass speculation about the bases for those attitudes. "Successful persuasion takes into account the reasons underlying the attitudes as well as the attitudes themselves."[47] If we can determine *why* an individual or group adheres to a particular view, and if we can show that individual or group *why* that view is held (people can seldom fully explain their attitudes and sometimes are unaware of their existence), we may be able to deal more effectively with the situation.

---

47. Karlins and Abelson, p. 92. See also section on bases and functions in this chapter.

For example, why were some hard-hats at loggerheads with students in 1969 and early 1970? Was patriotism the issue? Or was it that men who work hard with their hands to build could not stand idly by while another group, however small, seemed bent on the physical destruction of publicly owned buildings and facilities? Or was the issue increasing economic hardship for the hard-hats in contrast with the relatively easy life (from the hard-hat viewpoint) of the student "agitators"? In an effort to persuade the hard-hats to avoid future confrontations with the students, would it be safe to assume that the salient hard-hat attitude was "We should all back the President"? The point is that the *apparent* attitude may not be the *key* attitude, and it is the speaker's job to do more than make a superficial assumption about what impels people to action along certain lines in a given instance or series of instances.

STEP 3: Analysis from the Standpoint of
  Listener Attitudes Toward Message, Speaker, Situation

Once you know as much as you can about an audience's attitudes, you are ready to anticipate reactions to the content of the proposed talk. You are also in good position to make adjustments in the strategy of the message (motivation and goals, degree of tension to be aroused, reasoning and evidence, etc.), in the structure of the message (order of ideas, presentation of two sides of question versus one, etc.), and in consistency (introduction of message inconsistency and determination of the degree to which that approach should be used). What you have already absorbed about attitudes toward the message in this chapter and about message theory and practice in others will be helpful in this process of adjustment of content to attitudes and in the determination of what factors to employ in the endeavor to change attitudes.

The next obvious move is to take a look at what the audience will expect from you as the speaker. This strategy includes determining whether or not there will be any antipathy toward you on the part of the audience or on the part of influential individuals in it, finding out what advantages you may enjoy in interaction with this particular group, and deciding to do everything possible to meet and exceed what you see as reasonable audience expectations.

What will be the audience attitude and reaction toward the situation in general? This question calls for an examination of the physical, atmospheric, and other nonspeech and nonspeaker conditions to which the audience will be subjected. What group-consensus, group-pressure, group-leadership, or group-participation factors will be operative? Can anything supportive be done with music, light, amplifiers? Should the format include a questioning period? Besides doing a responsible job on the talk, what can you do about the situational surroundings to make the persuasive project a success with this audience?

STEP 4: Analysis from the Standpoint of
  Integrating Attitudinal Information with Overall Preparation

A final step in this process is the use "in reverse" of parts of the outline for critical analysis which appears near the close of Chapter 8. Section II of that outline lists a series of considerations for the "evaluation of choices made by the speaker." Paragraphs of typical questions are added to aid the analyst in his evaluation. It is possible to conceive of yourself as the speaker being evaluated and to use the evaluation pattern to determine how well you are preparing to relate purpose, motivation, attitudinal relationships, etc., to your image of the audience.

Persuasive communication, then, has many ingredients; four of them are based on your knowing something of the persuasibility and general character of the audience, knowing something of listener attitudes related to the communication situation, knowing something of the factors operative in any attempt to change those attitudes, and knowing how to go about using that knowledge to advantage in the persuasive project at hand.

. . . .

In conclusion . . .

Changing listener attitudes is one of the more difficult objectives in speech-communication. It can be reached partially and sometimes completely if, in the process of message preparation, the communicator-speaker will take the time to study not only listener attitudes but also factors affecting those attitudes. The persuasion planner must then make adaptive-to-the-listener adjustments in the characteristics of his message, of himself as speaker, and of the situational surroundings. When you plan a persuasive talk, prepare it well, and adapt it to the audience, you can reasonably expect one or more of these results: some change in listener perceptions, some change in beliefs or opinions, some change in the way individuals in the group feel about the topic under consideration, and some change in the action patterns concerned. If one or more of these things happen, you have successfully changed listener attitude.

. . . .

Speaking options

If a part of the basic course has been participation in problem-solving through discussion (Chapter 11), the students in the class will already be well on the way toward preparation of persuasive talks aimed at "influencing audience attitudes." This does not mean, of course, that all the members of a particular committee or discussion group should take exactly the same position; all it means is that the evidence and viewpoints presented in the small group offer a "mine" from which materials for a variety of persuasive positions can be extracted.

1. This project can be a straightforward 5–7 minute *persuasive effort in support of some value judgment*. The student endeavors to gain audience acceptance for an evaluative statement in any field (social, political, economic, artistic, etc.) He tries *to create* a new evaluative attitude or *to reinforce* one which already exists. For instance:

   A General Motors car is your best buy.
   Government bonds are a good investment.
   By and large, politicians are honest.
   Modern art leaves something to be desired.
   Communism *is* a threat to our way of life.

The township is an outmoded political entity.
The image of the American abroad is indeed "ugly."
The American Cancer Society deserves stronger support.

2. Here, in five to seven minutes, the student's objective is to convince his audience that *a serious problem exists* or, if the audience is generally aware that it exists, that *the problem is very serious.* The audience may or may not be aware that, for example:

City Hall is paying over-market-value prices for everything it buys!
The building of schools in this town costs twice as much per square foot as the type of building justifies.
We are being poisoned by air pollution.
Our "Greek organizations" discriminate on a basis of race.
The local crime situation is much worse than you think.

Caution: Be careful not to select a problem which your audience already recognizes as existing *and* serious. You will be wasting your time and, more important, theirs.

3. A 5–7 minute talk aimed at convincing the audience that *a particular solution, plan, or policy will solve a problem known to be serious.* If the local newspaper has been running a long and carefully documented series on corruption in voting practices in your city, it is possible to review the situation adequately in the introduction to a talk and then spend the bulk of your time in promoting a plan for solving the problem. Other examples of known problems calling for solution: It is known that the cities are losing important segments of their populations to the suburbs; less is known about ways and means to keep people in the city. It is known that young men must be drafted to serve in the armed forces; an acceptable way to handle the drafting has yet to be devised. When the rate of inflation begins to accelerate, there are almost as many plans for deceleration as there are economic experts proposing them.

To propose solution(s) of a problem, you must have an understanding of its causes, and your plan should be aimed at the elimination of them. Sometimes an attack on the symptoms is also in order as a part of the overall approach: If a primary cause of poverty is a lack of education, we can do something now to help the poor at the same time that we are working to improve educational opportunity.

Caution: Plans often cost money. Be prepared to estimate cost, to suggest a means of raising the necessary funds, and to justify the recommended expenditures. Avoid casual reference to "funds from the federal government." Washington doesn't readily provide funds on request. However, your investigation may disclose that there is already some kind of provision for "matching funds" through some federal legislation already passed. If so, your problem would then be to find a reasonable source for local or state funds.

4. A 6–8 minute problem-*and*-solution persuasive effort. This is a talk in which the student combines the salient features of the two preceding options. He undertakes to convince his audience (1) that an existing problem is serious enough to warrant concern and (2) that he has a sound plan outlining what can be done about it. (Since this is normally a more difficult talk to give than others aiming

at influencing an audience, there is often some provision for an extra minute or two in the presentation of it.) If you believe, for instance, that your audience is unaware of the extent of drug abuse in your community, you are first faced with the task of convincing your hearers that *the problem is really serious* (dangers to health, hidden costs, higher taxes, etc.); then you can go on to what you hope they will accept and support as a sensible plan for solving the problem.

Listening options

1. Use Chapter 8 (Listening: modes and methods) as the basis for "listening self-defensively" to one of the persuasive talks presented in class. Prepare a short reaction report in which you answer the questions posed in that section of Chapter 8. The report may be prepared in one of three forms: extemporaneous for presentation from notes, written in oral style to be read in class, or written in essay style to be turned in to the instructor.

2. Write a short paragraph commending one of the speakers for his recognition of and adaptation to an attitude which you feel is held by a majority of the members of the class. Or write a short paragraph in which you point out to a speaker that he fell short of recognizing a class attitude and failed to make adjustment to it. (All such paragraphs should be turned in to the instructor for handling in an appropriate and anonymous way.)

3. Write a short paragraph in which you point out that a speaker did or did not take advantage of one of the suggestions for *handling a factor affecting attitudes toward the message.*

4. Write a short paragraph in which you point out that a speaker did or did not take advantage of one of the suggestions for *handling a factor affecting attitudes toward the speaker.*

5. Write a short paragraph in which you point out that a speaker did or did not take advantage of one of the suggestions for *handling a factor affecting attitudes toward the situational surroundings.*

. . . .

Example of Outline of Problem-and-Solution Persuasive Speech

The organizational pattern which follows consists of excerpts from a student outline provided by Assistant Professor John Pacilio, Jr., University of Arizona.

Purpose: To convince the audience that the problem of smog is a serious threat to life and that we should work to solve it.

INTRODUCTION

Opening sentence(s): In 1952, smog covered the Greater London area and caused the deaths of hundreds of Londoners.

Personal competence: My first awareness of the problem of smog came when my father was working in the Los Angeles area.

Purpose and subject: Today I intend to present four ideas for your consideration:

I. Air pollution is not a new problem.
II. Today the problem is particularly serious.
III. Control of pollution is desirable.
IV. Practical solutions to this problem do exist.

Reason(s) to listen: If the right measures are taken, we can save millions of dollars and solve the air pollution problem at the same time.

BODY

(*Transition*: Many people are convinced that air pollution is a new problem. First, let us review evidence that—)

I. Air pollution is not a new problem.
   A. The problem of air pollution has existed for centuries.
      1. The first use of fire produced carbon dioxide, smoke, and ash.
      2. Accounts of medieval towns indicate that the air was foul.
   B. Smog is just a modern complication.
      1. The first smog known to cause fatalities occurred in Belgium in 1930.
      2. In 1948, in Donora, Pennsylvania, 20 were killed and almost 6,000 sickened by heavy smog.
      3. In 1952, smog caused up to 4,000 deaths in London.

(*Transition*: Air pollution, then, is not a new problem. Today—)

II. The problem is serious.
   A. The automobile is a major source of pollution.
      1. Nearly 150 chemicals are found in car exhausts.
      2. Millions of cubic yards of polluted air are daily poured into Arizona air.
   B. Public laws are ineffective.
      1. Arizona's laws don't provide for real control.
      2. Arizona statutes provide only for definition of nuisances and abatement of them.

(*Transition*: Let us see what we would gain in solving this problem.)

III. Air pollution control is desirable.
   A. Air pollution is costing two billion dollars a year in damage to crops, livestock, and property.
   B. Those who smoke apparently increase chances of dying from cancer by driving in heavy traffic.

(*Transition*: Can we, in fact, develop ways to control the smog?)

IV. Practical solutions to this problem do exist.
   A. The federal government is already setting purity standards for cars.
      1. The auto industry can supply the necessary equipment.
      2. Auto engineers can eliminate at least 50 percent of the hydrocarbons.
   B. The separate states can take action.
      1. California is spending millions to bring pollution under control.
      2. Arizona can also initiate an effective program.

CONCLUSION

Summary: You have seen that the problem of air pollution is not new and that today it is serious. You have also seen that there are benefits from solving the problem and that we can, in fact, solve it.

Concluding sentence(s): The only thing we need is action. Write to your local and national representatives and request support for bills that help solve this ever-growing problem. Do it now—while you're still able to breathe.

Notes on the outline

It would have been possible to cover the same ground under two main points rather than under four:
I. The problem of air pollution is growing steadily more serious.
   A. Air pollution has been a danger for a long time.
   B. Air pollution is especially threatening now.
II. We can solve the air pollution problem.
   A. Practical approaches to the solution now exist.
   B. Additional advantages would come from action now.

The advantage of the organization above is that it would be not only somewhat easier for the audience to grasp but also easier for the average speaker to handle.

Representative Student Speeches Aimed at Changing Attitudes

The examples that follow were selected from a series of student speeches published in 1970 by the Interstate Oratorical Association. They are reprinted here by permission of the Association.

No man need be an island

By Rebecca M. Ferris, *University of Kentucky*

> *No man is an island, entire of itself; . . . any man's death diminishes me, because I am involved in mankind.*

These lines of John Donne once represented hope for the alienated, security for the rejected and companionship for the lonely. Shelley suggests, "The eye sees what it brings to the seeing." I am alarmed by my own vision. I see an American people so involved with technological and industrial progress that they have neglected to realize the need for human advancement.

I am concerned because I see an American people striving vainly to solve man's fundamental problems of food, health, education, clothing, but paying too little attention, not through malice but carelessness, to an equally universal problem. The malady of which I am speaking is not a distant one—in fact, its closeness is frightening. Every day I see the problem reflected in the faces of my fellow students, members of minority groups, the elderly, newlyweds, hippies, and even the silent majority. Their expressions are typical of the lonely, the alienated, the rejected. Observation has persuaded me that Donne's philosophy is no longer applicable. For men are islands unto themselves; the death of one man diminishes no one. As Dale Wasserman writes in his play *Man of La Mancha*: "A man has died; some say he was a good man; I knew him not."

My concern is difficult to verbalize for people often think it sentimental or trite; but that doesn't make it any less universally ignored. The poet James Weldon Johnson expressed the problem when he wrote: "And God stepped out on space and He looked around and said, 'I'm lonely.'"

It is the problem of loneliness—alienation—with which I am concerned, for it is rampant in our time. As one writer noted: "This malady is not something remote; . . . it is democratically available for all."

Literature and life are replete with the lonely figure, each character having his own cause for isolation from the rest of mankind. Steinbeck, for instance, saw homelessness as a cause for loneliness and poignantly reflected it in his work *Of Mice and Men*. Socioeconomic forces caused the loneliness in the *Street Scene* of Elmer Rice and Anderson's *Winterset*. William Saroyan, in *The Time of Your Life*, reflected on the loneliness resulting from the conflict between the material and the spiritual. Each of us has experienced vicariously the doubting loneliness of Oedipus the King, the Melancholy Dane, and the Crucified Christ.

But we don't need books and plays to tell of loneliness. All we have to do is open our eyes to the lives around us. Observe your local cafeterias during the evening meal, noticing the number of older men and women who each evening eat alone at separate tables. Think of the lonely seclusion of the elderly in rest homes. Notice the aloneness of the single student watching television late at night in the student union lounge. Notice the students in your college housing units who constantly brag about their dates—but never seem to have any. Observe the reaction of the little child who is a newcomer to a neighborhood and the others won't let him play. Think of the seclusion of the retarded child. Remember the feeling you had when someone special didn't phone you as he promised. Recall the look in your father's eye when you forgot his birthday. Watch the loneliness of parents who can do nothing to help their children solve their problems. These are scenes of the lonely. Perhaps these isolates desire this sense of estrangement; whatever the cause of alienation, you, they, and I suffer for their separation. For whether we like it or not, we are involved in each other. Whether we like it or not, everybody needs somebody.

What seems particularly ironic about the existence of loneliness is that we live in an age of communication. Our technology has placed men on the moon and we watch and listen. Invention of the picture telephone and weather satellites represent man's eagerness to explore and to communicate. But man has failed to communicate on his own planet with his own kind. He has become too involved with travel and technology to realize or to remember, and perhaps the latter is worse, that the most exciting communication is that which occurs between two people face to face.

The implications of the existence of loneliness are frightening. Psychologists have told us that loneliness and alienation may result in both physical and psychological problems for the individual. Dr. A. H. Schmale, writing in the *Journal of Psychosomatic Medicine*, reveals that almost all with organic disease who were admitted to a general hospital had sustained some emotional crises prior to the onset of their physical symptoms. Dr. G. L. Engel cites evidence strongly suggestive that dispiriting events which produce hopelessness are factors in ulcerative colitis. The research of professors Maslow and Fromm indicates that when society does not permit people a way of life that produces rich satisfaction of human needs, physical or mental illness takes root. According to Harvard psychologist Sidney Jourard, "Nothing makes a man sick sooner than feeling...unwanted...and unneeded."

What can be done about the problem of loneliness? How can you and I reach the alienated, the lonely, the rejected? The solution is so simple you will scoff when you hear it. The answer? We must listen—simply listen to what other people have to say. We must stop the verbal game of double solitaire, for we have all talked and none of us listened for so long that we have made our fellowmen islands unto themselves. We must permit people to be themselves. One simple way to allow self-realization is to listen. Stop and think for a moment. I am a speech major; most of you are speech teachers. How many textbooks can you name which deal with effective listening? We pay lip service to the concept in speaking of the two-step flow of communication, audience analysis, idea adaptation, and so forth. But in comparison with the number of books in drama, debate, discussion, rhetoric, how many books deal with the specifics of effective listening? Perhaps even more significant are the few attempts at teaching effective listening.

Listening, it would seem to me, involves at least three things: first, we must care about people, for without caring, why bother to listen; and maybe we don't care, but if not, let's have the guts to admit that we don't care; secondly, effective listening means helping and allowing a friend to disclose his inner feelings freely and honestly without fear of laughter, censure or ridicule; thirdly, effective listening involves interpreting what has been disclosed in order to help the other person. The effective listener cares about and listens to—people. He is able to get into empathic contact with anybody who is ill, worried, troubled, concerned, anxious whether Negro or white, young or old, Protestant or Catholic, moral or immoral, hippy or conservative, silent majority or activist. If he cannot immediately relate to this person, he strives to learn his language, his view of the world, his values, his wants, so that he can then listen and understand. The effective listener cares about and listens to—people. You may be thinking that my concept of the effective listener is one which will never be attained by any one person. Perhaps you are right. But I believe that our value orientation is wrong if we place more emphasis on what is achieved rather than what is attempted.

I realize, of course, that listening cannot solve all our interpersonal problems. But how many people could we reach, how many could we pull back into the company of men if we would but listen? According to Dr. Jourard, "There is ample reason to suspect that people fall ill...because their past way of life...has failed to inspire...

and their future seems . . . to be devoid of . . . meaning." In his book *From Death Camp to Existentialism*, V. E. Frankl writes of those who survived incredible stress primarily because they could find some purpose for living. "It appears that man can inspire in man an attitude . . . which does affect . . . growth and learning." I suggest, therefore, that the manner in which we listen and relate to our fellows can and does make a significant difference.

Perhaps no man is an island. But in my experience he is, sealing himself off from those around him often because those around him don't care enough to listen. Remember those who dine at separate tables. Recall the despair in the eyes of the child. Remember the feeling you had when your special person didn't phone. Recall the lonely distance between parent and child.

The universal agony of loneliness may be corrected by the ecstasy of communication. Granted, communication is not an easy process—it requires effort and patience by both the sender and the receiver. On some occasions, channels may become crossed; but that is no reason to abandon the attempt.

Today I ask you to remember that loneliness and alienation are rampant in our time—and that you and I have the key to unlock man's barrier of seclusion. I appeal to you to use that key by never forgetting that everybody needs somebody. Perhaps when we do remember, then no man will be an island.

Custer had it coming

By H. Timothy Halverson, *Muskingum College, Ohio*

Separated from the mainland by an impassable body of water, Alcatraz was inescapable. On a clear day, prisoners could catch glimpses of San Francisco and its surrounding culture, yet even the most ingenious convicts realized that escape was impossible; they were doomed to live on the "rock," in society's shadow.

On a foggy morning in the early part of November, fourteen Indian college students arrived at Alcatraz. They told the press that they came to the island because it already had all the necessary features of a reservation: dangerously uninhabitable buildings, no fresh water, inadequate sanitation, and the certainty of total unemployment.

While reading about the sacrifice and dedication of these Indian college students, I realized my own very inadequate knowledge as to the causes that brought these Indians to the "rock." By seeking out information, I became concerned about the seriousness of the Indian problem. Soon it became very apparent that Alcatraz is symbolic of the imprisonment of all American Indians. Like the convict, he is unable to swim the chasm that separates him from the American mainstream. Yet, it is only because of our unawareness, apathy, and disregard that this problem exists. The American public must become aware of the Indian problem—aware that in society's shadow, the Indian is making his last stand for cultural survival.

An uneducated American public, a paternalistic Bureau of Indian Affairs, and the lack of economic and educational reform have created this Indian problem. Once free to roam this country, the Indian was socially and economically chained to the reservation. While Hollywood has glamorized this event, the Indian realizes the truth—the white man stole his land and killed his people. Forced into land locked jails, alienated from his own culture, cheated, swindled, and exploited by his "Christian friends," the one hundred Indians now occupying Alcatraz plead for public awareness and support. [Editor's note: Federal authorities removed the "occupying Indians" in 1971.] The recent Report of the Commission on National Goals revealed that "the economic position of the Indian is less favorable than that of any other minority group."

And the Indian problem is growing. His unemployment rate is 10 times the national average, his life span is 21 years shorter than his fellow citizens, and his average income is only $\frac{1}{4}$ of the national average. Inadequate sanitary facilities, contaminated water, poor education, and the highest suicide rate in the nation further reveal the Indian's burden. Yet, facts and statistics are incomplete. They alone cannot conjure up the picture of a "tiny two-room log cabin holding a family of thirteen at Fort Hall, or a gutted automobile body in which a Pine Ridge Sioux family huddles against the South Dakota winter." Hopefully, Lyndon Johnson expressed the public concern when he told Congress that "no enlightened nation, no progressive government, no progressive people can permit this shocking situation to continue."

Through attitudes of apathy, neglect, and ignorance, this dilemma was created. To correct the Indian's problem, the public must create new approaches and new attitudes to replace those that have failed.

Robert Bennett illustrates this need. Appointed in 1966 as the first Indian to head the Bureau of Indian Affairs, he resigned last July in utter disgust, charging that "the new Administration has completely ignored the Indians." The Bureau has been crippled, as Bennett's resignation points out, by an administration and general public that are shamefully unaware that the 652,000 Indians even exist. A change in public attitude could solve the Indian problem.

The small band of Indians that defiantly occupy Alcatraz are uncertain as to what direction the Indian must now move to create this necessary public response. The sense of urgency, however, is everywhere apparent. Signs, such as "Custer had it Coming" and "Better Red than Dead," catch the new mood of the American Indian. And while the Tom-Toms and the more militant Tom-a-hawks disagree over methods, all Indians agree that the great white father, the American public, is the greatest obstacle in their war of liberation.

An educated public must realize that Indians deeply resent their status as incompetent wards of the white man's government. Explaining the prevalent American attitude, the Indians cite the following legend: A white man sees a mountain and asks, "How can I change you?" An Indian, seeing the same mountain, asks, "How can I live with you?"

The Bureau of Indian Affairs, the public's direct overseer to the Indian, must reflect a change in this paternalistic Amerian attitude. At present, the Bureau, or BIA, takes care of the Indian's money, doles it out if his request is good, determines the use of his land, is in charge of the development of all Indian natural resources, educates his children, and dominates all aspects of Indian life—depriving the Indian of his manhood, self-respect, and the ability to make his own decisions. Even the local reservation authorities many times are unable to make immediate decisions without the approval from Washington. The BIA itself is enmeshed within the cumbersome structure of the Department of Interior where the considerations of the Bureau of Land Management and the Bureau of Reclamation overshadow the needs of the Indians.

Clearly the public, through the BIA, needs to reevaluate its objectives. The Bureau can no longer perpetuate the image of the great white father; instead, self-help and self-determination must be key objectives in this restructured approach. The BIA itself must be freed from the stranglehold of the Department of Interior, and a separate department must be created in which the concerns of the Indian are primary.

Alone, however, a restructured BIA is not the answer. The bow of his shoulder and slump of his body reveals the Indian's loss of pride. The Indians on Alcatraz are painfully aware that economic and educational reform must also occur if the Indian is to again stand tall with pride. The American public must take the initiative and show the Indian people a renewed faith in these forgotten Americans. As the late Robert F. Kennedy, chairman of the Subcommittee on Indian Affairs, stated in 1966, "our first Americans seem to be our last American concern."

A modern society cannot allow such conditions to exist. Teachers must be better trained, more funds need to be made available, and an Indian Peace Corps must be established. More and larger scholarships are necessary to provide the youth a chance to break the cycle of despair and despondency—a cycle inherent from one generation to the next—resulting in a suicide rate among the Indian youth five times the national average. Public awareness, yours and mine, must provide the Indian youth with an alternative to self-destruction.

Economic reform is also necessary if Indian liberation is to become a reality. At the crux of the problem is more jobs. Professor Gary Orfield of the University of Virginia feels that the creation of 40,000 jobs could solve the basic economic problem of the Indian community.

To solve the economic problem, the Indians must first control their own land. Many reservations, such as the Fort Hall Reservation, are controlled by white economic interests. As Peter Collier pointed out in his article, "The Red Man's Burden," at Fort Hall the Indians control only 17 percent of their land; the other 83 percent has been exploited by whites at an average profit of $200 an acre. The Indian must reap the profit of his own land.

Second, the Indian must develop his land. Irrigation projects, the creation of recreational sites, and the development of natural resources are necessary. The government must make long-range, low-interest loans available to the Indians so they can develop their own individual and community resources.

Third, tax incentives must be given to lure industries to relocate on the reservations, thereby trying to duplicate the success of Fairchild Camera Company. This company has had excellent results in Arizona employing Indians working under Indian management.

The Indian's ownership, development, and management of his land and his destiny is vital for economic liberation. The Indian asks to be more than a mere tourist attraction. They ask for self-respect and self-reliance.

Indians must no longer remain as mere anachronisms to the late night show which depicts these uneducated savages slaughtered by the talented and morally superior cowboys. The Indians argue for the future.

Last month, Earth Day brought the problem of pollution to the attention of the American public. Let us also set aside a day of awareness for the Indian; a day in which schools, news media, civic clubs, churches, and communities throughout the nation would inform America of the Red Man's Burden. An American Indian Day would arouse and awaken a slumbering public. It would create a public concern, and it would call for a dedicated people to join the Indian in fighting his last continuing war, the war for cultural survival.

An uneducated American public, a paternalistic BIA, educational and economic reform, these are the obstacles. Yet, in the words of one Indian, "We have a hard trail ahead of us, but we are not afraid of hard trails."

Symbolic Alcatraz lies separated from the American mainland. But Alcatraz does not have to be an island; the separating body of water is bridgeable. The gates of the prison must be opened, and her children must again run free.

To share the grief of Hammlyn Town

By Gregory Abels, *West Virginia University at Parkersburg*

There's a song in America. It's a song of love and brotherhood without obligation; of freedom and life without struggle. Composed worlds ago by prophets and played this day by the pusher, this refrain of sweet melodies runs through the ghettos, the suburbs, the factories, the schools—throughout the nation. It's the song of speed, uppers, bennies, acid, crystal, and the most entrancing of them all—the big H. Heroin—offering the needle for the need, for all needs. The lyrics have appeal, except for those who have listened long and caught the deceit. But long after the music faded, the necessity of escape lingers on. Fewer than 2 percent of those who succumb to the man with the song, the pusher of false happiness, ever return. The others are destined to lives of poverty, loneliness, crime, prison, illness, and always unhappiness. A portrait of hell? Or a snapshot of the future of young America?

Heroin, long considered the affliction of the hardened criminal, the skid-row derelict, the aging prostitute whose beauty is fading, has now reached the college campus, the high school classroom, and the junior high cafeteria. Elementary school children are singing songs of drug-induced highs and psychedelic dreams. They speak the jargon of the junkie. A recent *Newsweek* national poll reported the use of drugs "an accepted fact of life for 30 to 50 percent of all U.S. secondary school students." Addiction below age 25 jumped 40 percent from 1968 to 1969. Known teen-age deaths from heroin increased 183 percent in the past two years. Young America is listening to the man with the song. Dr. Donald Luria, president of the New York State Council on Drug Addiction, predicts that at the current rate of infiltration, hard drugs will be in every U.S. high school and college within the next two years. And the pushers continue to sing their songs. Unnoticed and seldom bothered by the authorities, they sell "death on the installment plan" to easily enticed young people who stop to listen. Those who destroy young lives for money no longer offer candy to the children; they offer "happiness," a phone number, a hastily scrawled message, a plastic bag of white powder, a needle, a name, an "experience"— an experience which if continued leads to eventual deterioration of the mind and body—or death.

We can no longer turn away and say that drug abuse is solely a problem within the ghetto where it seethed for so long. The man with the song may be found in nearly every American community.

Although it might seem reasonable to apprehend the man rather than focus on catching the juvenile user or possessor, government action has been relatively unsuccessful. Such programs as Operation Intercept along the Mexican-American border and the Controlled Dangerous Substances Act have been operating under the old outdated stereotype of the pusher. We're all familiar with the image. The dirty old man lurking in the shadows, hiding in the alley, playing cards in the backroom of the local pool hall—just waiting to ensnare an innocent, curious youth. But in reality the man with the song is often just another kid who happens to have some contacts—with dropouts, college students, or adults who can get the stuff. Just another kid who breaks in new addicts to support his own habit. Government programs must change their concepts to meet the operations of the new drug culture—to catch the pusher and hush his song.

And so it comes to you and me. There's a new song that we must sing. It rings of friendship, understanding and warmth. It's sung today by volunteer students and ex-addicts who work at small rehabilitation centers. The addict who comes to a center is received into a circle of friends rather than a clinical, sterile atmosphere. Attendants are not dressed in starched white uniforms, for theirs is simply a job of listening and caring. This is why the rehabilitation centers are so important. Our local center, typical of those being established in smaller communities, works with the addict in a three-phase program. The first phase seeks to acquaint the community with the available services. Although sympathetic to all, young or old, our primary concern is the youth. Volunteers, usually college age or younger, go into the schools and explain what the drugs are, how they affect the user, and how an addict may be treated. Youth listens to youth.

Secondly, we try to create a feeling of trust and security in the addict when he comes to the center. We talk to him, let him know we care, draw him out, let him talk with others with similar problems, try to help him realize that as an adolescent he has a special susceptibility to the man with the song. In addition to the normal curiosity of youth, he is under pressure from peer groups, a pressure hard to resist. Through awareness we try to prepare him to face the problems or situations that turned him to the promise of the needle. We have to convince him that users are not "cool," that junk is not "in," that the lyrics are not lasting.

And in the final treatment phase, qualified medical personnel take charge. To acquaint, to care, to treat—to act. This is the purpose of the center. It's a time-consuming process, usually taking from a year to two years. There is a relatively small amount of money available to combat addiction, and an even smaller number of sympathetic people willing to offer their services, for the job isn't easy. It isn't refreshing to spend a Saturday morning with an ex-honor student fighting withdrawal; it isn't fun to spend an evening trying to occupy a boy's mind with something other than his desperate need for a fix. But to hear one boy or girl making plans to help their friends break their habits, to share a former addict's joy when he receives his college acceptance, can be extremely rewarding. And a reformed addict is the best advertisement for a center. Those who are rehabilitated will reach out to other addicts, hopefully causing a multiplier effect. We can't hope to cure all the addicts with our new song—but we can cure some. And it is a beginning. But our song will never be finished if more isn't done. Volunteers are needed at all the existing centers, and if a center does not exist in a particular area, someone must start one. For if our song isn't finished, the history of our youth culture may someday read much like that of a little town in Germany many years ago.

Into that town one day came a man with a song. His music entered the hearts of the children as they crowded to listen, calling to one another to follow. The song of dreams entered the gardens, the houses, and the schools; and more and more the children came. Too late the parents rushed out to stop them. But the song had faded. And so had the children with their piper of dreams. How bitter was the grief that settled over Hammlyn Town.

If fools and folly rule the world, the end of man in our time may come as a rude shock, but it will no longer come as a complete surprise.

Abdul Rahman Pazhwak

13 / Debating issues in a free society

Congress shall make no law respecting an establishment of religion, or prohibiting the free exercise thereof; or abridging the freedom of speech, or of the press; or the right of the people peaceably to assemble and to petition the Government for a redress of grievances.

First Amendment, Constitution of the United States

If you live in an area reached by an educational television station, you may have seen an hour-long show called "The Advocates." It is a weekly discussion of a current public issue before a live audience. Two attorneys, known to have opposing points of view, are the primary speakers. As a part of his team, each attorney has three or four guest witnesses or experts. The meeting is moderated by an expert in the field under study, and there is a permanent chairman whose job it is to see that both sides get "equal time." After the debate, the people in the studio express their views by voting on the issue, and the TV viewers are also invited to vote by mail. The program is mentioned here because it is typical of constructive free speech at its best. If you have a chance to see it or a program similar to it, you will have a fine model for the debating of public issues.

Not all public debating is up to that high standard. In fact, there are those who from time to time make attempts to inhibit any kind of freedom of speech. For example, in 1968 and later, some public figures took the position that opponents of the Vietnam war were close to committing treason. The implication was that it was "un-American" to dissent and to criticize involvement in the war. (Apparently overlooking the cardinal principle that it is the right of any American to oppose a policy he does not consider to be in our national interest, those leaders had also forgotten their condemnation of the Nazis whose excuse for blindly following Hitler was that they had felt constrained to be loyal to their leader's policies, right or wrong.)

In addition to making occasional efforts to hinder or prohibit freedom of speech through legal maneuvers or through attempts to marshal public opinion against this constitutional right, governmental agencies are sometimes overzealous in "protecting us from ideas." It is not, of course, the province of government to so protect us; rather, it is the duty of any administration to see to it that we are fully informed and free to discuss any and all policies undertaken in our name through authorizations granted to it by us. For example, it is difficult to get permission to visit countries considered by any one administration to be "off limits" to our citizens. (A student discussion, speech, or debate could be profitably centered on questions such as: Should we be sheltered in this way? Are we morally and intellectually incompetent to judge for ourselves where we want to go and what ideas we wish to accept or reject?) In ages past, it was common for government or ecclesiastical agencies to decide what the people should read, hear, think, and say. Fortunately for us, the Constitution guarantees us the right of freedom of speech, and that means free access to ideas and freedom to debate and discuss them in any field, political, social, religious, economic, moral, and philosophical. We should be constantly on our guard against having any group, official or unofficial, chip away at this basic right.

What is Freedom of Speech?

In November, 1970, results of a survey by the Education Commission of the United States indicated that a majority of young people lack "any consistent understanding or conviction about the exercise of free speech."[1] In a random sampling across the country, about 90,000 individuals up to age 35 were asked if they would allow Americans to hear the following statements by radio or television: "Russia is better than the United States." "Some races of people are better than others." "It is not necessary to believe in God." Of those in the 26 to 35 age bracket, 68 percent said they would not permit the broadcast; 78 percent of the 17-year-olds and 94 percent of the 13-year-olds held the same view. Clearly, there is need for a better understanding of freedom of speech and of its importance to the preservation of our constitutional liberties.

As already suggested, *freedom of speech is the freedom to discuss and debate ideas and to try to change the views and attitudes of others who do not agree with us; it is not the freedom to do what we wish.* For instance, there are those who believe that a "war policy" of any kind is undesirable, and unless those citizens are silenced by force or intimidated by public opinion, they will continue to work for a change in policy. *This is their constitutional right.* However, so long as a "war policy" of any kind is in effect, it is the duty of every citizen to obey the rules, laws, decrees, and ordinances decided upon by the legally constituted governmental bodies. The individual citizen may try to change the views of the majority, but he cannot divorce himself from responsibility to pay his taxes, serve in the armed forces if called upon, and place himself under whatever controls are deemed necessary by the administration. The citizen who insists that he can do as he pleases if he does not agree with

---

1. As reported in the *Indianapolis Star*, November 18, 1970, p. 5.

policy believes neither in a government of free men working together to solve problems nor in a free democratic (will of the majority) government; he believes in anarchy.

Lest we think we are dealing with a new problem, we should again read Plato's *Apology*, in which Socrates, by declaring man's right to freedom of speech, is telling the city fathers of Athens that they cannot tell him what to think or say. In the *Crito*, recognizing his responsibilities as a citizen, he is subjecting himself to the laws of Athens, even though he does not as an individual consider them to be just.

An important distinction: The First Amendment forbids the abridging of *freedom of speech*, but it does not forbid the abridging of *speech*. This means (1) that such acts as libel, slander, incitement to crime, conspiracy to overthrow the government, and treason can be "abridged" and (2) that lawfully constituted agencies may specify conditions, procedures, and rules that must be observed in making arrangements for a public meeting. For example, if a city has an ordinance specifying that no two public meetings are to be permitted in the same general area of the city at the same time, the ordinance is one legitimately abridging speech (specifying conditions) but not abridging freedom of speech. In other words, the government "may regulate any aspects of the form, time, place or manner of speaking . . ., but must not use those powers so as actually to regulate substance or content."[2]

To be afraid of ideas, any idea, is to be unfit for self-government.

Alexander Meiklejohn

Two Key Decisions on Freedom of Speech

In 1924, Roger Baldwin, then director of the American Civil Liberties Union, and seven striking silkworkers were convicted of holding a meeting in Paterson, New Jersey, after being notified by the chief of police of that city that no further meetings of strikers could be held. (The strikers had been meeting daily before the issuance of the order.) The New Jersey Supreme Court, to which the case was appealed said, *"The right of the people to meet in public places to discuss in an open and public manner all questions affecting their substantial welfare and to vent their grievances, to protest against oppression, economic or otherwise . . . were rights . . . guaranteed them by . . . the Bill of Rights. . . ."*[3]

In July 1934, a known Communist, Dirk DeJonge, was indicted for arranging a Portland, Oregon, meeting to protest against the shooting of striking longshoremen by Portland police. Although the meeting was called to deplore violence, the prosecution held that the defendant belonged to a party advocating the overthrow of the American form of government. DeJonge's conviction was reversed by the U.S. Supreme Court in 1937. In effect, the Court held that "The holding of meetings for peaceable

---

2. From *Free Speech* by Robert M. O'Neil, copyright © 1966, by The Bobbs-Merrill Company, p. 64. Reprinted by permission of the publishers.

3. Reported in Williams, pp. 69–71.

political action cannot be proscribed," no matter by whom the meetings are called. Chief Justice Hughes went on to say, in part, that *the constitutional rights of free speech, free press, and free assembly must be protected "in order to maintain the opportunity for free political discussion, to the end that government may be responsive to the will of the people and that changes, if desired, may be obtained by peaceful means. Therein lies the security of the Republic, the very foundation of constitutional government."*[4]

Decisions in a Free Society

In a free society, one in which citizens make decisions themselves or delegate (by voting) responsibility for making decisions to others who represent them, the fundamental principle is that *power and authority continue to reside in the people*. They have the right and opportunity to influence local decisions through active personal participation in the decision-making process; they have the right and opportunity to influence the decisions of their representatives by means of face-to-face or telephone conversations, telegrams, letters, and the lobbying process. The average citizen resorts primarily to letters; if you have written to U.S. Senators or to members of the House of Representatives, you know that a reply arrives soon thereafter. The reply may not say what you want it to say, but you can be certain that your letter is tallied on the pro or con side of the issue on which you expressed an opinion. In the long run, senators and representatives vote the way they feel a majority of their constituents want them to vote; otherwise, they soon find themselves "retired." The crucial point to remember is that the elected officials in your town or city are working for *you*; the officials in the state capital are working for *you*; those in the national governmental offices are working for *you*. You are entitled to full and complete information on matters of public policy, and it is your constitutional right to speak freely on any such matter. *No individual and no official can abridge this right*. This fact will not, of course, deter some people from trying to abridge it; as indicated earlier, injunctions and other legal devices are sometimes used to hamper freedom of speech; sometimes parliamentary procedures are distorted (filibusters, etc.) to achieve that end; sometimes threats of physical violence are invoked; sometimes a matter of policy is discussed and settled without any affected citizen's being aware that the subject was coming up; and sometimes the public is purposely kept in ignorance about the significance of a topic, so that people will not interfere in "matters they know nothing about." It is not uncommon for the citizens of a community to discover that the members of the city council have made an important decision without consulting anyone outside their little group; it is not really unusual for an elected board to decide that contracts should be "negotiated" or that the high bidder on a contract is "more reliable" than any of the lower bidders; and it does happen that certain boards and elected groups meet "privately" to discuss problems without having citizens and reporters present—this practice facilitates rapid and "business-like" handling of affairs in the formal public meetings. These and other abuses of *the right of the citizen to know and to make his views known* occur (1) when citizens are

---

4. Williams, pp. 74–75.

ignorant of their rights or (2) when they do not care enough about civic problems to take an active interest in local, state, and national affairs.

When a nation silences criticism and dissent, it deprives itself of the power to correct its errors.

Henry Steele Commager

The Student and Freedom of Speech

It is often said that college and university educators have a primary responsibility to teach students how to think, not what to think. Although intellectual freedom (the right to search for "truth") follows naturally from that proposition, freedom of expression is obviously essential to the dissemination of new knowledge and ideas; it is even more important to the preservation of a political system in which personal and intellectual freedom is guaranteed. No student should be graduated without an understanding (1) of the constitutional basis for freedom of speech in this country, (2) of his stake in the guarding of that freedom from unconstitutional efforts to infringe upon it, and (3) of his legitimate exercise of it on and off the campus. Enough has already been said in this chapter about the first two points; let us now consider what freedom of speech means to the student in terms of "legitimate exercise" of it.

First of all, students of legal age have the right to vote, and fortunately for all of us, those who have not reached that age are joining with those who have in becoming increasingly involved in political activity and campaigning. Student groups are studying platforms and supporting candidates of their choice by manning telephones, doing office work, ringing doorbells, participating in fund-raising rallies, and doing anything and everything required to exert political influence. In fact, the students surpass many of their elders both in their interest in making our political system work and in their willingness to undertake the drudgery of campaign detail. Some of the work is done through such organizations as Young Republican Clubs, Young Democrat Clubs, and similar groups representing other political persuasions. Although free discussion of controversial issues, political or otherwise, is still restricted on some campuses, most schools now allow student organizations to express unpopular viewpoints on such issues. The larger schools have long been more permissive in their attitudes toward political organizations and their activities, but even the small denominational colleges are now moving toward acceptance of student rights to freedom of expression.[5]

In addition to feeling that they should have the right to be individually and collectively active in politics, many students feel that their organizations should be entitled "to hear in live confrontation an off-campus speaker enunciate any opinion, regardless of its public popularity and regardless of the speaker's political beliefs or

---

5. See Williamson and Cowan, pp. 39–60, for a report on campus political organizations and the relative freedom of students to discuss topics ranging from interracial marriage laws to sale of farm products to Russia.

association, his intellectual merits, or the possibility of causing a public disturbance."[6] They take the position that it is part of a college or university education to learn to pass judgment on ideas and that it is very much a part of the "American way" to grant a hearing to all ideas, wise and unwise, fair and unfair, unprejudiced and prejudiced, safe and dangerous. Listening to a speaker does not, after all, imply approval of him or of his views, and in the view of many educators and administrators, the majority of students are entirely capable of thinking for themselves. However, on this general issue (invitation of controversial speakers), "The acceptability of speakers varies widely, both from speaker to speaker and from school to school, but not even the most reputable of men can be heard in some schools."[7] For example, Dr. Ralph Bunche has served the United States and the United Nations with notable success; his appearance on some campuses would be "controversial" on one or both of two counts: his association with the United Nations and his being a black.

Students also believe that they should, through student government or appropriately designated student agencies, participate in institutional policy-making.[8] Decisions affecting them have been made and are being made with little or no attempt to determine student views or reactions in advance of a ruling. Students feel that they should have something to say about such matters as determination of codes of conduct, regulations and procedures in disciplinary actions, choice of faculty advisers by the organizations concerned, and the right to live off campus and travel at will.[9] Increasing numbers of colleges and universities are already consulting students through their membership on selected advisory boards; some have appointed students to voting membership on boards of trustees; others give student governments opportunity to discuss and debate academic problems, and the resulting resolutions are considered before a final decision is made. In fact, in matters directly affecting students, fewer and fewer decisions are now being made unilaterally by faculties or by administrators; the trend is toward unofficial and official consultation, so that students have an opportunity for democratic participation in the decision-making. Some of this decision-making takes place in conversational settings, some in informal and formal discussions (e.g., board meetings), some in public or semipublic debates, and some in large-group parliamentary "assemblies." Small-group decision-making has been treated in Chapter 11; public debates are discussed below; and large-group decision-making is the subject of Chapter 14.

Friendly Persuasion in Public Debate

At some point in practically every film epic of the "Wild West," one of the principals challenges another to a face-to-face "showdown." One modern counterpart of this

---

6. *Student Dimensions, Codification of Policy of the United States National Student Association* (Philadephia: U.S.N.S.A., 1963–64), p. 115. From E. G. Williamson and John L. Cowan, *The American Student's Freedom of Expression* (Minneapolis: University of Minnesota Press, 1966), p. 61. Reprinted by permission.
7. Williamson and Cowan, p. 84.
8. The transcript of a student discussion on this topic appears near the close of Chapter 11.
9. Williamson and Cowan, p. 7. (The student "wants" noted in this volume are a part of the final analysis and report based on 1000 questionnaires mailed to institutions of higher learning in 1964.)

practice is the challenge to direct confrontation in public debate which a person holding one point of view issues to one holding an opposite view. If the challenge is accepted, the debate takes place and the public or audience concerned makes a judgment on the issue(s) through the ballot or by some other appropriate action. (One who refuses to participate in a debate almost automatically lowers his personal standing and the credibility level of his position unless the reasons for the refusal are exceptionally good.) The Kennedy-Nixon television debates of 1960 were examples of such debates in the political arena; so were the celebrated Lincoln-Douglas debates of more than a century ago. Similar events are taking place with increasing frequency in all fields and at all levels, local, state, and national.

As we all know, the preparation of an informative talk or a persuasive speech is difficult enough, but at least there is seldom any direct opposition. You prepare the talk, deliver it, and then sit down. In real life, however, there are times when one is invited to speak on a controversial issue with the understanding that the speaker will be expected to answer questions from *opponents* as well as proponents and neutrals after the speech. On other occasions, the plan calls for a public debate in which one speaker debates a question with another who opposes his stand. Then there are times when one wants to stand up at a public meeting to refute remarks just made by another speaker. In a free democratic society, a situation calling for an opposing question or for an answering statement occurs often enough so that we should be well acquainted with approaches to refuting views with which we do not agree.

You will recall that Chapter 3 deals with the subject of common sense in reasoning. You will remember also that the problem of maintaining good relations with one another as human beings has been touched upon in various sections of this book, and that Chapter 11 carried a special emphasis on the respect one should have for the views of another and for his dignity as a person. Debate and the idea of refutation should not cause you to set aside what you have learned elsewhere and in this course about getting along with people. Debate is not used here in the sense of a "contest" to determine the "winner." It is used in the sense of "loyal opposition," the term used so long in the parliaments of the world to describe a minority's constructive examination and criticism of proposals made by the party or coalition in power. There is some truth in the axiom "No one ever won an argument." It is occasionally possible to show that someone is apparently wrong about his facts, about his conclusions, or about both; if you do so in a sharp and contentious manner, you not only run the risk of making an enemy of your "opponent," but you also lose the respect of the audience.

Approaches to Case Organization and Defense

Previous chapters (notably 11 and 12) have included suggestions aimed at helping you in the study of problems and solutions for them. When such problems fall into the category of public controversy at any level (local, state, national, international), special care is required in preparing the statement of your position and making ready to defend it. After you have done the best you can to uncover the facts, the questions below can be useful in checking or completing your analysis and in planning the broad structure of your speech.[10]

    I. What are the goals of our present plan or policy? Can they be consistently defended on a long-range basis?

   II. Is our present plan or policy helping us to achieve those goals? Is there any reasonable chance of our reaching them with the present approach?

  III. Will a change in plan or policy improve the chances of attaining our goals? If so, what am I (or are we) recommending?

Your organization of the "case" in support of an existing policy or in argument against it will ordinarily serve double duty by also providing adequate background for refuting attacks on your position. The following discussion offers suggestions and patterns you may wish to use in meeting opposing arguments.

A. Methods of refutation

1. *Question the goal(s) advocated.* Is the goal based on facts? Can we seek this goal consistently? What are the costs of achieving this goal?[11]
2. *Question the evidence.* Is the evidence accurate, representative, complete, from reputable sources, generally accepted as "true"? (See Chapters 3 and 8.)
3. *Question the conclusions drawn from the evidence.* (See Chapters 3 and 8.)
4. *Advance stronger evidence pointing to a different conclusion.* Sometimes the scales in public debate are tipped in a particular direction simply by the relative "weights" of evidence introduced by the participants.

B. Planning the refutation

1. *Listen carefully to the speaker* whose arguments you hope to refute.
2. *Try to outline his major arguments.* If the talk is well organized, you should find it easy to note the speaker's thesis (proposition, or resolution) along with his main contentions or points.

---

10. The three sets of questions are derived from Newman and Newman, pp. 3–15.
11. Questions from Newman and Newman, p. 6.

3. *Decide on the general approach you want to take.*
   a. Criticize the goals he wishes adopted, or use any one or more of the other methods of refutation.
   b. If he is trying to show that a serious problem exists, you will be trying to show that it is not so serious as alleged.
   c. If he attempts to show both that a particular problem is very serious and that he has a solution for it, you have the option of dismissing with a comment or two his remarks on the problem; that enables you to concentrate on attacking his solution.

      Or you can forget the solution and try to show that he is exaggerating the problem; then you can add whatever modifications you consider necessary to handle the problem under the present system.

      Or you can attack some of his arguments on the problem *and* some details of his proposal for a solution.

      Or you can admit that the problem is serious and propose what you hope will be accepted as a better plan for solution. If you choose this procedure, be sure that your proposal is *different in principle* from the one presented by the opposition. (You cannot make minor improvements on *his* general plan and call it another proposal.)
   d. If he proposes a solution for a problem that everyone agrees is serious, you can attack his solution (too costly, impractical, unmanageable, etc.), you can propose what you hope the audience will accept as a better solution, or you can both attack *and* propose.

C. Presenting the refutation

1. *Briefly review* for the audience the position of the opposing speaker and include references to main points and his support for them.
2. *Cite points on which you agree*, even if your agreement consists only in acknowledging that there is a problem. (You need not refute everything an opponent says; in addition to the fact that much of what he says may make good sense, you do not have the time to cover everything in detail.) Remember that any audience expects you to be fair.
3. *State the general approach to refutation* that you have decided upon. Just where are you going to concentrate your attack?
4. *Begin the refutation proper.*
   a. State the specific contentions which you oppose, and review their relationship to the "case." For instance, if you tell the audience that you are going to show that the problem is not so serious as the opposition contends, you should take up in order the points made by the opposition to support the idea that the problem *is* serious.
   b. *Attack the evidence and/or reasoning* advanced in support of those points you have listed as vulnerable.
   c. *Conclude* by pointing out that the evidence and/or reasoning do not support the view that the problem is severe.

In summary, remember that audiences appreciate having a speaker *state the point to be refuted, show its importance in relation to a main contention or to the case as a whole, refute it efficiently, and demonstrate the damage done to the case by the refutation.*

. . . .

Speaking options

1. Prepare a 5–7 minute persuasive speech in which you take a *position on a controversial topic.* (Review Chapter 12 with special reference to materials and the order in which they should be presented.) This kind of speech is often followed by three or four minutes devoted to defending one's position by answering questions from the audience. (This option and the next are planned on a basis of a possible allotment of ten minutes per student in a "final round.")
2. Find another student who is ready to take a position opposite to yours in a current controversy, and prepare for a 14-minute *public debate.* Controversial topics can be gleaned readily enough from earlier class discussions or from news and editorial items in print and broadcast media. The "proposition" should be worded affirmatively, for example, "A student's noncurrent disciplinary records should be periodically destroyed." The "pro" speaker has five minutes to state his affirmative position and the reasons for it. The "con" speaker has up to seven minutes for refutation and for a statement of his position. Then the "pro" speaker is given another two minutes to bring the debate to a close.[12] If time permits, there may be an audience question period of four to six minutes. In choosing a speaking option, you may want to consider the following typical examples of controversial topics.[13]

Should members of the United States Armed Forces be allowed freedom of speech (e.g., protesting a war) when off duty?

Should the censorship of books and magazines (or movies) be abolished in the United States?

Should restrictions be placed on passing out handbills (or picketing) on public property?

Should the use of loudspeakers and sound trucks be restricted?

Listening options[14]

Using your reaction to one of the student talks in the present series, write a one-page answer to any one set of questions below. Be prepared to use it as a base for comments in class or to turn it in to your instructor.

---

12. There are many good texts on argumentation and debate; one of them is Austin J. Freeley, *Argumentation and Debate*, 2nd ed. (San Francisco: Wadsworth, 1966). See the Bibliography for other citations.
13. From "III. Teaching Freedom of Speech Through the Use of Common Materials," by Thomas L. Tedford, The Speech Teacher, **16** (November 1967), p. 270. Questions reprinted by permission.
14. Item 4 is quoted from Frazier, p. 335. Items 1, 2, and 3 are based on similar items on the same page.

1. Did you agree on the analysis of issues as presented by the speaker? What were the issues? Were any important issues overlooked?
2. What is your evaluation of the sources used by the speaker? Was the evidence convincing? Were the conclusions warranted?
3. If refutation was attempted, did the speaker handle his refutation in an efficient manner? Diplomatically?
4. What were the most telling points that helped you in making up your mind on the topic at hand? What might have been added to make the talk more effective?
5. If a two-student debate was on the program for the day, what was the general atmosphere? Did each speaker seem to be aware that the other had some good reasons for his position? Did either of them make any concessions to the other? Did they go at the problem in "hammer and tongs" fashion? Or in a friendly and cooperative way through which each demonstrated a regard for the other and some understanding of his position?

. . . .

*All men make mistakes, but a good man yields
when he knows his course is wrong
and repairs the evil. The only sin is pride.*

Sophocles in Antigone

14 / Decision-making in parliamentary procedure

In a sense, this chapter is an extension of the preceding chapter on debating issues in a free society. Our right to speak freely is important enough in conversations, in discussions, and in informative or persuasive speaking situations in general. That right is crucial to the democratic process when an individual citizen takes a position on a controversial public question and undertakes to express it through a public statement, through testifying pro or con at a hearing, through publicly debating the issue with an opponent, or through presenting his views in open consideration of the issue by members of any informally or formally constituted body, club, organization, assembly, or legislature. As each of us knows, this last kind of "large-group debate" ends—and sometimes begins—in chaos unless the participating members or legislators operate under a detailed and strict set of rules for parliamentary procedure. These rules are the subject of this chapter.

You may be familiar with *Robert's Rules of Order*[1] and you are undoubtedly aware of the frequent specification of that small volume as the official rule book governing the conduct of meetings for American organizations of all kinds. All of us have attended a variety of formal meetings. On some occasions, we have been appalled by the waste of time and general confusion; on others, we have marveled at the efficiency and skill displayed. In some meetings, a few of the bolder spirits are permitted to monopolize the discussion; in others, everyone present has an opportunity to make himself heard if he wishes. We sometimes sympathize with the meeting chairman because of his total inability to maintain an orderly progression toward the goals of the day; at other times, we are filled with admiration for the chairman who knows what he is doing and fully understands the purpose and operation of the parliamentary rules under which the group is operating.

As our society becomes progressively better educated and cooperatively oriented, the number of meetings we attend steadily increases. As pointed out in Chapter 11, when a group consists of no more than nine or ten members, it can still carry on the

---

1. First published by General Henry Robert in 1876.

business of arriving at consensus on a relatively informal "committee" basis. When the number of members goes beyond ten, the group finds it increasingly difficult to get agreement without resorting to the "machinery" of parliamentary procedure. Without that machinery, large-group order and efficiency are achieved only by the undemocratic imposition of arbitrary authority; if neither the machinery nor the authority exists, the process of arriving at agreement degenerates into chaos. Since we are—and should always be—concerned about our democratic liberties as well as about our personal ability to chair or to participate intelligently in large-group formal meetings, it is very much in our interests as Americans and as individuals to gain some command over the elements of parliamentary debate.

The purpose of parliamentary procedure, then, is to provide a balance between democracy and efficiency in the discussion of whatever problem is "before the house." *Democracy* is assured through rules which promote (1) freedom of speech in debate, (2) concentration on one question or proposal at a time, (3) recognition of the equal rights of all members present, (4) protection of the rights of the minority, and (5) decision according to the will of the majority. *Efficiency* is achieved through an understanding of the rules and cooperative administration of them. It is not only necessary that the chairman know parliamentary methods; the members of a group should also be well versed in at least those procedural techniques which are common to the meetings they attend.[2]

In parliamentary procedure, a *motion* is a formal proposal or suggestion made by an individual—or by an individual for a group—in an official meeting of large committees, councils, boards, assemblies, etc. For instance, after being recognized by the chairman, someone says, "I *move* that we conduct a hunger march to raise money for the poor and hungry." Another individual who wants to support the idea says, "I *second* the motion." In this context, the word *move* is simply a formal synonym or substitute for *propose* or *suggest*, and the word *second* is the formal synonym or substitute for *support*. Some motions require that the idea be seconded before it can be turned over to those present for discussion; others require no such support.

In this volume, the focus is on those procedures which would occur in the normal course of initiating a motion, discussing it, and voting on its disposition. First, we consider a diagrammatic summary of the twelve *basic motions* commonly used to introduce and dispose of a main motion; this is followed by a section providing a brief explanation of each motion. Next are descriptions of the *special-problem motions*, which deal with the purely mechanical and incidental matters which are encountered occasionally in a meeting and which have nothing directly to do with the disposition of a motion under discussion.

Basic Motions and Examples

All twelve basic motions require a *second*.
All motions in **boldface** are open to *unlimited debate*.
Unless otherwise indicated, all motions are decided by *majority vote*.

---

2. There are many works available on parliamentary procedure. For two approaches, see the Hellman and Sturgis entries in the Bibliography. Students interested in this subject will find additional volumes listed there.

1. **Main motion.** "I move the adoption of the following resolution:

In-the-course-of-discussion motions
2. **To postpone indefinitely.** "I move that this motion be postponed indefinitely."
3. **To amend.** "I move to amend the motion by deleting the word 'certain' in line 2 of Section II."
4. *To refer to committee.* "I move to refer the motion to committee for further study." (Limited debate)
5. *To postpone definitely.* "I move that further discussion of this motion be postponed until the next meeting." (Limited debate)
6. *To limit debate* (two-thirds vote). "I move that further discussion of this motion be limited to a half-hour." (Limited debate)
7. *To vote immediately* (two-thirds vote). "I move to vote immediately on the motion before us." (No debate)
8. *To table.* "I move that the motion be tabled." (No debate)

The motions in this box are "subsidiary" or "affective" motions; they *affect* the way in which motions are discussed and handled. As indicated by the flow of arrows, one higher in number (e.g., 8) may be made when one lower in number (e.g., 4) is under consideration. There is no need for any of these motions if the discussion of the main motion can be brought to the decision stage without them. ("Limited debate" means debate limited to discussion of the *procedural action* proposed.)

Decision on motion
"All in favor, say 'Aye'   (or *raise your right hand*)   (or *stand up*)."
"All opposed, say 'No'   (or *raise your right hand*)   (or *stand up*)."

Reverse-decision motions
9. **To reconsider.** "I move to reconsider the motion passed earlier in this meeting in favor of the resolution on the Selective Service Act." (Only someone who voted in favor of the original motion may make this motion; it may be made at any time *in the same meeting or session.*)
10. **To repeal.** "I move to repeal the motion passed at the last meeting in favor of the resolution on. . . ."

When either of the above motions is made, it is a **Main motion.**

Stop-session motions
11. *To recess.* "I move that we recess for ten minutes." (Limited debate)
12. *To adjourn.* "I move that we adjourn." (No debate)

Description of basic motions

1. Main motion. This motion is used to introduce a proposal which you want the assembled group to consider. (The chairman should not permit anyone to "pave the way" for a motion by rambling along before getting to the "I move" stage; *there can be no debate unless there is a motion on the floor.*)

Main motions may be classified under two broad headings: (1) those proposing action and (2) those proposing statements of sentiment, commonly called resolutions. An example of a proposal of action: "I move that we appropriate $100 as a contribution to the United Fund." A resolution may be introduced with these words: "I move the adoption of the following resolution...." To make the motion complete would of course require the reading of the entire resolution. (Three resolutions appear verbatim at the end of Chapter 11.)

In-the-course-of-discussion motions

2. To postpone indefinitely. If seconded, this motion is debatable. If passed, it will put an end to further consideration of the main motion. It is used primarily by opponents of a motion who wish to put the measure to a "test vote" in order to make a preliminary assessment of strength of sides, identification of supporters and opponents, etc.

3. To amend. In the ordinary course of discussion of a main motion (and of others), the motion "to amend" occurs with considerable frequency. If a resolution has been distributed in advance of the meeting in which it is going to be brought up, some members of the group will already have ideas about changes which they would like to have incorporated in the document. Additional changes will occur to other members during the course of the meeting. On the principle that any motion, lengthy or short, should at the moment of the final vote on it represent the collective best judgment of the group, the amendment process is a vital part of "democracy in action."

As Sturgis points out,[3] any motion which is variable in wording can be amended. For instance, the motion "to recess" is amendable because the length of the time of the recess is open to discussion and change; on the other hand, the motion "to table" is not amendable because it may not contain any qualification as to time.

When a motion to amend has been made and seconded, *it becomes the center of discussion* until some action has been taken to dispose of it. A *first* motion to amend is called a "first-degree amendment."

While the motion to amend is being discussed, it is in order to make and to second a motion "to amend the amendment" under consideration. Until the proposed "amendment to the amendment" has been carried or lost, *it is the center of discussion.* A motion to amend an amendment is called a "second-degree amendment."

The rules do not permit a motion "to amend the proposed amendment to the proposed amendment to the motion." In other words, (1) a *first-degree amendment* (i.e., motion to amend the motion under consideration) is in order, and (2) a *second-degree amendment* (i.e., motion to amend the proposed amendment to the motion under consideration) is in order, but—fortunately for all of us—the complexity of trying to deal

---

3. Sturgis, p. 27.

with (3) a *third-degree amendment* (i.e., motion to amend the proposed amendment to the proposed amendment to the motion under consideration) is *out* of order.

For the sake of example, let us suppose than a resolution proposing additional controls on the sale of firearms has been moved and seconded.

Chairman: "Approval of the resolution which you have in your hands has been moved and seconded. Is there any discussion?"

Member 1 (after being recognized): "I move that the phrase 'or by any other method' be added after the word 'mail' in line 2 of Section I."

Member 2: "I second the motion."

Chairman: "It has been moved and seconded that the motion be amended by adding the phrase '....' Is there any discussion?"

Member 3 (after being recognized): "I move to amend the amendment by adding the words 'such as United Parcel Service' to the new wording proposed.

Member 4: "I second the motion."

Chairman: "It has been moved and seconded that the words 'such as United Parcel Service' be added to the proposed amendment after the words 'or by any other method.' Is there any discussion on this amendment to the amendment?"

(After disposal of this second-degree amendment, the members of the group would normally return to a discussion of the first-degree amendment and, after its disposal, to continuing consideration of the main motion.)

4. *To refer to committee.* It is occasionally the consensus of the group that additional study should precede further discussion and a final decision. A typical motion: "I move that the motion be referred to a committee appointed by the chairman and charged with the responsibility to report its findings as soon as possible."

5. *To postpone definitely.* Sometimes there is a reason why discussing a motion at a later time would be more appropriate than deciding upon it at the present time. Perhaps some pertinent information will not be available until later, or perhaps the leading spokesman for the measure cannot be present until a later time. Whatever the reason, one of the members interested in postponement simply says, "I move that further discussion of the measure be postponed until 9 a.m. tomorrow."

(If you want to be absolutely sure that the assembly will take up the matter without delay at that time, you insert the words "as a special order of business" at some proper place in the motion; in this particular example, it would come after the word "postponed." This "special order" provision requires a two-thirds vote, whereas the straight postponement requires only a majority vote.)

6. *To limit debate.* There is always the possibility that the members present in a meeting will have a tendency to continue the debate after almost everything bearing on the issue has been said. At this point, one of the members may say, "I move that further discussion of this motion be limited to ten minutes." After seconding and discussion, two-thirds of the members must favor the motion to make it effective.

7. *To vote immediately.*[4] This is a call for an immediate vote on the motion before the house. It is undebatable and, if seconded, requires a two-thrids vote to pass. If the motion is carried, the chairman *then* calls for a vote on the substantive motion, and at this point, of course, only a majority vote is required to carry that motion.

8. *To table.* This motion should be used for laying a motion on the table (that is, setting it aside for the moment in order to work on more pressing business) with the intention of taking it up again as soon as the opportunity arises. (The motion "to table" should not be used to "kill" a motion; the proposal "to postpone indefinitely" should be used for that purpose.)

Reverse-decision motions

9. To reconsider. ⎫ Both are main motions. See discussion of main motions at top of
10. To repeal.   ⎬ page 257.
                    ⎭

Stop-session motions

11. *To recess.* "I move that we recess for ten minutes." This motion can be made at any time an interruption is desired; it requires a second and is undebatable, except that it can be amended to change the length of time for the recess.

12. *To adjourn.* "I move that we adjourn." Specifications are the same as for the motion above, except that it cannot be amended.

Special-Problem Motions

A motion in this classification must be made as soon as the "special problem" arises. Therefore, within the bounds of good manners and discretion, you may *at any time* interrrupt either the chairman or the speaker who has the floor in order to introduce one of the following seven motions.

1. *Call for a more accurate vote count.* Whenever a member is dissatisfied with the Chairman's interpretation of a voice vote, he should interrupt whatever is going on immediately after the vote and say, "Mr. Chairman, I request a division of the assembly." The chairman will then take a second vote by having members stand or raise their right hands.

2. *Point of order.* If someone is not, in your opinion, following the proper parliamentary procedures, or if the rules are not being enforced, you may call the attention of the chairman to this lapse by saying, "Mr Chairman, a point of order." He will ask you to state your point and will then rule that the point of order is "well taken" or that it is not.

3. *Appeal from the chair's decision.* Whenever the chairman makes a ruling of any kind with which you do not agree on procedural grounds, you may immediately say,

---

4. In many manuals this is a motion "for the previous question." The terminology here is used by Sturgis, p. 67.

"Mr. Chairman, I appeal from the decision of the chair." *If someone seconds* your appeal, the motion is on the floor for debate. In this instance, the chairman may participate in the discussion by giving the reasons for his ruling. When the discussion is ended—or when someone makes a properly seconded motion "to vote immediately"—the chairman calls for a vote, first of those willing to sustain his ruling, and then of those agreeing with you. His final ruling will of course be in accord with the will of the majority voting on this issue.

4. *Parliamentary inquiry.* If you are not certain about whether or not it is proper to make a certain type of motion at a particular point in the proceedings, it is your privilege to stand and say, "Mr. Chairman, I rise to a parliamentary question." The chairman will ask you what your question is, and he will either answer it directly or, if an official parliamentarian is present, ask for advice and then answer.

5. *Request for information.* If, in the course of a discussion, it seems to you that some vital piece of information is missing, you may say, "Mr. Chairman, I rise for information." He will ask you to state what you want to know and, again, will either answer the question himself or try to obtain the answer from someone in the group. Another form of the same motion: "Mr. Chairman, will the speaker yield for a question?" If the speaker is willing to yield the floor temporarily, you then ask *him* whatever question you have in mind.

6. *Point of privilege.* If you cannot hear a speaker, or if it is too hot in the room, or if there is something about the physical arrangement of the chairs which could be improved, or if you notice that someone appears to be ill, you may say, "Mr. Chairman, I rise to a point of privilege." He will ask you to state your point, and if he agrees with you, he will take appropriate action. This motion is intended to cover any possible complaint or suggestion dealing with the "comfort" of those in the room.

7. *Suspension of the rules.* At any time that the members of the group, organization, or assembly wish to take action contrary to the bylaws or rules being observed, the rules may be suspended. The motion must contain the purpose for which the suspension is desired. For example, "I move to suspend the rules to allow the members to hear a nonmember." If the motion is seconded, the chairman immediately calls for a vote by having the members stand or raise their right hands. (This voting method is used whenever, as in this instance, a two-thirds vote is required.)

Administration and Order of Business

The description of motions in this volume is intentionally limited to those elements required for the routine parliamentary problems with which one has to deal in typical meeting. To become an expert in this field requires concentrated study of the intricacies of parliamentary detail; however, our purpose here is only to make it possible to acquire a basic competence in this kind of formal debate and to foster an appreciation of the guarantees it offers for freedom of speech on an equal basis for all involved.

The conduct of business in the formal larger-group situation (as distinguished from informal small-group process discussed in Chapter 11) requires the services of a chairman who does *not* take part in the discussion of substantive matters but who does preside and direct the proceedings; he should therefore have a reasonably thorough comprehension of the "rules."

Although the parliamentary process seems complicated, some of the problems in administering it can be solved through the understanding that *there are only twelve primary motions*. Three of these (the main motion and the motions "to amend" and "to vote immediately") occur with greater frequency than any of the others. Except for the "appeal from the chair's decision," the special-problem motions are easy to handle. The chairman must be prepared for any eventuality, of course, but he does not have to give a decision without consulting either (1) a chart or diagrammatic summary, such as the one suggested earlier in this chapter, or (2) the "parliamentarian." The latter should be an individual who has a thorough knowledge of the practical operational details of parliamentary procedure. (In the classroom, the instructor ordinarily serves in this capacity.) When a motion is made, the chairman should be well enough acquainted with the rules to know whether or not the motion is "in order." For instance, if the group is on the point of voting on a motion "to table," the chairman cannot allow the introduction of a motion "to amend."

The chairman should not in any way hamper or hinder free discussion and debate. However, he should be alert to opportunities to expedite the business "before the house." Whenever he is convinced that everyone in the group is ready for or wants to follow a certain procedure, he may suggest that it do so by asking, "Are there any objections to ...?" An example: "Are there any objections to voting immediately?" If no member objects, the procedure can be followed without further ado. If the chairman is confronted with a procedural question for which he does not have and cannot obtain the answer, he may make a ruling on a common-sense basis or simply turn the problem over to the assembly and say, "All those who believe that this motion is in order at this time, say '*Aye*.'" "All those opposed, '*No*.'" The chairman is then in a position to rule that the motion is accepted or rejected.

The chairman and members of a group may find the following "rules of thumb" useful.

1. All twelve basic motions (i.e., those outside the special-problem class) require a second.

2. All *substantive* basic motions (i.e., those having to do directly with debate on the merits of the proposal) are open to *unlimited debate*.
3. Of the seven basic motions having to do with *procedural* matters, three are not debatable: "to vote immediately," "to table," and "to adjourn." *Debate would in each case defeat the purpose of the motion.*
4. The four remaining *procedural* motions ("to refer to committee," "to postpone definitely," "to limit debate," and "to recess") are debatable only because they are subject to amendment on details of time, number of people on a committee, etc.; therefore, they are *subject to debate limited to such details.*
5. Of the special-problem motions, only two require a second: "appeal from the chair's decision" and "suspension of the rules." (The "appeal" motion is subject to limited debate because there is, in this instance, an obvious difference of opinion on how a procedural rule should be interpreted. No debate is permitted on a motion to suspend the rules.)
6. A decision is always reached by a majority voice vote, *unless the motion stands in the way of the principle of unlimited debate or overturns the rules.* The motions "to limit debate," "to vote immediately," or "to suspend the rules" are in the latter category and require a two-thirds vote to pass. All two-thirds votes should of course be taken by a show of hands or by a standing vote.

A *quorum* (number of members who must be present to make a meeting "legal") normally consists of a majority of the members in good standing. If a *quorum* is present, all votes are computed on the basis of the number of members voting. For example, if 21 members are present and constitute a *quorum* and if three of these do not vote, a majority would then number 10, and a two-thirds vote would be 12.

When the chairman is faced with several members standing to seek recognition at the same time, he should consider the following factors in determining who should be recognized.

1. If the member who proposed the motion wants to speak on it (after it has been seconded), he should be given that opportunity.
2. General practice then requires that an opposing speaker be "given the floor." If the chairman is uncertain about the approach to be taken by potential speakers, he announces, "The chair will recognize an opposing speaker." Then he makes a choice of one in that category.
3. On the principle of alternation of views, the next speaker should be one supporting the motion.
4. Within the framework above, the chairman should give preference to a speaker who has not yet had anything to say.
5. If only one member is asking for the floor at a given time, the chairman has no problem. Under these circumstances, two or more members opposing the motion or two or more members favoring it may follow in succession.

In other words, the elements of common sense underlie parliamentary regulations and practice, and if you understand the general principles involved, you will have no real difficulty in the role of chairman (or of a participating member).

The only other officer essential to the efficient conduct of business is the secretary. This member keeps a record of the progress of the meeting. The normal order of business is (1) the reading of the minutes of the previous meeting; (2) reports of standing committees; (3) reports of any special committees; (4) unfinished business, such as motions pending at the end of the last meeting, followed by motions postponed from earlier meetings to this specific time; and finally (5) new business. Items to come up under "new business" are often determined in advance by an agenda committee; if no such committee exists, the chairman usually introduces items on which decisions should be made, and members of the group are also free to make motions on matters which they feel require attention.

As a part of the record-keeping, the secretary is expected to keep *an exact record of each motion and of its disposition.* A part of the record-keeping can be made easier through the use of typewritten, dittoed, or mimeographed forms. An example of such a form follows.

```
                      MAIN MOTION no. _____
    Moved by _____     Date _____
    that _____
    _____
    Seconded by _____    No second _____   (check)
    Carried _____ (check)        Lost _____ (check)
    Other disposition (specify) _____
```

Similar forms could be used for amendments to main motions and for amendments to amendments to main motions, with appropriate blank spaces in the titles to allow for proper identification by number. Other details would be the same as those in the form for main motions, except that the last item would be omitted.

A member who reads a lengthy motion or resolution should give a copy of it to the secretary. If the recording system suggested above is being used, he simply clips the supplied text to a blank and writes "attached" on the line provided for wording of the motion. The chairman should be able to depend on the secretary for exact information on the wording or status of a motion at any time during the course of a meeting. However, it is *not* the secretary's duty to keep a record of what is said in the course of discussion and debate on a measure. After a meeting is adjourned, it is the secretary's responsibility to write the "minutes" by briefly but accurately recording (1) disposition of all main motions and amendments introduced, (2) only those procedural motions which passed, and (3) all motions still pending when the meeting came to an end. The motions listed in the third group are brought up at the next meeting under "unfinished business." These minutes, limited strictly to motions made and to their disposition, are ready by the secretary at the opening of the next session; they enable the group to begin where it "left off" with no uncertainty about what happened in the previous meeting.

Duties of "Assembly" Members

As a member of a group engaged in parliamentary debate, you are expected to exercise courtesy and tact at all times in the process of presenting and disposing of motions. To obtain the floor you stand and try to get the attention of the chairman by saying, "Mr. Chairman." If he chooses to "recognize" you, he will state your name. Then for example, you say, "Mr. Chairman, I move the adoption of this resolution favoring guaranteed employment for United States citizens. It reads as follows: Whereas..." When you finish the reading, you give a copy of the resolution to the secretary and return to your seat. Provided there is a second to your motion, the chairman says, "You have heard the motion presenting the resolution favoring guaranteed employment for United States citizens. It has been seconded by [name of person seconding]. Is there any discussion?" From this point forward, the discussion follows the patterns previously outlined in this chapter. If you have something to say about a particular motion, do not hesitate to seek recognition from the chairman in order to exert influence for or against a proposal. Be alert to special-problem situations and the motions available for solving them. Remember, however, that the "case" being presented in support of a motion is the primary business of the assembly; concentrate on it and on what you can contribute *in cooperation* with others who agree with you. Be ready to compromise on minor issues and amendments; otherwise, take what you consider to be a reasonable position and try to win the assent of enough others to pass or defeat a measure. (If you need a short "time out" for some face-to-face personal negotiation, the motion "to recess" is useful for that purpose.)

Participation and listening options

As previously noted in the discussion of the main motion, that particular motion is used to introduce either (1) the proposal of some specific action or (2) a statement of sentiment called a resolution. Almost any proposal falling into those categories may be suitable as a base for practice in parliamentary procedure. If a group or groups in the class have already prepared resolutions (suggested as an optional activity in Chapter 11), one or more of those statements will provide measures for deliberation by the "assembly."

It will be necessary to have an organizational meeting a few days before deliberations are to begin. Resolutions already available for proposal should be noted, placed on the agenda, and immediately—or shortly thereafter—distributed to the members of the class. At this time, a different chairman should also be appointed for each class meeting to be devoted to debate; ordinarily, the number of class meetings approximates the number of resolutions to be considered, with the tacit agreement that no one resolution will be discussed for more than one class period. Different secretaries may also be selected. (The chairmen and secretaries can be volunteers for these tasks, or they can be appointed by the instructor.)

Two or three class periods between the organizational meeting and the actual beginning of debate should be used for study of parliamentary procedure and for some "dry run" practice in it. For this purpose, one of the sample resolutions at the end of Chapter 11 can be debated in its present form or with modifications made in it by general committee effort conducted in the classroom.

On the first day of "official" deliberations, the student chairman for that day opens the meeting by calling it to order. Then, on the imaginative assumption that this session is one continuing business conducted on previous days, he directs this question to the secretary: "What business is now before the house?" The secretary responds, "The following resolutions have been reported out of committee in this order: [the titles of the resolutions on the previously determined agenda]." The chairman then opens the way for debate by saying, "The first resolution before us is.... What is your pleasure?" This question from the chairman is the signal for one of the members of the committee proposing that particular resolution to move its adoption. After the motion is seconded, the "assembly" debates the measure until a decision is reached or until the end of that particular period. If no decision is achieved by the end of the period, the motion should be "tabled" *for action in a later period if there is time to take it up again.* (The secretary for each class period must pass on to the secretary for the next period a complete record of what happened in the period for which he was responsible.)

The second period of deliberation opens with the chairman of the day calling for order. The secretary for that day then reports what happened in the previous session. When the secretary concludes, the chairman asks if there are any additions or corrections. "If not, the minutes will stand approved as read." Following the pattern of the previous day, he asks what business is now before the house, and the secretary reads the title of the second resolution. (This resolution *may* have already been introduced on the preceding day; if so, deliberation is now continued on it to the point of decision, but not beyond the end of the second class period.)

In other words, if there are four resolutions to be considered, no more than four class periods are normally used for deliberation on them. If an end to debate on the first measure is forced by the end of the class period in which it is introduced, further debate on it depends on whether or not the other resolutions are handled expeditiously enough to allow returning to the first one on a subsequent day of the series. The number of class periods allotted to these deliberative sessions will determine the number of chairmen and secretaries required. (The chairman and the secretary for a given session are invariably chosen from those students whose resolutions are not likely to come up on that day.)

As far as the "speech-making" is concerned, students intending to propose, support, or oppose a certain resolution should prepare short statements of their arguments. If there are five students on a committee, responsibility for a part of the total case can be assigned to each of the five. If a majority of the students on a committee favors a particular measure and a minority of the same committee does not, the minority may, if it wishes, propose a resolution of its own and try to win support for it. (This second proposal from one committee should be considered only if it is possible to do so within the time allotted to consideration of the majority report.)

The instructor usually acts as parliamentarian. He should be careful not to volunteer his services unless specifically asked to do so by a chairman. Some instructors prefer to use ten minutes at the end of each period for a critique of student handling of content and procedure in that particular session. If there is no preference for this short-critique-per-day plan, a final period may be used for a critique of the entire series. Both students and instructor may find the following topical order[5] helpful in assessing individual and collective performance.

A. Courteous and cooperative attitude.
B. General understanding of parliamentary procedure.
C. Effectiveness in speaking from the standpoints of:
   1. evidence and reasoning;
   2. delivery.
D. Success in enlisting support as seen in:
   1. working with "partisans";
   2. winning over "neutrals";
   3. lessening influence of "opponents."
E. Overall contribution to efficient handling of business.

. . . .

---

5. Adapted from criteria used by critics judging performance of "legislators" in student legislative assemblies sponsored by the Purdue University Department of Communication.

*Come my friends,
'Tis not too late to seek a newer world.*

Tennyson in Ulysses

Appendix A / Use of the library

It is assumed that one has a subject in mind when he undertakes to look for materials to be used in any form of speech-communication. Knowing how to use library facilities is of course an indispensable skill. College and university libraries normally offer students a free booklet describing the location and use of reference works, periodicals, and general collections. With or without such a booklet, librarians as a group are willing to make suggestions aimed at helping the student find the answers to his research problems.

The general reference desk of any library is an excellent place to start your search for information. There you will usually find the standard sources of facts and statistics, biographical summaries of the *Who's Who* variety, indexes to specific fields in the arts and sciences, the more general *Readers' Guide to Periodical Literature*, encyclopedias of all kinds, current periodicals, popular magazines, and daily newspapers. (See Appendix B for a supplementary list of standard library aids and reference works.) Then you can check the card catalog for authors, titles, or subject matter related to the project at hand. If you know, for instance, that a man named Beardsley wrote a book on logic, you can turn to the appropriate "B" card file and find a card listing the call number for the book under his name, "Beardsley, Monroe C." If you know only the title of the book, *Thinking Straight*, you will find another card for it under "T." If you simply want to find a book on logic, cards for such books will be found under "L." Card-catalog systems vary from library to library, but it is no great chore to become familiar with the system—Library of Congress or Dewey—used at your institution, and it will save you time and trouble to do so at the earliest possible time in your undergraduate career.

How to take notes is a matter for the individual to decide. One good method is to use standard 3 × 5 cards. For *each* book, article, or other source from which you take information, use *one* card to write the pertinent bibliographical data: author; title of article; title of magazine, periodical, or book; etc. If you don't know how to record such data in an organized fashion, ask the librarian to refer you to a manual of style. If you have only a few bibliographical cards, no coding system will be necessary; if you have more than ten, however, you may want at some stage in the process to assign a number to each book or article to facilitate subsequent note-taking. You may of course have several numbers assigned to one author if you use several of his works. Two authors with the same names present no problem, since the code numbers assigned will be different. Two examples of bibliographical cards are shown below.

Bibliographical card for book

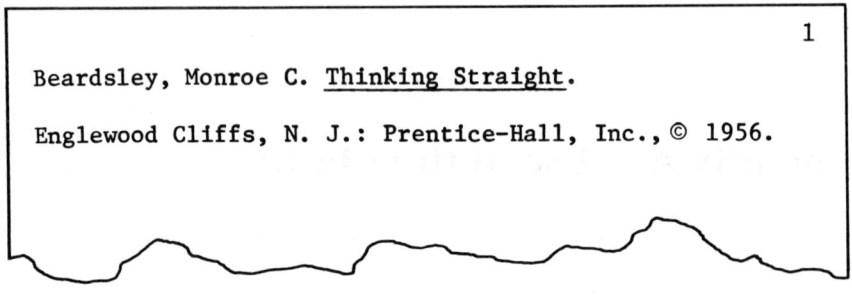

```
                                                              1
Beardsley, Monroe C. Thinking Straight.
Englewood Cliffs, N. J.: Prentice-Hall, Inc., © 1956.
```

Bibliographical card for article

```
                                                              2
Solmsen, Friedrich.  "Aristotelian Tradition in Ancient
Rhetoric," American Journal of Philology, LXII (January,
1941), 35-50.
```

As you take notes, *keep them short*. It is best to use only one side of a card for ease in later handling. At the top left of the note card, put the last name of the author; at the top right, put the code number you wish to assign to the particular article or book. Examples of note cards follow.

Note card from Beardsley

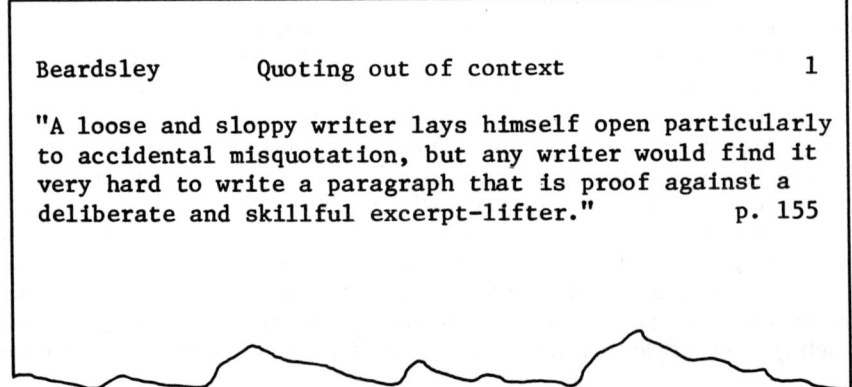

```
Beardsley         Quoting out of context               1
"A loose and sloppy writer lays himself open particularly
to accidental misquotation, but any writer would find it
very hard to write a paragraph that is proof against a
deliberate and skillful excerpt-lifter."        p. 155
```

The "title" at the top center of the note card is the topic to which you believe the quotation has reference. Sometimes you will leave that space blank, either permanently or until you have decided just where a particular piece of evidence can be used. The number 1 on the Beardsley card indicates that the book is his *Thinking Straight*. Remember that *the page number is vital*; always note the exact page or pages from which you take a quotation or other information. Use quotation marks. If you prefer to paraphrase a passage, the absence of quotation marks will tell you at a later date that you did not quote verbatim.

Note card from an article

```
Ruch      Personality Testing for Employment Selection     15

"Personality testing has been under fire for a decade,
but the use of psychological testing in employee
selection nonetheless has increased at a rapid pace.
A recent study conducted among personnel directors
indicated that psychological tests of all kinds showed
a steady increase within a five-year period."      p. 58

(Also on p. 58 are two bar graphs which could be blown
up to show the increase in the use of personality
tests.)
```

All cards from the Ruch article[1] would carry the number 15 in the upper right corner. Note that the Ruch card carries both a quotation and a "mental note" or reminder that some illustrative material is available here for use as a visual aid. A card can carry any kind of information, of course, but only related items should be on any one card. Long quotations can ordinarily be shortened by using the familiar device of three ellipsis dots (. . .) to indicate omission of a nonessential word or words.

As your note-taking proceeds, you will want to file the cards according to some planned system. One way is to place the *bibliographical* cards in alphabetical order by authors in one section. The *contents* note cards are then placed in succeeding sections under topical heads which you may find useful during the organizing and outlining steps that will follow. We say "may find useful" because outlines change in the process of constructing them, and your successes and failures in finding materials will often dictate the changes to be made.

---

1. Floyd L. Ruch, "Personality: Public or Private," *Psychology Today*, **1** (October 1967), pp. 46 ff. The assumption in this instance would be that the Ruch article is the fifteenth source from which you took notes. (The quotation is reprinted from *Psychology Today* Magazine, October 1967. Copyright © Communications/Research/Machines/Inc.)

Appendix B / Library aids

General indexes to magazine articles

Poole's Index to Periodical Literature. An alphabetical list of the subjects of materials appearing in 470 American and English magazines in the period from 1802 through 1906.

19th Century Readers' Guide to Periodical Literature. An index by author, subject, and illustrator to 51 periodicals in the period from 1890 through 1899.

Readers' Guide to Periodical Literature (1900 to date). The best index to articles published in this century. Each entry includes the name, volume, and date of the magazine or journal, along with the name of the author, the title of the article, and the paging for it. Following the general pattern of card catalogs, entries are listed under author, subject, and title when necessary.

Typical indexes to newspapers

New York Times Index. An author and subject index to all issues of that newspaper from 1913 to date.

The Official Index to the Times. An author, subject, and title index to the *London Times* from 1914 to date.

Typical specialized indexes

Agricultural Index (1916 to date).
Education Index (1929 to date).
Engineering Index (1884 to date).
Public Affairs Information Service (1915 to date).
Social Sciences and Humanities Index (1916 to date).

Three primary encyclopedias

Encyclopaedia Britannica, 14th edition, 24 volumes
Encyclopedia Americana, 30 volumes
Collier's Encyclopedia, 24 volumes

Typical specialized encyclopedias

Cyclopedia of American Agriculture, 4 volumes.
Cyclopedia of Education, 5 volumes.
Encyclopaedia of the Social Sciences, 15 volumes.

Biographical dictionaries

Dictionary of National Biography, 22 volumes and supplements. Biographies of famous British men and women who are no longer living.

Dictionary of American Biography, 20 volumes. The American equivalent of the *Dictionary of National Biography*.

Who's Who (Great Britain, 1849 to date). An annual review of the lives of important British men and women living at the time of the publication of a given volume.

Who's Who in America (1899 to date). The American equivalent, published every two years.

Miscellaneous aids

Bartlett's Familiar Quotations

Cambridge Modern History, 13 volumes. Useful coverage of almost any subject of consequence in modern history.

Rand McNally Commercial Atlas and Marketing Guide. Data about manufacturing, marketing, transportation, etc.

Roget's Thesaurus. A dictionary of synonyms and antonyms.

The World Almanac and Book of Facts (1868 to date). Details on what is happening each year in every field.

And if all else fails, the volume listed below—or one like it—is available at the reference desk of every library.

Winchell's Guide to Reference Books. A first-rate listing and evaluation of approximately 7500 reference works. Especially valuable as a tool for the finding of additional bibliographies and reference guides to such fields as philosophy, religion, the social sciences, general science, the fine and applied arts, literature, biography, geography, and history.

Appendix C / Focus on common materials

Some course outlines permit or require students to center their studies on major problems or areas for the duration of the course. One pattern for this approach allows the students to choose to work in one or more fields, for example, urban affairs, foreign policy, interior affairs, armed services.[1] The individual student can of course work independently and separately in preparing and executing a series of speaking and participation options within a chosen field. If some kind of group or committee organization is desired, a practical number of committees or interest groups is three or four to a class (four to six students in each group). The particular fields chosen will vary with the times; such committee titles as "health and welfare," "education," and others can be readily substituted in order always to have individuals or student groups studying vital issues of the day. (The specific topics or issues taken up and under scrutiny within the subordinate areas will naturally be still narrower in scope.) The problem-area designations will ordinarily be changed from semester to semester, from term to term, or from year to year. For example, one pattern could be:

Interest-group committees	*Problem areas*
Urban Affairs	Law Enforcement
Foreign Policy	The United States in Asia
Interior Affairs	Civil Disturbances
Armed Services	Arms Procurement Policies

A plan of this kind focuses student attention on current issues at the same time that it narrows the search for a specific speech topic. For a first assignment on "Presenting one's point of view," for example, a student might choose to take any one or more of the following positions.

---

1. For a guide to materials and research suggestions on four additional topical units (population control, business ethics, teacher education, and campus revolt), see Brandes and Walwik.

Whether or not you get justice depends on the kind of lawyer you can afford.

The hands of justice are tied by Supreme Court rulings protecting criminals.

The Government does not keep the people informed.

Black rioters are simply "hoods" taking advantage of a situation.

Violent tactics are a necessary last resort in the struggle of blacks for redress of grievances.

The "selective" draft is too selective.

The young men of America are patriotic.

Calling a dissenter a Communist doesn't make him one.

If the committee plan is used in whole or in part, the general area to be studied by a particular interest-group committee can be determined by the instructor, with the choice of particular issues left to the students. For instance, if in any one year our foreign policy problems seem to be focused in the Mediterranean area, the Foreign Policy Committee will of course want to concentrate its attention on that area. In any event, there is some evidence that students may perform at higher levels when working in a chosen field than when searching for subjects and moving from topic to topic in a number of fields; on the other hand, there is always the danger that one or two students in a committee will depend on the research efforts of the others in the same group. Nevertheless, if the course plan includes or permits provision for student concentration of effort on specific areas, the students may work individually or they may be grouped in small committees of five to seven students for the duration of the course.

For the sake of example, let us assume that from one to five students in a class declared an interest in working on the problem area of "selective service." Depending on administrative policy, they would be permitted to work individually in that area, or they could become members of a student committee doing research and preparing for both individual and group performances. Either as an individual or as a member of such a committee, each student would find his preparations for performance affected in one or more of the following ways.

1. A *first individual assignment* (or conversation with another student) could be based on such a statement as "Decisions to draft or not to draft specific individuals depend too much on local interpretations of rules by draft boards." (Preparing for the assignment and participating in it would provide "leads" on areas which could be investigated in getting ready for the information report to come.)

2. An *information report* could be one showing exactly how the Selective Service System operates or how it affects all of us directly or indirectly. (The data and other materials collected for this report would provide at least a partial base for participation in the third project, a problem-solving discussion.)

3. Participation in *small-group discussion* would require problem-solving effort on the part of the group or committee to which he belonged. The specific problem could be "the uncertainties of students in facing the possibility of being drafted." (Ideas discussed and conclusions reached in this project could be used in preparation for the next performance, the persuasive speech. In addition, a group or committee "bill" or resolu-

tion could be prepared for appropriate action in a final project devoted to parliamentary debate.)

4. A *persuasive speech* could be one advocating a change in the selection procedures of the SSS. (Materials and experience gained in this assignment could be used to good advantage in debating or in undertaking to support or to oppose "bills" in project 6 below.)

5. An *analytical-listening report* could be based on a speech explaining draft policy, on one opposing the draft, or on one favoring retention of the present system. Or the report could deal with a discussion or meeting at which some aspect of the committee organization of the U.S. Congress was discussed, attacked, or defended.

6. By the time for *participation in a debate*, the student would be the beneficiary of four or five prior projects in his chosen "problem area." With some additional work and practice, he would be ready to perform at a relatively high level of efficiency in facing questions after presenting a controversial point of view, in facing questions after debating an issue with another student, or in working with his committee and other interested students in securing passage of a "bill" in a final parliamentary debate series involving all the members of the class.

Within the bounds of a selected "problem area," then, it is possible for each student in a class to work individually on some projects and to work cooperatively on others.

Appendix D / Topical bibliographies

The bibliographies below may be helpful to individual students or committees wishing to work on ecological topics, on freedom of speech, or on various approaches to changing some of the operational ground rules in Congress.

Protecting and restoring our environment

Part I [1]

Blake, Peter. *God's Own Junkyard.* New York: Holt, Rinehart and Winston, Inc., 1964.

Brown, Harrison S. *The Challenge of Man's Future.* New York: Viking, 1954.

Carson, Rachel. *Silent Spring.* Boston: Houghton Mifflin, 1962.

Commoner, Barry. *Science and Survival.* New York: Viking, 1967.

De Bell, Garrett, ed. *The Environmental Handbook.* New York: Ballantine, 1970.

Douglas, William O. *A Wilderness Bill of Rights.* Boston: Little, Brown, 1965.

Dubos René. *So Human An Animal.* New York: Scribner's, 1968.

Ehrlich, Paul R. *The Population Bomb.* New York: Ballantine, 1968.

Goldman, Marshall I. *Controlling Pollution: The Economics of a Cleaner America.* Englewood Cliffs, N.J.: Prentice-Hall, 1967.

Graham, Frank, Jr. *Disaster by Default: Politics and Water Pollution.* New York: Evans, 1966.

Graham, Frank, Jr. *Since Silent Spring.* Boston: Houghton Mifflin, 1970.

Leopold, Aldo. *A Sand County Almanac.* New York: Oxford University Press, 1949.

---

1. Contributed by Frank Graham, Jr., author of *Since Silent Spring* and other works on the environment.

Mumford, Lewis. *The City in History: Its Origins, Its Transformations, Its Prospects.* New York: Harcourt, Brace and World, 1961.

Nash, Roderick, ed. *The American Environment: Readings in the History of Conservation.* Reading, Mass.: Addison-Wesley, 1968.

Novick, Sheldon. *The Careless Atom.* Boston: Houghton Mifflin, 1969.

Rienow, Robert, and Leona Train Rienow. *Moment in the Sun.* New York: Dial, 1967.

Rudd, Robert L. *Pesticides and the Living Landscape.* Madison. Univeristy of Wisconsin Press, 1964.

Udall, Stewart L. *The Quiet Crisis.* New York: Holt, Rinehart and Winston, 1963.

Part II [2]

Benarde, Melvin A. *Our Precarious Habitat.* New York: Norton, 1970.

Boughey, Arthur S. *Ecology of Populations.* New York: Macmillan, 1968.

Dasmann, Raymond F. *Environmental Conservation.* 2nd ed. New York: Wiley, 1968.

Elton, Charles S. *Animal Ecology.* London: Methuen, 1927.

Ewald, William R., Jr., ed. *Environment for Man: The Next Fifty Years.* Bloomington: Indiana University Press, 1967.

Hardin, Garrett, ed. *Population, Evolution and Birth Control: A Collage of Controversial Ideas.* San Francisco: Freeman, 1969.

Kormondy, Edward J. *Concepts of Ecology.* Englewood Cliffs, N.J.: Prentice-Hall, 1969.

Odum, Eugene P. *Ecology.* New York: Holt, Rinehart and Winston, 1969.

Shepard, Paul, and Daniel McKinley, eds. *Subversive Science: Essays Toward an Ecology of Man.* New York: Houghton Mifflin, 1969.

Whittaker, Robert H. *Communities and Ecosystems.* New York: Macmillan, 1970.

Young, Louise B., ed. *Population in Perspective.* New York: Oxford University Press, 1968.

Freedom of speech

Beman, Lamar T., ed. *Selected Articles on Censorship of Speech and the Press.* New York: AMS Press, 1969.

Bosmajian, Haig. *The Principles and Practice of Freedom of Speech.* Boston: Houghton Mifflin, 1971.

Capaldi, Nicholas, ed. *Clear and Present Danger: The Free Speech Controversy.* New York: Pegasus, 1969.

Chafee, Zecariah. *Free Speech in the United States.* Cambridge, Mass.: Harvard University Press, 1941.

Emerson, Thomas I. *Toward a General Theory of the First Amendment.* New York: Random House, 1966.

---

2. Contributed by Professor Ronald L. Giese, Director, Natural Resources and Environmental Science Program, Purdue University.

Emerson, Thomas I. *The System of Freedom of Expression*. New York: Random House, 1970.

Haiman, Franklyn S. *Freedom of Speech: Issues and Cases*. New York: Random House, 1965.

Hook, Sydney. *Heresy, Yes—Conspiracy, No!* New York: Day, 1953.

Hook, Sydney. *Paradoxes of Freedom*. Berkeley: University of California Press, 1962.

Hudon, Edward G. *Freedom of Speech and Press in America*. Washington: Public Affairs Press, 1963.

Meiklejohn, Alexander. *Political Freedom*. New York: Oxford University Press (Galaxy Book), 1965.

O'Neil, Robert M. *Free Speech*. New York: Bobbs-Merrill, 1966.

Rice, George P., Jr. *Law for the Public Speaker*. Boston: Christopher, 1958.

Shapiro, Martin. *Freedom of Speech: The Supreme Court and Judical Review*. Englewood Cliffs, N.J.: Prentice-Hall, 1966.

Williamson, E. G., and John L. Cowan. *The American Student's Freedom of Expression*. Minneapolis: University of Minnesota Press, 1966.

Congressional reorganization[3]

Bolling, Richard. *House Out of Order*. New York: Dutton, 1965.

Burns, James MacGregor. *Congress on Trial: The Legislative Process and the Administrative State*. New York: Harper and Row, 1949.

Burns, James MacGregor. *Deadlock of Democracy: Four-Party Politics in America*. Englewood Cliffs, N.J.: Prentice-Hall, 1963.

Clark, Joseph S. *Congress: The Sapless Branch*. New York: Harper and Row, 1964.

Clark, Joseph S., et al. *The Senate Establishment*. New York: Hill and Wang, 1963.

Hinckley, Barbara. *The Seniority System in Congress*. Bloomington: Indiana University Press, 1971.

Kirby, James C., Jr. *Congress and the Public Trust: Report of the Association of the Bar of the City of New York, Special Committee on Congressional Ethics*. New York: Atheneum, 1970.

Task Force on Financing Congressional Campaigns. *Electing Congress: The Financial Dilemma*. New York: Twentieth Century Fund, 1970.

---

3. From *Common Cause* release, "Making Congress Work," November 1970.

Appendix E / Bibliography of speech collections

Aly, Bower, and Lucile F. Aly, eds. *Speeches in English*. New York: Random House, 1968.

Arnold, Carroll C., Douglas Ehninger, and John C. Gerber, eds. *The Speaker's Resource Book*. 2nd ed. Chicago: Scott, Foresman, 1966.

Black, Edwin, and Harry P. Kerr, eds. *American Issues*. New York: Harcourt, Brace and World, 1961.

Boase, Paul H., ed. *The Rhetoric of Christian Socialism*. New York: Random House, 1969.

Bormann, Ernest G., ed. *Forerunners of Black Power: The Rhetoric of Abolition*. Englewood Cliffs, N. J.: Prentice-Hall, 1971.

Bosmajian, Haig A., ed. *Readings in Speech*. 2nd ed. New York: Harper and Row, 1971.

Bosmajian, Haig A., and Hamida Bosmajian, eds. *The Rhetoric of the Civil-Rights Movement*. New York: Random House, 1969.

Brandes, Paul D., ed. *The Rhetoric of Revolt*. Englewood Cliffs, N. J.: Prentice-Hall, 1971.

Congressional Digest. Washington Congressional Digest Corporation, 1921–. Published monthly.

Golden, James L., and Richard D. Rieke, eds. *The Rhetoric of Black Americans*. Columbus, Ohio: Charles E. Merrill, Company, 1971.

Hildebrandt, Herbert W., ed. *Issues of Our Time: A Summons to Speak*. New York: Macmillan, 1963.

Hurd, Charles, ed. *A Treasury of Great American Speeches*. Rev. ed. New York: Hawthorne, 1970.

Linkugel, Wil A., R. R. Allen, and Richard L. Johannesen, eds. *Contemporary American Speeches*. 2nd ed. Belmont, Calif.: Wadsworth, 1969.

Lomas, Charles W., ed. *The Agitator in American Society*. Englewood Cliffs, N. J.: Prentice-Hall, 1968.

McBath, James H., and Walter R. Fisher, eds. *British Public Addresses, 1828—1960.* Boston: Houghton Mifflin, 1971.

Matson, Floyd W. *Voices of Crisis: Vital Speeches on Contemporary Issues.* New York: Odyssey, 1967.

O'Neill, Daniel J. *Speeches by Black Americans.* Encino, Calif.: Dickenson, 1971.

Scott, Robert L., and Wayne Brockriede, eds. *The Rhetoric of Black Power.* New York: Harper and Row, 1969.

Smith, Arthur L., and Stephen Robb, eds. *The Voice of Black Rhetoric.* Boston: Allyn and Bacon, 1971.

Stewart, Charles J., ed. *On Speech-Communication: An Anthology of Contemporary Writings and Messages.* New York: Holt, Rinehart and Winston, 1972.

Vital Speeches of the Day. Southold, N. Y.: City News, 1934—. Published biweekly.

Williams, Jamye Coleman, and McDonald Williams, eds. *The Negro Speaks.* New York: Noble and Noble, 1970.

Zacharias, Donald W., ed. *In Pursuit of Peace: Speeches of the Sixties.* New York: Random House, 1970.

General bibliography

Books marked with asterisks are especially useful for supplementary reading. If possible, they should be placed on a library reserve list along with others selected by students or instructors.

Aggertt, Otis, J., and Elbert R. Bowen. *Communicative Reading.* 2nd ed. New York: Macmillan, 1963.

Alexander, Hubert G. *Language and Thinking.* Princeton, N. J.: D. Van Nostrand, 1967.

Argyle, Michael. *Social Interaction.* New York: Atherton, 1969.

Auer, J. Jeffery, ed. *The Rhetoric of Our Times.* New York: Appleton-Century-Crofts, 1969.

Barnlund, Dean C., ed. *Interpersonal Communication: Survey and Studies.* Boston: Houghton Mifflin, 1968.

*Barnlund, Dean C., and Franklyn S. Haiman. *The Dynamics of Discussion.* Boston: Houghton Mifflin, 1960.

*Beardsley, Monroe C. *Thinking Straight.* Englewood Cliffs, N. J.: Prentice-Hall, 1956.

Bennis, Warren G., Edgar H. Schein, Fred I. Steele, and David E. Berlew, eds. *Interpersonal Dynamics: Essays and Readings on Human Interaction.* rev. ed. Homewood, Ill.: Dorsey, 1968.

Berelson, Bernard, and Gary A. Steiner. *Human Behavior: An Inventory of Scientific Findings.* New York: Harcourt, Brace and World, 1964.

Berlo, David K. *The Process of Communication.* New York: Holt, Rinehart and Winston, 1960.

Berne, Eric. *Games People Play.* New York: Grove, 1964.

*Bettinghaus, Erwin P. *Persuasive Communication.* New York: Holt, Rinehart and Winston, 1968.

Birdwhistell, Ray L. *Kinesics and Context: Essay on Body Motion Communication.* Philadelphia: University of Pennsylvania Press, 1970.

Borden, George A., Richard B. Gregg, and Theodore G. Grove. *Speech Behavior and Human Interaction.* Englewood Cliffs, N. J.: Prentice-Hall, 1969.

Bormann, Ernest G. *Discussion and Group Methods.* New York: Harper and Row, 1969.

Bosmajian, Haig A., ed. *The Principles and Practice of Freedom of Speech.* Boston: Houghton Mifflin, 1971.

Bosmajian, Haig A., ed. *The Rhetoric of Nonverbal Communication.* Glenview, Ill.: Scott, Foresman, 1971.

Bowers, John Waite, and Donovan J. Ochs. *The Rhetoric of Agitation and Control.* Reading, Mass.: Addison-Wesley, 1971.

Brandes, Paul D. "II. The Common Materials Approach to the Teaching of Speech," *The Speech Teacher,* **16** (November 1967), pp. 265—268.

Brandes, Paul D., and Theodore J. Walwik. *A Research Manual for the Performance Course in Speech.* New York: Harper and Row, 1967.

Brehm, Jack W., and Arthur R. Cohen. *Explorations in Cognitive Dissonance.* New York: Wiley, 1962.

Brink, Edward L., and William T. Kelley. *The Management of Promotion.* Englewood Cliffs, N. J.: Prentice-Hall, 1963.

Brooks, Robert D., and Thomas M. Scheidel. "Speech as Process: A Case Study," *Speech Monographs,* **35** (March 1968), pp. 1—7.

*Brown, Charles T., and Charles van Riper. *Speech and Man.* Englewood Cliffs, N. J.: Prentice-Hall, 1966.

Brown, Roger. *Social Psychology.* New York: Free Press, 1965.

Brown, Roger. *Words and Things.* New York: Free Press, 1958.

Burton, Dwight L., and John S. Simmons, eds. *Teaching English.* New York: Holt, Rinehart and Winston, 1965.

*Campbell, James H., and Hal W. Hepler, eds. *Dimensions in Communication: Readings.* 2nd ed. Belmont, Calif.: Wadsworth, 1970.

Cherry, Colin. *On Human Communication,* 2nd ed. Cambridge, Mass.: MIT Press, 1966.

Cohen, Arthur R. *Attitude Change and Social Influence.* New York: Basic Books, 1964.

Collins, Barry E., and Harold Guetzkow. *A Social Psychology of Group Processes for Decision-Making.* New York: Wiley, 1964.

*Condon, John C., Jr. *Semantics and Communication.* New York: Macmillan, 1966.

Davitz, Joel R., et al. *The Communication of Emotional Meaning.* New York: McGraw-Hill, 1964.

Dewey, John. *Logic: The Theory of Inquiry.* New York: Holt, Rinehart and Winston, 1964 printing of 1938 copyright.

Duker, Sam, ed., *Listening: Readings.* New York: Scarecrow Press, 1966.

Edwards, Allen J., and Dale P. Scannell. *Educational Psychology.* Scranton, Pa.: International Textbook, 1968.

*Ehninger, Douglas, and Wayne Brockriede. *Decision by Debate*. New York: Dodd, Mead, 1963.

Eisenson, Jon, J. Jeffery Auer, and John V. Irwin. *The Psychology of Communication*. New York: Appleton-Century-Crofts, 1963.

Ewbank, Henry Lee, and J. Jeffery Auer. *Discussion and Debate*, 2nd ed. New York: Appleton-Century-Crofts, 1951.

Fishbein, Martin. "An Investigation of the Relationships Between Beliefs About an Object and the Attitude Toward That Object," *Human Relations*, **16** (August 1963), pp. 233–239.

Fogarty, Daniel. *Roots for a New Rhetoric* (in Columbia University Series of Teachers College Studies in Education). New York: Bureau of Publications, Teachers College, Columbia University, 1959.

Frazier, Alexander. "Making the Most of Speaking-and-Listening Experiences," *The English Journal*, **46** (September 1957), pp. 330–338, 365.

*Freeley, Austin J. *Argumentation and Debate*. 2nd ed. San Francisco: Wadsworth, 1966.

Gardner, John W. *Excellence: Can We Be Equal and Excellent Too?* First Colophon edition. New York: Harper and Row, 1962.

Getzels, Jacob W., and Philip W. Jackson, *Creativity and Intelligence*. New York: Wiley, 1962.

Giffin, Kim, and Bobby R. Patton, eds. *Basic Readings in Interpersonal Communication*. New York: Harper and Row, 1971.

Goffman, Erving. *Behavior in Public Places*. New York: Free Press, 1963.

Goffman, Erving. *The Presentation of Self in Everyday Life*. Garden City, N.Y.: Doubleday (Anchor Book), 1959.

*Haiman, Franklyn S. *Freedom of Speech*. New York: Random House, 1965.

*Hall, Edward T. *The Silent Language*. New York: Fawcett World Library printing of 1963.

Haney, William V. *Communication and Organizational Behavior*. Rev. ed. Homewood, Ill.: Irwin, 1967.

*Hayakawa, S. I. *Language in Thought and Action*. 2nd ed. New York: Harcourt Brace and Jovanovich, 1964.

*Hellman, Hugo E. *Parliamentary Procedure*. New York: Macmillan, 1966.

Hildebrandt, Herbert W. "I. A Rationale for Non-Fragmented Topics," *The Speech Teacher*, **16** (November 1967), pp. 259–264.

Holm, James N. *Productive Speaking for Business and the Professions*. Boston: Allyn and Bacon, 1967.

*Holtzman, Paul D. *The Psychology of Speakers' Audiences*. Glenview, Ill.: Scott, Foresman, 1970.

Hook, Sidney. *Paradoxes of Freedom*. Berkeley: University of California Press, 1962.

Hovland, Carl I., ed. *The Order of Presentation in Persuasion*. New Haven: Yale University Press, 1957.

Hovland, Carl I., and Irving L. Janis, eds. *Personality and Persuasibility*. New Haven: Yale University Press, 1959.

Hovland, Carl I., Irving L. Janis, and Harold H. Kelley. *Communication and Persuasion*. New Haven: Yale University Press, 1963.

*Howell, William S., and Ernest G. Bormann. *Presentational Speaking for Business and the Professions*. New York: Harper and Row, 1971.

Hudon, Edward Gerard. *Freedom of Speech and Press in America*. Washington, D.C.: Public Affairs Press, 1963.

*Johannesen, Richard L., ed. *Ethics and Persuasion*. New York: Random House, 1967.

Johnson, Martha, and Don Richardson. "Listening Training in the Fundamentals of Speech Class," *The Speech Teacher*, **17** (November 1968), pp. 293–296.

*Johnson, Wendell. *People in Quandaries*. New York: Harper and Row, 1946.

Kahn, Robert L., and Charles F. Cannell. *The Dynamics of Interviewing*. New York: Wiley, 1957.

*Karlins, Marvin, and Herbert I. Abelson. *Persuasion: How Opinions and Attitudes Are Changed*. 2nd ed. New York: Springer, 1970.

Kibler, Robert J., and Larry L. Barker, eds. *Conceptual Frontiers in Speech-Communication: Report of the New Orleans Conference on Research and Instructional Development*. New York: Speech Association of America, 1969.

Kiesler, Charles A., Barry E. Collins, and Norman Miller. *Attitude Change: A Critical Analysis of Theoretical Approaches*. New York: Wiley, 1969.

Kiesler, Charles A., and Sara B. Kiesler. *Conformity*. Reading, Mass.: Addision-Wesley, 1969.

Kuhlen, Raymond G., ed. *Studies in Educational Psychology*. Waltham, Mass.: Blaisdell, 1968.

Larson, Carl E., and Frank E. X. Dance, eds. *Perspectives on Communication*. Milwaukee: Speech Communication Center, University of Wisconsin/Milwaukee, 1968.

*Lee, Irving J. *How to Talk with People*. New York: Harper and Row, 1952.

McGuire, William J. "The Nature of Attitudes and Attitude Change," in *The Handbook of Social Psychology*, Gardner Lindzey and Elliot Aronson, eds., III, pp. 136–314. 2nd ed. Reading, Mass.: Addison-Wesley, 1969.

March, James G., and Herbert A. Simon. *Organizations*. New York: Wiley, 1958.

Maslow, A. H. *Motivation and Personality*. New York: Harper and Row, 1954.

Miller, George A. *Language and Communication*. New York: McGraw-Hill, 1951.

Mills, Glen E. *Reason in Controversy*. Boston: Allyn and Bacon, 1964.

Nadeau, Ray. "Hermogenes on Stases," *Speech Monographs*, **31** (November 1964), pp. 369–373.

Newman, Robert P., and Dale R. Newman. *Evidence*. Boston: Houghton Mifflin, 1969.

Nichols, Ralph G. "Do We Know How to Listen? Practical Helps in a Modern Age," *The Speech Teacher*, **10** (March, 1961), pp. 118–124.

*Nichols, Ralph G., and Leonard A. Stevens. *Are You Listening?* New York: McGraw-Hill, 1957.

*Oliver, Robert T., and Dominick A. Barbara. *The Healthy Mind in Communion and Communication.* Springfield, Ill.: Thomas, 1962.

*O'Neil, Robert M. *Free Speech.* New York: Bobbs-Merrill, 1966.

Osgood, Charles E., and Thomas E. Sebeok, eds. *Psycholinguistics: A Survey of Theory and Research Problems* (printed with *A Survey of Psycholinguistic Research, 1954—1964* by A. Richard Diebold, and with *The Psycholinguists* by George A. Miller). Bloomington: Indiana University Press, 1965.

Perelman, Chaim. *The Idea of Justice and the Problem of Argument,* trans. by John Petrie. New York: The Humanities Press, 1963.

Perelman, Chaim, and L. Olbrechts-Tyteca. *The New Rhetoric: A Treatise on Argumentation,* trans. by John Wilkinson and Purcell Weaver. Notre Dame, Ind.: University of Notre Dame Press, 1969.

Phillips, Gerald M. *Communication and the Small Group.* New York: Bobbs Merrill, 1966.

Remmers, H. H., ed. *Anti-Democratic Attitudes in American Schools.* Evanston, Ill.: Northwestern University Press, 1963.

Richards, I. A. *The Philosophy of Rhetoric.* New York: Oxford University Press, 1965.

Rokeach, Milton, et al. *The Open and Closed Mind.* New York: Basic Books, 1960.

Rosenberg, Milton J., et al. *Attitude Organization and Change.* New Haven: Yale University Press, 1960.

Ruechelle, Randall C. "An Experimental Study of Emotional and Intellectual Appeals in Persuasion," *Speech Monographs,* **35** (March 1958), pp. 49—58.

Ruesch, Jurgen, and Gregory Bateson. *Communication: The Social Matrix of Psychiatry.* New York: Norton, 1951.

Ruesch, Jurgen, and Weldon Kees. *Nonverbal Communication.* Berkeley: University of California Press, 1970.

Ruitenbeek, Hendrik M. *The Individual and the Crowd.* New York: New American Library (Mentor), 1964.

Salomon, Louis B. *Semantics and Common Sense.* New York: Holt, Rinehart and Winston, 1966.

Sapir, Edward. *Culture, Language, and Personality.* Berkeley: University of California Press, 1956.

Scheidel, Thomas M., and Laura Crowell. "Idea Development in Small Discussion Groups," *Quarterly Journal of Speech,* **50** (April 1964), pp. 140—145.

Schramm, Wilbur, ed. *The Process and Effects of Mass Communication,* 5th printing. Urbana: Ill.: University of Illinois Press, 1961.

Schramm, Wilbur, ed. *The Science of Human Communication.* New York: Basic Books, 1963.

*Scott, Robert L., ed. *The Speaker's Reader: Concepts in Communication.* Glenview, Ill.: Scott, Foresman, 1969.

Secord, Paul F., and Carl W. Backman. *Social Psychology*, New York: McGraw-Hill, 1964.

Sereno, Kenneth K., and C. David Mortenson, eds. *Foundations of Communication Theory*. New York: Harper and Row, 1970.

Sesonske, Alexander. "Saying, Being, and Freedom of Speech," *Philosophy and Rhetoric*, 1 (January 1968), pp. 25–37.

Shannon, Claude E., and Warren Weaver. *The Mathematical Theory of Communication*. Urbana: University of Illinois Press, 1949.

Shepherd, Clovis R. *Small Groups*. San Francisco: Chandler, 1964.

Sherif, Carolyn W., Muzafer Sherif, and Roger Nebergall. *Attitude and Attitude Change*. Philadelphia: Saunders, 1965.

Smith, Alfred G., ed. *Communication and Culture*. New York: Holt, Rinehart and Winston, 1966.

Smith, G. Kerry, ed. *Stress and Campus Response*. San Francisco: Jossey-Bass, 1968.

Solomon, Arthur, with Steven Perry and Robert Devine. *Interpersonal Communication: A Cross-Disciplinary Approach*. Springfield, Ill.: Thomas, 1970.

Sommer, Robert. *Personal Space*. Englewood Cliffs, N. J.: Prentice-Hall, 1969.

Steele, Edward D., and W. Charles Redding. "The American Value System: Premises for Persuasion," *Western Speech*, **26** (Spring 1962), pp. 83–91.

Steiner, Ivan D., and Martin Fishbein, eds. *Current Studies in Social Psychology*. New York: Holt, Rinehart and Winston, 1965.

*Sturgis, Alice. *Sturgis Standard Code of Parliamentary Procedure*. 2nd ed. New York: McGraw-Hill, 1966.

Tagiuri, Renato, and Luigi Petrullo, eds. *Person Perception and Interpersonal Behavior*. Stanford: Stanford University Press, 1958.

Tedford, Thomas L. "III. Teaching Freedom of Speech Through the Use of Common Materials," *The Speech Teacher*, **16** (November 1967), pp. 269–270.

Thompson, Wayne N. *Modern Argumentation and Debate*. New York: Harper and Row, 1971.

Weaver, Carl H., and Warren L. Strausbaugh. *Fundamentals of Speech Communication*. New York: American Book, 1964.

Weaver, Richard. *The Ethics of Rhetoric*. Chicago: Henry Regnery 1965.

Weinberg, Harry L. *Levels of Knowing and Existence*. New York: Harper and Row, 1959.

Whorf, Benjamin Lee. *Language, Thought, and Reality*, ed. by John B. Carroll. Cambridge, Mass.: MIT Press, 1956.

Wiksell, Wesley. *How to Conduct Meetings*. New York: Harper and Row, 1966.

*Wilcox, Roger P. *Oral Reporting in Business and Industry*. Englewood Cliffs, N. J.: Prentice-Hall, 1967.

Williams, Chester S. *Right of Free Speech* (in Our Freedoms Series). Evanston, Ill.: Row, Peterson, 1940.

Williamson, E. G., and John L. Cowan. *The American Student's Freedom of Expression.* Minneapolis: University of Minnesota Press, 1966.

*Windes, Russel R., and Arthur Hastings. *Argumentation and Advocacy.* New York: Random House, 1965.

Index

This index is limited to page citations for (1) topics discussed and (2) writers quoted or cited in the text proper. A book or article by more than one author is entered under the name of the first-cited author, and only the last names appear (e.g., Hovland, Janis, and Kelley). In reference to the work of one author, his full name is given. Complete citations for all book references may be found in the General Bibliography immediately preceding this Index.

abstraction, process of, 34–35
Alexander, Hubert G., 12
analogy; *see* reasoning
analysis, of discussion problem, 170
 of a speech, 122–126
analyst, 121, 122; *see also* listening
 analytically
argument, checking of, 56–57
 concept of, 44–45
 order of, 217–218
Argyle, Michael, 17, 132
Aristotle, 42, 45, 54, 112, 144, 221
attention; *see* cues
attitude(s), 20, 209–230; *see also* factors
 affecting attitudes
 bases and functions, 212–213
 definitions and distinctions, 20, 210–212
 diagram of factors affecting change of, 214
 observable stimuli (message, speaker, situation), 213–214
 relation to beliefs, 20, 210
 relation to common premise and value premises, 211–212
 relation to opinions, 210–211

attitude analysis from standpoints of:
 integration of attitudinal information, 229–230
 listener attitudes (specific), 228–229
 listener attitudes toward message, speaker, situation, 229
 listener persuasibility, 227–228
attitude change as seen through:
 listener response, 226–227
 observable effects, 227
authorities, in reasoning, 49–50

Bacon, Francis, 59
Barnlund and Haiman, 165, 170, 172, 180
Beardsley, Monroe C., 26, 46, 47
behavior, as communicative goal, 15, 20
 factors affecting group behavior, 174
belief, definition of, 20; *see also* attitude(s)
Berelson and Steiner, 68, 140, 165, 169, 172, 211, 212
Berlo, David, 19, 20
Berlo, Lemert, and Mertz, 222
Bettinghaus, Erwin P., 222, 223
Bill of Rights, 3, 245

Birdwhistell, Ray L., 11
Bosmajian, Haig A., 17
Brandes, Paul D., 158
Brink and Kelley, 71, 76, 118, 140
Brooks and Scheidel, 16
Brown, Roger, 58, 218, 221
Brown and Van Riper, 9, 26, 71, 76

Campbell, George, 10, 144
causal relations; *see* reasoning
chairman's duties, in discussion, 175–180
  in introductions, 81–83
  in parliamentary procedure, 260–262
character, confidence-generating, 112; *see also* ethical appeal
Chase, Stuart, 24, 25
Cherry, Colin 2, 10, 26
classification, process of, 35–36
  reasoning by, 54
Cohen, Arthur R., 212, 216, 217, 220, 223, 224
Collins and Guetzkow, 169, 172, 174
common materials, focus on, 274–276
communication, hope for future of, 5–6
  importance of, 1–6
  political, 3–4
  practical, 4–5
  social, 2–3
comparison; *see* reasoning
conclusions to speeches, preparation of, 102
Condon, John C., Jr., 27
conflict, as cue, 74
Confucius, 44
contrast, as cue, 74
control, confidence-generating, 112
conversations, characteristics of, 132–133
  definition of, 131–132
  interaction in, 135
  motivation of, 133–134
  purposes of, 132
Cooper, Wyatt, 83
Cousins, Norman, 109
critic; *see* analyst
cues:
  conflict, 74
  intensity, 73
  movement, 73
  novelty and contrast, 74
  precision in language, 74
  proximity, 73
  reference to familiar, 74

  selection of, 72–74
  size, 73

debating issues, 243–253
deduction, concept of, 45–46
definition, problems in, 36–37
delivery, preparation stages of, 104–113
Dewey, John, 52, 169, 170
discussion:
  case study approaches to, 167
  definitions and objectives, 165–166
  evaluating discussion, 180–182
  interpersonal environment, 172–173
  interpersonal finesse, 177–178
  learning approaches to, 166–167
  model, factors affecting group behavior, 174
  patterns, formal and informal, 167–168
  planning discussion series, 178–180
  problem-solving approaches to, 167
  task environment, 169–172
  task finesse, 176–177
  types of questions, 166
dissent, right to, 3–4, 243–246
dissonance, cognitive, 219

Edwards and Scannell, 140
effect-to-causes *and* effect-to effect; *see* reasoning
Ehninger and Brockriede, 56
Eisenson, Auer, and Irwin, 11
emotive appeal, 31–32, 75–77, 125, 217
enthymeme, deductive pattern of, 45–46
ethical appeal *or* ethos, 16, 112, 220–223
Ewbank and Auer, 46
example, as support; *see* reasoning

fact, definition of, 38–39
  as support; *see* reasoning
factors affecting attitudes toward:
  message, 215–220
  situation, 223–226
  speaker, 220–223
fallacies, detection of, 57
familiar, reference to, as cue, 74
feedback, 12–13, 16, 19
  external, 12–13
  internal, 12
Festinger, Leon, 10, 219
Fishbein, Martin, 20, 210, 211
Frazier, Alexander, 84, 253

freedom of speech, 3–4
  abridging of, 245
  definition of, 243–245
  key decisions in, 245–246
  in relation to students, 247–248
Freeley, Austin J., 56, 252

Gann, Ernest, 131
generalization; *see* reasoning
gestures and bodily action, 106–107
goals, communicative, 20–21
  motivating, 69–71; *see also* motivation
Goffman, Erving, 11
graphs, bar and line, 150–154
group cohesion, as interaction factor in discussion, 173
group consensus, 223–224
group leadership, 225
group participation, 225–226
group pressure, 224–225

Haney, William V., 60
Harrison, Randall, 94
Hayakawa, S. I., 2, 3, 35, 62, 93, 118, 168
Hilgard and Bower, 142
Holtzman, Paul D., 15, 42, 44, 72, 127, 223
Hovland, Carl I., 10, 212, 216, 221
Hovland and Janis, 212, 214
Hovland, Janis, and Kelley, 212, 216, 217, 222, 223, 224, 225
Howell and Bormann, 77, 137, 150
Human Rights Declaration, 3

idea messages, questioning of, 119
impromptu speaking, 86–87
induction, concept of, 45
inference, definition of, 39
information, presenting of, 140–164
informational talk, definition of, 143
  importance of, 144
  types of, 143
  visual aids in, 145–157
intensity, as cue, 73
interaction, levels of, 19–20
  person-to-person, 131–139
interpersonal environment; *see* discussion
interviews, characteristics of, 132–133
  definitions, 131–132
  interaction in, 136–137
  motivation, 133–134
  purposes, 132

introduction, of an individual, 82
  of a speaker, 82
  to speeches, 101–102
Isocrates, 112

Jacobs, Herbert A., 48
James, William, 10
Janis, Irving, 10
Johnson, Arlee, 94, 95
Johnson, Wendell, 35
judgment, definition of, 40

Kahn and Cannell, 133
Karlins and Abelson, 212, 214, 215, 216, 217, 221, 222, 224, 226, 228
Katz, Elihu, 225
Kerr, Harry P., 183
Kiesler, Collins, and Miller, 212
Kuhlen, Raymond G., 69

language, 2–3, 5, 24–41
  care in use of, 38–40
  as control agency, 5
  determination of meaning of, 25–27
  precision in, as cue, 74
  symbolic and presymbolic, 2–3
language choice, in adopting direct style, 32
  in appealing to senses, 29–30
  in evoking word pictures, 30
  in expressing feeling, 31–32
  in relying on action words, 30–31
language problems, in abstraction, 34–35
  in classification, 35–36
  in definition, 36–37
language sensitivity, to allness, 26–27
  to context, 26
  to self-qualification, 27
  to slanting, 26
Lasswell, Harold, 10
Lazarsfeld, Paul, 10
leadership, as interaction factor in discussion, 172
learning, "laws" of, 141–142
  theories of, 140–141
Lee, Irving J., 127, 168, 176
Lewin, Kurt, 10
library, use of, 269–271
library aids, 270–273
listening, 114–127
  actively 114–117

analytically, 121–127
options; *see* speaking-listening options
self-defensively, 117–121
logical appeal; *see* reasoning

Maccoby, Nathan, 10
manuscript, speaking from, 108–110
Maslow, A. H., 68, 69, 70, 71
materials, ways to find and assimilate:
   adopt point of view, 93
   read editorials, etc., 92
   review experiences, 91–92
   talk with experts, 92
McGuire, William J., 210, 211, 212, 226, 227
Mehrabian, Albert, 17
message, components of, 11–19
message consistency, 218–220
message strategy, 215–217
message structure, 217–218
Miller, George A., 11, 140
Mills, Glen E., 56
motivation, definition of, 68–69; *see also* goals
movement, as cue, 73

Nadeau, Ray, 169
Newman and Newman, 48, 250
Nichols and Stevens, 115, 116, 127
noises, interfering or reinforcing, 11, 13
nonverbal dimensions (signs):
   in discussion, 172, 177–178, 181–182
   in group influence on attitude change, 223–226
   in interacting person-to-person, 134
   in listening actively, 115
   in speech-communication planning and preparation, 94, 106–107, 111–112; *see also* visual aids
   in speech-communication process, 13–14, 17–18, 21–23
notes, handling of, 107–108
novelty, as cue, 74

O'Neil, Robert M., 245
opinion, definition of, 210–211; *see also* attitudes
order of business; *see* parliamentary procedure
organizing and outlining:
   rationale for, 94–95
   spatial pattern, 98–99
   step pattern, 95–97
   topical pattern, 99–100

parliamentary procedure, 254–266
   basic motions, 257–259
   definition, 255
   diagram, 256
   order of business, 260–264
   purpose, 255
   special-problem motions, 259–260
perception, definition of, 60; *see also* person perception
   communication and, 60–61
   self-concept and, 62–64
Perelman, Chaim, 42, 47, 58, 67
Perelman and Olbrechts-Tyteca, 42, 44, 47
person perception:
   definition, 65
   modes, 65–66
   relation to speech-communication, 66–67
person-to-person interacting; *see* interaction
persuasion, susceptibility to, 214–215; *see also* attitude(s)
Phillips, Gerald M., 168, 170
planning for communication event, 91–103
Plato, 218, 245
point of view, presenting of, 88–89
potential-realization, goals of, 70
premise, as in "common premise," 42–44
   in syllogistic reasoning, 45–46
presence, as complex of controlled and uncontrolled personal factors, 13–14
   confidence-generating, 111–112
probability, concept of, 46–47
propaganda, recognition of, 57–58
proximity, as cue, 73
Public Broadcast Laboratory, 76

Quintilian, 112
quorum, definition of, 262
quotations in reasoning, 49–50

Rankin, Paul T., 4
rapport, 75–77
reading, interpretative, 85
reasoning, checking of, 55–58
reasoning, fundamental concepts in:
   argument, 44–45
   common premise, 42–44
   deduction, 45–46
   induction, 45
   probability, 46–47

reasoning, materials of:
  examples, 49
  facts and statistics, 48–49
  quotations, 49–50
reasoning, patterns in:
  analogy, 52
  causal relations, 52–54
  classification, 54–55
  comparison, 51
  generalization, 51
reasoning, process of, 43–59
refutation, methods of, 250–252
resolutions, examples of, 206–208
Rice, George P., Jr., 3
Robert, General Henry, 254
Rosenberg et al., 212
Ruch, Floyd L., 271
Ruechelle, Randall C., 76

sales messages, questioning of, 118–119
Scheidel and Crowell, 171
Schlesinger, Arthur M., 76
Schramm, Wilbur, 10, 72, 73, 212
Secord and Backman, 54, 55, 169
secretary, duties in parliamentary procedure, 263
self-concept, definition of, 62
  as affected by perception, 62–63
  relation to speech-communication, 63–64
Shannon and Weaver, 11
Shepherd, Clovis R., 169
Sherif, Sherif, and Nebergall, 212
signs or signals; see nonverbal dimensions
size, as cue, 73
small-group process; see discussion
source credibility; see ethical appeal
spatial pattern; see organizing
speaking-listening options:
  changing attitudes, 230–232
  debating issues, 252–253
  interacting person-to-person, 135–136, 138–139
  parliamentary procedure, 264–266
  participating in discussion, 182–184
  presenting information, 157–159
speech, abridging of, 245
speech, freedom of; see freedom of speech
speech collections, bibliography of, 280–281

speech-communication, definition of, 15
  process of, 9–23
statistics:
  definitions of average (mean), median, and mode, 151
  in reasoning, 48–49
status, as interaction factor in discussion, 173
Steele and Redding, 43, 44
Steiner and Fishbein, 20, 210, 212
step pattern; see organizing
Sturgis, Alice, 257, 259
subject, choice of; see materials
syllogism, rhetorical, 45–46
symbols, manipulation of, 12; see also language

task environment; see discussion
Tedford, Thomas L., 252
tension, confidence-generating, 111
timing, suggestions on, 108
topical bibliographies:
  congressional reorganization, 279
  ecology, 277–278
  freedom of speech, 278–279
topical pattern; see organizing
Toulmin, Stephen, 56
transitions, 100–101

values, American, 43–44
visual aids, 145–157
  actual objects, 146
  diagrams, 149
  drawings, 147
  graphs, 150–154
  models, mock-ups, 147
voice, suggestions on, 106

warrant in Toulmin system, 56, 57
Weaver and Strausbaugh, 71
Weinberg, Harry L., 52, 54, 70, 77
Weiss, Walter, 221
White, Robert W., 69
Whorf, Benjamin Lee, 25, 41
Williams, Chester S., 245, 246
Williams, Frederick, 150
Williamson and Cowan, 247, 248
Winans, James, 10
words, meanings of, 25–27